THE GENDERED SOCIETY

Michael S. Kimmel

State University of New York at Stony Brook

SECOND EDITION

New York   Oxford

OXFORD UNIVERSITY PRESS

2004

Oxford University Press

Oxford   New York
Auckland   Bangkok   Buenos Aires   Cape Town   Chennai
Dar es Salaam   Delhi   Hong Kong   Istanbul   Karachi   Kolkata
Kuala Lumpar   Madrid   Melbourne   Mexico City   Mumbai
Nairobi   São Paulo   Shanghai   Taipei   Tokyo   Toronto

Published by Oxford University Press, Inc.
198 Madison Avenue, New York, New York 10016
http://www.oup-usa.org

Oxford is a registered trademark of Oxford University Press

ISBN: 0-19-514975-0

Printing number: 9 8 7 6 5 4 3 2 1

Printed in the United States of America
on acid-free paper

For Sandi,
who found her voice

CONTENTS

PREFACE

As this book enters its second edition, it's been adopted widely around the country and is in the process of translation into several languages. It's personally gratifying, of course, but more gratifying is the embrace of its vision of a world in which gender inequality is but a distant anachronism, and a serious intellectual confrontation with gender inequality, and the differences that such inequality produces, is a central part of the struggle to bring such a world about. I'm proud to contribute to that struggle.

For this edition, I've thoroughly revised the book, trying to incorporate the suggestions and respond to the criticisms various reviewers and readers have offered. I've not modified my view on some issues (such as sex role theory) as much as some critics might have liked, and my critique of biological differences has, if anything, grown sharper. I've also added a new section on the gendered body, and reframed chapter 10 around that new theme.

As a gender scholar and father of a four-year-old son, I'm often asked if having a son has forced me to change my views about biological difference. "Now you'll see that it's all biological!" one old friend cackled.

Well, first off, speaking as a social scientist, it would be really bad social science to generalize from a sample of one, with no comparative group to measure against. That's not to say people don't engage in such bad social science reasoning all the time, assuming somehow that their children are all children, and that the differences that they might see between a son and daughter somehow reflect what I call the Interplanetary Theory of Gender (that men are from Mars and women from Venus).

If anything, watching Zachary grow has only increased my awareness of the constant daily barrage of messages that children receive from the world around them about what is appropriate behavior for boys and girls. If difference was so "natural," I'm continually thinking, why does it need to be so methodically and continuously forced on children, and why would it have to be so coercively reinforced at every turn? I'm more convinced than ever that gender difference must be produced, even when it is hardly there, because the entire system of gender inequality depends on it.

That said, I do think it's equally true that children are born with certain personalities—that they are oriented toward different styles of expression and have different abilities and interests. I often think it might be a good idea to resurrect that old anthropological term *temperament* to describe it. Zachary seemed to have a particular temperament from birth, and his first four years have only made him more, well, Zachary-like.

What seems most marked in his temperament is the range of affective expression that he has. He certainly loves rough and tumble play, whether it's wrestling with me, or playing with various superheroes. (When he recently asked his grandparents for a Barbie, I was somewhat surprised, since his choices until then had been Buzz Lightyear and Batman. But Barbie has simply become another superhero, and she flies around, apparently happily, with Spider-Man and the gang.) And he also seems remarkably attuned to others' feelings, compassionate and caring. When a child in his preschool is crying, Zachary will offer a hug, comfort, or ask what's wrong.

It is this "other" side of boys' lives—the compassion, caring, and love that comes so *naturally* and is so obviously hardwired—that we often watch being systematically excised from boys' lives. The demands of boyhood, which have nothing whatever to do with evolutionary imperatives or brain chemistry, cripple boys, forcing them to renounce those feelings and suppress and deny the instinct to care. And those who deviate will be savagely punished.

And is there not a parallel process at work for the girls who love to run with him in the playground, who can out-swing him on the monkey bars, who are fearless adventurers in their play? Do not the demands of girlhood require the cultivation of physical helplessness, the loss of voice?

It seems to me, then, four years into the adventure of parenthood, that the task of caregivers and parents of girls, as so many wise and rigorous scholars have demonstrated, is to empower them to retain their voice, to remain as fully confident and competent as they already are. For boys, it is to hold open the opportunity to remain whole, to retain the natural, biological capacity for compassion and empathy, and to enable them to draw on a full—and fully human—emotional palette.

Such a child-rearing protocol will inevitably confront gender inequality, for that is, I believe, the foundation on which the edifice of gender difference is built. But adopting that protocol will enable our children to be so much more fully human.

For this edition, I've been happily reunited with my editor, Peter Labella, whose friendship and editorial guidance spans more than a decade. It's also been a pleasure to work with Sean Mahoney and Christine D'Antonio on this project. I've benefited from close readings of new material from Lisa Machoian, and continued help on various sections from Will Courtenay, Erich Goode, and Joe Pleck.

My family and friends are my foundation; Amy and Zachary are the axis around which my world revolves. If our friends are the families we choose, I could not have chosen better.

This book is for my sister, Sandi, with respect for the path she has chosen, delight at her new adventure, and a lifetime of love.

MSK
Brooklyn, NY

CHAPTER 1

INTRODUCTION

Human Beings: An Engendered Species

In no country has such constant care been taken as in America to trace two clearly distinct lines of action for the two sexes, and to make them keep pace with the other, but in two pathways which are always different.

—ALEXIS DE TOCQUEVILLE
DEMOCRACY IN AMERICA (1835)

Daily, we hear how men and women are different. They tell that we come from different planets. They say we have different brain chemistries, different brain organization, different hormones. They say our different anatomies lead to different destinies. They say we have different ways of knowing, listen to different moral voices, have different ways of speaking and hearing each other.

You'd think we were different species, like, say lobsters and giraffes, or Martians and Venutians. In his best-selling book, pop psychologist John Gray informs us that not only do women and men communicate differently, but they also "think, feel, perceive, react, respond, love, need, and appreciate differently."[1] It's a miracle of cosmic proportions that we ever understand one another!

Yet, despite these alleged interplanetary differences, we're all together in the same workplaces, where we are evaluated by the same criteria for raises, promotions, bonuses, and tenure. We sit in the same classrooms, eat in the same dining halls, read the same books, and are subject to the same criteria for grading. We live in the same houses, prepare and eat the same meals, read the same newspapers, and tune into the same television programs.

What I have come to call this "interplanetary" theory of complete and universal *gender difference* is also typically the way we explain another universal phenomenon: *gender inequality*. Gender is not simply a system of classification, by which biological males and biological females are sorted, separated, and socialized into equivalent sex roles. Gender also expresses the universal inequality between women and men. When we speak about gender we also speak about hierarchy, power, and inequality, not simply difference.

So the two tasks of any study of gender, it seems to me, are to explain both difference and inequality, or, to be alliterative, *difference* and *dominance*. Every general explanation of gender must address two central questions, and their ancillary derivative questions.

First: *Why is it that virtually every single society differentiates people on the basis of gender?* Why are women and men perceived as different in every known society? What are the differences that are perceived? Why is gender at least one—if not the central—basis for the division of labor?

Second: *Why is it that virtually every known society is also based on male dominance?* Why does virtually every society divide social, political, and economic resources unequally between the genders? And why is it that men always get more? Why is a gendered division of labor also an unequal division of labor? Why are women's tasks and men's tasks valued differently?

It is clear, as we shall see, that there are dramatic differences among societies regarding the type of gender differences, the levels of gender inequality, and the amount of violence (implied or real) that is necessary to maintain both systems of difference and domination. But the basic facts remain: *Virtually every society known to us is founded upon assumptions of gender difference and the politics of gender inequality*.

On these axiomatic questions, two basic schools of thought prevail: biological determinism and differential socialization. We know them as "nature" and "nurture," and the question of which is dominant has been debated for a century in classrooms, at dinner parties, by political adversaries, and among friends and families. Are men and women different because they are "hardwired" to be different, or are they different because they've been taught to be? Is biology destiny, or is it that human beings are more flexible, and thus subject to change?

Most of the arguments about gender difference begin, as will this book, with biology (in chapter 2). Women and men *are* biologically different, after all. Our reproductive anatomies are different, and so are our reproductive destinies. Our brain structures differ, our brain chemistries differ. Our musculature is different. Different levels of different hormones circulate through our different bodies. Surely, these add up to fundamental, intractable, and universal differences, and these differences provide the foundation for male domination, don't they?

The answer is an unequivocal maybe. Or, perhaps more accurately, yes and no. There are very few people who would suggest that there are no differences between males and females. At least, I wouldn't suggest it. What social scientists call *sex differences* refer precisely to that catalog of anatomical, hormonal, chemical, and physical differences between women and men. But even here, as we shall see, there are enormous ranges of female-ness and male-ness. Though our musculature differs, plenty of women are physically stronger than plenty of men. Though on average our chemistries are different, it's not an all-or-nothing proposition—women do have varying levels of androgens, and men have varying levels of estrogen in their systems. And though our brain structure may be differently lateralized, males and females both do tend to use both sides of their brain. And it is far from clear that these biological differences automatically and inevitably lead men to dominate women. Could we not imagine, as some writers already have, a culture in which women's biological abilities to bear and nurse children might be seen as the expression of such ineffable power—the ability to create life—that strong men wilt in impotent envy?

In fact, in order to underscore this issue, most social and behavioral scientists now use the term *gender* in a different way than we use the word *sex*. Sex refers to the biological apparatus, the male and the female—our chromosomal, chemical, anatomical organization. Gender refers to the meanings that are attached to those differences within a culture. Sex is male and female; gender is masculinity and femininity—what it means to be a man or a woman. Even the Supreme Court understands this distinction. In a 1994 case, Justice Antonin Scalia wrote:

> The word "gender" has acquired the new and useful connotation of cultural or attitudinal characteristics (as opposed to physical characteristics) distinctive to the sexes. That is to say, gender is to sex as feminine is to female and masculine is to male.[2]

And while biological sex varies very little, gender varies enormously. What it means to possess the anatomical configuration of male or female means very different things depending on where you are, who you are, and when you are living.

It fell to anthropologists to detail some of those differences in the meanings of masculinity and femininity. What they documented is that gender means different things to different people—that it varies cross-culturally. (I discuss and review the anthropological evidence in chapter 3.) Some cultures, like our own, encourage men to be stoic and to prove their masculinity. Men in other cultures seem even more preoccupied with demonstrating sexual prowess than American men. Other cultures prescribe a more relaxed definition of masculinity, based on civic participation, emotional responsiveness, and the collective provision for the community's needs. And some cultures encourage women to be decisive and competitive, whereas others insist that women are naturally passive, helpless, and dependent. What it meant to be a man or a woman in seventeenth-century France, or what it means among Aboriginal peoples in the Australian outback at the turn of the twenty-first century are so far apart that comparison is difficult, if not impossible. The differences between two cultures is often greater than the differences between the two genders. If the meanings of gender vary from culture to culture, and vary within any one culture over historical time, then understanding gender must employ the tools of the social and behavioral sciences and history.

The other reigning school of thought that explains both gender difference and gender domination is *differential socialization*—the "nurture" side of the equation. Men and women are different because we are taught to be different. From the moment of birth, males and females are treated differently. Gradually we acquire the traits, behaviors, and attitudes that our culture defines as "masculine" or "feminine." We are not necessarily born different; we become different through this process of socialization.

Nor are we born biologically predisposed toward gender inequality. Domination is not a trait carried on the Y chromosome; it is the outcome of the different cultural valuing of men's and women's experiences. Thus, the adoption of masculinity and femininity implies the adoption of "political" ideas that what women do is not as culturally important as what men do.

Developmental psychologists have also examined the ways in which the meanings of masculinity and femininity change over the course of a person's life. The issues confronting a man about proving himself and feeling successful will change, as will the social institutions in which he will attempt to enact those experiences. The meanings of femininity are subject to parallel changes, for example, among prepubescent women, women in child-bearing years, and postmenopausal women, as they are different for women entering the labor market and those retiring from it.

Although we typically cast the debate in terms of *either* biological determinism *or* differential socialization—nature versus nurture—it may be useful to pause for a moment to observe what characteristics they have in common. Both schools of thought share two fundamental assumptions. First, both "nature lovers" and "nurturers" see women and men as markedly different from each other—truly, deeply, and irreversibly different. (Nurture does allow for some possibility of change, but they still argue that the process of socialization is a process of making males and females different from each other—differences that are normative, culturally necessary, and "natural.") And both schools of thought assume that the differences *between* women and men are far greater and more decisive (and worthy of analysis) than the differences that might be observed *among* men or *among* women. Thus, both "nature lovers" and "nurturers" subscribe to some version of the interplanetary theory of gender.

Second, both schools of thought assume that gender domination is the inevitable outcome of gender difference, that difference causes domination. To the biologists, it may be because pregnancy and lactation make women more vulnerable and in need of protection, or because male musculature makes them more adept hunters, or that testosterone makes them more aggressive with other men and with women too. Or it may be that men have to dominate women in order to maximize their chances to pass on their genes. Psychologists of "gender roles" tell us that, among other things, men and women are taught to devalue women's experiences, perceptions, and abilities, and to overvalue men's.

I argue in this book that both of these propositions are false. First, I hope to show that the differences between women and men are not to be nearly as great as are the differences among women or among men. Many perceived differences turn out to be differences based less on gender than on the social positions people occupy. Second, I will argue that gender difference is the product of gender inequality, and not the other way around. In fact, gender difference is the chief outcome of gender inequality, because it is through the idea of difference that inequality is legitimated. As one sociologist recently put it, "The very creation of difference is the foundation on which inequality rests."[3]

Using what social scientists have come to call a "social constructionist" approach—I explain this in chapter 5—I will make the case that neither gender difference nor gender inequality is inevitable in the nature of things, nor, more specifically, in the nature of our bodies. Neither are difference and domination explainable solely by reference to differential socialization of boys and girls into sex roles typical of men and women.

When proponents of both nature and nurture positions assert that gender inequality is the inevitable outcome of gender difference, they take, perhaps inadvertently, a political position that assumes that inequality may be lessened, or that its most negative effects may be ameliorated, but that it cannot be eliminated—precisely because it is based upon intractable differences. On the other hand, to assert, as I do, that the exaggerated gender differences that we see are not as great as they appear and that they are the result of inequality allows a far greater political latitude. By eliminating gender inequality, we will remove the foundation upon which the entire edifice of gender difference is built.

What will remain, I believe is not some non-gendered androgynous gruel, in which differences between women and men are blended and everyone acts and thinks in exactly the same way. Quite the contrary. I believe that as gender inequality decreases, the differences among people—differences grounded in race, class, ethnicity, age, sexuality *as well as* gender—will emerge in a context in which each of us can be appreciated for our individual uniqueness as well as our commonality.

MAKING GENDER VISIBLE FOR BOTH WOMEN AND MEN

To make my case, I shall rely upon a dramatic transformation in thinking about gender that has occurred over the past thirty years. In particular, three decades of pioneering work by feminist scholars, both in traditional disciplines and in women's studies, has made us aware of the centrality of gender in shaping social life. We now know that gender is one of the central organizing principles around which social life revolves. Until the 1970s, social scientists would have listed only class and race as the master statuses that defined and proscribed social life. If you wanted to study gender in the 1960s in social science, for example, you would have found but one course designed to address your needs—"Marriage and the Family"—which was sort of the "Ladies Auxiliary" of the social sciences. There were no courses on gender. But today, gender has joined race and class in our understanding of the foundations of an individual's identity. Gender, we now know, is one of the axes around which social life is organized and through which we understand our own experiences.

In the past thirty years, feminist scholars properly focused most of their attention on women—on what Catharine Stimpson has called the "omissions, distortions, and trivializations" of women's experiences—and the spheres to which women have historically been consigned, such as private life and the family.[4] Women's history sought to rescue from obscurity the lives of significant women who had been ignored or whose work has been minimized by traditional androcentric scholarship, and to examine the everyday lives of women in the past—the efforts, for example, of laundresses, factory workers, pioneer homesteaders, or housewives to carve out lives of meaning and dignity in a world controlled by men. Whether the focus has been on the exemplary or the ordinary, though, feminist scholarship has made it clear that gender is a central axis in women's lives.

But when we think of the word *gender*, what gender comes to mind? It is not unusual to find, in courses on History of Gender, Psychology of Gender, or Sociology of Gender, that the classroom is populated almost entirely by women. It's as if only women had gender and were therefore interested in studying it. Occasionally, of course, some brave young man will enroll in a Women's Studies class. You'll usually find him cringing in the corner, in anticipation of feeling blamed for all the sins of millennia of patriarchal oppression.

It's my intention in this book to build upon the feminist approaches to gender by also making masculinity visible. We need, I think, to integrate men into our curriculum. Because it is men—or, rather masculinity—that is invisible.

"What?!" I can hear you saying. "Did he just say 'integrate men into the curriculum'? Men are invisible? What's he talking about?! Men aren't invisible. They're everywhere."

And, of course, that's true. Men are ubiquitous in universities and professional schools, and in the public sphere in general. And it's true that if you look at the college curriculum, every course that doesn't have the word *women* in the title is about men. Every course that isn't in "women's studies" is de facto a course in "men's studies"—except we usually call it history, political science, literature, chemistry.

But when we study men, we study them as political leaders, military heroes, scientists, writers, artists. Men, themselves, are invisible *as men*. Rarely, if ever, do we see a course that examines the lives of men as men. What is the impact of gender on the lives of these famous men? How does masculinity play a part in the lives of great artists, writers, presidents, etc. How does masculinity pay out in the lives of "ordinary" men—in factories and on farms, in union halls and large corporations? On this score, the traditional curriculum suddenly draws a big blank. Everywhere one turns there are courses about men, but virtually no information on masculinity.

Several years ago, this yawning gap inspired me to undertake a cultural history of the idea of masculinity in America, to trace the development and shifts in what it has meant to be a man over the course of our history.[5] What I found is that American men have been very articulate in describing what it means to be a man, and in seeing whatever they have done as a way to prove their manhood, but that we haven't known how to hear them.

Integrating gender into our courses is a way to fulfill the promise of women's studies—by understanding men as gendered as well. In my university, for example, the course on nineteenth-century British literature includes a deeply "gendered" reading of the Brontës, that discusses their feelings about femininity, marriage, and relations between the sexes. Yet not a word is spoken about Dickens and masculinity, especially about his feelings about fatherhood and the family. Dickens is understood as a "social problem" novelist, and his issue was class relations—this despite the fact that so many of Dickens's most celebrated characters are young boys without fathers, and who are searching for authentic families. And there's not a word about Thomas Hardy's ambivalent ideas about masculinity and marriage in, say, *Jude the Obscure*. Hardy's grappling with premodernist conceptions of an apathetic universe is what we discuss. And my wife tells me that in her nineteenth-century American literature class at Princeton, gender was the main topic of conversation when the subject was Edith Wharton, but the word was never spoken when they discussed Henry James, in whose work gendered anxiety erupts variously as chivalric contempt, misogynist rage, and sexual ambivalence. James, we're told, is "about" the form of the novel, narrative technique, the stylistic powers of description and characterization. Certainly not about gender.

So we continue to act as if gender applied only to women. Surely the time has come to make gender visible to men. As the Chinese proverb has it, the fish are the last to discover the ocean.

This was made clear to me in a seminar on feminism I attended in the early 1980s.[6] In that seminar, in a discussion between two women, I first confronted this invisibility of gender to men. During one meeting, a white woman and a black woman were discussing whether all women were, by definition, "sisters," because they all had essentially the same experiences and because all women faced a common oppression by men. The white woman asserted that the fact that they were both women bonded them, in spite of racial differences. The black woman disagreed.

"When you wake up in the morning and look in the mirror, what do you see?" she asked.

"I see a woman," replied the white woman.

"That's precisely the problem," responded the black woman. "I see a *black* woman. To me, race is visible every day, because race is how I am *not* privileged in our culture. Race is invisible to you, because it's how you are privileged. It's why there will always be differences in our experience."

At this point in the conversation, I groaned—more audibly, perhaps, than I had intended. Since I was the only man in the room, someone asked what my response had meant.

"Well," I said, "when I look in the mirror, I see a human being. I'm universally generalizable. As a middle-class white man, I have no class, no race, no gender. I'm the generic person!"

Sometimes, I like to think that it was on that day that I *became* a middle-class white man. Sure, I had been all those before, but they had not meant much to me. Until then, I had thought myself generic, universally generalizable. Since then, I've begun to understand that race, class, and gender didn't refer only to other people, who were marginalized by race, class, or gender privilege. Those terms also described me. I enjoyed the privilege of invisibility. The very processes that confer privilege to one group and not another group are often invisible to those upon whom that privilege is conferred. What makes us marginal or powerless are the processes we see. Invisibility is a privilege in another sense—as a luxury. Only white people in our society have the luxury not to think about race every minute of their lives. And only men have the luxury to pretend that gender does not matter.

Consider another example of how power is so often invisible to those who have it. Many of you have email addresses, and you send email messages to people all over the world. You've probably noticed that there is one big difference between email addresses in the United States and email addresses of people in other countries: Their addresses end with a "country code." So, for example, if you were writing to someone in South Africa, you'd put "za" at the end, or "jp" for Japan, or "uk" for England (United Kingdom), or "de" for Germany (Deutschland). But when you write to people in the United States, the email address ends with "edu" for an educational institution, "org" for an organization, "gov" for a federal government office, and "com" or "net" for commercial Internet providers. Why is it that the United States doesn't have a country code?

It is because when you are the dominant power in the world, everyone else needs to be named. When you are "in power," you needn't draw attention to yourself as a specific entity, but, rather, you can pretend to be the generic, the universal, the generalizable. From the point of view of the United States, all other countries are "other" and thus need to be named, marked, noted. Once again, privilege is invisible. In the world of the Internet, as Michael Jackson sang, "We are the world."

There are consequences to this invisibility: Privilege, as well as gender, remains invisible. And it is hard to generate a politics of inclusion from invisibility. The invisibility of privilege means that many men, like many white people, become defensive and angry when confronted with the statistical realities or the human consequences of racism or sexism. Since our privilege is invisible, we may become defensive. Hey, we may even feel like victims ourselves. Invisibility "creates a neurotic oscillation between a sense of entitlement and a sense of unearned privilege," as journalist Edward Ball put it, having recently explored his own family's history as one of the largest slave-owning families in South Carolina.[7]

The continued invisibility of masculinity also means that the gendered standards that are held up as the norm appear to us to be gender-neutral. The illusion of gender neutrality has serious consequences for both women and men. It means that men can maintain the fiction that they are being measured by "objective" standards; for women, it means that they are being judged by someone else's yardstick. At the turn of the century, the great sociologist Georg Simmel underscored this issue when he wrote:

> We measure the achievements and the commitments . . . of males and females in terms of specific norms and values; but these norms are not neutral, standing above the contrasts of the sexes; they have themselves a male character. . . . The standards of art and the demands of patriotism, the general mores and the specific social ideas, the equity of practical judgments and the objectivity of theoretical knowledge . . . —all these categories are formally generically human, but are in fact masculine in terms of their actual historical formation. If we call ideas that claim absolute validity objectivity binding, then it is a fact that in the historical life of our species there operates the equation: objective = male.[8]

Simmel's theoretical formulation echoes in our daily interactions. Recently, I was invited to be a guest lecturer in a course on Sociology of Gender taught by one of my female colleagues. As I entered the lecture hall, one student looked up from her notes and exclaimed, "Finally, an objective opinion." Now, I'm neither more nor less "objective" than my colleagues, but, in this student's eyes, I was seen as objective—the disconnected, disembodied, deracinated, degendered, voice of scientific and rational objectivity. I am what objectivity looks like! (One ironic result is that I could probably say more outlandish things in a classroom than my female colleagues could. If a female, or African American, professor were to make a statement such as, "White Men are privileged in American society," our students might respond by saying, "Of course you'd say that. You're biased." They'd see such a normative statement as revealing the inherent biases of gender or race, a case of special pleading. But when I say it? As objective fact, transmitted by an objective professor, they'll probably take notes.)

Such an equation that "objective = male" has enormous practical consequences in every arena of our lives, from the elementary school classroom to professional and graduate schools, and in every workplace we enter. As Simmel writes, "Man's *position of power* does not only assure his relative superiority over the woman but it assures that his standards become generalized as generically human standards that are to govern the behavior of men and women alike."[9]

THE CURRENT DEBATE

I believe that we are, at this moment, having a national debate about masculinity in this country—but that we don't know it. For example, what gender comes to mind when I invoke the following current American problems: "teen violence," "gang violence," "suburban violence," "drug violence," "violence in the schools?" And what gender comes to mind when I say the words "suicide bomber" or "terrorist hijacker"?

Of course, you've imagined men. And not just any men—but younger men, in their teens and twenties, and relatively poorer men, from the working class or lower middle class.

But how do our social commentators discuss these problems? Do they note that the problems of youth and violence is really a problem of young *men* and violence? Do they ever mention that everywhere ethnic nationalism sets up shop, it is young men who are the shopkeepers? Do they ever mention masculinity at all?

No. Listen, for example, to the voice of one expert, asked to comment on the brutal murder of Matthew Shepard, a gay twenty-one-year-old college student at the University of Wyoming. After being reminded that young men account for 80 percent to 90 percent of people arrested for "gay bashing" crimes, the reporter quoted a sociologist as saying that "[t]his youth variable tells us they are working out identity issues, making the transition away from home into adulthood."[10] This *"youth* variable"? What had been a variable about age and gender had been transformed into a variable about age. Gender had disappeared. That is the sound of silence, what invisibility looks like.

Now, imagine that these were all women—all the ethnic nationalists, the militias, the gay bashers. Would that not be *the* story, the *only* story? Would not a gender analysis be at the center of every single story? Would we not hear from experts on female socialization, frustration, anger, PMS, and everything else under the sun? But the fact that these are men earns nary a word.

Take one final example. What if it had been young girls who opened fire on their classmates in West Paducah, Kentucky, in Pearl, Mississippi, in Jonesboro, Arkansas, or in Springfield, Oregon? And what if nearly all the children who died were boys? Do you think that the social outcry would demand that we investigate the "inherent violence" of Southern culture, or simply express dismay that young "people" have too much access to guns? I doubt it. And yet no one seemed to mention that the young boys who actually committed those crimes were simply doing—albeit in dramatic form at a younger age—what American men have been taught to do for centuries when they are upset and angry. Men don't get mad; they get even. (I explore the gender of violence in chapter 11.)

I believe that until we make gender visible for both women and for men we will not, as a culture, adequately know how to address these issues. That's not to say that all we have to do is address masculinity. These issues are complex, requiring analyses of the political economy of global economic integration, of the transformation of social classes, of urban poverty and hopelessness, of racism. But if we ignore masculinity—if we let it remain invisible—we will never completely understand them, let alone resolve them.

THE PLURAL AND THE POWERFUL

When I use the term *gender,* then, it is with the explicit intention of discussing both masculinity and femininity. But even these terms are inaccurate because they imply that there is one simple definition of masculinity and one definition of femininity. One of the important elements of a social constructionist approach—especially if we intend to dislodge the notion that gender differences alone are decisive—is to explore the differences *among* men and *among* women, since, as it turns out, these are often more decisive than the differences between women and men.

Within any one society at any one moment, several meanings of masculinity and femininity coexist. Simply put, not all American men and women are the same. Our experiences are also structured by class, race, ethnicity, age, sexuality, region. Each of these axes modifies the others. Just because we make gender visible doesn't mean that we make these other organizing principles of social life invisible. Imagine, for example, an older, black, gay man in Chicago and a young, white, heterosexual farm boy in Iowa. Wouldn't they have different definitions of masculinity? Or imagine a twenty-two-year-old wealthy Asian American heterosexual woman in San Francisco and a poor white Irish Catholic lesbian in Boston. Wouldn't their ideas about what it means to be a woman be somewhat different?

If gender varies across cultures, over historical time, among men and women within any one culture, and over the life course, can we really speak of masculinity or femininity as though they were constant, universal essences, common to all women and to all men? If not, gender must be seen as an ever-changing fluid assemblage of meanings and behaviors. In that sense, we must speak of *masculinities* and *femininities,* and thus recognize the different definitions of masculinity and femininity that we construct. By pluralizing the terms, we acknowledge that masculinity and femininity mean different things to different groups of people at different times.

At the same time, we can't forget that all masculinities and femininities are not created equal. American men and women must also contend with a particular definition that is held up as the model against which we are expected to measure ourselves. We thus come to know what it means to be a man or a woman in our culture by setting our definitions in opposition to a set of "others"—racial minorities, sexual minorities. For men, the classic "other" is, of course, women. It feels imperative to most men that they make it clear—eternally, compulsively, decidedly—that they are unlike women.

For most men, this is the "hegemonic" definition—the one that is held up as the model for all of us. It is as Virginia Woolf wrote in 1938, "the quintessence of virility, the perfect type of which all the others are imperfect adumbrations."[11] The hegemonic definition of masculinity is "constructed in relation to various subordinated masculinities as well as in relation to women," writes sociologist R. W. Connell. The sociologist Erving Goffman once described this hegemonic definition of masculinity like this:

> In an important sense there is only one complete unblushing male in America: a young, married, white, urban, northern, heterosexual, Protestant, father, of college education, fully employed, of good complexion, weight, and height, and a recent record in sports. . . . Any male who fails to qualify in any one of these ways is likely to view himself—during moments at least—as unworthy, incomplete, and inferior.[12]

Women contend with an equally exaggerated ideal of femininity, which Connell calls "emphasized femininity." Emphasized femininity is organized around compliance with gender inequality, and is "oriented to accommodating the interests and desires of men." One sees emphasized femininity in "the display of sociability rather than technical competence, fragility in mating scenes, compliance with men's desire for titillation and ego-stroking in office relationships, acceptance of marriage and childcare as a response to labor-market discrimination against women."[13] Emphasized femininity exaggerates gender difference as a strategy of "adaptation to men's power" stressing empathy and nurturance; "real" womanhood is described as "fascinating" and women are advised that they can wrap men around their fingers by knowing and playing by the "rules." In one research study, an eight-year-old boy captured this emphasized femininity eloquently in a poem he wrote:

If I were a girl, I'd have to attract a guy
wear makeup; sometimes.
Wear the latest style of clothes and try to be likable.
I probably wouldn't play any physical sports like football or soccer.
I don't think I would enjoy myself around men
in fear of rejection
or under the pressure of attracting them.[14]

GENDER DIFFERENCE AS "DECEPTIVE DISTINCTIONS"

The existence of multiple masculinities and femininities dramatically undercuts the idea that the gender differences we observe are due solely to differently gendered people occupying gender-neutral positions. Moreover, that these masculinities and femininities are arrayed along a hierarchy, and measured against one another, buttresses the argument that domination creates and exaggerates difference.

The interplanetary theory of gender assumes, whether through biology or socialization, that women act like women, no matter where they are, and that men act like men no matter where they are. Psychologist Carol Tavris argues that such binary thinking leads to what philosophers call the "law of the excluded middle," which, as she reminds us, "is where most men and women fall in terms of their psychological qualities, beliefs, abilities, traits and values."[15] It turns out that many of the differences between women and men that we observe in our everyday lives are actually not *gender* differences at all, but differences that are the result of being in different positions or in different arenas. It's not that gendered individuals occupy these ungendered positions, but that the positions themselves elicit the behaviors we see as gendered. The sociologist Cynthia Fuchs Epstein calls these "deceptive distinctions" because, while they appear to be based on gender, they are actually based on something else.[16]

Take, for example, the well-known differences in communication patterns observed by Deborah Tannen in her best-selling book *You Just Don't Understand*. Tannen argues that women and men communicate with the languages of their respective planets—men employ the competitive language of hierarchy and domination to get ahead; women create webs of inclusion with softer, more embracing language that ensures that everyone feels O.K. At home, men are the strong silent types, grunting monosyllabically to their wives, who want to use conversation to create intimacy.[17]

But it turns out that those very same monosyllabic men are very verbal at work, where they are in positions of dependency and powerlessness, and need to use conversation to maintain a relationship with their superiors at work; and their wives are just as capable of using language competitively to maximize their position in a corporate hierarchy. When he examined the recorded transcripts of women's and men's testimony in trials, anthropologist William O'Barr concluded that the witnesses' occupation was a more accurate predictor of their use of language than was gender. "So-called women's language is neither characteristic of all women, nor limited only to women," O'Barr writes. If women use "powerless" language, it may be due "to the greater tendency of women to occupy relatively powerless social positions" in society.[18] Communication differences turn out to be "deceptive distinctions" because rarely do we observe the communication patterns of dependent men and executive women.

We could take another example from the world of education, which I explore in chapter 6. Aggregate differences in girls' and boys' scores on standardized math tests have led people to speculate that while males have a natural propensity for arithmetic figures, females have a "fear of math." Couple this with their "fear of success" in the workplace and you might find that women manage money less effectively—with less foresight, less calculation, less care. The popular writer Colette Dowling, author of the best-selling 1981 book *The Cinderella Complex* (a book that described that underneath their apparent ambition, competence, and achievement, women "really" were waiting for Prince Charming to rescue them and carry them off into a romantic sunset, a future in which they could be as passive and helpless and they secretly wanted to be), recently interviewed sixty-five women in their late fifties about money matters and found that only two had *any* investment plans for their retirements. Broke and bankrupt after several best-sellers and single again herself, Dowling argues that this relates to "conflicts with dependency. Money savvy is connected with masculinity in our culture," she told an interviewer. "That leaves women with the feeling that if they want to take care of themselves and are good at it, the quid pro quo is they'll never hook up with a relationship." Because of ingrained femininity, women end up shooting themselves in the foot.[19]

But such assertions fly in the face of all available research, argues the financial expert Jane Bryant Quinn, herself the author of a best-seller about women and money. "It *is* more socially acceptable for women not to manage their money," she told the same interviewer. "But the Y chromosome is not a money management chromosome. In all the studies, if you control for earnings, age and experience, women are the same as men. At 23, out in the working world staring at a 401(k) plan, they are equally confused. But if those women quit working, they will know less and less about finance, while the man, who keeps working, will know more and more."[20] So it is our experience, not our gender, that predicts how we'll handle our retirement investments.

What about those enormous gender differences that some observers have found in the workplace (the subject of chapter 8)? Men, we hear, are competitive social climbers who seek advancement at every opportunity; women are cooperative team builders who shun competition and may even suffer from a "fear of success." But the pioneering study by Rosabeth Moss Kanter, reported in *Men and Women of the Corporation,* indicated that gender mattered far less than opportunity. When women had the same opportunities, networks, mentors, and possibilities for advancement, they behaved just as the men did. Women were not successful because they lacked opportunities, not because they feared success; when men lacked opportunities, they behaved in stereotypically "feminine" ways.[21]

Finally, take our experiences in the family, which I examine in chapter 6. Here, again, we assume that women are socialized to be nurturing and maternal, men to be strong and silent, relatively emotionally inexpressive arbiters of justice—that is, we assume that women do the work of "mothering" because they are socialized to do so. And again, sociological research suggests that our behavior in the family has somewhat less to do with gender socialization than with the family situations in which we find ourselves.

Research by sociologist Kathleen Gerson, for example, found that gender socialization was not very helpful in predicting women's family experiences. Only slightly more than half the women who were primarily interested in full-time motherhood were, in fact, full-time mothers; and only slightly more than half the women who were primarily interested in full-time careers had them. It turned out that marital stability, husbands' income, women's workplace experiences, and support networks were far more important than gender socialization in determining which women ended up full-time mothers and which did not.[22]

On the other side of the ledger, research by sociologist Barbara Risman found that despite a gender socialization that downplays emotional responsiveness and nurturing, most single fathers are perfectly capable of "mothering." Single fathers do not hire female workers to do the typically female tasks around the house; they do those tasks themselves. In fact, Risman found few differences between single fathers and mothers (single or married) when it came to what they did around the house, how they acted with their children, or even in their children's emotional and intellectual development. Men's parenting styles were virtually indistinguishable from women's, a finding that led Risman to argue that "men can mother and that children are not necessarily better nurtured by women than by men."[23]

These findings also shed a very different light on other research. For example, some recent researchers found significant differences in the amount of stress that women and men experience on an everyday basis. According to the researchers, women reported higher levels of stress and lower numbers of "stress-free" days than did men. David Almeida and Ronald Kessler sensibly concluded that this was not a biologically based difference, a signal of women's inferiority in handling stress, but rather an indication that women had more stress in their lives, since they had to balance and juggle more family and work issues than did men.[24]

Almeida and Kessler's findings were reported with some fanfare in newspapers, which with few exceptions recounted new significant gender differences. But what Almeida and Kessler actually found was that women, as Kessler noted, "tend to the home, the plumber, their husband's career, their jobs, and oh yes, the kids." By contrast, for men, it's "How are things at work? The end."[25] And they found this by asking married couples, both husbands and wives, about their reactions to such "stressors." What do you think their findings would have been had they asked single mothers and single fathers the same questions? Do you think they would have found any significant gender differences at all? More likely, they would have found that trying to juggle the many demands of a working parent is likely to generate enormous stress both for men and for women. Again, it's the structure, not the gender, that generates the statistical difference.

Based on all this research, you might conclude, as does Risman, that "if women and men were to experience identical structural conditions and role expectations, empirically observable gender differences would dissipate."[26] I am not fully convinced. There *are* some differences between women and men, after all. Perhaps, as this research suggests, those differences are not as great, decisive, or as impervious to social change as we once thought. But there are some differences. It will be my task in this book to explore both those areas where there appear to be gender differences but where there are, in fact few or no differences, and those areas where gender differences are significant and decisive.

THE MEANING OF MEAN DIFFERENCES

Few of the differences between women and men are hardwired into all males to the exclusion of all females, or vice versa. Although we can readily observe differences between women and men in rates of aggression, physical strength, math or verbal achievement, caring and nurturing, or emotional expressiveness, it is not true that all males and no females are aggressive, physically strong, and adept at math and science, and all females and no males are caring and nurturing, verbally adept, or emotionally expressive. What we mean when we speak of gender differences are mean differences, differences in the average scores obtained by women and men.

These mean scores tell us something about the differences between the two groups, but they tell us nothing about the distributions themselves, the differences *among* men or *among* women. Sometimes these distributions can be enormous: There are large numbers of caring or emotionally expressive men, and of aggressive and physically strong women. (See figure 1.1.) In fact, in virtually all the research that has been done on the attributes associated with masculinity or femininity, the differences among women and among men are far greater than the mean differences between women and men. We tend to focus on the mean differences, but they may tell us far less than we think they do.

What we think they tell us, of course, is that women and men are different, from different planets. This is what I will call the interplanetary theory of gender difference—that the observed mean differences between women and men are decisive and that they come from the fact that women and men are biologically so physically different.

For example, even the idea that we are from different planets, that our differences are deep and intractable, has a political dimension: To call the "other" sex the "opposite" sex obscures the many ways we are alike. As the anthropologist Gayle Rubin points out:

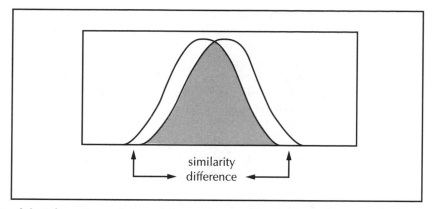

similarity
difference

Figure 1.1. Schematic rendering of the overlapping distributions of traits, attitudes, and behaviors by gender. Although mean differences might obtain on many characteristics, these distributions suggest far greater similarity between women and men, and far greater variability among men and among women.

> Men and women are, of course, different. But they are not as different as day and night, earth and sky, yin and yang, life and death. In fact from the standpoint of nature, men and women are closer to each other than either is to anything else—for instance mountains, kangaroos, or coconut palms. . . . Far from being an expression of natural differences, exclusive gender identity is the suppression of natural similarities.[27]

The interplanetary theory of gender difference is important not because it's right—in fact, it is wrong far more often than it is right—but because, as a culture, we seem desperately to *want* it to be true. That is, the real sociological question about gender is not the sociology of gender differences—explaining the physiological origins of gender difference—but the sociology of knowledge question that explores why gender difference is so important to us, why we cling to the idea of gender difference so tenaciously, why, I suppose, we shell out millions of dollars for books that "reveal" the deep differences between women and men, but will probably never buy a book that says, "Hey, we're all Earthlings!"

That, however, is the message of this book. Virtually all available research from the social and behavioral sciences suggests that women and men are not from Venus and Mars, but are both from planet Earth. We're not opposite sexes, but neighboring sexes—we have far more in common with each other than we have differences. We pretty much have the same abilities, and pretty much want the same things in our lives.

The Politics of Difference and Domination

Whether we believe that gender difference is biologically determined or is a cultural formation, the interplanetary theory of gender difference assumes that gender is a property of individuals, that is, that gender is a component of one's identity. But this is only half the story. I believe that individual boys and girls become gendered—that is, we learn the "appropriate" behaviors and traits that are associated with hegemonic masculinity and exaggerated femininity, and then we each, individually, negotiate our own path in a way that feels right to us. In a sense, we each "cut our own deal" with the dominant definitions of masculinity and femininity. That's why we are so keenly attuned to, and so vigorously resist gender stereotypes—because we believe that they do not actually encompass our experiences.

But we do not cut our own deal by ourselves, in gender-neutral institutions and arenas. The social institutions of our world—workplace, family, school, politics—are also gendered institutions, sites where the dominant definitions are reinforced and reproduced, and where "deviants" are disciplined. We become gendered selves in a gendered society.

To speak of a gendered society is not the same thing as pointing out that rocket ships and skyscrapers bear symbolic relationships to a certain part of the male anatomy. Sometimes function takes precedence over symbolic form. It is also only partially related to the way we use metaphors of gender to speak of other spheres of activity—the way, for example, the worlds of sports, sex, war, and work each appropriate the language of the other sphere.

When we say that we live in a gendered society we imply that the organizations of our society have evolved in ways that reproduce both the differences between women and men and the domination of men over women. Institutionally, we can see how the structure of the workplace is organized around demonstrating and reproducing masculinity: The temporal and spatial organization of work both depend upon the separation of spheres (distance between work and home and the fact that women are the primary child care providers).

As it did with respect to the invisibility of gendered identity, assuming institutional gender neutrality actually serves to maintain the gender politics of those institutions. And it also underscores the way we often assume that if you allow individuals to express a wider range of gender behaviors, they'll be able to succeed in those gender-neutral institutions. So we assume that the best way to eliminate gender inequality in higher education or in the workplace is to promote sameness—that is, we're only unequal because we're different.

This, however, creates a political and personal dilemma for women in gendered institutions. It's a no-win proposition for women when they enter the workplace, the military, politics, or sports—arenas that are already established to reproduce and sustain masculinity. To the extent that they become "like men" in order to succeed, they are seen as having sacrificed their femininity. Yet to the extent to which they refuse to sacrifice their femininity, they are seen as different, and thus gender discrimination is legitimate as the sorting of different people into different slots.[28] Women who succeed are punished for abandoning their femininity—rejected as potential partners, labeled as "dykes," left off the invitation lists. The first women who entered the military, or military colleges, or even Princeton and Yale when they went coeducational in the late 1960s were seen as being "less" feminine, as being unsuccessful as women. Yet had they been more "successful" as women, they would have been seen as less capable soldiers or students.[29] Thus, gender inequality creates a double bind for women—a double bind that is based on the assumption of gender difference and the assumption of institutional gender neutrality.

There's a more personal side to this double bind. Often, men are perplexed by the way their wives have closets filled with clothes, yet constantly complain that they have "nothing to wear." Men often find this behavior strange, probably the behavior of someone who must have come from another planet. After all, we men typically alternate among only three or four different color shirts and suits, which we match with perhaps five or six different ties. Navy blue, charcoal gray, black—what could be so difficult about getting dressed?

But women who work enter a gendered institution in which everything they wear "signifies" something. So they look at one business-like dress and tell themselves, "No, this is too frumpy. They'll never take me seriously as a woman in this dress!" So they hold up a slinkier and tighter outfit and think, "In this little number, all they'll see in me is a woman, and they'll never take me seriously as an employee." Either way—corporate frump or sexy babe—women lose, because the workplace is, itself, gendered, and standards of success, including dressing for success, are tailored to the other sex.

Both difference and domination are produced and reproduced in our social interactions, in the institutions in which we live and work. Though the differences between us are not as great as we often assume, they become important in our expectations and observations. It will be my task in this book to examine those differences—those that are real and important—as well as to reveal those that are neither real nor important. I will explore the ways in which gender inequality provides the foundation for assumptions of gender difference. And, finally, I will endeavor to show the impact of gender on our lives—how we become gendered people living gendered lives in a gendered society.

EXPLANATIONS OF GENDER

ORDAINED BY NATURE

Biology Constructs the Sexes

A devil, a born devil, on whose nature
Nurture can never stick! On whom my pains,
Humanely taken, all, all lost, quite lost!

—SHAKESPEARE
THE TEMPEST (ACT IV, SCENE 1)

Oprah: Do you think society will change if it were proven be-
yond a shadow of a doubt that you were born that way?

Gay twin: It would be easier . . . the acceptance, but you under-
stand that people still don't accept Blacks and Hispanics and
handicapped . . . Gays are right in there with them . . . peo-
ple don't accept obese people.

Oprah (chagrined): I forgot about that. Let's take a break.

Aside from his exasperated cry of "women—what do they want?" Sigmund Freud's most famous line is probably the axiom, "Anatomy is destiny." Though it's not clear that Freud ever intended that it be taken literally, a large number of biologists believe that the differences in anatomy are decisive, and provide the basis for the differences in men's and women's experiences. One recent researcher proclaimed his belief that "the differences between the males and females of our species will ultimately be found in the cell arrangements and anatomy of the human brain."[1] To biologists, the source of human behavior lies neither in our stars nor in ourselves, as Caesar had suggested to Brutus—but rather in our cells.

Biological explanations hold a place of prominence in our explanations of both gender *difference* and gender *inequality*. For one thing, biological explanations have the ring of "true" science to them: since their theories are based on "objective scientific facts," the arguments of natural scientists are extraordinarily persuasive. Secondly, biological explanations seem to accord with our own observations: Women and men *seem* so different to us most of the time—so different, in fact, that we often appear to be from different planets.

There's also a certain conceptual tidiness to biological explanations, since the social arrangements between women and men (gender inequality) seem to stem directly and inevitably from the differences between us. Biological arguments reassure us that what *is* is what should be, that the social is natural. Finally, such reassurances tell us that these existing inequalities are not our fault, that no one is to blame, really. We cannot be held responsible for the way we act—hey, it's biological! (Such claims are made by conservatives and liberals, by feminists and misogynists, and by homophobes and gay activists.) What's more, if these explanations are true, no amount of political initiative, no amount of social spending, no great policy upheavals will change the relationships between women and men.

This chapter will explore some of the various biological evidence that is presented to demonstrate the natural, biologically based differences between the sexes, and the ways in which social and political arrangements (inequality) directly flow from those differences. Biological differences can tell us much about the ways in which men and women behave. The search for such differences can also tell us a lot about our culture—about what we want so desperately to believe, and why we want to believe it.

BIOLOGICAL DIFFERENCES, THEN AND NOW

The search for the biological origins of the differences between women and men is not new. What is new, at least for the past few centuries, is that scientists have come to play the central role in exploring the natural differences between males and females.

Prior to the nineteenth century, most explanations of gender difference had been the province of theologians. God had created man and woman for different purposes, and those reproductive differences were decisive. Thus, for example, did the Rev. John Todd warn against woman suffrage which would "reverse the very laws of God" and its supporters who tried to convince women that she would "find independence, wealth and renown in man's sphere, when your only safety and happiness is patiently, lovingly, and faithfully performing the duties and enacting the relations of your own sphere."[2]

By the late nineteenth century, under the influence of Darwin and the emerging science of evolutionary biology, scientists jumped into the debate, wielding their latest discoveries. Some argued that woman's normal biological processes made her unfit for the public world of work and school. For example, in his book, *A Physician's Counsels to Woman in Health and Disease* (1871), Dr. W. C. Taylor cautioned women to stay home and rest for at least five or six days a month:

> We cannot too emphatically urge the importance of regarding these monthly returns as periods of ill-health, as days when the ordinary occupations are to be suspended or modified. . . . Long walks, dancing, shopping, riding and parties should be avoided at this time of month invariably and under all circumstances.[3]

In his pathbreaking work, *On the Origin of Species* (1859), Darwin had posed several questions. How do certain species come to be the way they are? Why is there such astonishing variety among those species? Why do some species differ from others in some ways and remain similar in other ways? He answered these questions with the law of natural selection. Species adapt to their changing environments. Those species that adapt well to their environments are reproductively successful, that is, their adaptive characteristics are passed on to the next generation, while those species that are less adaptive do not pass on their characteristics. Within any one species, a similar process occurs, and those individuals who are best suited to their environment pass on their genes to the next generation. Species are always changing, always adapting.

Such an idea was theologically heretical to those who believed that God had created all species, including human beings, intact and unchanging. And Darwin did believe that just as the species of the lower animal world evidenced differences between males and females, so too did human beings. "Woman seems to differ from man in mental disposition, chiefly in her greater tenderness and lesser selfishness," he wrote in *The Descent of Man*. Man's competitiveness, ambition, and selfishness "seem to be his natural and unfortunate birthright. The chief distinction in the intellectual powers of the two sexes is shown by man's attaining to a higher eminence, in whatever he takes up, than can woman—whether requiring deep thought, reason, or imagination, or merely the uses of the senses and the hands."[4]

No sooner had the biological differences between women and men been established as scientific fact than writers and critics declared all efforts to challenge social inequality and discrimination against women to be in violation of the "laws of nature." Many writers argued that women's efforts to enter the public sphere—to seek employment, to vote, to enter colleges—were misguided for they place women's social and political aspirations over the purposes for which their bodies had been designed. Women were not to be *excluded* from voting, from the labor force or from higher education as much as they were, as the Rev. Todd put it, "to be exempted from certain things which men must endure."[5] This position was best summed up by a participant in a debate about woman suffrage in Sacramento, California, in 1880:

> I am opposed to woman's sufferage [sic] on account of the burden it will place upon her. Her delicate nature has already enough to drag it down. Her slender frame, naturally weakened by the constant strain attendant upon her nature is too often racked by diseases that are caused by a too severe tax upon her mind. The presence of passion, love, ambition, is all too potent for her enfeebled condition, and wrecked health and early death are all too common.[6]

Social scientists quickly jumped on the biological bandwagon—especially Social Darwinists, who shortened the time span necessary for evolution from millennia to one or two generations and who causally extended Darwin's range from ornithology to human beings. In their effort to legitimate social science by allying it with natural law, Social Darwinists applied Darwin's theory in ways its originator had never imagined, distorting his ideas about natural selection to claim decisive biological differences among races, nations, families, and, of course, between women and men. For example, the eminent French sociologist Gustav LeBon, who would later become famous for his theory of the collective mind and the irrationality of the crowd, believed that the differences between women and men could be explained by their different brain structure. He wrote in 1879:

In the most intelligent races, as among the Parisians, there are a large number of women whose brains are closer in size to those of gorillas than to the most developed of male brains. . . . All psychologists who have studied the intelligence of women . . . recognize today that they represent the most inferior forms of human evolution and that they are closer to children and savages than to an adult civilized man. They excel in fickleness, inconstancy, absence of thought and logic, and incapacity to reason. Without doubt, there exist some distinguished women, very superior to the average man, but they are as exceptional as the birth of any monstrosity, as, for example, of a gorilla with two heads . . .[7]

Much of the debate centered on whether or not women could be educated, especially in colleges and universities. One writer suggested that a woman "of average brain" could attain the same standards as a man with an average brain "only at the cost of her health, of her emotions, or of her morale." Another prophesied that women would grow bigger and heavier brains and their uteruses would shrink if they went to college. Perhaps the most famous social scientist to join this discussion was Edward C. Clarke, Harvard's eminent professor of education. In his best-selling book *Sex in Education: or; A Fair Chance for the Girls* (1873), Clarke argued that women should be exempted from higher education because of the tremendous demands made upon their bodies by reproduction. If women went to college, Clarke predicted, they would fail to reproduce, and it would require "no prophet to foretell that the wives who are to be mothers in our republic must be drawn from transatlantic homes."[8] (Clarke's invocation of the threat to civilization posed by immigrants reproducing faster than native-born whites is common to the conflation of racism and sexism of the era.)

The evidence for such preposterous biological claims? Simple. It turned out that college-educated women were marrying less often and bearing fewer children than non-college-educated women. It must have been those shriveled wombs and heavier brains. And it also appeared that 42 percent of all women admitted to mental institutions were college-educated, compared with only 16 percent of the men. Obviously, collegiate education was driving women crazy. Today, of course, we might attribute this difference in fertility or in mental illness among college-educated women to enlarged opportunities or frustrated ambitions, respectively, but not to shrinking wombs. Clarke's assertions remain a striking example of the use of correlational aggregate social science data for decidedly political purposes.

The implicit conservatism of such arguments was as evident at the turn of the last century as it is now. "How did woman first become subject to man as she is now all over the world?" asked James Long. "By her nature, her sex, just as the negro is and always will be, to the end of time, inferior to the white race, and therefore, doomed to subjection; but happier than she would be in any other condition, just because it is the law of her nature."[9]

Today, biological arguments generally draw their evidence from three areas of research: (1) evolutionary theory, from sociobiology to "evolutionary psychology"; (2) brain research; and, (3) endocrinological research on sex hormones, before birth and again at puberty. The latter two areas of research are also used to describe the biologically based differences between heterosexuals and homosexuals, which are, as we shall see, often expressed in gender terms.[10]

THE EVOLUTIONARY IMPERATIVE: FROM SOCIAL DARWINISM TO SOCIOBIOLOGY AND EVOLUTIONARY PSYCHOLOGY

Evolutionary biologists since Darwin have abandoned the more obviously political intentions of the Social Darwinists, but the development of a new field of sociobiology in the 1970s revived evolutionary arguments again. Edward Wilson, a professor of entomology at Harvard, helped to found this school of thought, expanding his original field of expertise to include human behavior as well as bugs. All creatures, Wilson argued, "obey" the "biological principle," and all temperamental differences (personalities, cultures) derive from the biological development of creatures undergoing the pressure of evolutionary selection. The natural differences that result are the source of the social and political arrangements we observe today. As Wilson and fellow sociobiologist Richard Dawkins put it, "[F]emale exploitation begins here." Culture has little to do with it, as Wilson argues, for "the genes hold culture on a leash."[11]

One of the major areas that sociobiologists have stressed is the differences in male and female sexuality, which they believe to be the natural outgrowth of centuries of evolutionary development. Evolutionary success requires that all members of a species consciously or unconsciously desire to pass on their genes. Thus, males and females develop reproductive "strategies" to ensure that our own genetic code passes on to the next generation. Sociobiologists often use a language of intention and choice, referring to "strategies," which makes it sound as if our genes were endowed with instrumental rationality and each of our cells acted in a feminine or masculine way. Thus, they seem to suggest that the differences we observe between women and men today have come from centuries of advantageous evolutionary choices.

Take, for example, the size and the number of the reproductive cells themselves. Add to that the relative cost to male and female in producing a healthy offspring, and—presto!—you have the differences between male and female sexual behavior at a typical college mixer this weekend. "He" produces billions of tiny sperm; "she" produces one gigantic ovum. For the male, reproductive success depends upon his ability to fertilize a large number of eggs. Toward this end, he tries to fertilize as many eggs as he can. Thus, males have a "natural" propensity toward promiscuity. By contrast, females require only one successful mating before their egg can be fertilized, and therefore they tend to be extremely choosy about which male will be the lucky fellow. What's more, females must invest a far greater amount of energy in gestation and lactation, and have a much higher reproductive "cost," which their reproductive strategies would reflect. Females, therefore, tend to be monogamous, choosing the male who will make the best parent. "A woman seeks marriage to monopolize not a man's sexuality, but, rather, his political and economic resources, to ensure that her children (her genes) will be well provided for," writes journalist Anthony Layng. As sociobiologist Donald Symons puts it, women and men have different "sexual psychologies":

> Since human females, like those of most animal species, make a relatively large investment in the production and survival of each offspring—and males can get away with a

relatively small one—they'll approach sex and reproduction, as animals do, in rather different ways from males. . . . Women should be more choosy and more hesitant, because they're more at risk from the consequences of a bad choice. And men should be less discriminating, more aggressive and have a greater taste for variety of partners because they're *less* at risk.

Not surprisingly, Symons notes, this is "what we find":

Selection favored the basic male tendency to be aroused sexually by the sight of females. A human female, on the other hand, incurred an immense risk, in terms of time and energy, by becoming pregnant, hence selection favored the basic female tendency to discriminate with respect both to sexual partners and to the circumstances in which copulation occurred.[12]

The dilemma for these monogamous females, then, is how to extract parental commitment from these recalcitrant rogue males, who would much prefer to be out fertilizing other females than home with the wife and kids. Her strategy is to "hold out" for emotional, and therefore parental, commitment *before* engaging in sexual relations. Thus, women are not only predetermined to be monogamous, but they also link sexual behavior to emotional commitment, extracting from those promiscuous males all manner of promises of love and devotion before they will finally "put out." Thus, males are hardwired genetically to be promiscuous sexual predators, ever on the prowl for new potential sexual conquests, while females have a built-in biological tendency toward monogamy, fantasies of romantic love and commitment coupled with sexual behavior, and a certain sexual reticence that can only be activated by chivalric male promises of fealty and fidelity.

Other evolutionary arguments examine other aspects of reproductive biology to spell out the differences between men and women, and thereby explain the social inequality between them. For example, the separation of spheres seems to have a basis far back in evolutionary time. "In hunter-gatherer societies, men hunt and women stay at home. This strong bias persists in most agricultural and industrial societies, and, on that ground alone, appears to have a genetic origin," writes Edward Wilson. "My own guess is that the genetic bias is intense enough to cause a substantial division of labor in the most free and most egalitarian of future societies."[13] Lionel Tiger and Robin Fox emphasize the social requirements for the evolutionary transition to a hunting and gathering society. First, the hunting band must have solidarity and cooperation, which requires bonding among the hunters. Women's biology—especially their menstrual cycle—puts them at a significant disadvantage for such consistent cooperation, while the presence of women would disrupt the cooperation necessary among the men and insinuate competition and aggression. They also are possessed of a "maternal instinct." Thus, it would make sense for men to hunt, and for women to remain back home raising the children.[14]

From such different reproductive strategies and evolutionary imperatives come different temperaments, the different personalities we observe in women and men. The newest incarnation of sociobiology is called "evolutionary psychology," which declares an ability to explain psychological differences between women and men through their evolutionary trajectories. Men are understood to be more aggressive, controlling, and managing—skills that were honed over centuries of evolution as hunters and fighters. After an equal amount of time raising children and performing domestic tasks, women are said to be more reactive, more emotional, "programmed to be passive."[15]

Finally, these differences also enable scientists to try and explain such behaviors as inter-species violence and aggression. Sociobiologist David Barash combines sociobiology with New Age platitudes when he writes that "genes help themselves by being nice to themselves." Unfortunately, this doesn't necessarily mean being nice to others. Selfish genes do not know the Golden Rule. For example, Barash explains rape as a reproductive adaptation by men who otherwise couldn't get a date. Following their study of scorpion flies and mallard ducks, Barash, Thornhill, and other evolutionists argue that men who rape are fulfilling their genetic drive to reproduce in the only way they know how. "Perhaps human rapists, in their own criminally misguided way, are doing the best they can to maximize their fitness," writes Barash. Rape, for men, is simply an "adaptive" reproductive strategy of the less successful male—sex by other means. If you can't pass on your genetic material by seduction, then pass it on by rape.[16]

In their book *A Natural History of Rape,* Thornhill and Craig Palmer amplify these arguments, and make wildly unfounded assertions in the process. Rape, they write, is "a natural, biological phenomenon that is a product of human evolutionary heritage."[17] The male's biological predisposition is to reproduce, and their reproductive success comes from spreading their seed as far and wide as possible, women are actually the ones with the power, since they get to choose which males will be successful. "But getting chosen is not the only way to gain sexual access to females," they write. "In rape, the male circumvents the females' choice."[18] Rape is the evolutionary mating strategy of losers, males who cannot otherwise get a date. Rape is an alternative to romance; if you can't always have what you want, you take what you need.

Don't blame the men, though—or even their genetic imperatives. It's really women's fault. "As females evolved to deny males the opportunity to compete at ovulation time, copulation with unwilling females became a feasible strategy for achieving copulation," write Richard Alexander and K. M. Noonan. Women, then, are biologically programmed to "hold out"—but they better not do it too long. If women were only a little bit more compliant, men wouldn't be forced to resort to rape as a reproductive tactic.[19]

EVOLUTIONARY PSYCHOLOGY: A "JUST-SO" STORY

Do these evolutionary arguments make sense? Does their evidence add up to basic, irreconcilable differences between women and men, made necessary by the demands of evolutionary adaptation? While there is a certain intuitive appeal to these arguments—since they give our contemporary experiences the weight of history and science—there are simply too many convenient lapses in reasoning for us to be convinced.

The theory may tidily describe the intricate mating rituals of fruit flies or brown birds, or *seem* applicable to an urban singles bar or the dating dynamics of high school and college students, but it is based on an interpretation of evidence that is selective and conforms to preconceived ideas. It is as if these sociobiologists observe what is normative—that men are more likely than women to separate love and sex, that men feel entitled to sexual contact with women, that men are more likely to be promiscuous—and read it back into our genetic coding. Such explanations always fall into teleological traps, reasoning backward to fill existing theoretical holes. It is so because it is supposed to be so. Besides, the time span is too short. Can we explain each single sexual encounter by such grand evolutionary designs? I would bet that most of our conscious "strategies" at college mixers have more immediate goals than to ensure our reproductive success.

Some arguments go far beyond what the data might explain and into areas that are empirically untestable. Biologist Richard Lewontin, a passionate critic of sociobiology, argues that "no evidence at all is presented for a genetic basis of these characteristics [religion, warfare, cooperation] and the arguments for their establishment by natural selection cannot be tested, since such arguments postulate hypothetical situations in human prehistory that are uncheckable." And fellow evolutionary biologist Stephen Jay Gould denies that there is "any direct evidence for genetic control of specific human social behavior."[20]

Some sociobiological arguments seem to assume that only one interpretation is possible from the evidence. But there could be others. Psychologists Carol Tavris and Carole Wade, for example, ask why parents—women or men—would "invest" so much time and energy in their children when they could be out having a good time? While sociobiologists argue that we are "hardwired" for such altruistic behavior, because our children are the repository of our genetic material, Tavris and Wade suggest that it may be simple economic calculation: In return for taking care of our offspring when they are young and dependent, we expect them to take care of us when we are old and dependent—a far more compact and tidy explanation.[21]

Some sociobiological arguments are based on selective use of data, ignoring those data that might be inconvenient. Which species should we use as the standard of measurement? Among chimpanzees and gorillas, for example, females usually leave home and transfer to new tribes, leaving the males at home with their mothers; among baboons, macaques, and langurs, however, it's the males who leave home to seek their fortune elsewhere. So which sex has the wanderlust, the natural predisposition to leave home? Sociobiologists tend to favor male-dominant species to demonstrate the ubiquity of male dominance. But there are other species. For example, baboons seem to be female-dominant, with females determining the stability of the group and deciding which males are trustworthy enough to be their "friends." Then there is the female chimpanzee. She has sex with lots of different males, often up to fifty times a day during peak estrus. She flirts, seduces, and does everything she can to attract males—whom she then abandons as she moves on to the next customer. Would we say that such evidence demonstrates that females are genetically programmed toward promiscuity and males toward monogamy? And sociobiologists tend to ignore other behavior among primates. For example, sexual contact with same sex others is "part of the normal sexual repertoire of all animals, expressed variously over the lifetime of an individual."[22] But few posit a natural predisposition toward homosexuality.

Some arguments are just plain wrong in light of empirical evidence. Take the argument about how women's menstrual cycle debilitates them so that they were inevitably and correctly left behind in the transition to hunting and gathering. Katherine Dalton's research on English schoolgirls showed that 27 percent got poorer test scores just before menstruation than at ovulation. (She does not say how much worse they did.) But 56 percent showed no change in test grades and 17 percent actually performed better at premenstruation. And what about that "maternal instinct"? How do we explain the enormous popularity of infanticide as a method of birth control throughout Western history, and the fact that it was women who did most of the baby killing? Infanticide has probably been the most commonly practiced method of birth control throughout the world. One historian reported that infanticide was common in ancient Greece and Rome and that "every river, dung heap and cesspool used to be littered with dead infants." In 1527, a priest commented that "the latrines resound with the cries of children who have been plunged into them."[23]

And finally, what is one to make of the argument that rape is simply sex by other means for reproductively unsuccessful males? Such arguments ignore the fact that most rapists are not interested in sex but in humiliation and violence, motivated more by rage than by lust. Most rapists have regular sex partners, quite a few are married. Many women well outside of reproductive age, either too young or too old, are raped. And why would some rapists hurt and even murder their victims, thus preventing the survival of the very genetic material that they are supposed to be raping in order to pass on? And why would some rapists be homosexual rapists, passing on their genetic material to those who could not possibly reproduce? And what about rape in prison? Using theories of selfish genes or evolutionary imperatives to explain human behavior cannot take us very far.

"[S]election favored males who mated frequently," argue Thornhill and Palmer; therefore, "rape increased reproductive success."[24] But why should this be true? Might it not also be the case that being hardwired to be good lovers and devoted fathers enabled us to be reproductively successful? One might argue that selection favored males who mated *well,* since successful mating is more than spreading of seed. After all, human males are the only primates for whom skillful lovemaking, enhancing *women's* pleasure, is normative, at least in many societies. Being an involved father probably assured reproductive success far better than rape. After all, babies are so precious, so fragile that they need extraordinary—and extraordinarily long!—care and devotion. Infants conceived during rape would have a far lower chance of survival, which is probably one reason why we invented love. Infants conceived in rape might well have been subject to infanticide—historically, the most common form of birth control before the modern era.

Is rape "natural"? Of course it is. As is *any* behavior or trait found among human primates. If it exists in nature, it's natural. Some "natural" beverages contain artificial—"social"—additives that give them their color, their texture, their taste, their "meaning" or "significance." This is equally true of rape. Telling us that it is natural tells us nothing about it except that it is found in nature.

Sociobiology and evolutionary psychology provide us with what Rudyard Kipling called a "just-so" story—an account that uses some evidence to tell us how, for example, an elephant got its trunk, or a tiger its stripes. These are children's fables, understood by the reader to be fictions, but convenient, pleasant and, ultimately, useful fictions.

Could we not use the same evidence and construct a rather different "just-so" story? Try this little thought experiment. Let's take the same evidence about sperm and eggs, about reproductive strategies, about different levels of parental investment that the sociobiologists use, and add a few others. Let's also remember that human females are the only primate females who do not have specified periods of estrus, that is, they are potentially sexually receptive at any time of their reproductive cycle, including when they are incapable of conception. What could be the evolutionary reproductive "strategy" of this? And let's also remember that the human clitoris plays no part whatsoever in human reproduction, but is solely oriented toward sexual pleasure. And don't forget that in reality, most women do not experience peaks of sexual desire during ovulation (which is what evolutionary biologists would predict, since they must ensure reproductive success) but actually just before and just after menstruation (when they are almost invariably infertile, though the ratio of female to male hormones is lowest).[25] And finally, let's not forget that when a baby is born, the identity of the mother is obvious, though that of the father is not. Until very recently, with the advent of DNA tests, fathers could never be entirely certain that the baby was theirs; after all, how did they know their partner had not had sexual contact with another male?

From this evidence one might adduce that human females are uniquely equipped biologically—indeed, that it is their sexual strategy—to enjoy sex simply for its physical pleasure and not for its reproductive potential. And if the reproductive goal of the female is to ensure the survival of her offspring, then it would make sense for her to deceive as many males as possible into thinking that the offspring was theirs. That way, she could be sure that all of them would protect and provide for the baby, since none of them could risk the possibility of his offspring's death and the obliteration of his genetic material. So might not women's evolutionary "strategy" be promiscuity?[26]

Actually, that's what you might conclude from the Bari people of Venezuela, where female promiscuity ensures that a woman's offspring stand a better chance of survival. Among the Bari, the man who impregnates the female is considered the primary father, but other men with whom the mother also has sex during her pregnancy consider themselves secondary fathers and spend a good deal of time making sure the child has enough fish or meat to eat.[27] And it may be not that far off from what we do as well. One recent study found that women reported that their partners increased their attentiveness and "monopolization" behavior—calling them often to check on their whereabouts, for example—just as they began to ovulate. But the women found that they fantasized far more about cheating on their partners at the same time. (They reported no increase whatever in sexual thoughts about their partners—so much for their evolutionary predisposition toward fidelity.) While this suggests that the men had good reason to be more guarding and jealous, it also suggests that women "instinctively want to have sex with as many men as possible to ensure the genetic quality of their offspring, whereas men want to ensure that their own genes get reproduced," according to a journalist reporting on the story. Equally selfish genes, and equally a "war between the sexes"—but one with completely different interpretation.[28]

Another biological fact about women might make life even more confusing for males seeking to determine paternity. Barbara McClintock's research about women's menstrual cycles indicated that in close quarters, women's cycles tended to become increasingly synchronous; that is, over time, women's cycles will tend to converge with those of their neighbors and friends. (McClintock noticed this among her roommates and friends while an undergraduate at Harvard in the early 1970s.)[29] What's more, in cultures where artificial light is not used, all the women will tend to ovulate at the full moon and menstruate at the new moon. While this might be an effective method of birth control in nonliterate societies (to prevent pregnancy, you must refrain from sex when the moon approaches fullness), it also suggests that unless women were controlled, paternity could not be established definitively.

If males were as promiscuous as females they would end up rather exhausted and haggard from running around hunting and gathering for all those babies who might *or might not* be their own. How were they to know, after all? In order to ensure that they did not die from exhaustion, males might "naturally" tend toward monogamy, extracting from women promises of fidelity before offering up a lifetime of support and protection to the potential offspring from those unions. Such males might invent ideals of female chastity, refuse to marry (sexually commit to) women who were not virgins, and develop ideologies of domesticity that would keep women tied to the household and children to prevent them from indulging in their "natural" disposition toward promiscuity.

In fact, there is some persuasive evidence on this front. Since getting pregnant is often difficult (it takes the average couple three or four months of regular intercourse to become pregnant), then being a faithful and consistent partner would be a far better reproductive strategy for a male. "Mate guarding" would enable him to maximize his chances of impregnating the woman and minimize the opportunities for other potential sperm bearers.[30]

Of course, I'm not suggesting that this interpretation supplant the one offered by evolutionary psychologists. But the fact that one can so easily use the exact same biological evidence to construct an entirely antithetical narrative suggests that we should be very cautious when the experts tell us there is only one interpretation possible from these facts. "Genes do not shout commands to us about our behavior," writes the celebrated ecologist Paul Ehrlich. "At the very most, they whisper suggestions."[31]

"HIS" BRAIN AND "HER" BRAIN

Biologists have also focused on the brain to explain the differences between women and men. This approach, too, has a long history. In the eighteenth century, experts measured women's brains and men's brains and argued that, since women's brains were smaller and lighter, they were inferior. Of course, it later turned out that women's brains were not smaller and lighter relative to body size and weight, and thus were not predictive of any cognitive differences. The late nineteenth century was the first heyday of brain research, as researchers explored that spongy and gelatinous three-pound blob in order to discover the differences between whites and blacks, Jews and non-Jews, immigrants and "normal" or "real" Americans, criminals and law-abiding citizens. For example, the great sociologist Emile Durkheim succumbed to such notions, when he wrote, "[W]ith the advance of civilization the brain of the two sexes has increasingly developed differently. . . . [T]his progressive gap between the two may be due both to the considerable development of the male skull and to a cessation and even a regression in the growth of the female skull." And another turn-of-the-century researcher argued that the brain of the average "grown-up Negro partakes, as regards his intellectual faculties, of the nature of the child, the female, and the senile White." (One can only speculate where this put older black women.) But the fact is that none of these hypothesized differences turned out to have any scientific merit; they all satisfied political and racist assumptions.[32]

Brain research remains a particularly fertile field of study and scientists continue their search for differences between women and men in their brains. One writes that "many of the differences in brain function between the sexes are innate, biologically determined, and relatively resistant to change through the influences of culture." Popular books proclaim just how decisive these differences are. The male brain is "not so easily distracted by superfluous information"; it is a "tidier affair" than the female brain, which appears "less able to separate emotion from reason."[33] (Notice that these statements did not say—though they easily might have, based on the same evidence—that the female brain is capable of integrating *more* diverse sources of information and *better* able to synthesize feelings and thought.)

That brain research fits neatly (a male brain trait?) into preconceived ideas about men's and women's roles is hardly a coincidence. In most cases, brain researchers (like many other researchers) find exactly what they are looking for, and what they are looking for are the brain-based differences that explain the observable behavioral differences between adult women and men. One or two historical examples should suffice. The "science" of craniology was developed in the late nineteenth century to record and measure the effect of brain differences among different groups. But the scientists could never agree on exactly which measures of the brain to use. They *knew* that men's brains had to be shown to be superior, but different tests yielded different results. For example, if one used the ratio of brain surface to body surface, then men's brains would "win"; but if one used the ratio of brain weight to body weight, women's brains would appear superior. No scientist could rely on such ambiguity; more decisive methods had to be found to demonstrate that men's brains were superior.[34]

Test scores were no better as indicators. At the turn of the century, women were found to be scoring higher on comprehensive examinations at New York University. Since scientists "knew" that women were not as smart as men, some other explanation had to be sought. "After all, men are more intellectual than women, examination papers or no examination papers," commented the dean of the college, R. Turner. "Women have better memories and study harder, that's all. In tasks requiring patience and industry women win out. But when a man is both patient and industrious he beats a woman any day." (It is interesting to see that women's drive, ambition, and industriousness is used against them, instead of labeling it men's impulsiveness, impatience, and laziness.) In the 1920s, when IQ tests were first invented, women scored higher on those tests as well. So the experimenters changed the questions.[35]

Contemporary brain research has focused on three areas: (1) the differences between right and left hemisphere; (2) the differences in the tissue that connects those hemispheres; and (3) the ways in which males and females use different parts of their brains for similar functions.[36]

Some scientists have noticed that the right and left hemispheres of the brain seem to be associated with different cognitive functions and abilities. Right-hemisphere dominance is associated with visual and spatial abilities, such as the ability to conceive of objects in space. Left-hemisphere dominance is associated with more practical functions, such as language and reading. Norman Geschwind and Peter Behan, for example, observed that sex differences begin in the womb when the male fetus begins to secrete testosterone that washes over the brain, selectively attacking parts of the left hemisphere and slowing its development. Thus, according to Geschwind, males tend to develop "superior right hemisphere talents, such as artistic, musical, or mathematical talent." Geschwind believes that men's brains are more lateralized, with one half dominating over the other, while women's brains are less lateralized, with both parts interacting more than in men's.[37]

One minor problem with this research, though, is that scientists can't seem to agree on which it is "better" to have and, not so coincidentally, which side of the brain dominates for which sex. In fact, they keep changing their minds about which hemisphere is superior, and then, of course, assigning that superior one to men. Originally, it was the *left* hemisphere that was supposed to be the repository of reason and intellect, while the right hemisphere was the locus of mental illness, passion, and instinct. So males were thought to be overwhelmingly more left-brained than right-brained. By the 1970s, though, scientists had determined that the truth lay elsewhere, and that the right hemisphere was the source of genius, talent, creativity, and inspiration, while the left brain was the site of ordinary reasoning, calculation, and basic cognitive function. Suddenly males were hailed as singularly predisposed toward right-brainedness. One neuroscientist, Ruth Bleier, reanalyzed Geschwind and Behan's data and found that in more than five hundred fetal brains from ten to forty-four weeks of gestation, the authors had found no significant sex differences—this despite the much-trumpeted testosterone bath.[38]

Perhaps it wasn't which half of the brain dominates, but the degree to which the brain was lateralized—that is, had a higher level of differentiation between the two hemispheres—that determined sex differences. Buffery and Gray found that female brains were more lateralized than male brains, which, they argued, interfered with spatial functioning, and made women less capable at spatial tasks. That same year, Levy found that female brains were *less* lateralized than male brains, and so he argued that *less* lateralization interferes with spatial functioning. (There is virtually no current evidence for either of these positions, but that has not stopped most writers from believing Levy's argument.)[39] One recent experiment shows how the desperate drive to demonstrate difference actually leads scientists to misinterpret their own findings. In 1997, a French researcher, Jean Christophe Labarthe, tried to demonstrate sex differences in visual and spatial abilities. Two-year-old boys and girls were asked to build a tower and a bridge. For those of average birth weight or better (greater than 2500 grams), there was no difference whatever in ability to build a tower, although 21 percent of the boys and only 8 percent of the girls could build a bridge. On children whose birth weight was less than 2500 grams, though, there were no differences for either skill. From this skimpy data, Labarthe concludes that boys are better at bridge building than girls—instead of the far more convicing (if less mediagenic) finding that birth weight affects visual and spatial functioning![40]

Some research suggests that males use only half their brains while performing some verbal tasks, such as reading or rhyming, while females draw on both sides of their brains. A recent experiment reveals as much about our desire for difference as about difference itself. Researchers from the Indiana University school of medicine measured brain activity of ten men and ten women as they listened to someone read a John Grisham thriller. A majority of the men showed exclusive activity on the left side of their brains, while the majority of the women showed activity on both sides of the brain. While some might suggest that this provides evidence to women who complain that their husbands are only "half-listening" to them, the study mentions little about what the minority of males or females were doing—especially when the total number was only ten to begin with. Besides, what if they had been listening instead to a Jane Austen novel? Might the males have "needed" both sides of their brain to figure out a plot that was a bit less action-packed? Would the females have been better able to relax that side of their brain that has to process criminal intrigue and murder?[41]

If these tacks weren't convincing, perhaps both males and females use both halves of their brains, but use them *differently*. In their popular book detailing these brain differences, Jo Durden-Smith and Diane deSimone suggest that in the female left hemisphere, language tends to serve as a vehicle for communication, whereas for males it is a tool for more visual-spatial tasks, such as analytical reasoning. Similarly, they argue, in the right hemisphere males assign more neural space to visual-spatial tasks, while females have more room left over for other types of nonverbal communication skills, such as emotional sensitivity and intuition.[42]

But don't the differences in mathematical ability and reading comprehension provide evidence of different sides of the brain being more dominant among females and males? While few would dispute that different sides of the brain account for different abilities, virtually all humans, both men and women, use both sides of their brains to reasonably good effect. If so, argues the neuropsychiatrist Jerre Levy, "then males may be at a double disadvantage in their emotional life. They may be emotionally less sophisticated. And because of the difficulty they may have in communicating between their two hemispheres, they may have restricted verbal access to their emotional world."[43]

It is true that males widely outnumber females at the genius end of the mathematical spectrum. But does that mean that males are, on average, more mathematically capable and females more verbally capable? Janet Hyde, a psychologist at the University of Wisconsin, has conducted a massive amount of research on this question. She reviewed 165 studies of verbal ability that included information about more than 1.4 million people and included writing, vocabulary, reading comprehension. She found no gender differences in verbal ability. But when she analyzed 100 studies of mathematical ability, representing the testing of nearly 4 million students, she did find some modest gender differences. In the general studies, females outperformed males in mathematics, except in those studies designed only for the most precocious individuals.[44] What Hyde and her colleagues—and virtually every single study ever undertaken— found is that there is a far greater range of differences *among* males and *among* females than there is *between* males and females. That is to say that the variance within the group far outweighs the variance between groups, despite the possible differences between the mean scores of the two groups.

But what if it's not the differences between the hemispheres, or even that males and females use the same hemispheres differently? Perhaps it's the connections *between* the hemispheres. Some researchers have explored the bundle of fibers known as the *corpus collosum* that connect the two hemispheres and carry information between them.

A subregion of this connecting network, known as the splenium, was found by one researcher to be significantly larger and more bulbous in shape in females. This study of fourteen brains at autopsy suggested that this size difference reflected less hemispheric lateralization in females than in males, and that this affected visual and spatial functioning. But subsequent research failed to confirm this finding. One researcher found no differences in the size of the corpus callosum between males and females. What's more, in magnetic resonance imaging (MRI) tests on living men and women, no differences were found between women and men.[45]

But that doesn't stop some popular writers from dramatic and facile extrapolation. Here's Robert Pool, from his popular work, *Eve's Rib:* "Women have better verbal skills than men on average; the splenium seems to be different in women and men, in shape if not in size; and the size of the splenium is related to verbal ability, at least in women." And a recent popular book by psychologist Michael Gurian claims that only females with "boys' brains" can grow up to be architects, since girls' brains are organized to promote nurture, the love and caring for children. (Not only is such a statement insulting to women—as if mathematical reasoning and spatial ability was somehow "beyond" them—but it's also insulting to men, especially to fathers who seem to be fully capable of care and nurturing children.)[46]

In fact, there seems to be little consistent evidence for significant brain differences between women and men. Even neuropsychologist Doreen Kimura understands that "in the larger comparative context, the similarities between human males and females far outweigh the differences." And Jonathan Beckwith, professor of microbiology and molecular genetics at Harvard Medical School argues that "[e]ven if they found differences, there is absolutely no way at this point that they can make a connection between any differences in brain structure and any particular behavior pattern or any particular aptitude."[47]

If there is no evidence of these arguments, why do they persist? One brain researcher, Marcel Kinsbourne, suggests that it is "because the study of sex differences is not like the rest of psychology. Under pressure from the gathering momentum of feminism, and perhaps in backlash to it, many investigators seem determined to discover that men and women 'really' are different. It seems that if sex differences do not exist, then they have to be invented."[48]

THE GAY BRAIN

One of the most interesting and controversial efforts by scientists who study the biological origins of behavior has been the search for biological origins of sexual orientation. Recent research on brain structure and endocrinological research on hormones has suggested a distinctly homosexual "essence," which will emerge regardless of the cultural conditions that shape its opportunities and experiences. This research on the origins of sexual *orientation* is related to research on the basis of sex differences between women and men because, culturally, we tend to understand sexuality in terms of gender. Gender stereotypes dominate the discussion of sexual orientation; we may assume, for example, that gay men are not "real" men, that is, are not sufficiently masculine, identify with women, and even adopt feminine affect and traits. Similarly, we may assume that lesbians are insufficiently feminine, identify with and imitate men's behaviors, etc. Homosexuality, our stereotypes tell us, is a *gender* "disorder."[49]

We have a century-long historical legacy upon which we draw such stereotypic ideas. Homosexuality emerged as a distinct identity in the late nineteenth century, when it was regarded as an "inborn, and therefore irrepressible drive" according to one Hungarian physician. Earlier, there were homosexual *behaviors,* of course, but identity did not emerge from nor inhere in those behaviors. By the turn of the century, though, "the homosexual" was characterized by a form of "interior androgyny, a hermaphroditism of the soul," writes Foucault. "The sodomite had been a temporary aberration; the homosexual was now a species." Since Freud's era, we have assumed that male homosexuality, manifested by effeminacy, and lesbianism, manifested by masculine affect, might not be innate, but were, nonetheless, intractable products of early childhood socialization, and that differences between gays and straights, once established, proved the most telling in their lives' trajectories.[50]

In recent decades, biological research has emerged as central in the demonstration of the fundamental and irreducible differences between homosexuals and heterosexuals. And, it should not surprise us that researchers have found what they hoped to find—that homosexual men's brains and hormone levels more closely resemble those of females than those of heterosexual males. Science, again, has attempted to prove that the stereotypes of gay men and lesbians are based not in cultural fears and prejudices, but in biological fact. For example, in the 1970s, Dorner and his associates found that homosexual men possess a "predominantly female-differentiated brain" caused by a "deficiency" of androgen during the hypothalamic organizational phase in prenatal life, and which may be activated to homosexual behavior by normal or about-normal androgen levels in adulthood.[51]

More recently, Simon LeVay focused on the structure of the brain in an effort to uncover the etiology of homosexuality. Hoping that science can demonstrate "the origins of sexual orientation at a cellular level," LeVay gives no credence to environmental determination of sexuality. "If there are environmental influences, they operate very early in life, at the fetal or early-infancy stages, when the brain is still putting itself together," he argues. "I'm very much skeptical of the idea that sexual orientation is a cultural thing." LeVay noticed that, among primates, experimental lesions in the medial zone of the hypothalamus did not impair sexual functioning, but did suppress mounting attempts by the male monkeys on female monkeys. He also noticed that the size of this region of the brain was different in men and women. In his experiment, LeVay examined the brain tissues of forty-one deceased people. Nineteen of these had died of AIDS and were identified as part of the risk group "homosexual and bisexual men"; sixteen other men were presumed to be heterosexual because there was no evidence to the contrary (six had died of AIDS and the other ten from other causes); and six were women who were presumed heterosexual (one had died of AIDS). These brains were treated and compared. Three of the four sections revealed no differences, but a fourth section, the anterior hypothalamus, a region about the size of a grain of sand, was found to be different among the groups. LeVay found that the size of the same area among the presumably heterosexual men was approximately twice the size of the same area for the women and the presumably gay men.[52]

But several problems in his experiments give us pause. LeVay and his colleagues failed to measure the cell number or density because "of the difficulty in precisely defining the neurons belonging to INAH 3," the area of the brain involved. A number of the "homosexual" men (five of the nineteen) and of the women (two of the six) appeared to have areas of the brain as large as those of the presumed heterosexual men. And in three of the presumed heterosexual men, this area of the brain was actually very small. What's more, the sources of his data were widely varied. All the gay men in his sample died of AIDS, a disease known to affect the brain. (Reduced testosterone occurs among AIDS patients, and this alone may account for the different sizes.) And all the brains of gay men were preserved in a formaldehyde solution that was of a different strength than the solution in which the brains of heterosexual men were preserved, because of the fears of HIV transmission, although there was no effort to control for the effect of the formaldehyde on the organs. It is possible that what LeVay may have been measuring was the combined effect of HIV infection and preservation in high densities of formaldehyde solution on postmortem brain structure, rather than differences in brain structure between living heterosexuals and homosexuals. A recent effort to replicate LeVay's findings failed, and one researcher went farther, suggesting that "INAH-3 is not necessary for sexual behavior in men, whether they chose men or women as their partners."[53]

More recently, researchers have found that the brains of male transsexuals more closely resembled the brains of women than heterosexual, "normal" men. Dutch scientists at the Netherlands Institute for Brain Research examined the hypothalamus sections of forty-two men and women, six of whom were known to be transsexuals, and nine of whom were gay men, while the rest were presumed to be heterosexual. Again, they found that the hypothalamus in the transsexual men and women was smaller than in the heterosexual or homosexual men. While they were careful *not* to interpret their findings in terms of sexual orientation, since the heterosexual and homosexual men's brains were similar, they did take their research to signal sex differences, since the male transsexuals were men who felt themselves to be women. However, the variance may also be a result of transsexual surgery and the massive amounts of female hormones the male transsexuals took, which might have had the effect of shrinking the hypothalamus, just as the surgery and hormones also resulted in other anatomical changes (loss of facial and body hair, breast growth, etc.).[54]

Another recent study finds that the sounds emitted by the inner ears of lesbians fall in between the sounds emitted by men and heterosexual women, forming a sort of "intermediate" zone between the two groups. (Lesbian emissions were stronger than men's, but weaker than heterosexual women's.) Before we get carried away, though, I should mention that the research found no differences whatever between gay men and heterosexual men on such emissions.[55] "You can't assume that because you find a structural difference in the brain that it was caused by genes," says researcher Marc Breedlove. "You don't know how the difference got there." Another adds that we "are still unsure whether these signs are causes or effects."[56] Personally, I'm more concerned about the sounds of bias and false difference that flow *into* our ears than the sounds that come out of them.

THE SEARCH FOR THE GAY GENE

Other biological research has attempted to isolate a gay gene, and thus show that sexual orientation has its basis in biology. For example, research on pairs of monozygotic twins (twins born from a single fertilized egg that splits in utero) suggests that identical twins have a statistically far higher likelihood of having similar sexualities (either both gay or both straight) than dizygotic twins (twins born from two separate fertilized eggs). One genetic study involved eighty-five pairs of twins in the 1940s and 1950s. All forty pairs of monozygotic twins studied shared the same sexual orientation; if one twin was heterosexual, the other was also; if one twin was homosexual, so too was the other twin. Such data were so perfect that subsequent scientists have doubted their validity.[57]

More recently, Bailey and Pillard collected data on gay men who were twins, as well as on gay men who had adoptive brothers who lived in the same home before age two. The 161 respondents were drawn from responses to ads placed in gay periodicals and included 56 monozygotic twins, 54 dizygotic twins, and 57 adoptive brothers. Respondents were asked about their brothers' sexuality and were asked permission to contact those brothers. About three-fourths of the brothers participated in the study. Bailey and Pillard found that in 52 percent of the monozygotic pairs, and in 22 percent of the dizygotic pairs, and in 11 percent of the adoptive pairs, both brothers were homosexual or bisexual.[58]

Such findings were widely interpreted to mean that there is some biological foundation for men's sexual contact with other men. But several problems remain. The study was generated from self-identified homosexuals, not from a sample of twins.[59] What's more, there was no independent measure of the environment in which these boys grew up, so that what Bailey and Pillard might have measured is the predisposition of the environments to produce similar outcomes among twins. After all, biological predisposition should be more compelling than one-half. And the fact that fraternal twins of homosexual men were twice as likely as other biological brothers to be gay would mean that environmental factors *must* be present, since dizygotic twins share no more genetic material than other biological brothers. The increase in concordance could be just as convincingly explained by a continuum of similarity of treatment of brothers— from adoptive to biological to dizygotic to monozygotic—without any genetic component whatever.

Actually, what is most interesting in the twin studies is how little concordance there actually is. After all, having identical genetic material and the same family and environmental conditions should produce a greater concordance than, at best, half. There is, however, some evidence that homosexual orientations tend to occur more frequently in family constellations. Psychiatrist Richard Pillard and psychologist James Weinrich questioned fifty heterosexual and fifty-one homosexual men and their siblings. Only 4 percent of the heterosexual men had brothers who were homosexual (the same percentage that had been found by Kinsey's studies in the 1940s), while about 22 percent of the gay men had gay or bisexual brothers. "This is rather strong evidence that male homosexuality clumps in families," said Weinrich, although there was no indication of the biological or genetic origin of this relationship. And the correlation, incidentally, did not hold true for women, as about the same percentage of the sisters of both groups said they had sisters who were lesbian. None said his or her parents were gay. This gender disparity might suggest that more than biology is at work here, and that gender identity may have more to do with inequality than with genetics.[60]

Recently, sociologists Peter Bearman and Hannah Bruckner examined all the studies that purported that opposite-sex twins are more likely to be gay than those who are not. They concluded that there were no hormonal connections whatever, and that the level of sex stereotyping in early childhood socialization is a far better predictor of behavioral outcome than whether or not one has a twin of the opposite sex. Predicting sexual orientation from that evidence is sort of like predicting penis size from shoe size—there's not even a correlation, but if there were, it would be specious.[61]

ESTROGEN AND TESTOSTERONE: HORMONAL BASIS FOR GENDER DIFFERENCES

Sex differentiation faces its most critical events at two different phases of life: (1) fetal development, when primary sex characteristics are determined by a combination of genetic inheritance and the biological development of the embryo that will become a boy or a girl; and (2) puberty, when the bodies of boys and girls are transformed by a flood of sex hormones that cause the development of all the secondary sex characteristics. Breast development in girls, lowering of boys' voices, the development of facial hair for boys, and the growth of pubic hair for both are among puberty's most obvious signs.

A significant amount of biological research has examined each of these two phases in an attempt to chart the hormonal bases for sex differentiation. Much of this research has focused on the links between sex hormones and aggression in adolescent boys, between sex hormones and aggression in women, and on problems of normal hormonal development and the outcomes for gender identity development. Summarizing his reading of this evidence, sociologist Steven Goldberg writes that since "men and women differ in their hormonal systems" and "every society demonstrates patriarchy, male dominance and male attainment," it is logical to conclude that "the hormonal renders the social inevitable."[62]

Earlier, we saw how Geschwind and Behan found that during fetal development it is the "testosterone bath" secreted by slightly more than one-half of all fetuses that begins sex differentiation in utero. (All embryos, remember, begin as "female.") Geschwind and Behan found that this testosterone bath selectively attacks the left hemisphere, which is why males favor the right hemisphere. But the implication of fetal hormonal research is that the secretion of sex hormones has a decisive effect on the development of gender identity, and on the expressions of masculinity and femininity. We've all heard the arguments about how testosterone, the male sex hormone, is not only the driving force in the development of masculinity in males, but is also the biological basis of human aggression, which is why males are more prone to violence than women. We should remember that women and men have both testosterone *and* estrogen, although typically in dramatically different amounts. On average, men do have about ten times the testosterone level that women have, but the range among men varies greatly, and some women have levels higher than some men.

In recent years, research has suggested some correlations between levels of testosterone and body mass, baldness, self-confidence, and even the ability and willingness to smile. Some wildly inflated claims about the effects of testosterone have led to both popular misconceptions and a variety of medical interventions to provide remedies. In one recent book, for example, psychologist James Dabbs proclaims that "testosterone increases masculinity," which was translated by a journalist into the equation that "lust is a chemical" as he looked forward to his "biweekly encounter with a syringe full of manhood."[63] And, of course, today men can purchase testosterone patches to boost one's daily testosterone level, or "AndroGel," a product that seems to promise masculinity in a tube.[64]

While the claims made for testosterone are often ridiculous, ministering less to science and more to men's fears of declining potency, there are some experiments on the relationship between testosterone and aggression that appear convincing. Males have higher levels of testosterone and higher rates of aggressive behavior than females do. What's more, if you increase the level of testosterone in a normal male, his level of aggression will increase. Castrate him—or at least a rodent proxy of him—and his aggressive behavior will cease entirely. Though this might lead one to think that testosterone is the cause of the aggression, Stanford neurobiologist Robert Sapolsky warns against such leaps of logic. He explains that if you take a group of five male monkeys arranged in a dominance hierarchy from 1–5, then you can pretty much predict how everyone will behave toward everyone else. (The top monkey's testosterone level will be higher than the ones below him, and levels will decrease down the line.) Number 3, for example, will pick fights with numbers 4 and 5, but will avoid and run away from numbers 1 and 2. If you give number 3 a massive infusion of testosterone, he will likely become more aggressive—but only toward numbers 4 and 5, with whom he has now become an absolute violent tormentor. He will still avoid numbers 1 and 2, demonstrating that the "testosterone isn't causing aggression, it's exaggerating the aggression that's already there."[65]

It turns out that testosterone has what scientists call a "permissive effect" on aggression: It doesn't cause it, but it does facilitate and enable the aggression that is already there. What's more, testosterone is produced *by* aggression, so that the correlation between the two may in fact have the opposite direction than previously thought. In his thoughtful book, *Testosterone and Social Structure,* Theodore Kemper notes several studies in which testosterone levels were linked to men's experiences. In studies of tennis players, medical students, wrestlers, nautical competitors, parachutists, and officer candidates, winning and losing determined levels of testosterone, so that the levels of the winners rose dramatically, while those of the losers dropped or remained the same. Kemper suggests that testosterone levels vary depending upon men's experience of either dominance, "elevated social rank that is achieved by overcoming others in a competitive confrontation," or eminence, where elevated rank "is earned through socially valued and approved accomplishment." Significantly, men's testosterone levels prior to either dominance or eminence could not predict the outcome; it was the experience of rising status due to success that led to the elevation of the testosterone level. (These same experiences lead to increases in women's testosterone levels as well.)[66]

Several recent studies have made the earlier facile correlation quite a bit more interesting. A Finnish study found no difference in testosterone levels between violent and nonviolent men. But among the violent men, levels of testosterone did correlate with levels of hostility: the violent men with higher levels of testosterone were diagnosed with Antisocial Personality Disorder. This supports the notion that testosterone has a permissive effect on aggression, since it correlates with hostility *only* among the violent men. And a UCLA researcher found that men with *low* testosterone were more likely to be angry, irritable and aggressive than men with normal or high levels of testosterone. While Sapolsky's statement that "testosterone is probably a vastly overrated hormone" may be an understatement, these last studies raise some troubling concerns, especially when compared with the questions about sexual orientation and hormone levels (see below).[67]

Some recent research approaches the relationship between testosterone and aggression from the other side. It turns out that marriage and fatherhood tend to depress the amount of testosterone in a man's body. In one study of fifty-eight Boston-area men (nearly all of whom were Harvard graduate or professional students), unmarried men had higher levels than did married men, and that difference increased only slightly when the married man had a child. Those married men with children who spent a lot of time doing child care had even lower levels. Actually, the testosterone levels differed only slightly, and only in the evening; samples taken in the morning, when one had rested, showed no differences at all. Yet from these results, massive leaps of logic followed. Since testosterone facilitates competition and aggression, fathers with children were opting out of this typically masculine activity. "Maybe it's very adaptive for men to suppress irritability," commented Peter Ellison, one of the study's authors. "Maybe the failure to do that places the child at risk." Maybe. Or maybe Harvard graduate students have lower testosterone levels than other men in Boston. Or maybe by the end of the day, trying to balance work and family life, an involved father is simply depleted. (Stress reduces levels of testosterone.) From such tiny and inconsistent differences, one should leap to no conclusions whatever.[68]

Some therapists, though, go much farther and prescribe testosterone for men as a sort of chemical tonic, designed to provide the same sort of pep and "vim and vigor" that tonics and cure-alls promised at the turn of the last century. Happy consumers swear by the results, and some clinicians have even diagnosed a medically treatable malady (which should enable it to be covered by insurance) called "andropause" or "male menopause," treatable by hormone-replacement therapy for men.[69]

Much of the research on hormones and gender identity has been by inference—that is, by examining cases where hormones did not work properly, or where one biological sex got too much of the "wrong" hormone. In some of the more celebrated research on fetal hormone development, Money and Ehrhardt reported on girls who had androgenital syndrome (AGS)—a preponderance of male hormones (androgens) in their systems at birth—and another set of girls whose mothers had taken progestins during pregnancy. All twenty-five girls had masculine appearing genitalia, and had operations to "correct" their genitals. The AGS girls also were given constant cortisone treatments to enable their adrenal glands to function properly.[70]

Money and Ehrhardt's findings were interesting. The girls and their mothers reported a higher frequency of tomboy behavior in these girls. They enjoyed vigorous outdoor games and sports, preferred toy cars and guns to dolls, and attached more importance to career plans than to marriage. However, they showed no more aggression or fighting than other girls. Later research seemed to confirm the notion that "prenatal androgen is one of the factors contributing to the development of temperamental differences between and within the sexes."[71]

Appearances, however, can be deceiving. Medical researcher Anne Fausto-Sterling argues that several problems make Ehrhardt and her colleagues' research less convincing than it at first may seem. The research suffered from "insufficient and inappropriate" controls: cortisone is a powerful drug, and the AGS girls underwent calamitous surgery (including clitoridectomy), and there were no independent measures of their effects. Further, their "method of data collection is inadequate" because it was based entirely on interviews with parents and children, with no impartial direct observation of these reported behaviors. Finally, "the authors do not properly explore alternative explanations of their results," such as parental expectations and differential treatment of their very "different" children.[72]

Another set of experiments examined the other side of the equation—boys who received higher-than-average doses of prenatal estrogen from mothers who were treated with estrogen during their pregnancies. Yalom, Green, and Fisk found that boys who received "female" hormones in utero were less active and less athletic than other boys. However, all the boys' mothers were chronically and seriously ill during their infancy and childhood (which was not true for the control sample of normal boys). Perhaps the boys had simply been admonished against loud and boisterous play in the house so as not to disturb their mothers, and had simply *learned* to be content while playing quietly or reading.[73]

About the relationship between women's hormones and behaviors, we have the research on PMS. During the days just before menstruation, some women seem to exhibit symptoms of dramatic and wildly unpredictable mood changes, outbursts of violence, anger, and fits of crying. Alec Coppen and Neil Kessel studied 465 women and observed that they were more irritable and depressed during the premenstrual phase than during mid-cycle. Such behaviors have led physicians to label this time PMS, for the associated symptoms of Premenstrual Syndrome. PMS has been listed as a disease in the DSM III, which guides physicians (and insurance companies) in treating illnesses. PMS has even been successfully used as a criminal defense strategy for a woman accused of violent outbursts. Arguing that PMS is a form of temporary insanity, two British women have used PMS as a successful defense in their trials for the murder of their male partners.

The politics of PMS parallel the politics of testosterone. "If you had an investment in a bank, you wouldn't want the president of your bank making a loan under those raging hormonal influences at that particular period," one physician noted. "There are just physical and psychological inhabitants that limit a female's potential." Happily, PMS occurs for only a few days a month, while unpredictably high levels of testosterone in men may last all month. Perhaps these presumed bank investors might want to rethink their investment strategies. Or consider this observation by feminist writer Gloria Steinem: During those days immediately preceding her menstrual period (the PMS days), a woman's estrogen level drops to its lowest point in the monthly cycle. Thus, just before menstruation, women, at least hormonally, more closely resemble men than at any other point in their cycle![74] Perhaps, then, the only sensible purely biological solution would be to have every corporation, government office, and—especially—military operation run by gay men, whose levels of testosterone would presumably be low enough to offset the hormone's propulsion toward aggression, while they would also be immune to the "raging hormonal influences" of PMS.

HORMONES AND HOMOSEXUALITY

The research on the relationship between hormones and homosexuality might lead us in that direction, were we politically disposed to go there. However, most research on the relationship between prenatal hormones and sexual orientation has had exactly the opposite political agenda. At the turn of the century, many theorists held that homosexuals were "inverts," creatures of one sex (their "true" sex) trapped in the body of the other. Some argued that homosexuality was "caused" by hormonal imbalances in utero that left males effeminate and therefore desiring men, and left women masculine, and therefore desiring women. In the 1970s, the German researcher Günter Dorner, director of the Institute for Experimental Endocrinology at Humboldt University in Berlin, and his associates argued that low levels of testosterone during fetal development, a rather tepid hormonal bath, would predispose males toward homosexuality. If rats did not receive enough of their appropriate sex hormone during fetal development, "then something would go wrong with the formation of the centers and with later sexual behavior," reported two journalists. "Adult rats would behave in ways like members of the opposite sex. They would become, in a sense, 'homosexual.' "[75]

Such research fit neatly with the era's antigay political agenda, suggesting as it did that male homosexuality was the result of insufficient prenatal masculine hormones, or inadequate masculinity. Treatment of homosexuality—indeed, perhaps its cure—might be effected simply by injecting higher doses of testosterone into these men, whose recharged virility would transform them into heterosexuals with higher sex drives. When such an experiment was attempted, researchers found that the men's sex drive did indeed increase as a result of the testosterone injections. However, the object of their lusts did not change: They simply desired more sex with men! Hormone levels may affect sexual urges, and especially the intensity or frequency of sexual activity, but they are empirically and logically irrelevant to studies of sexual object choice.

Could prenatal stress account for a disposition toward homosexuality? In another series of studies, Dorner and his colleagues argued that more homosexual men are born during wartime than during peacetime. Their evidence for this claim was that a high proportion of the 865 men treated for venereal disease in six regions of the German Democratic Republic were born between 1941 and 1947. They theorized that since prenatal stress leads to "significant decrease in plasma testosterone levels" among rat fetuses, which also leads to increased bisexual or homosexual behaviors among the adult rats, why not among humans? Dorner theorized that war led to stress, which led to a lowering of androgens in the male fetuses, which encouraged the development of a homosexual orientation. Based on this trajectory, Dorner concluded that the prevention of war "may render a partial prevention of the development of sexual deviation."[76] (Well, perhaps—but only because wartime tends to place men together in foxholes without women, where they may engage in homosexual activity more frequently than during peacetime.)[77]

Even if these data were convincing, a purely endocrinological account fails to satisfy. For example, one could just as easily construct a purely psychodynamic theory. For example: In wartime, children tend to grow up more often without a father or to be separated from other members of the family. If homosexuality really occurs more frequently during wartime, it would be just as reasonable to take this as "proof" of certain psychodynamic theories of homosexuality, for example, the lack of a father, or a particularly close bond between mother and son.

Another "just-so" story? Perhaps. But, then, so are explanations about aggregate levels of testosterone during wartime. While these arguments may not be convincing, they continue to exert significant influence over our commonsense explanations of gender difference.

The most interesting recent research on the relationship between prenatal hormones and sexual orientation has been carried out by U. C. Berkeley psychologist Marc Breedlove and his students. Breedlove is a far more careful researcher than most, and he is also far more cautious in the claims he makes. Breedlove measured the lengths of the index and ring fingers (second and fourth digits) and calculated the ratios between them for both heterosexual women and lesbians, and for gay and heterosexual men. It's well known that for average women, the two fingers are usually the same length, while among average men, the index finger is more often significantly shorter than the fourth. This is assumed to be an effect of prenatal androgens on male fetuses. Breedlove found that the ratio between the two fingers was more "masculine" among the lesbians than the heterosexual women; that is, that lesbians' index fingers were significantly shorter than their ring fingers. He found no differences between gay and straight men (both were equally "masculine"), although another study did find significant differences between the two, with gay men's finger ratios being somewhat more "masculine" than heterosexual men's.[78]

Breedlove believed that the difference between lesbians and heterosexual women was due to the effect of increased prenatal androgens among the lesbians—thus rendering them more "masculine." Now, this accords with traditional stereotypes that suggest homosexuality is related to gender nonconformity. But one must be careful about overstating these stereotypes, since Breedlove found the exact opposite among men. Breedlove also found a relationship between birth order and sexual orientation for men. The greater the number of older brothers a man had, the higher the likelihood that he would be homosexual. Breedlove hypothesized that this also was the result of postnatal androgenization of subsequent children. While this might not appear controversial, it accords with other studies that find that gay men's levels of testosterone are significantly *higher* than those of heterosexual men. That is, gay men are more "real men" than straight men. (Other research that supports the argument that gay men are "hyper-masculine" includes studies that find gay men's penis size is greater than straight men's, despite the fact that gay men undergo puberty a bit earlier and are therefore slightly shorter than straight men, and that gay men report significantly higher amounts of sexual behavior.) "This calls into question all of our cultural assumptions that gay men are feminine," said Breedlove in an interview—a thought that biological determinists and their political allies will not especially comforting.[79]

Pubertal Hormonal Influences: The Research on Hermaphrodites

One of the most intriguing tests of hormonal research has been carried out on hermaphrodites. Here, at the boundaries of biological sex, we can observe more clearly the processes that are often too difficult to see in "normal" biological development. Hermaphrodites are organisms that have both male and female characteristics. True hermaphrodites have either one ovary and one testicle, or else a single organ with both types of reproductive tissue. They are exceedingly rare. Less rare, however, are those whose biological sex is ambiguous.[80]

Take the most celebrated case: Two relatively isolated villages in the Domincan Republic seemed to produce a larger than expected set of cases of genetically male hermaphrodites for at least three generations. These were babies born with internal male structures, but with sex organs that resembled a clitoris more than they did a penis. Moreover, the testes had not descended at all, leaving what appeared to be a scrotum that resembled labia, as well as an apparently closed vaginal cavity. Their condition was the result of an extremely rare deficiency in a steroid 5-alpha reductase. Eighteen of these babies were raised as girls and studied by a team of researchers from Cornell University.[81]

After relatively uneventful childhoods, during which they played and acted like other little girls, their adolescence became somewhat more traumatic. They failed to develop breasts, and noticed a mass of tissue in their groins that turned out to be testicles beginning a descent. At puberty, their bodies began to produce a significant amount of testosterone, which made their voices deepen, their muscles develop, and facial hair appear. Suddenly, these youngsters were no longer like the other girls! And so, all but one of them switched and became males. One remained a female, determined to marry and have a sex change operation. (Another decided he was a male, but continued to wear dresses and act as a female.) All the others were successful in making the transition; they became men, found typically masculine jobs (woodchoppers, farmers, miners), and married women.

Imperato-McGinley and her colleagues interpreted these events as a demonstration of the effect of prenatal and pubertal sex hormones. They argued that a prenatal dose of testosterone had created "male" brains, which had remained dormant within ambiguous and female-appearing physiological bodies. At puberty, a second secretion of testosterone activated these genetically masculine brains, and the youngsters made the transition without too much psychological trauma.

They didn't, however, do it alone. The other villagers had made fun of them, calling them *guevadoches* ("eggs [testicles] at twelve") or *machihembra* ("first woman, then man"). But after they had made the move to become males, their neighbors were more encouraging, and offered advice and gifts to ease the transition. Moreover, one might argue that these children had a less fixed relationship between early gender development and adolescent gender patterns precisely because of their ambiguous genital development. After three generations, they might have come to assume that a girl does not always develop into a woman. Anthropologist Gilbert Herdt argues that such "gender polymorphic" cultures have the ability to deal with radical gender changes across the life cycle far more easily than do "gender dimorphic" cultures, such as the United States, where we expect everyone to be either male or female for their entire lives.[82] One might also ask what would have happened had these been little boys who, it turned out, had actually been female, and were therefore invited to make a transition to being adult women? Who would choose to stay a girl if she could end up becoming a boy, especially in a culture in which the sexes are highly differentiated and males enjoy privileges that females do not? Would boys find a transition to becoming girls as easy?

Recent survey data suggest a somewhat different interpretation. Junior high school students in north midwestern states (Michigan, Wisconsin, Minnesota, North and South Dakota) were asked what they would do if the next morning they awoke to find themselves transformed into the opposite sex. The girls thought about the question for a while, expressed modest disappointment, and then described the kinds of things they would do if they were suddenly transformed into boys. Become a doctor, fireman, policeman, or baseball player were typical answers. The boys, by contrast, took virtually no time before answering. "Kill myself" was the most common answer when they contemplated the possibility of life as a girl.[83]

THE POLITICS OF BIOLOGICAL ESSENTIALISM

Biological arguments for sex differences have historically tended to be politically conservative, suggesting that the social arrangements between women and men—including social, economic, and political discrimination based on sex—were actually the inevitable outcome of nature working in its mysterious ways. Political attempts to legislate changes in the gender order, or efforts to gain civil rights for women, or for gay men and lesbians, have always been met with biological essentialism: Don't fool with Mother Nature! James Dobson, a former professor of pediatrics and founder of Focus on the Family, a right-wing advocacy group, puts the case starkly:

> I feel it is a mistake to tamper with the time-honed relationship of husband as loving protector and wife as recipient of that protection. . . . Because two captains sink the ship and two cooks spoil the broth, I feel that a family must have a leader whose decisions prevail in times of differing opinions. . . . [T]hat role has been assigned to the man of the house.[84]

Social scientists have also jumped on the biological bandwagon. For example, sociologist Steven Goldberg, in his book *The Inevitability of Patriarchy,* argues that since male domination is ubiquitous, eternal, it simply has to be based on biological origins. There is simply too much coincidence for it to be social. Feminism, Goldberg argues, is therefore a war with nature:

> Women follow their own physiological imperatives. . . . In this, and every other society [men] look to women for gentleness, kindness, and love, for refuge from a world of pain and force. . . . In every society basic male motivation is the feeling that the women and children must be protected. . . . [T]he feminist cannot have it both ways: if she wishes to sacrifice all this, all that she will get in return is the right to meet men on male terms. She will lose.[85]

Politically, unequal social arrangements are, in the end, ordained by nature.[86]

But the evidence—occasionally impressive, often uneven—is far from convincing. If male domination is natural, based on biological imperatives, why, asks sociologist Cynthia Fuchs Epstein, must it be coercive, held in place by laws, traditions, customs, and the constant threat of violence for any woman who dares step out of line? Why would women want to enter male spheres such as colleges and universities, politics and the labor force, the professions, and the military, for which they are clearly biologically ill-suited?

Ironically, in the past decade, conservatives who argue that biological bases account for both sex differences and sexuality differences have been joined by some women and some gay men and lesbians, who have adopted an essentialism of their own. Some feminists, for example, argue that women should be pleased to claim "the intuitive and emotional strengths given by their right-hemisphere, in opposition to the over-cognitive, left-hemisphere-dominated, masculine nature."[87] Often a feminist essentialism uses women's experiences as mothers to describe the fundamental and irreducible differences between the sexes, rather than evolution, brain organization or chemistry. Sociologist Alice Rossi argues that, because of their bodies, "women have a head start in easier reading of an infant's facial expressions, smoothness of body motions, greater ease in handling a tiny creature with tactile gentleness."[88]

Similarly, the research on the biological bases of homosexuality suggests some unlikely new political allies, and a dramatic shifting of positions. Gay brain research may have generated little light on the etiology of sexual orientation, but it has certainly generated significant political heat. In a way, the promotion of gay essentialism is a political strategy to normalize gayness. "It points out that gay people are made this way by nature," observes Robert Bray, the director of public information of the National Gay and Lesbian Task Force. "It strikes at the heart of people who oppose gay rights and who think we don't deserve our rights because we're choosing to be the way we are." Michael Bailey and Richard Pinnard, the authors of the gay twin study, opined in a *New York Times* op-ed essay that a "biological explanation is good news for homosexuals and their advocates." "If it turns out, indeed, that homosexuals are born that way, it could undercut the animosity gays have had to contend with for centuries," added a cover story in *Newsweek*. Such an understanding would "reduce being gay to something like being left handed, which is in fact all that it is," commented gay journalist and author Randy Shilts in the magazine. And Simon LeVay, whose research sparked the recent debate, hoped that homophobia would dissipate as the result of this research, since its basis in prejudice about the unnaturalness of homosexual acts would vanish.

Gays would become "just another minority," just another ethnic group, with an identity based on primordial characteristics.[89]

This political implication is not lost on conservatives, who are now taking up the social constructionist, "nurture" mantle on sexual orientation as firmly as they argue for intractable biologically based differences between women and men. A decade ago, then–Vice President Dan Quayle argued that homosexuality was a matter of choice—"the wrong choice" he added quickly. Attorney General John Ashcroft agrees that it is "a choice which can be made and unmade." Such thinking leads to the politically volatile though scientifically dubious "conversion" movement which holds that, through intensive therapy, gay men and lesbians can become happy and "healthy" heterosexuals.[90]

Others are less convinced. Gay historian John D'Emilio wondered if "we really expect to bid for real power from a position of 'I can't help it?' "[91] What's more, such naturalization efforts are vulnerable to political subversion by the very forces they are intended to counteract. Antigay forces could point to a brain defect, and suggest possible prenatal interventions for prevention and postnatal "cures." The headline in the *Washington Times* heralding LeVay's research shouted: "Scientists Link Brain Abnormality, Homosexuality." LeVay himself acknowledges this danger, commenting that "the negative side of it is that with talk of an immutable characteristic, you then can be interpreted as meaning a defect or a congenital disorder. You could say that being gay is like having cystic fibrosis or something, which should be aborted or corrected in utero." And no sooner did he say that than James Watson, Nobel laureate for his discovery of the double helix in genetics, suggested that women who are found to be carrying the gene for homosexuality ought to be allowed to abort the child. "If you could find the gene which determines sexuality and a woman decides she doesn't want a homosexual child, well, let her," he said in an interview.

What this debate ignores is what we might call the *sociology* of gay essentialism: the ways in which gender remains the organizing principle of the homosexual essence. First, notice how essentialist research links homosexuality with gender inversion, as if *women* were the reference point against which gay and straight men were to be measured. Gay men, it turns out, have "female" brain structures, thus making gay men into hermaphrodites—women's brains in men's bodies—a kind of neurological third sex. But if gay men and women had similar brain structures, then the headline in the *Washington Times* cited above might have more accurately problematized heterosexual men, the numerical minority, as the deviant group with the brain abnormalities.

More significantly, though, these studies miss the social organization of gay sex—the ways in which the who, what, where, when, how, and how many are governed by gender norms. In their sexual activities, rates of sexual encounters and variations, gay men and lesbians are far greater gender *conformists* that they are nonconformists. Gay men's sexuality looks strikingly like straight men's sexuality—except for the not-completely-incidental detail of the gender of their object choice. Regardless of sexual orientation, virtually all sex research points to one conclusion: Gender, *not sexual orientation,* is the organizing principle of sexual behavior. Gay men and straight men seek masculine sex; sex is confirmation of masculinity. Straight women and lesbians experience feminine sex; sex is confirmation of femininity.[92]

The gender organization of sexuality also explains who believes it. Recent surveys have shown that, overwhelmingly, it is gay *men* who believe that their homosexuality is natural, biological, and inborn. Lesbians are more likely to believe that their homosexuality is socially constructed.[93] Gay men lean toward essentialist explanations, Vera Whisman argues, because gender privilege gives them the possibility of access to higher status positions; if their homosexuality is biological, it can be overlooked and they can claim their "rightful" (read: masculine) status. Lesbian sexuality is seen by lesbians as more socially and historically contingent because lesbians are doubly marginalized, and their sexuality and gender identity are often, but not always conditioned by an ideological connection to feminism. As lesbian-feminist writer Charlotte Bunch argues:

> Woman identified Lesbianism is, then, more than a sexual preference, it is a political choice. It is political because relationships between men and women are essentially political, they involve power and dominance. Since the Lesbian actively rejects that relationship and chooses women, she defies the established political system.[94]

For lesbians, sexual behavior implies a political statement about living outside the mainstream; gay men see it as an accident of birth, to be overcome by being overlooked.

Conclusion

Biological research holds significant sway over our thinking about the two fundamental questions in the study of gender: the *differences* between women and men, and the gendered *inequalities* that are evident in our social lives. But from the perspective of a social scientist, they have it backward. Innate gender differences do not automatically produce the obvious social, political, and economic inequalities we observe in contemporary society. In fact, the reverse seems to be true: Gender inequality, over time, ossifies into observable differences in behaviors, attitudes, and traits. If one were to raise a person in a dark room and then suddenly turn the lights on, and the person had a difficult time adjusting to the light, would you conclude that they had genetic eye problems compared to the population that had been living in the light all that time?

There are many problems with the research on biological bases for gender difference, and more and greater problems with the extrapolation of those differences to the social world of gender inequality. Consider the problem of what we might call anthropomorphic hyperbole. Neurobiologist Simon LeVay writes that "Genes demand instant gratification."[95] What are we to make of such an obviously false statement? Genes do not "demand" anything. And which genes is he talking about anyway? Some genes simply control such seemingly unimportant and uninteresting things as eye color or the capacity to differentiate between sweet and sour tastes. Others wait patiently for decades until they can instruct a man's hair to begin to fall out. Still others are so undemanding that they may wait patiently for several generations, until another recessive mate is found after multiple attempts at reproduction. Genes may play a role in the sexual decision making of a species, or even of individual members of any particular species; they do so only through that individual's interaction with his or her environment. They cannot possibly control any particular decision made by any particular individual at any particular time. With whom you decide to have sex this weekend—or even if you *do* have sex—is not determined by your genes, but by you.

Another problem in biological research has been the casual assumption that causation always moves from physiology to psychology. Just because one finds a correlation between two variables doesn't permit one to speculate about the causal direction. As biologist Ruth Hubbard argues:

> If a society put half its children into short skirts and warns them not to move in ways that reveal their panties, while putting the other half into jeans and overalls and encouraging them to climb trees, play ball, and participate in other vigorous outdoor games; if later, during adolescence, the children who have been wearing trousers are urged to "eat like growing boys" while the children in skirts are warned to watch their weight and not get fat; if the half in jeans runs around in sneakers or boots, while the half in skirts totters about on spike heels, then these two groups of people will be biologically as well as socially different.[96]

We know, then, what we *cannot* say about the biological bases for gender difference and gender inequality. But what *can* we say? We can say that biological differences provide the raw materials from which we begin to create our identities within culture, within society. "Biological sexuality is the necessary precondition for human sexuality," writes historian Robert Padgug. "But biological sexuality is only a precondition, a set of potentialities, which is never unmediated by human reality, and which becomes transformed in qualitatively new ways in human society."[97]

At the conclusion to his powerful indictment of Social Darwinism, first published in 1944, the eminent historian Richard Hofstadter pointed out that biological ideas such as survival of the fittest,

> whatever their doubtful value in natural science, are utterly useless in attempting to understand society; that the life of man in society, while it is incidentally a biological fact, has characteristics that are not reducible to biology and must be explained in the distinctive terms of a cultural analysis; that the physical well-being of men is a result of their social organization and not vice versa; that social improvement is a product of advances in technology and social organization, not of breeding or selective elimination; that judgments as to the value of competition between men or enterprises or nations must be based upon social and not allegedly biological consequences . . .[98]

Scientists have yet to discover the gene on which is carried the belief in nature over nurture; it is not yet clear which half of the brain blots out evidence of cultural or individual variation from evolutionary imperatives. Is human gullibility for pseudoscientific explanations carried on a particular chromosome? Scientists—social, behavioral, natural, biological—will continue to disagree as they hunt for the origins of human behavior. What they must all recognize is that people behave differently in different cultures, and that even similar behaviors may mean different things in different contexts.

Americans seem to want desperately to believe that the differences between women and men are significant, and that those differences can be traced to biological origins.

A recent cover story in *Newsweek* promised to explain "Why Men and Women Think Differently," although the article within revealed problems with every bit of evidence, and concluded that "the research will show that our identities as men and women are creations of both nature and nurture. And that no matter what nature deals us, it is we—our choices, our sense of identity, our experiences in life—who make ourselves what we are."[99]

How we do that, how we create identities out of our experiences, how we understand those experiences, and the choices we make—these are the province of social science, which tries to explore the remarkable diversity of human experience. While biological studies can suggest to us the basic building blocks of experience and identity, it is within our cultures, our societies, and our families that those building blocks are assembled into the astonishingly diverse architecture that constitutes our lives.

Spanning the World

Cross-Cultural Construction of Gender

*If a test of a civilization be sought, none can be so sure as the
condition of that half of society over which the other half has
power.*

—HARRIET MARTINEAU,
SOCIETY IN AMERICA (1837)

Biological models assume that biological sex determines gender, that innate biological differences lead to behavioral differences, which in turn lead to social arrangements. By this account, social inequalities are encoded into our physiological composition. Biological anomalies alone should account for variation. But the evidence suggests otherwise. When children like the Dominican pseudohermaphrodites are raised as the other *gender* they can easily make the transition to the other *sex*. And how do we account for the dramatic differences in the definitions of masculinity and femininity around the world? And how come some societies have much wider levels of gender inequality than others? On these questions, the biological record is mute.

What's more, biology is not without its own biases, though these have been hard to detect. Some anthropologists argue that biological models projected contemporary Western values onto other cultures. These projections led evolutionists such as Steven Goldberg to ignore the role of women and the role of colonialism in establishing gender differences in traditional cultures. Anthropologists such as Karen Sacks suggest that biological researchers always assumed that gender *difference* implied gender *inequality,* since Western notions of difference do usually lead to and justify inequality. In other words, gender difference is the *result* of gender inequality—not the other way around.[1]

Anthropological research on cultural variations in the development of gender definitions arose, in part, in response to such casual biological determinism. The more we found out about other cultures, the more certain patterns emerged. The evolutionary and ethnographic world offers a fascinating diversity of cultural constructions of gender. Yet, some themes do remain constant. Virtually all societies manifest some amount of difference between women and men, and virtually all exhibit some form of male domination, despite variations in gender definition. So, anthropologists have also tried to explore the link between the near-universals of gender difference and gender inequality. Some search for those few societies in which women hold positions of power; others examine those rituals, beliefs, customs, and practices that tend to increase inequality and those that tend to decrease it.

THE VARIATIONS IN GENDER DEFINITIONS

When anthropologists began to explore the cultural landscape, they found far more variability in the definitions of masculinity and femininity than any biologist would have predicted. Men possessed of relatively similar levels of testosterone, with similar brain structure and lateralization, seemed to exhibit dramatically different levels of aggression, violence, and, especially, aggression toward women. Women with similar brains, hormones, and ostensibly similar evolutionary imperatives have widely varying experiences of passivity, PMS, and spatial coordination. One of the most celebrated anthropologists to explore these differences was Margaret Mead, whose research in the South Seas (Samoa, Polynesia, Indonesia) remains, despite some significant criticism, an example of engaged scholarship, clear writing, and important ideas. Mead was clear that sex differences were "not something deeply biological," but rather were learned, and once learned, became part of the ideology that continued to perpetuate them. Here's how she put it:

> I have suggested that certain human traits have been socially specialized as the appropriate attitudes and behavior of only one sex, while other human traits have been specialized for the opposite sex. This social specialization is then rationalized into a theory that the socially decreed behavior is natural for one sex and unnatural for the other, and that the deviant is a deviant because of glandular defect, or developmental accident.[2]

In *Sex and Temperament in Three Primitive Societies* (1935), Mead explored the differences in those definitions, while in several other books, such as *Male and Female* (1949) and *Coming of Age in Samoa* (1928), she explored the processes by which males and females become the men and women their cultures prescribe. No matter what she seemed to be writing about, though, Mead always had one eye trained on the United States. In generating implicit comparisons between our own and other cultures, Mead defied us to maintain the fiction that because it is so here, it must be right and cannot be changed.

In *Sex and Temperament,* Mead directly took on the claims of biological inevitability. By examining three very different cultures in New Guinea, she hoped to show the enormous cultural variation possible in definitions of masculinity and femininity, and, in so doing, enable Americans better to understand both the cultural origins and the malleability of their own ideas. The first two cultures exhibited remarkable similarities between women and men. Masculinity and femininity were not the lines along which personality differences seemed to be organized. Women and men were not the "opposite" sex. For example, all members of the Arapesh culture appeared gentle, passive, and emotionally warm. Males and females were equally "happy, trustful, confident," and individualism was relatively absent. Men and women shared child rearing; both were "maternal," and both discouraged aggressiveness among boys and girls. Both men and women were thought to be relatively equally sexual, though their sexual relationships tended to be "domestic" and not "romantic" or, apparently what we might call passionate. Although female infanticide and male polygamy were not unknown, marriage was "even and contented." Indeed, Mead pronounced the political arrangements "utopian." Here's how she summed up Arapesh life:

quiet and uneventful co-operation, singing in the cold dawn, and singing and laughter in
the evening, men who sit happily playing to themselves on hand-drums, women holding
suckling children to their breasts, young girls walking easily down the centre of the village, with the walk of those who are cherished by all about them.[3]

By contrast, Mead describes the Mundugamor, a tribe of headhunters and cannibals, who also viewed women and men as similar, but expected both sexes to be equally
aggressive and violent. Women showed little "maternal instinct"; they detested pregnancy and nursing, and could hardly wait to return to the serious business of work and
war. "Mundugamor women actively dislike child-bearing, and they dislike children,"
Mead writes. "Children are carried in harsh opaque baskets that scratch their skins,
later, high on their mother's shoulders, well away from the breast." Among the Mundugamor, there was a violent rivalry between fathers and sons (there was more infanticide
of boys than of girls), and everyone experienced a fear that they were being wronged
by others. Quite wealthy (partly as a result of their methods of population control), the
Mundugamor were, as Mead concludes, "violent, competitive, aggressively sexual, jealous, ready to see and avenge insult, delighting in display, in action, in fighting."[4]

Here, then, were two tribes that saw gender differences as virtually nonexistent.
The third culture Mead described was the Tchambuli, where, as in the United States,
women and men were seen as extremely different. This was a patrilineal culture in
which polygyny was accepted. Here, one sex was composed primarily of nurturing and
gossipy consumers who spent their days dressing up and going shopping. They wore
curls and lots of jewelry, and Mead describes them as "charming, graceful, coquettish."
These, incidentally, were the men, and they liked nothing better than to "go off re-
splendent in feathers and shell ornaments to spend a delightful few days" shopping.
The women were dominant, energetic, economic providers. It was they who fished,
an activity upon which the entire culture depended, and it was they "who have the
real positions of power in the society." Completely unadorned, they were efficient,
business-like, controlled all the commerce and diplomacy of the culture, and were the
initiators of sexual relations. Mead notes that the Tchambuli were the only culture she
had ever seen "where little girls of ten and eleven were more alertly intelligent and
more enterprising than little boys." She writes that "[w]hat the women will think, what
the women will say, what the women will do lies at the back of each man's mind as he
weaves his tenuous and uncertain web of insubstantial relations with other men." By
contrast, "the women are a solid group, confused by no rivalries, brisk, patronizing,
and jovial."[5]

What Mead found, then, were two cultures in which women and men were seen
as similar, and one culture in which they were seen as extremely different from each
other, but the reverse of the model familiar to us. Each culture, of course, believed that
women and men were the way they were because their biological sex *determined* their
personality. None of them believed that they were the outcome of economic scarcity,
military success, or cultural arrangements.

Mead urged her readers to "admit men and women are capable of being molded
to a single pattern as easily as a diverse one."[6] She demonstrated that women and men
are *capable* of similar or different temperaments, but she did not adequately explain
why women and men turn out to be different or the same. What are the determinants

of women's and men's experiences? Nor did she explain why male domination seems to be nearly universal, despite the three exceptions she studied. These questions have been taken up by other anthropologists.

The Centrality of the
Gender Division of Labor

In almost every society, labor is divided by gender (as well as age). Certain tasks are reserved for women, others for men. How do we explain this gender division of labor, if not by some biologically based imperatives?

One school of thought, functionalism, maintains that a sex-based division of labor was necessary for the preservation of the society. As society became increasingly complex, there arose a need for two kinds of labor: hunting and gathering. Functionalists differ as to whether this division of labor had any *moral* component, whether the work of one sex was more highly valued than the work of the other. But they agree that the sex-based division of labor was functionally necessary for these societies. Such models often assume that because the sex-based division of labor arose to meet certain social needs at one time, its preservation is an evolutionary imperative, or at least an arrangement that is not to be trifled with casually.

On the other hand, since the sex-based division of labor has a history, it is not biologically inevitable; societies have changed and will continue to change. And it's a very recent history at that. "The sexual division of labor as we know it today probably developed quite recently in human evolution," writes anthropologist Adrienne Zihlman.[7] Moreover, this sex-based division of labor is far more varied than we might have assumed. In some cultures, women build the house; in others, they do the cooking. But in a few, it's the reverse. In most cultures women are responsible for child care. But not in all cultures, and they are certainly not doing it all. In some cultures, tasks are dramatically skewed and labor rigidly divided; others offer far more flexibility and fluidity. Today, a sex-based division of labor is functionally anachronistic, and the biological bases for specific social tasks being assigned to either men or women have long been eroded. In the place of such foundations, though, lie centuries of social customs and traditions that today contribute to our gender ideologies about what is appropriate for one sex and not the other. The gender-based division of labor has become a part of our culture, not a part of our physical constitution.

In fact, our physical constitutions have become less determinative in the assignment of tasks and the choosing of careers. It may even be true that the less significance there is to real physical differences, the more emphasis we place on them ideologically. For example, men no longer need to have physical strength to be powerful and dominant. The most highly muscular men, in fact, appear in cultural sideshows of body-building competitions, but they do no more physical labor than the average suburban husband mowing the lawn and shoveling snow. As for women, the technologies of family planning and sexual autonomy—birth control technology, legal abortion, and institutional child care—have freed them from performing only child care duties, and enabled them to participate in the institutions of the public sphere.

Once free, women have entered every area of the public sphere. A century ago, women campaigned to enter the college classroom, the polling place, the professions, the work world. More recently, it's been the military and military colleges that have opened their doors to women, the latter by court order. Today, very few occupations exist for which only women or only men are strictly biologically suited. What occupations do you know of that *biologically* only women or only men could perform? Offhand, I can think of only three: for women, wet nurse and surrogate mother; for men, professional sperm donor. None of these is exactly a career of choice for most of us.

If a sex-based division of labor has outlived its social usefulness or its physical imperatives, it must be held in place by something else: the power of one sex over the other. Where did that power come from? How has it developed? How does it vary from culture to culture? What factors exaggerate it; what factors diminish it? These are among the questions that anthropologists have endeavored to answer.

THEORIES OF GENDER
DIFFERENTIATION AND MALE DOMINATION

Several theorists have tried to explain the sexual division of labor and gender inequality by reference to large, structural forces that transform societies' organizing principles. For example, in the late nineteenth century, Friedrich Engels applied ideas that he developed with his collaborator, Karl Marx, and assigned to private property the role of central agent in determining the division of labor by sex. In *The Origins of the Family, Private Property and the State,* Engels suggested that the three chief institutions of modern Western society—a capitalist economy, the nation-state, and the nuclear family—emerged at roughly the same historical moment—and all as a result of the development of private property. Prior to that, Engels asserts, families were organized on a communal basis, with group marriage, male-female equality, and a sexual division of labor without any moral or political rewards going to males or females. The birth of the capitalist economy created wealth that was mobile and transferable—unlike land, which stays in the same place. Capitalism meant private property, which required the establishment of clear lines of inheritance. This requirement led, in turn, to new problems of sexual fidelity. If a man were to pass his property on to his son, he had to be sure that his son was, indeed, *his.* How could he know this in the communal group marriage of precapitalist families?

Out of this need to transmit inheritance across generations of men the traditional nuclear family emerged, with monogamous marriage and the sexual control of women by men. And if inheritance were to be stable, these new patriarchs needed to have clear, binding laws, vigorously enforced, that would enable them to pass their legacies on to their sons without interference from others. This required a centralized political apparatus (the nation-state) to exercise sovereignty over local and regional powers that might challenge them.[8]

Some contemporary anthropologists continue in this tradition. Eleanor Leacock, for example, argues that prior to the rise of private property and social classes, women and men were regarded as autonomous individuals, who held different positions that were held in relatively equal esteem. "When the range of decisions made by women is considered," she writes, "women's autonomous and public role emerges. Their status was not as literal 'equals' of men . . . but as what they were—female persons, with their own rights, duties and responsibilities, which were complementary to and in no way secondary to those of men." In her ethnographic work on the Labrador peninsula, Leacock shows the dramatic transformation of women's former autonomy by the introduction of the fur trade. The introduction of a commercial economy turned powerful women into home-bound wives. Here again, gender inequality, introduced by economic shifts, resulted in increasing differences in the meanings of masculinity and femininity.[9]

Karen Sacks examined four African cultures, and found that the introduction of the market economy shifted basically egalitarian roles toward male dominance. As long as the culture was involved in producing goods for their own use, men and women were relatively equal. But the more involved the tribe became in a market exchange economy, the higher the level of gender inequality and the lower the position of women. Conversely, when women and men shared access to the productive elements of the society, the result was a higher level of sexual egalitarianism.[10]

Another school of anthropological thought traces the origins of male domination to the imperatives of warfare in primitive society. How does a culture create warriors who are fierce and strong? Anthropologist Marvin Harris has suggested two possibilities. It can provide different rewards for the warriors, based on their dexterity or skill. But this would limit the solidarity of the fighting force and sow seeds of dissent and enmity among the soldiers. More effective would be to reward virtually all men with the services of women, excluding only the most inadequate or cowardly. Warrior societies tend to practice female infanticide, Harris observes, ensuring that the population of females remains significantly lower than that of males (and thus the males will be competing for the women). Warrior societies also tend to exclude women from the fighting force, since their presence would reduce the motivation of the soldiers and upset the sexual hierarchy. In this way, warfare leads to female subordination as well as patrilinearity, since the culture will need a resident core of fathers and sons to carry out its military tasks. Males come to control the society's resources, and, as a justification for this, develop patriarchal religion as an ideology that legitimates their domination over women.[11]

Two other groups of scholars use different variables to explain the differences between women and men. Descent theorists, such as Lionel Tiger and Robin Fox, stress the invariance of the mother-child bond. Men, by definition, lack the tie that mothers have with their children. How, then, can they achieve that connection to the next generation, the connection to history and society? They form it with other men in the hunting group. This is why, Tiger and Fox argue, women must be excluded from the hunt. In all societies, men must somehow be bound socially to the next generation, to which they are not inextricably, biologically connected. Male solidarity and monogamy are the direct result of men's needs to connect with social life.[12] Alliance theorists such as Claude Lévi-Strauss are less concerned with the need to connect males to the next generation than they are with the ways that relationships among men come to organize social life. He argues that men turn women into sex objects whose exchange (as wives) cements the alliances among men. Both descent and alliance theorists treat these themes as invariant and natural, rather than as the outcomes of historical relationships that vary dramatically not only over time but also across cultures.[13]

Determinants of Women's Status

Virtually every society of which we have knowledge revels some differentiation between women and men, and virtually every society exhibits patterns of gendered inequality and male domination. Yet the variety within these universals is still astounding. Gender differences and gender inequality may be more or less pronounced. It is not simply the case that the higher the degree of gender differentiation, the greater the gender inequality, although this is generally the pattern. One could, conceivably, imagine four such possibilities—high or low levels of gender differentiation coupled with either high or low levels of gender inequality.

What, then, are the factors that seem to determine women's status in society? Under what conditions is women's status improved, and under what conditions is it minimized? Economic, political, and social variables tend to produce different cultural configurations. For example, one large-scale survey of different cultures found that the more a society needs physical strength and highly developed motor skills, the larger will be the differences in socialization between males and females. It also seems to be the case that the larger the family group the larger the differences between women and men. In part this is because the isolation of the nuclear family means that males and females will need to take each other's roles on occasion, so that strict separation is rarely enforced.[14]

One of the key determinants of women's status has been the division of labor around child care. Women's role in reproduction has historically limited their social and economic participation. While no society assigns all child care functions to men, the more that men participate in child care and the more free women are from child-rearing responsibility, the higher women's status tends to be. There are many ways to free women from sole responsibility. In non-Western societies, several customs evolved, including child nurses who care for several children at once, sharing child care with husbands or with neighbors, and assigning the role of child care to tribal elders, whose economic activity has been curtailed by age.[15]

Relationships between children and their parents have also been seen as keys to women's status. Sociologist Scott Coltrane found that the closer the relationship between father and son, the higher the status of women is likely to be. Coltrane found that in cultures where fathers are relatively uninvolved, boys define themselves *in opposition* to their mothers and other women, and therefore are prone to exhibit traits of hypermasculinity, to fear and denigrate women as a way to display masculinity. The more mothers and fathers share child rearing, the less men belittle women. Margaret Mead also emphasized the centrality of fatherhood. Most cultures take women's role in child rearing as a given, whereas men must learn to become nurturers. There is much at stake, but nothing inevitable: "every known human society rests firmly on the learned nurturing behavior of men."[16]

That men must learn to be nurturers raises the question of masculinity in general. What it means to be a man varies enormously from one culture to another, and these definitions have a great deal to do with the amount of time and energy fathers spend with their children. Such issues are not simply incidental for women's lives either; it turns out that the more time men spend with their children, the less gender inequality is present in that culture. Conversely, the more free women are from child care—the more that child care is parceled out elsewhere and the more that women control their fertility—the higher will be their status. Coltrane also found that women's status depended upon their control over property, especially after marriage. A woman's status was invariably higher when she retained control over her property after marriage.

Interestingly, recent research on male bonding, so necessary to those theories that stress warfare or the necessity of attaching males to the social order, also seems to bear this out. Sociologist and geographer Daphne Spain argues that the same cultures in which men developed the most elaborate sex-segregated rituals were those cultures in which women's status was lowest. Spain mapped a number of cultures spatially, and found that the farther the distance the men's hut was from the center of the village, the more time the men spent at their hut, and the more culturally important were the men's rituals, the lower was women's status. "Societies with men's huts are those in which women have the least power," she writes. If you spend your time away from your hut, off at the men's hut with the other men, you'll have precious little time, and even less inclination, to spend with your family and sharing in child rearing![17]

Similarly, anthropologist Thomas Gregor found that all forms of spatial segregation between males and females are associated with gender inequality. The Mehinaku of central Brazil, for example, have well-institutionalized men's huts where the tribal secrets are kept and ritual instruments are played and stored. Women are prohibited from entering. As one tribesman told Gregor, "[T]his house is only for men. Women may not see anything in here. If a woman comes in, then all the men take her into the woods and she is raped."[18]

These two variables—the father's involvement in child rearing (often measured by spatial segregation) and women's control of property after marriage—emerge as among the central determinants of women's status and gender inequality. It is no wonder that they are also determinants of violence against women, since the lower women's status in a society, the higher the likelihood of rape and violence against women. In one of the most wide-ranging comparative studies of women's status, Peggy Reeves Sanday found several important correlates of women's status. Contact was one. Sex segregation was highly associated with women's lower status; as if separation were "necessary for the development of sexual inequality and male dominance." (By contrast, a study of a sexually egalitarian society found no ideology of the desirability of sex segregation.) Of course, women's economic power, that crucial determinant, is "the result of a sexual division of labor in which women achieve self-sufficiency and establish an independent control sphere." In addition, in cultures that viewed the environment as relatively friendly, women's status was significantly higher; cultures that saw the environment as hostile were more likely to develop patterns of male domination.[19]

Finally, Sanday found that women had the highest levels of equality, and thus the least frequency of rape, when both genders contributed about the same amounts to the food supply. When women contributed equally, men tended to be more involved in child care. Ironically, when women contributed a lot, their status was also low. So, women's status tended to be lower when they contributed either very little or a great deal, and more equal when their contribution was about equal.

Following Tavris and Wade, we can summarize the findings of cross-cultural research on female status and male dominance. First, male dominance is lower when men and women work together, with little sexual division of labor. Sex segregation of work is the strongest predictor of women's status. Second, male dominance is more pronounced when men control political and ideological resources that are necessary to achieve the goals of the culture, and when men control all property. Third, male dominance is "exacerbated under colonization"—both capitalist penetration of the countryside and industrialization generally lower women's status. Male dominance is also associated with demographic imbalances between the sexes: the higher the percentage of marriageable men to marriageable women, the lower is women's status. And, finally, environmental stresses tend to exaggerate male domination.[20]

THE CROSS-CULTURAL EXPLANATIONS OF RAPE

The quotation above, cited by Gregor, and the research of Peggy Reeves Sanday and others suggest that rape is not the evolutionary reproductive strategy of the less successful males, but rather a cultural phenomenon by which relations between men are cemented. Rape may be a strategy to ensure continued male domination or a vehicle by which men can hope to conceal maternal dependence, according to ethnographers, but it is surely not an alternative dating strategy. In her ethnographic study of a gang rape at the University of Pennsylvania, Sanday suggests that gang rape has its origins in both the gender inequality that allows men to see women as pieces of meat, and in men's needs to demonstrate their masculinity to one another. Gang rape cements the relations among men. But more than that, gang rape permits a certain homoerotic contact between men. When one participant reported his pleasure at feeling the semen of his friends inside the woman as he raped her, Sanday sensed a distinct erotic component. The woman was the receptacle, the vehicle by which these men could have sex with one another and still claim heterosexuality. Only in a culture that degrades and devalues women could such behaviors take place. Rape, then, is hardly an evolutionary strategy by which less successful males get to pass on their reproductive inheritance. It is an act that occurs only in those societies where there is gender inequality and by men who may be quite "successful" in other forms of mating but believe themselves entitled to violate women. It is about *gender*, not about *sex*, and it is a way in which gender inequality produces gender difference.[21]

RITUALS OF GENDER

One of the ways that anthropologists have explored the cultural construction of gender is by examining specific gender rituals. Their work suggests that the origins of these rituals lie in nonbiological places. Since questions of reproduction and child rearing loom so large in the determination of gender inequality, it makes sense that a lot of these rituals are concerned with reproduction. And since spatial segregation seems to be highly associated with gender difference and gender inequality, ritual segregation—either in space or time—may have also been a focus of attention. For example, the initiation of young males has been of particular concern, in part because of the relative disappearance of such formal cultural rituals in the contemporary United States. Initiation rituals provide a sense of identity and group membership to the men who participate in them. Many cultures, especially settled agricultural and pastoral societies, include circumcision, the excision of the foreskin of a boy's penis, in a ritual incorporating a male into the society. The age of this ceremony varies; one survey of twenty-one cultures that practice circumcision found that four perform it in infancy, ten when the boy is about ten years old (before puberty), six perform it at puberty, and one waits until late adolescence.

Why would so many cultures determine that membership in the world of adult men requires genital mutilation? Indeed, circumcision is the most common medical procedure in the United States. Theories, of course, abound. In the Jewish Bible, circumcision is a visible sign of the bond between God and man, a symbol of man's obedience to God's law. (In Genesis 17:10–11, 14, God commands Abraham to circumcise Isaac as a covenant.) But it also seems to have been seen as a trophy. Successful warriors would cut off their foes' foreskins to symbolize their victory, and to permanently disfigure and humiliate the vanquished foe. (In 1 Samuel 18:25, King Saul demands that David slay one hundred enemies and bring back their foreskins as a bride-price. David, a bit overeager, brings back two hundred.)

In other cultures, ethnographers suggest that circumcision creates a visible scar that binds men to one another, and serves as a rite of passage to adult masculinity. Whiting, Kluckhohn, Anthony argue that it symbolically serves to sever a boy's emotional ties to his mother, and therefore to assure appropriate masculine identification. Other writers point out that cultures that emphasize circumcision of young males tend to be those where both gender differentiation and gender inequality are greatest. Circumcision, which is always a public ceremony, simultaneously cements the bonds between father (and his generation) and son (and his generation), links the males together, and excludes women, visibly and demonstrably. Circumcision, then, tends to be associated with male domination.[22] As do other forms of male genital mutilation. In a very few cultures, for example, the penis is ritually bled by cutting. Such cultures still believe in bleeding as a cure for illness—in this case, illness brought about by sexual contact with women, who are believed to be impure and infectious. And we know of four cultures that practice hemi-castration, the removal of one testicle. In one culture, people believe it prevents the birth of twins.[23]

Female circumcision is also practiced in several cultures, though far fewer than male circumcision. This consists either of clitoridectomy, in which the clitoris is cut away, or infibulation, in which the labia majora are sewn together with only a very small opening left to allow for urination. It is interesting that female circumcision is often performed by adult women. In other cultures, it is performed by the brother of the girl's father. Clitoridectomy is widespread in Africa, but few other places, and it invariably takes place in societies that also practice male circumcision. The World Health

Organization estimates that 130 million girls and women have undergone some form of cutting.[24] Infibulation seems to be most widely practiced in East Africa and Somalia, and its goal is to prevent sexual intercourse, while the goal of clitoridectomy is simply to prevent sexual pleasure, and thereby sexual promiscuity. Here is the description of the practice from one who underwent it, a Sudanese woman now working as a teacher in the Middle East:

> I will never forget the day of my circumcision, which took place forty years ago. I was six years old. One morning during my school summer vacation, my mother told me that I had to go with her to her sisters' house and then to visit a sick relative in Halfayat El Mulook [in the northern part of Khartoum, Sudan]. We did go to my aunt's house, and from there all of us went straight to [a] red brick house [I had never seen].
>
> While my mother was knocking, I tried to pronounce the name that was on the door. Soon enough I realized that it was Haija Alamin's house. She was the midwife who performed circumcisions on girls in my neighborhood. I was petrified and tried to break loose. But I was captured and subdued by my mother and two aunts. They began to tell me that the midwife was going to purify me.
>
> The midwife was the cruelest person I had seen. . . . [She] ordered her young maid to go buy razors from the Yemeni grocer next door. I still remember her when she came back with the razors, which were enveloped in purple wrappings with a crocodile drawing on it.
>
> The women ordered me to lie down on a bed [made of ropes] that had a little hole in the middle. They held me tight while the midwife started to cut my flesh without anesthetics. I screamed till I lost my voice. The midwife was saying to me "Do you want me to be taken into police custody?" After the job was done I could not eat, drink, or even pass urine for three days. I remember one of my uncles who discovered what they did to me threatened to press charges against his sisters. They were afraid of him and they decided to bring me back to the midwife. In her sternest voice she ordered me to squat on the floor and urinate. It seemed like the most difficult thing to do at that point, but I did it. I urinated for a long time and was shivering with pain.
>
> It took a very long time [before] I was back to normal. I understand the motives of my mother, that she wanted me to be clean, but I suffered a lot.[25]

It is interesting that both cultures that circumcise men and those that circumcise women tend to be those where men's status is highest. The purpose of the ritual reveals some of this difference. For men, it is a marking that simultaneously shows that all men are biologically *and culturally* alike—and that they are different from women. Thus, it can be seen as reinforcing male dominance. Historically, there was some evidence that male circumcision was medically beneficial, as it reduced the possibilities of penile infection by removing the foreskin, a place where bacteria could congregate. This is no longer the case; rates of penile infection or urethral cancer show no differences between those who have or have not been circumcised. Among advanced industrial societies, only in the United States are the majority of men circumcised, although that rate has dropped from over 95 percent in the 1960s to about two-thirds today. Australia has the second highest rate, about 10 percent.

For women, circumcision has never been justified by medical benefits; it directly impedes adequate sexual functioning and is designed to curtail sexual pleasure. Female circumcision is nearly always performed when women reach the age of puberty, that is, when they are capable of experiencing sexual pleasure, and seems to be associated with men's control over women's sexuality. Currently, political campaigns are being waged to prohibit female circumcision as a violation of women's human rights. However, many of its defenders suggest that such campaigns are motivated by Western values. They insist that afterward, women are revered and respected as members of the culture. (There are no widespread political campaigns against male circumcision, though some individuals have recently begun to rethink the ritual as a form of genital mutilation, and a few men are even undergoing a surgical procedure designed to replace the lost foreskin.)[26]

One of the more interesting theories about the prevalence of these reproductive and sexual rituals has been offered by Jeffrey and Karen Paige in their book, *The Politics of Reproductive Ritual*. Paige and Paige offer a materialist interpretation of these rituals, locating the origins of male circumcision, couvade, and purdah in the culture's relationship with its immediate material environment. Take couvade, for example. This is a ritual that men observe when their wives are having babies. Generally, they observe the same food taboos as their wives, restrict their ordinary activities, and even seclude themselves during their wives' delivery and postpartum period. What could possibly be the point of this? Some might think it is anthropologically "cute," as the men often even imitate the symptoms of pregnancy, in apparent sympathy for their wives. But Paige and Paige see it differently. They argue that couvade is significant in cultures where there are no legal mechanisms to keep the couple together or to assure paternity. Couvade is a way for men to fully claim paternity, to know that the baby is theirs. It is also a vehicle by which the men can control women's sexuality by appropriating control over paternity.[27]

Paige and Paige also examine the politics of purdah, the Islamic requirement that women conceal themselves at all times. Ostensibly, this is to protect women's chastity and men's honor—women must be completely covered because they "are so sexy, so tempting, so incapable of controlling their emotions and sexuality, the men say, that they are a danger to the social order." It is as if by concealing women, they can harness women's sexuality. But this is only half the story. It also suggests that *men* are so susceptible to temptation, so incapable of resistance, such easy prey, that they are likely to fall into temptation at any time. In order to protect women from *men's* sexual rapaciousness, men must control women and take away the source of the temptation.[28]

HOW MANY GENDERS ARE THERE?

We've explored the relationship between levels of gender difference and levels of inequality. But in some cultures, gender itself doesn't seem to be that important, certainly not the central organizing principle of social life. In fact, it hardly matters at all. What accounts for that difference?

The discussion of gender difference often assumes that differences are based on some biological realities that sort physical creatures into their appropriate categories. Thus, we assume that because there are two biological sexes (male and female) there must only be two genders (men and women). But some research challenges such bipolar assumptions. Some societies recognize more than two genders—sometimes three or four. Research on Native American cultures is particularly fascinating and provocative. The Navaho, for example, appear to have three genders—one for masculine men, one for feminine women, and another, called the *nadle,* for those whose sex was ambiguous at birth. One could decide to become a nadle or be born one; either way, they perform tasks assigned to both women and to men and dress as the gender whose tasks they are performing, though they are typically treated as women, and addressed using feminine kinship terms. But let's not jump to conclusions: being treated as a woman was a promotion, not a demotion in Navaho society, where women historically had higher status than men and were accorded special rights and privileges, including sexual freedom, control over property, and authority to mediate disputes. Nadles were free to marry either males or females, with no loss of status.[29]

Another custom among some Native American cultures is the *berdache,* which is also found in Southeast Asia and the South Pacific. Berdaches are members of one biological sex who adopt the gender identity of the other sex, although such a practice is far more common for males than for females. In his pathbreaking study, *The Spirit and the Flesh,* anthropologist Walter Williams explored the world of the berdache in detail. These were men who dressed, worked, and generally acted as women—though

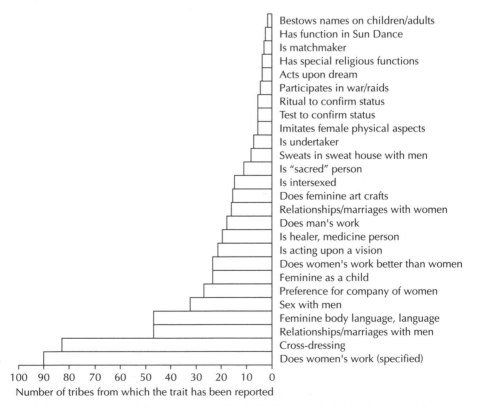

Figure 3.1. Components of the woman-man (male-bodied "berdache") role. From Sabine Lang, *Men as Women, Women as Men,* University of Chicago Press, 1998, p. 256.

everyone knew that they were biologically males. Among the Crow in North America, the berdache were simply males who did not want to become warriors.[30]

Consider how we treat males who dress and act like women. We treat them like freaks, deviants, or assume they must be homosexual. They are outcasts; acting like a berdache in this culture is not recommended if you value your health and your life. Among the Native American cultures of the Great Plains, though, the berdaches are revered as possessed of special powers, enjoy high social and economic status, and frequently control the tribe's ritual life. The reasoning is straightforward and logical: By being men who act like women, the berdaches are sexually indifferent to women, something that other men are not capable of being. Surely, they must be possessed of some supernatural power to be able to resist the charms of females! Only the berdache can be counted on to administer fairly without seeking to advance his claim on a specific woman whom he might fancy. Anthropologist Sabine Lang documented the wide range of cross-gender activities engaged in by berdaches in Native American cultures[31] (see figure 3.1).

There is one case of what might be called female berdaches. Among the Nahane, a Native American culture, a married couple might decide that they had too many daughters and too few sons to hunt for them when they got old. They would choose one of their daughters to live like a man. When she was about five years old, the dried ovaries of a bear were tied to her belt, and she was treated as if she were a boy from then on. As an adult, she would most likely have lesbian sexual relations.[32]

The Mohave seem to have four genders and permit both women and men to cross genders to carefully demarcated roles. A boy who showed preferences for feminine clothing or toys would undergo a different initiation at puberty and become an *alyha*. He would then adopt a female name, paint his face as a woman, perform female roles, and marry a man. When they married, the alyha would cut his upper thigh every month to signify "his" menstrual period, and he would learn how to simulate pregnancy and childbirth. Martin and Voorhies suggest how this was accomplished:

> Labor pains, induced by drinking a severely constipating drug, culminate in the birth of a fictitious stillborn child. Stillborn Mohave infants are customarily buried by the mother, so that an alyha's failure to return to "her" home with a living infant is explained in a culturally acceptable manner.[33]

If a Mohave female wanted to cross genders, she would undergo an initiation ceremony to become a *hwame*. Hwame lived men's lives—hunting, farming, and the like, and assumed paternal responsibility for children, though they were prohibited from assuming positions of political leadership. Neither hwame nor alyha is considered deviant.

In the Middle East, we find a group of Omani males called *xanith* who are biologically males, but whose social identity is female. They work as skilled domestic servants, dress in men's tunics (but in pastel shades more associated with feminine colors), and sell themselves in passive homosexual relationships. They are permitted to speak with women on the street (other men are prohibited). At sex-segregated public events, they sit with the women. However, they can change their minds—and their gender experiences. If they want to be seen as males, they are permitted to do so, and they then may engage in heterosexual sex. Others simply grow older and eventually quit the homosexual prostitution; they are then permitted to become "social men." Some "become" women, even going as far as marrying men. And still others move back and forth between these positions throughout their lives, suggesting a fluidity of gender identity that would be unthinkable to those who believe in biological determinism.

SEXUAL DIVERSITY

These studies of gender fluidity are also complemented by studies of sexual variation. Taken together, they provide powerful arguments about the cultural construction of both gender and sexuality. Anthropologists have explored remarkable sexual diversity, and thus have suggested that biological arguments about the natural-ness of some activities and arrangements may be dramatically overstated. Take homosexuality, which evolutionary biologists would suggest is a biological "aberration" if ever there were one, because homosexuality is not reproductive, and the goal of all sexual activity is to pass on one's genetic code to the next generation. Not only is homosexual activity ubiquitous in the animal kingdom, but it is also extraordinarily common in human cultures—so common, in fact, that it would appear to be "natural." What varies is not the presence or absence of homosexuality—that's pretty much a constant—but the ways in which homosexuals are treated in those cultures. We've already seen that many cultures honor and respect those who transgress gender definitions and adopt the gender of the other sex. Some of these might be considered "homosexual," if your definition of homosexual has only to do with the biological sex of your sex partner.

Even by that definition, though, we find astonishing variation in the ways in which homosexuals are regarded. In 1948, anthropologist Clyde Kluckohn surveyed North American Indian tribes and found homosexuality accepted by 120 of them and rejected by fifty-four. Some cultures (Lango in east Africa, Koniag in Alaska, and Tanala in Madagascar) all allow homosexual marriages between men. Some cultures have clearly defined homosexual roles for men and women, with clearly defined expectations.[34]

In a remarkable ethnography, Gilbert Herdt described the sexual rituals of the Sambia, a mountain people who live in Papua New Guinea. The Sambia practice ritualized homosexuality as a way to initiate young boys into full adult manhood. Young boys ritually daily fellate the older boys and men so that they (the younger boys) can receive the vital life fluid (semen) from the older men and thus become men. "A boy must be initiated and [orally] inseminated, otherwise the girl betrothed to him will outgrow him and run away to another man," was the way one Sambia elder put it. "If a boy doesn't eat semen, he remains small and weak." When they reach puberty, these boys are then fellated by a new crop of younger boys. Throughout this initiation, the boys scrupulously avoid girls, and have no knowledge of heterosexuality until they are married. Neither the boys nor the older men think of themselves as engaging in homosexual behavior: The older men are married to women, and the younger men fully expect to be. There is no adult homosexuality among the Sambia. But these young boys must become, as Herdt puts it, "reluctant warriors." How else are the boys to receive the vital life force that will enable them to be real men and warriors?[35]

Nearby, also in Melanesia, are the Keraki, who engage in a related practice. There, the boys are sodomized by older men, because the Keraki believe that without the older men's semen, the boys will not grow to be men. This ritual practice occurs until the boys hit puberty and secondary sex characteristics appear—facial hair, dropped voice—at which point the ritual has accomplished its task. When an anthropologist asked Kerki men if they had been sodomized, many responded by saying, "Why, yes! Otherwise how should I have grown?" Other ritualized homosexual practices have been reported from other cultures.[36] Interestingly, such ritual practices, as among the Sambia and Keraki, are more evident in cultures in which sex segregation is high and women's status is low. This conforms to other ethnographic evidence that suggests that elaborate rituals of male bonding have the effect of excluding women from ritual life, and thus correlate with women's lower status. Sex segregation is almost always associated with lower status for women—whether among the Sambia or among cadets at the Citadel.[37]

If all this sounds extraordinarily exotic, remember this: In every major city in the United States, there is a group of young men, many of whom are married and virtually all of whom consider themselves to be heterosexual, who have sex with other men for money. These gay hustlers will perform only certain acts (anal penetration) or will only allow certain acts (they permit their clients to fellate them, but will not reciprocate). By remaining the "insertor" in homosexual acts, these men do not identify as homosexual, but as men. Men are insertors, whether with women or with men, so as long as they remain insertors, they believe their masculinity is not compromised. "Objectively," you may argue, they are engaging in gay sex. But by their definition, homosexuality equals passivity in sexual contact, having sex like a woman. And by that definition, they are not having gay sex. Whatever you might make of this, though, suddenly the Sambia do not look completely alien; they look more like distant cousins.

Some cultures take permissiveness regarding homosexuality to a remarkable level. Among the Aranda of Australia, Siwans of Northern Africa, and Keraki of New Guinea, every male is homosexual during adolescence and bisexual after marriage. The purpose of this is to divert adolescent sex away from young girls and prevent teenage pregnancy, and therefore to keep the birth rate down in cultures that have very scarce resources. The well-studied Yanomamo have an institutionalized form of male homosexuality as well as female infanticide. This warrior culture feared population explosion and the depletion of resources to females.[38]

The Etero and the Marind-anim, both in New Guinea, prefer homosexuality to heterosexuality, even though they maintain heterosexual marriages. How, you might ask, do they solve the problem of reproduction? The Etero place a taboo on heterosexual sex for most of the year, but prohibit gay sex when the moon is full (and thus when all the women are ovulating). For the Marind-anim, even that much sexual contact with the opposite sex is undesirable. Their birth rate is so low that this warrior culture organizes raids every year, during which it kidnaps the babies of other cultures, raising them to be happy, healthy—and, of course, homosexual—Marind-anim.[39]

One Melanesian society, called "East Bay" in William Davenport's ethnographic study, practices full adult bisexuality. Nearly every male has extensive homosexual sexual contact throughout his life, though all are also heterosexual and married to women. (None are exclusively homosexual, only a few exclusively heterosexual.) Women and men are seen as relatively equal in terms of sexual drive, and there are no taboos against contact with women.[40]

SEXUAL CUSTOMS AS GENDER DIVERSITY

Sexual customs display a dizzying array that, taken together, imply that sexual behavior is anything but organized around reproduction alone. Where, when, how, and with whom we have sex varies enormously from culture to culture. Ernestine Friedel, for example, observed dramatic differences in sexual customs between two neighboring tribes in New Guinea. One, a highland tribe, believes that intercourse makes men weaker, and that women are naturally prone to tempt men, threatening them with their powerful sexuality. They also find menstrual blood terrifying. These sexual ideologies pit women against men, and many men would rather remain bachelors than risk contact with women. As a result, population remains relatively low, which this culture needs because they have no new land or resources to bring under cultivation. Not far away, however, is a very different culture. Here, both men and women enjoy sex and sex play. Men worry about whether women are sexually satisfied, and they get along relatively well. They have higher birth rates, which is manageable because they live in a relatively abundant and uncultivated region, where they can use all the hands they can get to farm their fields and defend themselves.[41]

Sex researchers have explored the remarkable cultural diversity of sexual behaviors, and in so doing have exposed the ethnocentrism of those arguments that stress the inevitability and naturalness of our own behaviors. Take the typical American couple, Mr. and Mrs. Statistical Average. They're white, middle-aged, married, and have sex about twice a week, at night, in their bedroom, alone, with the lights off, in the "missionary position"—the woman on her back, facing the man who lies on top of her. The encounter—from the "do you want to?" to kissing, foreplay, and intercourse (always in that order), and finally to "Goodnight sweetheart"—lasts about fifteen minutes. Now consider other cultures: Some cultures never have sex outside. Others believe that having sex indoors would contaminate the food supply (usually in the same hut). What about our rates of sexual contact? The Zande have sex two or three times a night, and then once again upon awakening. Chaga men have about ten orgasms a night, and Thonga men try to have sex with as many as three or four of their wives each night. But few beat the Marquesa: While it's not uncommon for a Marquesan man to have thirty or more orgasms a night, it is normal to have at least ten. Older married men are exempted: They have only about three or four a night. By contrast, the Yapese have sex only once a month or so. During this encounter, the man sits with his back against the side of the hut and his legs straight out. The woman straddles him, and he inserts his penis into her vagina a little bit, and then proceeds to stimulate her for several hours while she has dozens of orgasms.[42]

While for us, kissing is a virtually universal initiation of sexual contact—"first base" as it were—other cultures find it disgusting because of the possibility of exchanging saliva. "Putting your lips together?" say the Thonga or the Siriono. "But that's where you put food!" Some cultures practice almost no foreplay at all, but go directly to intercourse; others prescribe several hours of touching and caressing, in which intercourse is a necessary but sad end to the proceedings. Some cultures include oral sex in their lovemaking; others have never even considered it. Alfred Kinsey found that 70 percent of the American men he surveyed in 1948 had only had sex in the missionary position and that 85 percent had an orgasm within two minutes of penetration. In his survey of 131 Native American cultures, Clyde Kluckhohn found the missionary position preferred in only seventeen.[43]

In our culture, it is men who are supposed to be the sexual initiators, and women who are supposed to be sexually resistant. We've all heard stories about men giving women aphrodisiacs to make them more sexually uninhibited. The latest is a drug called Rohypnol, the "date rape drug," which men apparently put in unsuspecting women's drinks to make them more "compliant" or at least unconscious (which, in these men's minds, may amount to the same thing). How different are the Trobriand Islanders, where women are seen as sexually insatiable and take the initiative. Or the Tukano-Kubeo in Brazil. Here, women are the sexual aggressors, and may even avoid getting pregnant or abort because it would mean forgoing sex. Women commit adultery, not men, but they justify it by saying that it was "only sex." Taukno-Kubeo men secretly give the women anaphrodisiacs to cool them out.[44]

These are but a few examples. When questioned about them, people in these cultures give the same answers we would. "It's normal," they'll say. And they've developed the same kind of self-justifying arguments that we have. The Bambara, for example, believe that having sex during the day would produce albino children, while the Masai believe daytime sex can be fatal. So members of these cultures have sex only at night, and apparently, there are no albinos born and no fatalities during sex. The Chenchu, by contrast, believe that sex at night will lead to the birth of blind babies. So they only have sex during the day, and thus avoid having blind children. The Yurok believe that practicing cunnilingus will keep the salmon from running. No oral sex, no shortage of salmon. Such sexual variety suggests that the biological imperative toward reproduction can take many forms, but that none is more "natural" than any other.

ANTHROPOLOGY AS HISTORY

Anthropological research has helped to expose the faulty logic of those who argue that the universality of gender difference or of male domination are somehow natural and inevitable. By exploring the variety of meanings that have accompanied the cultural definitions of masculinity and femininity, and by examining cultural configurations that either magnify or diminish gender inequality, cross-cultural research has taken us beyond apparent biological imperatives. In another sense, anthropological research on our earlier human ancestors has also provided a historical retort to biological inevitability. Take, for example, the arguments we saw earlier that male domination was a natural development in the shift to hunting and gathering societies. Remember the story: Men's superior physical strength led them naturally toward hunting, while weaker women stayed home and busied themselves with gardening and child rearing. Tidy and neat—but also, it appears, historically wrong.

It turns out that such stories actually read history backward, from the present to the past, seeking the historical origins of the patterns we find today. But recent research suggests that meat made up a rather small portion of the early human diet, which meant that all that celebrated hunting didn't count for much at all. And those weapons men invented, the great technological breakthrough that enabled cultures to develop—

placing cultural development squarely on the backs of men? Turns out that the great technological leap was more likely slings that women with babies developed so they could carry both baby and food. It may even be true that the erect posture of human beings derives not from the demands of hunting, but the shift from foraging for food to gathering and storing it. While celebrants of "masculinist" evolution credited the demands of the hunt for creating the necessity of social (male) bonding for the survival of the community, surely it is the bond between mother and infant that literally and materially ensures survival. Painting a more accurate anthropological picture would require that we acknowledge that females were not simply passive and dependent bearers of children, but were active participants in the technological and economic side of life.[45]

Another way to look at this is suggested by Helen Fisher. She notes startling similarities between contemporary American culture and early human cultures. What we have inherited as the biologically "natural" system—nuclear families, marriages with one partner for life, the dramatic separation of home and workplace—all seem to be relatively recent cultural inventions that accompany settled agricultural societies. On the other hand, divorce and remarriage, institutionalized child care, and women and men working equally both at home and away are more typical of the hunting and gathering societies that preceded them—and had lasted for millions of years. It may be, Fisher suggests, that after a brief evolutionary rest stop in a settled agricultural domain (during which time male domination, warfare, and monotheism all developed), we are returning to our "true" human evolutionary origins. "As we head back to the future," she suggests, "there's every reason to believe the sexes will enjoy the kind of equality that is a function of our birthright."[46]

If this sounds a bit too mythical, there is a school of feminist anthropology that goes much farther. Most anthropologists agree with Michelle Rosaldo, who concluded that "human cultural and social forms have always been male dominated," or with Bonnie Nardi who finds "no evidence of truly egalitarian societies. In no societies do women participate on an equal footing with men in activities accorded the highest prestige."[47] But one school of feminist anthropologists sees such universality as "an ethnological delusion," and they argue that there are, and there have been, societies in which women and men were equal. What's more, there may have also been societies in which women were the dominant sex. Based on archeological excavations in Crete and elsewhere, Marija Gimbutas and Riane Eisler and others have argued that Neolithic societies were Goddess-worshiping, gender-equal virtual Gardens of Eden, in which women and men may have occupied separate spheres, but were equal and mutually respectful. Symbolized, Eisler writes, by the chalice—the symbol of shared plenty—these ancient peoples evidenced a "partnership" model of human interaction.[48]

Then, the story goes, the barbarians invaded, instituting male domination, a single omnipotent male God, and unleashing "the lethal power of the blade"—a violent and hierarchical world drenched in the blood of war and murder. We've been living under such a brutal dominator model—"in which male dominance, male violence, and a generally hierarchic and authoritarian social structure was the norm"—ever since. In such a world, "having violently deprived the Goddess and the female half of humanity of all power, gods and men or war ruled," Eisler writes, and "peace and harmony would be found only in the myths and legends of a long lost past."[49]

Another "just-so" story? Perhaps. I'm always skeptical of arguments that point to a dimly lit historical past for our models of future social transformation, since they so often rely on selective evidence and often make for retrogressive politics. And I'm equally uneasy with sweeping categorizations of "female" peace-loving cultures being swept aside by brutally violent "male" ones. After all, the contemporary world, for all its murderous, rapacious, and bloodthirsty domination, is *far* less violent than hunter-gatherer societies. Ethnographic data suggest that only about 10 percent of societies rarely engage in war; most cultures are engaged in conflict either continuously or more than once a year. The same !Kung bushmen celebrated by Eisler as the "harmless people," have a murder rate higher than Detroit or Washington, D.C. "The sad archeological evidence," writs Frances Fukuyama, "indicates that systematic mass killings of men, women, and children occurred in Neolithic times. There was no age of innocence."[50]

On the other hand, why would we want to believe that male domination is somehow natural and inevitable? Some of Eisler's arguments are on firm evolutionary footing: It is likely, for example, that descent was originally traced through matrilinearity. This would make descent far more certain in cultures that did not understand the relationship between sexual intercourse and birth nine months later. And one can believe the credible evidence that women played a greater role in early human societies, without assuming one momentous calamity of invasion when that Edenic world was forever lost.

There is even some evidence of cultures that, while not fully female-dominated, evince women's power in all public and private arenas. Peggy Sanday's fascinating study of the matrilineal Minangkabau of Western Sumatra, one of the largest ethnic groups in Indonesia, is a case in point. Instead of looking for a mirror-image world, in which women wield power as men do, Sanday finds instead a culture in which women's ways of governing parallel men's and at times even supplant them. Here, women are self-confident and independent of their husbands, and while men hold many of the formal political offices, women "rule without governing." They "facilitate social bonding outside the machinations of political power" that enable "the men's job of adjudicating disputes according to the rules of adat [customs] and consensus decision-making."[51]

If the anthropologists have demonstrated anything, it is the rich diversity in human cultural arrangements and the disparate definitions of gender and sexuality that we have produced within our cultures. Several theories explain the historical origins of these patterns and suggest ways we can modify or abandon some historically coercive or exploitative practices without doing damage to our evolutionary legacy. Cultural relativism also suggests that, in this enormous cultural variety and historical evolution of custom and culture, we shed those customs we no longer need, even if once they served some societal purpose. "Assertions of past inferiority for women should therefore be irrelevant to present and future developments," writes Eleanor Leacock.[52] Still, questions linger. Given such diversity of sexuality and gender, why is male dominance so universal? If it's not inevitable, how do we explain its persistence? Here, the answers may be a bit closer to home.

"So, That Explains It"

Psychological Perspectives on Gender Development

Upon no subject has there been so much dogmatic assertion based on so little scientific evidence, as upon male and female types of mind.

—JOHN DEWEY
"IS COEDUCATION INJURIOUS TO GIRLS?" (1911)

There's a famous cartoon of two babies, a boy and a girl, standing together. They're both holding open their diapers and peering down at their genitals. The caption reads, "So, that explains the difference in our salaries." The cartoon adopts a popular idea about the theories of Sigmund Freud, the founder of psychoanalysis. Freud believed that the anatomical differences between males and females led them toward different personalities, that sex did determine temperament. However, he did not believe that such differences were programmed into males and females at birth. On the contrary, Freud saw his work as challenging those who held that the body contained all the information it needed at birth to become an adult man or woman. He believed that the observed differences between women and men were traceable to our different experiences from infancy onward, especially in the ways we were treated in our families.

Gender identity, Freud maintained, was a crucial part of personality development—perhaps *the* most crucial part. Gender was acquired, molded through interactions with family members and with the larger society. And it wasn't an easy acquisition; the route to appropriate gender identity was perilous, and included the constant possibility of gender identity failure, which was manifest most clearly in sexual nonconformity, especially homosexuality. Of course, biology does play some role here: Freud and his followers believed that visible anatomical differences were decisive in the development of the child, and especially that sexual energy, located in the body, propelled the child's experiences that determined gender identity.

The Freudian Legacy

Freud proposed a stage theory of individual gender development, one in which each individual passes through a number of stages on his or her path to identity. These stages are set into motion by two factors: the composition or structure of the psyche and the realities of life. Four elements comprise Freud's model of the psyche: id, ego, superego, and the external world. These elements together form the basic architecture of the self, and each has a decisive role to play in the formation of personality. Id represents our desire to satisfy our basic animal needs for food, shelter, and pleasure. All drives and energy, id knows only that it wants gratification, but has neither morality nor the means to acquire what it wants. Freud calls the id "a cauldron filled with seething excitations."[1]

Unfortunately, the external world does not exist to satisfy our wants and desires, so id's desires are constantly thwarted. How we cope with those frustrations determines personality development. The ego, the rational problem-solving portion of our personality, takes the impulses of the id and translates them into strategies for gratification that will be effective. The ego must discipline the id, tame it, and seek possible sources of gratification for it. Another part of the psyche, the superego, is an outgrowth of ego's efforts to seek socially effective and appropriate outlets for gratification of id's desires. Freud calls it an "internalized externality"—superego sees the limited possibilities for gratification offered by society as legitimate. Superego is the seat of morality and it assists the ego in selecting effective strategies toward socially approved goals.

From these four elements, individuals fashion their psychological constitution: their drives for gratification, the limited possibilities offered by the world, the moralizing inner voice that tells us we do not deserve gratification, and the rational strategizer that tries to keep all these forces in balance. It is hard work, serving three "tyrannical masters"; as Freud writes, "[T]he ego, driven by the id, confined by the superego, repulsed by reality, struggles to master its economic task of bringing about harmony among the forces and influences working in and upon it; and we can understand how it is that so often we cannot suppress a cry, 'Life is not easy!' "[2] Freud proclaimed the mission of psychoanalysis was to strengthen the ego, to enable it to win this battle of wills. Not only did the personality development depend upon it, but also the future of civilization.[3] Unless ego finds socially acceptable directions in which to channel the potentially destructive impulses of the id, we cannot build and sustain the institutions of our culture.

These different components of the self emerge gradually through a child's development as the ego tries to navigate its way through the narrow straits presented by the incessant demands of the id and the imperious claims of the superego. In a way, Freud's theory of development is a rather sad story, as each successive stage does not provide nearly the pleasures of the one it replaces—we grow by giving up things that give us pleasure—and, since ego is often not strong enough to undertake such a struggle, there are the omnipresent dangers of temporary backsliding to earlier stages in our fantasies (neurosis) or a dramatic break with reality and the attempt to live in that earlier stage (psychosis).

Prior to birth, Freud believed, all the infant's desires are gratified; in the womb we are sensuously content. But birth expels us from this enveloping Eden; hungry and alone, we can take nothing for granted. Now the infant transfers gratification to the mother's breast, seeking pleasure through ingesting food. This Freud calls the "oral stage." But just as the ego accommodates itself to this source of gratification it's removed by weaning. In the next stage, the "anal stage," gratification is achieved not through taking food in but by giving food back, as in urination and defecation. These bodily functions are now a source of pleasure, but no sooner do we discover the joys of excretory creation that can compensate for the loss of the breast than we are toilet-trained, forced to repress that source of gratification until it is socially appropriate to do it, until, that is, it's convenient for grown-ups. Finally, after oral denial and anal repression, we reach what Freud calls the "genital stage." And here's where gender comes in.

Until now, both boys and girls have experienced roughly the same things. But after the resolution of the anal crisis, our paths diverge sharply. In this stage it is our task to "become" either masculine or feminine. Freud believed that this process was more difficult for boys than for girls, since from the beginning a girl learns to identify with her mother as a female, and this identification remains continuous into adulthood. In contrast, a boy must detach himself from his identification with his mother, *disidentify* with her, and identify with his father, a process that requires unlearning one attachment and forming a new one. This is made more difficult because mothers commonly offer a great deal of affection and caring, whereas fathers are often less affectionate and more authoritarian.

This critical moment for the boy is called the Oedipal crisis, after the play by Sophocles, *Oedipus the King*. The resolution of the Oedipal crisis is vital—the boy learns to desire sex with women and to identify as a man. This is crucial in Freudian theory: *The boy achieves gender identity and sexual orientation at the same moment in time.* During the Oedipal stage, the boy desires sexual union with mother, but he also realizes that he is in competition with his father for her affections. With his sexual desire for his mother thwarted by his father, the little boy sexualizes his fear of the father, believing that if he were to compete sexually with his father, his father would castrate him. The boy's ego resolves this state of terror of castration by transferring the boy's identification from mother to father, so that, symbolically, he can have sexual access to mother. Thus, the boy must break the identification with his mother, repudiate her, and identify with his father. This is a great shock—mother has been the source of warmth and love, and is the object of his desire; father has been a more distant source of authoritarian power, and is the source of the boy's terror. But by identifying with father the little boy ceases being "feminine" (identified with mother) and becomes masculine, as he simultaneously becomes heterosexual, symbolically capable of sexual relations with mother-like substitutes. Almost literally, as the 1930s popular song put it, he will "want a girl just like the girl that married dear old Dad."

For girls, Freud believed that the path was complementary, but not nearly as traumatic. Girls retain their identification with mother, but must renounce their sexual desire for her. They do this by acknowledging that they are incapable of sexual relations with mother, because they lack the biological equipment that makes such relations possible. This is why Freud believed that women experience "penis envy." The little girl understands that her only chance for sexual gratification is to retain her identification with mother and to be sexually possessed by a man who can satisfy her so that she can have a baby, which will be her source of feminine gratification. In the process, she transfers the location of sexual gratification from the clitoris (an "atrophied penis" in Freud's terms) to the vagina, that is, she develops feminine, passive sexuality. Again, gender identity and sexual organization go hand in hand.

Three issues are worth noting in this account of gender identity and sexuality. First, Freud dislocates gender and sexuality from the realm of biology. Gender identity and sexuality are psychological achievements—difficult, precarious, and full of potential pitfalls (an absent father may prevent a boy from transferring his identification from his mother, for example). Gender and sexuality are accomplished within the family, Freud argues, not activated by internal biological clocks. Second, Freud links gender identity to sexual orientation, making homosexuality a developmental *gender* issue rather than an issue of immorality, sin, or biological anomaly. Homosexuals are simply those who have either failed to renounce identification with mother in favor of father (gay men) or those who have failed to retain their ties of identification to mother (lesbians). (This idea also served as the basis for therapeutic interventions designed to "cure" homosexuals by encouraging gender-appropriate behaviors.) Third, Freud restates with new vigor traditional gender stereotypes as if they were the badges of successful negotiation of this perilous journey. A boy must be the sexual initiator, and scrupulously avoid all feminine behaviors, lest he be seen as having failed to identify with father. A girl must become sexually passive, wait for a man to be attracted to her, so that she can be fulfilled as a woman. Femininity means fulfillment not as a lover, but as a mother.

It's important to remember that though Freud postulated homosexuality was the failure of the child to adequately identify with the same-sex parent, and was therefore a problem of gender identity development, he did not believe in either the criminal persecution or psychiatric treatment of homosexuals. In fact, when Freud was contacted by a woman whose son was homosexual, he patiently explained why he did not think her son needed to be "cured":

> Homosexuality is assuredly no advantage, but it is nothing to be ashamed of, no vice, no degradation; it cannot be classified as an illness; we consider it to be a variation of the sexual function. . . . Many highly respectable individuals of ancient and modern times have been homosexuals, several of the greatest men among them. . . . It is a great injustice to persecute homosexuality as a crime—and a cruelty too. . . .
>
> What analysis can do for your son runs in a different line. If he is unhappy, neurotic, torn by conflicts, inhibited in his social life, analysis may bring him harmony, peace of mind, full efficiency, whether he remains homosexual or gets changed.[4]

It took another forty years before the American Psychiatric Association declassified homosexuality as a mental illness.

Today, popular stereotypes about homosexuality continue to rely on Freudian theories of gender development. Many people believe that homosexuality is a form of gender nonconformity; that is, effeminate men and masculine women are seen in the popular mind as likely to be homosexual, while masculine men's and feminine women's gender-conforming behavior leads others to expect them to be heterosexual.

Freud's theories have been subject to considerable debate and controversy. He based his theories about the sexuality of women on a very small sample of upper-middle class women in Vienna, all of whom were suffering from psychological difficulties that brought them to treatment with him in the first place. (Freud rejected the idea that they had been the victims of sexual abuse and incest, although many of them claimed they had been.) His theories of male development were based on even fewer clinical cases and on his own recollections of his childhood and his dreams. These are not the most reliable scientific methods, and his tendency to make sexuality the driving force of all individual development and all social and group processes may tell us more about his own life, and perhaps contemporary Vienna, than about other societies and cultures. Some researchers have argued that many of Freud's patients were actually telling the truth about their sexual victimization and not fantasizing about it, and that, therefore, it is not the fantasies of children but the actual behavior of adults that form the constituent elements in the construction of children's sexual view of the world.[5]

Although many today question Freud's theories on methodological, political, or theoretical grounds, there is no question that these theories have had a remarkable impact on contemporary studies and on popular assumptions about the relationship between gender identity and sexual behavior and sexual orientation. If gender identity and sexual orientation were *accomplished,* not inherent in the individual, then it was the parents' fault if things didn't turn out "right." Magazine articles, child-rearing manuals, and psychological inventories encouraged parents to do the right things and to develop the right attitudes, traits, and behaviors in their children; thus, the children would achieve appropriate gender identity and thereby ensure successful acquisition of heterosexual identity. A 1936 psychological inventory developed by Lewis Terman and Catherine Cox Miles in their monumental study, *Sex and Personality,* presented an inventory of behaviors, attitudes, and traits that enabled parents and teachers to monitor the child's successful acquisition of masculinity or femininity.[6]

Terman and Miles utilized a broad range of empirical measures to test gender identity, and constructed a continuum from Masculinity to Femininity, along which any individual could be placed according to answers on a series of questions. (The systematic—even obsessive—enterprise to find all possible measures of gender identity is itself an indication of the perceived significance of successful gender identity.) As a result of inventories such as the M-F test, gender identity came to be associated with a particular bundle of attitudes, traits, and behaviors, which, once acquired, could be seen as indicators of successful gender acquisition. When embraced by social science in the 1940s, these inventories became the basis for sex role theory.

The M-F test was perhaps the single most widely used means to determine successful acquisition of gender identity, and was still being used until the 1960s. The test was quite wide-ranging, including Rorschach-like interpretations of inkblots, which were coded for gender appropriateness, as well as identification, sentence completion, and some empirical questions. Here is a small sample of the questions on the M-F test. (If you want to keep your own score on these few items—to make sure that your own gender identity is progressing "normally"—you should score it the way that Terman and Miles suggested in 1936: If the response is "masculine," give yourself a "+"; if feminine, score with a "−." Interesting how these little value judgments creep into scientific research!)

Gendered Knowledge. In the following completion items there are right and wrong answers, and it was assumed that the more "boyish" would know the right answer to questions 2, 3, and 5, and the more girlish would know the answers to items 1 and 4. Girls who knew the answers to 2, 3, and 5 would be scored as more "masculine."

1. Things cooked in grease are: boiled (+), broiled (+), fried (−), roasted (+).
2. Most of our anthracite coal comes from: Alabama (−), Colorado (−), Ohio (−), Pennsylvania (+).
3. The "Rough Riders" were led by: Funston (−), Pershing (−), Roosevelt (+), Sheridan (−).
4. Red goes best with: black (−), lavender (+), pink (+), purple (+).
5. The proportion of the globe covered by water is about: 1/8 (−), 1/4 (−), 1/2 (−), 3/4 (+).

Gendered Feelings. The test also included a variety of stimuli that were thought to provoke certain emotions. Respondents were to answer whether these things caused (a) a lot, (b) some, (c) little, or (d) none of the expected emotion. For example:

- Does: being called lazy; seeing boys make fun of old people; seeing someone cheat on an exam make you ANGRY?
- Does: being lost; deep water; graveyards at night; Negroes [this is actually on the list!] make you AFRAID?
- Does: a fly caught on sticky fly paper; a man who is cowardly and can't help it; a wounded deer make you feel PITY?
- Does: boys teasing girls; indulging in "petting"; not brushing your teeth; being a Bolshevik make you feel that a person is WICKED?

To score this section, give yourself a minus (−) for every answer in which you said the thing caused a LOT of the emotion, except for the answer, "being a Bolshevik," which was obviously serious enough for men to get very emotional about. On all others, including being afraid of Negroes, however, high levels of emotion were scored as feminine.

Gendered Occupations, Appearances, Books. The test also included possible careers and their obvious sex-typing, such as librarian, auto racer, forest ranger, florist, soldier, and music teacher. There were lists of character traits (loud voices, men with beards, tall women) that those tested were asked to like or dislike, and a list of children's books (*Robinson Crusoe, Rebecca of Sunnybrook Farm, Little Women, Biography of a Grizzly*) that they either liked, didn't like, or had not read.

Gendered People. There was a list of famous people whom one either liked, disliked, or did not know (Bismarck, Lenin, Florence Nightingale, Jane Addams). Obviously, not having read a book or not knowing about a famous person could be seen as gender confirming or nonconfirming.

There were also questions about what you might like to draw if you were an artist (ships or flowers), what you might like to write about if you were a newspaper reporter (accidents or theater), and where you might like to travel if you had plenty of money (hunt lions in Africa or study social customs; learn about various religions or see how criminals are treated). Finally, the test included some self-reporting about the respondent's own behaviors and attitudes. Such Yes or No items (here listed with the scoring of a Yes answer) included:

- Do you rather dislike to take your bath? (+)
- Are you extremely careful about your manner of dress? (−)
- Do people ever say you talk too much? (+)
- Have you ever been punished unjustly? (+)
- Have you ever kept a diary? (−)

The research by Terman and Miles enabled a new generation of psychologists to construct a continuum between masculinity and femininity, along which any individual could be located, and thereby chart the acquisition of gender identity by examining the traits, attitudes, and behaviors appropriate to each gender. If a boy or girl exhibited the appropriate traits and attitudes, parents could be reassured that their child was developing normally. If, however, the child scored too high on the "inappropriate" side of the continuum, intervention strategies might be devised to facilitate the adoption of more appropriate behaviors. Artistic boys would be pushed toward rough and tumble play; tomboys would be forced into frilly dresses to read quietly a book such as *Rebecca of Sunnybrook Farm* instead of climbing a tree. Behind these interventions lay the spectre of the sissy, the homosexual male, whom Terman and Miles and other psychologists believed had gender identity problems. Following Freud, they believed that homosexuality was a gender disorder. As another psychologist, George W. Henry, wrote in 1937:

> In a large majority of . . . cases the tendencies to homosexuality as shown by attitude and behavior can be observed in early childhood. . . . To the extent that his interests, attitude and behavior are out of harmony with his actual sex he is likely to meet with circumstances which will accentuate his deviation. Boys appear to be somewhat more vulnerable than girls and if they show undue feminine tendencies special care should be exercised to give them opportunity to develop masculine characteristics.[7]

Freudian psychoanalytic theory spawned several different traditions in psychology. Some developmental psychologists sought to chart the sequences or stages of gender and sexual development, as children pass through psychological stages that correspond to physical changes. Other psychologists used various statistical tests to more precisely measure the differences between males and females at certain ages. Feminist psychoanalysts took Freud and his followers to task for their implicit or explicit use of masculinity as the normative reference against which all developmental stages were plotted and understood. And, finally, some psychologists sought to specify the social requirements for both masculine and feminine sex roles.

Theories of *cognitive development* locate the trigger of gender development and gender identity formation slightly later in life than early childhood. These psychologists argue that children are born more or less gender neutral; that is, no important biological differences between boys and girls at birth explain later gender differences. As they grow, children process new information through "cognitive filters" that enable them to interpret information about gender. Swiss psychologist Jean Piaget examined the developmental sequences in children's self-perception and their views of the world. Children are active participants in their own socialization, Piaget argued, not simply the passive objects of social influence. Piaget applied this model to cognitive development, pointing out the sequences of tasks and mental processes appropriate to children of various ages.[8]

Lawrence Kohlberg applied this Piagetian model of sequential cognitive development to the acquisition of a stable gender identity. One of the central developmental tasks of early childhood, Kohlberg argued, is to label oneself as either male or female. The point in time at which children learn "I am a boy" or "I am a girl" is a point after which self-identification seems fixed. The decision is *cognitive,* part of the pattern of mental growth in the organism. Early in life, children develop a gendered mental filter, after which new information from the social world is interpreted and acted upon in terms of its appropriateness to their gender identity. Even by age two, children have relatively stable and fixed understandings of themselves as gendered, and this categorization, Kohlberg argues, "is basically a cognitive reality judgment rather than a product of social rewards, parental justifications, or sexual fantasies." Things, persons, and activities are labeled, "this is appropriate to who I am" or "this is not appropriate to who I am." Messages coded in certain ways get through to boys, those coded in other ways get through to girls.[9]

According to this theory, children's early gender identities depend on concrete, physical cues such as dress, hair style, and body size in their categorization of the world into two genders. Boys never wear dresses and have short hair; girls do wear dresses and have long hair. Many children believe that they can change their gender by getting haircuts or changing their clothing, since they believe gender identity is concrete and attached to physical attributes. Some children become upset if their parents engage in gender-inappropriate conduct (Daddy carries Mommy's purse, Mommy changes the tire). It is not until age five or six that most children have the cognitive machinery to recognize gender as an attribute of the person and not the result of the material props that we use to display gender.

By this view, the acquisition of a gender identity is a switching point in the child's life. After age six, the child sees the world in *gender* terms. The child cannot go back, because the process of acquiring gender identity is irreversible after age three or four. All gender role performances that are socially coded as appropriate for men or women become, thereafter, more easily acquired by the child who possesses the "correct" filter. Because so many aspects of behavior depend on gender identity, the acquisition of an irreversible filter is necessary to human development, to be expected in all societies.

Social learning of gender does not end in childhood. Acquisition of gender identity may begin early, but it continues throughout the life cycle. Young children label themselves "boy" or "girl" at an early age, after which the child actively begins to use the label to make sense of the world. However, this label, demonstrated by the capacity to express the sentence "I am a boy (girl)" in a number of ways and situations, does not exhaust the content of gender roles or pick out unerringly the appropriate gender-typed stimuli. The child does not know most of the things that an adult knows or believes or likes or feels. The two- or three-year-old girl does not know that a woman is not likely to become president. She knows only that she uses the word "girl" to label herself, and that she is comfortable with that label. Gender identity is more fluid than young children believe, and our gender socialization continues throughout our lives. And, equally important, we are active agents in our own socialization, not simply the passive receptors of cultural blueprints for appropriate gender behaviors.

Since there is no "natural" relationship between gender identity and gender-role performances, the young child who "knows" its gender possesses a label with very little content. However, the label is used to organize the new things that are experienced. This is done by observing who (in gender terms) leaves the house to go to work, who is in charge of the labor of the household, and who plays with cars or dolls (or at least who they see playing with them in the media). All of these activities are more or less gender typed, mostly by who does them rather than by what is done. In addition, all children hear verbal exhortations of what boys do/don't do and what girls do/don't do. Children naturally tend to imitate models of behavior, even if that imitation is not reinforced, and this includes the vast amount of gender-typical behavior that is performed in front of them. Children swim in an ocean of gendered conduct, and it is terribly difficult to swim against the tide.[10]

From this point of view, the stability of the sense of a gendered self does not depend upon biological differences at birth, the experiences of early childhood, or a cognitive filter. It depends on the way that a child's day-to-day situations continuously stabilize his/her sense of being a boy or a girl. Since men and women each have different social learning histories, we find gender differences in the behaviors and values of children and adults. To understand our own sexuality, we must first look at the kinds of arrangements we have made for the ways in which men and women are supposed to behave in our society and the ways they conceive of themselves. If you conceive of yourself as a woman, and you are put in circumstances where people in your society expect women to react in a certain way, the fact that you think of yourself as a woman shapes the way you react to those circumstances. Thus, in a society, there are always two factors that affect gendered behavior: the demands of the social situation, and one's prior experience of being a girl or a boy or a woman or a man.

FEMINIST CHALLENGES TO PSYCHOANALYSIS AND DEVELOPMENTAL PSYCHOLOGY

Freud's theory of psychosexual development offered a very different kind of challenge to assumptions of biological inevitability. Rather than focus on variation, as did anthropologists, Freud stressed the universality of sex differences, but argued that such differences were produced—learned by children in interactions with their families and the larger society. He saw nothing inevitable about becoming either masculine or feminine, nor about becoming heterosexual. Sexual orientation and gender identity were achievements.

Many women have dismissed Freud's arguments because he argued that their development was the result of their coming to terms with the shame that would naturally follow from the realization that they did not have penises. Not only did this place an absurd emphasis on a little flap of tissue, but penis envy meant that women would always see themselves as inferior to men. What's more, Freud asserted that female development required the repudiation of the clitoris, the source of sexual agency and pleasure, for the more "mature" sexuality of vaginal receptivity.

No sooner had Freud published his theories than women challenged the centrality of penis envy in girls' development. Karen Horney's 1922 essay, "On the Genesis of the Castration Complex in Women," suggested that a theory that posited one half of the human race to be unsatisfied was itself theoretically problematic. It was, rather, "the actual social subordination of women" that provided the context for women's development. Since then, women have patiently explained that it was men, not women, who saw the possession of a penis as such a big deal. After all, without one, how could they know what it felt like? As one psychoanalyst put it:

> It is the male who experiences the penis as a valuable organ and he assumes that women also must feel that way about it. But a woman cannot really imagine the sexual pleasure of a penis—she can only appreciate the social advantages its possessor has.[11]

Perhaps women had a more political and social "privilege envy" than anything to do with the body.

In fact, some argued, Freud had it backward. Women did not have penis envy as much as men experienced "womb envy." Women, after all, can produce babies, apparently (at least in those cultures in which a rather uneventful moment nine months earlier is not remembered or not considered as significant) all by themselves! No matter what men do, they cannot create life. Bruno Bettleheim and several others suggested that the origins of women's subordination stemmed from men's fears of women's reproductive powers, and they pointed to male initiation rituals that imitated birth throes as an indication of ritual appropriation masking significant envy.[12]

Another line of critique has been to reverse Freud's initial proposition. Instead of asking how and why women come to see themselves as inferior to men, why not ask how men come to see themselves as superior to women? Several feminist writers such as Nancy Chodorow, Lillian Rubin, Dorothy Dinnerstein, and Jessica Benjamin have posed that question.[13] Inspired by the object-relations school of psychoanalytic thought, these theorists pointed to the more deeply embedded masculine biases in Freud's formulation. Freud argued that the final achievement of gender development was individual autonomy—freedom from dependency on the mother and thus freedom from the need for group identification. Autonomy was achieved in the boy's renunciation of identification with his mother, and subsequent identification with father. However, in *The Reproduction of Mothering*, Chodorow argued that Freud inadvertently revealed the sources of men's sense of superiority, and, thus, of male domination.[14]

What if, she argued, we were to suggest that the capacities for intimacy, connection, and community were healthy adult experiences. That would mean that the stage *before* the Oedipal crisis—when both boys and girls are deeply attached to their mother—was crucial. What happens is that boys lose that capacity for connection and intimacy in the break with mother and the shift to father, while girls retain that capacity. What's more, such a shift is so traumatic for boys—and yet so necessary in our culture—that they must demonstrate constantly that they have successfully achieved it. Masculinity comes to be defined as the distance between the boy and his mother, between himself and being seen as a "Mama's boy" or a sissy. So he must spend a significant amount of time and energy demonstrating his successful achievement of this distance, which he does by devaluing all things feminine—including girls, his mother, femininity, and, of course, all emotions associated with femininity. Male domination requires the masculine devaluation of the feminine. As Chodorow puts it:

> A boy, in his attempt to gain an elusive masculine identification, often comes to define his masculinity in largely negative terms, as that which is not feminine or involved with women. There is an internal and external aspect to this. Internally, the boy tries to reject his mother and deny his attachment to her and the strong dependency on her that he still feels. He also tries to deny the deep personal identification with her that has developed during his early years. He does this by repressing whatever he takes to be feminine inside himself, and, importantly, by denigrating whatever he considers to be feminine in the outside world.

Thus, Freud provided a decidedly "feminist" reading of male domination. He just didn't know it, so fixated was he on the break with mother as the crucial moment in *human* development.[15]

Kohlberg's ideas about the stages of cognitive and moral development have also come under critical scrutiny from feminist scholars. Kohlberg's stages proceeded from very concrete and practical rules to the application of universal ethical principles. But when girls and boys were evaluated, girls seemed "arrested" at the third stage of moral development, a stage that stresses mutual interpersonal expectations and relationships. (Kohlberg argued that this difference followed logically from the more remote and abstracted nature of the boy's relationship with his father compared with the girl's more interdependent relationship with her mother.) Carol Gilligan, one of Kohlberg's students, was not persuaded, and believed the different types of moral reasoning ought not be hierarchically ranked. In her pathbreaking book, *In a Different Voice,* Gilligan suggested that such stages appear only when men's lives were regarded as the norm. In her interviews with Harvard women undergraduates, Gilligan found very different criteria for moral decision making. She heard another moral voice besides the "ethic of justice"—that abstract, universal, ethical paradigm Kohlberg proposed as the final stage of moral development. There was also an "ethic of care," stressing intimacy and connectedness, that seemed to be followed more often by women. From this, Gilligan suggested that the origins of aggression might be different for women and men. For men, the ethic of justice demands the blind and indifferent application of sanctions; aggression stems from constraints on individual autonomy. Women, Gilligan writes, hear a different voice, wherein "lies the truth of an ethic of care, and the tie between the relationship and responsibility, and the origins of aggression in the failure of connection."[16]

Gilligan's work unleashed a broad controversy among feminist psychologists that has continued to ripple through the larger culture. Gilligan's work *seemed* to support arguments that women and men were fundamentally, irretrievably, and irreconcilably different. Other work building on that premise followed quickly, including works on cognition and epistemology and popular works that emphasized differences between women's and men's linguistic and mythical spheres.[17] Ironically, groups that sought to exclude women from various arenas attempted to use Gilligan's arguments to legitimate discrimination. If women and men are so obviously different, their reasoning went, then excluding women from certain positions would not be discrimination, but really a way to honor and respect differences. Historically, men who argued against woman suffrage made exactly the same case that Gilligan made. Here, for example, is an anti-suffragist, writing in 1914:

> One practical difficulty in the way of the participation of women in public affairs we might as well put bluntly. They do not seem to be intellectually fit for it. . . . [I]t is very rare to find a woman who has a statesmanlike mind. The ordinary woman is interested in persons rather than in principles. Only when a principle is embodied in a person is she aroused to any enthusiasm. She sees the picturesque aspects of a cause, but does not readily follow an economic process. . . . She is more likely to be interested in little things which touch her own life than in great things which determine the destinies of nations.

More recently, the Citadel and Virginia Military Institute cited the differences between women and men as justifications for excluding women from their state-supported corps of cadets, and fire departments sought to exclude women from entering their ranks. (Given that the legal code requires the indifferent application of the law and adherence to abstract principles, one might have also predicted a move to exclude women from serving as judges.)[18]

Gilligan herself was more circumspect, and deplored efforts to use her findings "to rationalize oppression." What she found is that "educationally advantaged North American males have a strong tendency to focus on issues of justice when they describe an experience of moral conflict and choice; two thirds of the men in our studies exhibited a 'justice focus.' One-third of the women we studied also showed a justice focus. But one third of the women focused on care, in contrast to only one of the 46 men." Moreover, "one third of both females and males articulate justice and care concerns with roughly equal frequency." The psychological patterns Gilligan observed, she argued, are "not based on any premise of inherent differences between the sexes, but solely on the different nature of their experiences." To extrapolate from these data to claim that *men* and *women* differ on moral voices would be to distort her findings into stereotypes; she writes:

> The title of my book was deliberate; it reads, "in a *different* voice," not "in a *woman's* voice." In my introduction, I explain that this voice is not identified by gender but by theme. Noting as an empirical observation the association of this voice with women, I caution the reader that "this association is not absolute, and the contrasts between male and female voices are presented here to highlight a distinction between two modes of thought and to focus a problem of interpretation rather than to represent a generalization about either sex." In tracing development, I "point to the interplay of these voices within each sex and suggest that their convergence marks times of crisis and change." No claims, I state, are made about the origins of these voices or their distribution in a wider population, across cultures or time (p. 2). Thus, the care perspective in my rendition is neither biologically determined nor unique to women. It is, however, a moral perspective different from that currently embedded in psychological theories and measures, and it is a perspective that was defined by listening to both women and men describe their own experience.[19]

Subsequent research has failed to replicate the binary gender differences in ethics; most researchers "report no average differences in the kind of reasoning men and women use in evaluating moral dilemmas, whether it is care-based or justice-based."[20]

Despite these disclaimers and the general lack of evidence of categorical gender differences, a generation of feminist essentialists have used Gilligan's work as a touchstone text. Observed differences between women and men are read backward into male and female biology in much the same way that biological essentialists were seen to have done. Perhaps the most celebrated of these efforts was Deborah Tannen, who presented evidence that men and women use language differently. Men, she argues, use language to establish their position in a hierarchy. To men, conversations "are negotiations in which people try and achieve and maintain the upper hand if they can, and protect themselves from some others' attempts to put them down and push them around." They interrupt more often, ignore comments from others, and make more declarations of facts and opinions. Women, by contrast, use conversation to establish and maintain relationships. To them, conversations are "negotiations for closeness in which people try and seek and give confirmation and support, and to reach consensus." They negotiate in private, ask more questions to maintain the flow of conversation, use more personal pronouns. Often when women speak, they end a declarative sentence with a slight rise in tone, as if ending it with a question mark.[21]

Like Gilligan, Tannen claims that she has simply identified two distinct patterns and that one is not "better" than the other. Unlike Gilligan, though, Tannen ascribes the difference between these patterns entirely to gender. Nor are her biases as concealed as she might have thought. For example, Tannen writes that men's need for autonomy and independence can be a "hindrance," since "there are times when they do not have all the information needed to make a decision." By contrast, women "make better managers because they are more inclined to consult others and involve employees in decision making."[22]

But are such observed differences between women and men real? Here, the evidence is less conclusive. For example, studies of interruption suggest a far more complicated picture, that women interrupt women and men interrupt men at about the same rates, while men interrupt women far more than women interrupt men—a finding that led researchers to conclude that it's not the gender of the speaker, but the gender of the person to whom one is speaking that makes the difference. This also seems to be the case with silence—that the same man, silent and uncommunicative at home, is quite talkative at work, where he uses conversation to make sure everyone feels all right. Again, it is not the gender of the silent one, but his or her relative power in the situation.

Feminist psychologists exposed an androcentric bias in the psychological literature of gender identity and development. With men as the normative standard against which both men and women were evaluated, women always seemed to be coming up short. As Gilligan demonstrated, when psychologists began to shift their framework, and to listen closely to the voices of women, new patterns of development emerged. This bias also had consequences in the lives of real people. For example, the *Diagnostic and Statistical Manual of Mental Disorders* (DSM), published by the American Psychiatric Association, is the diagnostic bible of mental illness professionals. For some time, the DSM has listed such mental illnesses as "premenstrual dysphoric disorder"

(PDD), which is their version of PMS. So each woman potentially suffers from a specific mental illness for up to one week a month—which adds up to about 25 percent of her adult life. (Homosexuality was recently removed from the manual.) Psychologist Paula Caplan suggested that the DSM instead consider adding a new set of diagnoses, including "Delusional Dominating Personality Disorder" (DDPD) to classify sexist behavior as symptomatic of mental illness. And what about "John Wayne syndrome" or "macho personality disorder," she asks? Her quiz to identify DDPD goes a long way toward exposing the gender biases in those ostensibly gender-neutral manuals (see figure 4.1).

DEVELOPMENTAL DIFFERENCES

So what are the real, and not the imagined or produced psychological differences between women and men? Developmental psychologists have pointed to some significant differences between males and females that emerge as we grow. Yet even these are differences between the means of two distributions, in which there is more variation *among* men and *among* women than there is *between* women and men. When psychologists Eleanor Maccoby and Carol Jacklin surveyed more than sixteen hundred empirical studies from 1966 to 1973, they found only four areas with significant and consistent sex differences: (1) girls have relatively higher verbal ability; (2) boys have better visual and spatial ability; (3) boys do better on mathematical tests; (4) boys were consistently more aggressive than girls. In fact, Maccoby and Jacklin conclude that their work

> revealed a surprising degree of similarity in the rearing of boys and girls. The two sexes appear to be treated with equal affection, at least in the first five years of life (the period for which most information is available); they are equally allowed and encouraged to be independent, equally discouraged from dependent behavior; . . . there is even, surprisingly, no evidence of distinctive parental reaction to aggressive behavior in the two sexes. There ARE differences, however. Boys are handled and played with somewhat more roughly. They also receive more physical punishment. In several studies boys were found to receive both more praise and more criticism from their caretakers—socialization pressure, in other words, was somewhat more intense for boys—but the evidence on this point is inconsistent. The area of greatest differentiation is in very specifically sex-typed behavior. Parents show considerably more concern over a boy's being a "sissy" than over a girl's being a tomboy. This is especially true of fathers, who seem to take the lead in actively discouraging any interest a son might have in feminine toys, activities, or attire.[23]

Males and females can be trained for a vast array of characteristics, and individual variations along this array overlap extensively. Since only small actual differences are found between girls and boys, how do we account for the relative ineffectiveness of socialization activities (toys, play, television, schools) in shaping the behavior of children in psychological experiments, and yet the continuing assignment to children and adults of roles on the basis of gender typing? Our answer can only be speculative. It appears that most psychological experiments offer boys and girls an opportunity to perform similar tasks without labeling the tasks as gender appropriate. In these con-

DO YOU RECOGNIZE THIS MAN?*

A quiz you'll never see in *Cosmo* and *Redbook*

Men who meet at least six of the following criteria may have Delusional Dominating Personality Disorder! Warning: DDPD is pervasive, profound, and a maladaptive organization of the entire personality! (Check as many as apply.)

I. Is he . . .

❑ unable to establish and maintain meaningful interpersonal relationships?

❑ unable to identify and express a range of feelings in himself (typically accompanied by an inablility to identify accurately the feelings of other people)?

❑ unable to respond appropriately and empathically to the feelings and needs of close associates and intimates (often leading to the misinterpretation of signals from others)?

❑ unable to derive pleasure from doing things for others?

2. Does he . . .

❑ use power, silence, withdrawal, and/or avoidance rather than negotiation in the face of interpersonal conflict or diffculty?

❑ believe that women are responsible for the bad things that happen to him, while the good things are due to his own abilities, achievements, or efforts?

❑ inflate the importance and achievements of himself, males in general, or both?

❑ categorize spheres of functioning and sets of behavior rigidly according to sex (like believing housework is women's work)?

❑ use a gender-based double standard in interpreting or evaluating situations or behavior (considering a man who makes breakfast sometimes to be extraordinarily good, for example, but considering a woman who sometimes neglects to make breakfast deficient)?

❑ feel inordinately threatened by women who fail to disguise their intelligence?

❑ display any of the following delusions:

• the delusion that men are entitled to the services of any woman with whom they are personally associated;

• the delusion that women like to suffer and be ordered around;

• the delusion that physical force is the best method of solving interpersonal problems;

• the delusion that men's sexual and aggressive impulses are uncontrollable;

• the delusion that pornography and erotica are identical;

• the delusion that women control most of the world's wealth and/or power but do little of the world's work;

• the delusion that existing inequalities in the distribution of power and wealth are a product of the survival of the fittest and that, therefore, allocation of greater social and economic rewards to the already privileged are merited.

3. Does he have . . .

❑ a pathological need to affirm his social importance by displaying himself in the company of females who meet any three of these criteria:

• are conventionally physically attractive; *or*

• are younger;

• are shorter;

• weigh less;

• appear to be lower on socioeconomic criteria; *or*

• are more submissive . . . than he is?

❑ a distorted approach to sexuality, displaying itself in one or both of these ways:

• a pathological need for flattery about his sexual performance and/or the size of his genitalia;

• an infantile tendency to equate large breasts on women with their sexual attractiveness.

❑ emotionally uncontrolled resistance to reform efforts that are oriented toward gender equity?

The tendency to consider himself a "New Man" neither proves nor disproves that the subject fits within this diagnostic category.

Some women also fit many of these criteria, either because they wish to be as dominant as men or because they feel men should be dominant.

Freely adapted, with permission, from *They Say You're Crazy:
How the World's Most Powerful Psychiatrists Decide Who's Normal* (Addison-Wesley, 1995) by Paula J. Caplan.

Figure 4.1. *Hypothetical Diagnostic Tool for Delusional Dominating Personality Disorder (DDPD)* by Paula J. Caplan.

texts, males and females perform mostly alike. It would appear that the real power of gender typing resides less in the child than in the environments in which the child finds itself. The social environment is filled with gendered messages and gendered activities. Even if the child possesses no fixed and permanent gender role, social arrangements will continually reinforce gender differences. In a gender-neutral experiment, social requirements are removed, and so the child does not behave in accord with a gender stereotype. Perhaps it is not internalized beliefs that keep us in place as men or women, but rather our interpersonal and social environments. As there is considerable variation in what men and women actually do, it may require the weight of social organization and constant reinforcement to maintain gender-role differences.

THE SOCIAL PSYCHOLOGY OF SEX ROLES

In their effort to understand the constellation of attitudes, traits, and behaviors that constituted appropriate gender identity, some social psychologists elaborated and extended original classifications of the M-F scale offered by Terman and Miles. If masculinity and femininity could be understood as points on a continuum, a variety of abnormal behaviors could possibly be understood as examples of gender-inappropriate behavior.[24] In the years after World War II, for example, some psychologists hypothesized that the propensity toward fascism and Nazism stemmed from distorted assertions of gender identity. The authors of *The Authoritarian Personality* posited a typology of behaviors, based on the M-F scale, that suggested that femininity and masculinity can describe both an internal psychological identification and an external behavioral manifestation. Their typology thus created four possible combinations instead of two:

		INTERNAL PSYCHOLOGICAL ORGANIZATION	
		Masculine	Feminine
EXTERNAL BEHAVIORAL MANIFESTATION	Masculine	MM	MF
	Feminine	FM	FF

Two of the cells, upper left and lower right, would be considered "gender appropriate"—males and females whose internal psychological identification matches their external behaviors. Those males whose scores placed them in the upper right cell—internally feminine, externally masculine—also scored highest on measures of racism, authoritarianism, and hypermasculinity. The authors proposed that such attitudes were the means for those who were insecure about their masculinity to cover up their insecurities—by more rigid adherence to the most traditional norms.[25]

This notion became common wisdom in 1950s America, and was used to study juvenile delinquency, Southern resistance to integration and civil rights, and male resistance to feminism. A more recent study has also included homophobia. It resonated in popular advice about schoolyard bullies—that they are the *least* secure about their masculinity, which is why they have to try and prove it all the time. One's response to a bully—"Why don't you pick on someone your own size?"—will always fall on deaf ears, because the goal is not to compete but to win, so that insecure masculinity can be (however momentarily) reassured. It doesn't work, of course, since the opponent was no real match, and so the bully has to do it all over again. Interestingly, Sanford and his colleagues found that the men who scored in the lower left cell—externally feminine and internally masculine—were the most creative, artistic, and intelligent. It took a very secure man, indeed, to stray from the behavioral norms of masculinity, they suggested.

While Sanford and his colleagues had developed a typology of inner identities and external behaviors, Miller and Swanson saw a developmental sequence. All children, both males and females, begin their lives as "FF"—totally identified with and behaving like mother. Boys then pass through the Oedipal stage, or "FM," during which they continue to identify with mother but begin to make a break from that identification, while they simultaneously acquire superficial masculine traits and behaviors. Finally, males arrive at "MM," both internal identification and external behaviors that are gender appropriate. Thus, authoritarianism, racism, sexism, and homophobia might now be seen as examples of psychological immaturity, a kind of arrested development. (The potential fourth stage, "MF," was dropped from the study.)[26]

A second trajectory that coincided with these studies was the work of Talcott Parsons and other sociologists who sought to establish the societal necessity for masculinity and femininity. Parsons argued that society had two types of major functions—production and reproduction—and that these required two separate institutional systems, the occupational system and the kinship system, which, in turn, required two types of roles that needed to be filled in order for it to function successfully. Instrumental roles demanded rationality, autonomy, and competitiveness; expressive roles required tenderness and nurturing so that the next generation could be socialized. In this way, Parsons shifted the emphasis of sex-role identity development away from the "need" of the infant to become either masculine or feminine to the need of society for individuals to fill specific slots. Fortunately, Parsons argued, we had two different types of people who were socialized to assume these two different roles.

Parsons suggested, however, that the allocation of roles to males and females did not always work smoothly. For example, in Western societies, the isolation of the nuclear family and the extended period of childhood meant that boys remained identified with mother for a very long time. What's more, the separation of spheres meant that girls had their appropriate role model immediately before them, while boys did not have adequate role models. Thus, he argued, their break with mother and their need to establish their individuality and masculinity often were accompanied by violent protest against femininity, and angry repudiation of the feminine became a way for the boy to purge himself of feminine identification. He "revolts against identification with his mother in the name of masculinity," Parsons writes, equating goodness with femininity, so that becoming a "bad boy" becomes a positive goal. This, Parsons suggests, has some negative consequences, including a "cult of compulsive masculinity":

Western men are peculiarly susceptible to the appeal of an adolescent type of assertively masculine behavior and attitudes which may take various forms. They have in common a tendency to revolt against the routine aspects of the primarily institutionalized masculine role of sober responsibility, meticulous respect for the rights of others, and tender affection towards women. Assertion through physical prowess, with an endemic tendency toward violence and hence the military ideal, is inherent in the complex and the most dangerous potentiality.[27]

For the girl, the process is somewhat different. She has an easier time because she remains identified with mother. Her rebellion and anger come from recognizing "masculine superiority"—"the fact that her own security like that of other women is dependent on the favor—even 'whim'—of a man." Suddenly, she realizes that the qualities that she values are qualities that may handicap her. She may express the aggression that would invariably follow upon such frustration by rebelling against the feminine role altogether: She may become a feminist.

By the 1970s, sex role theory was, itself, facing significant critical scrutiny. Some thinkers found the binary model between roles, system needs, and males and females just a bit too facile and convenient, as well as politically conservative—as if changing roles meant disrupting the needs that *society* had. Others stressed the coercive nature of these roles: If they were natural and met readily evident needs, why did so many people rebel against them, and why did they need to be so rigorously enforced? Some sociologists, like William J. Goode, stressed that roles were not descriptive but prescriptive, to better underscore this coercive aspect.

Two significant challenges came from social psychologists themselves. Sandra Bem and others explored the *content* of sex roles. The Bem Sex Role Inventory (BSRI) tested respondents on their perception of sixty different attributes, twenty of which were coded as "feminine," twenty as "masculine," and twenty more were "fillers." Although this replaced a continuum with categorical sex roles, Bem discovered that the most psychologically well-adjusted and intelligent people were those who fell in between the polar oppositions of masculinity and femininity. It was, she argued, *androgyny,* "the combined presence of socially valued, stereotypic, feminine and masculine characteristics," that best described the healthily adjusted individual. Several studies seemed to bear out the desirability of an androgynous personality constellation over a stereotypically feminine or masculine one. But subsequent studies failed to confirm the validity of these measures, and androgyny was discredited as a kind of wishy-washy nonpersonality, rather than the synthesis of the best of both worlds.[28] What's more, conceptually, dividing male and female traits into two categories makes it impossible to integrate power and gender inequality in the discussion; twenty years after her initial studies, Bem notes that the scale "reproduces . . . the very gender polarization that it seeks to undercut."[29]

While proponents of androgyny challenged the content of sex role theory, Joseph Pleck challenged the form. In a series of articles that culminated in his book, *The Myth of Masculinity,* Pleck advanced the idea that the problem was not that men were having a hard time fitting into a rational notion of masculinity but that the role itself was internally contradictory and inconsistent. Instead of simply accepting the sex role as a package, Pleck operationalized what he called the Male Sex Role Identity (MSRI) model into a discrete set of testable propositions. These included:

1. Sex role identity is operationally defined by measures of psychological sex typing, conceptualized in terms of psychological masculinity and/or femininity dimensions.
2. Sex role identity derives from identification-modeling and, to a lesser extent, reinforcement and cognitive learning of sex-typed traits, especially among males.
3. The development of appropriate sex role identity is a risky, failure-prone process, especially for males.
4. Homosexuality reflects a disturbance of sex role identity.
5. Appropriate sex role identity is necessary for good psychological adjustment because of an inner psychological need for it.
6. Hypermasculinity indicates insecurity in sex role identities.
7. Problems of sex role identity account for men's negative attitudes and behavior toward women.
8. Problems of sex role identity account for boys' difficulties in school performance and adjustment.
9. Black males are particularly vulnerable to sex role identity problems.
10. Male adolescent initiation rites are a response to problems of sex role identity.
11. Historical changes in the character of work and the organization of the family have made it more difficult for men to develop and maintain their sex role identities.

When virtually all of these turned out to be empirically false, Pleck argued that the male sex role itself was the source of strain, anxiety, and male problems. Psychology was thus transformed from the vehicle that would help problematic men adapt to their rational sex role into one of the origins of their problems, the vehicle by which men had been fed a pack of lies about masculinity. The sex role system itself was the source of much of men's anxieties and pain. In its place, Pleck proposed the Male Sex Role Strain model (MSRS):

1. Sex roles are operationally defined by sex role stereotypes and norms.
2. Sex roles are contradictory and inconsistent.
3. The proportion of individuals who violate sex roles is high.
4. Violating sex roles leads to social condemnation.
5. Violating sex roles leads to negative psychological consequences.
6. Actual or imagined violation of sex roles leads individuals to overconform to them.
7. Violating sex roles has more severe consequences for males than females.
8. Certain characteristics prescribed by sex roles are psychologically dysfunctional.
9. Each gender experiences sex role strain in its work and family roles.
10. Historical changes cause sex role strain.

The net effect of this new model is to shift the understanding of problems from the men themselves to the roles that they are forced to play.[30] Subsequent research has explored different groups of men's grappling with these contradictory role specifications, and the problematic behaviors (such as sexual risk taking) that are expressions of men's efforts to reconcile contradictory role demands.[31]

But there remain problems with sex role theory that even these two ambitious efforts could not resolve. For one thing, when psychologists discussed the "male" sex role or the "female" sex role, they posited a single, monolithic entity, a "role," into which all boys and all girls were placed. Through a process of socialization, boys acquired the male sex role, girls, the female one. Imagine two large tanks, into which all biological males and females are placed. But all males and all females are not alike. There are a variety of different "masculinities" or "femininities" depending on class, race, ethnicity, age, sexuality, and region. If all boys or all girls were to receive the same socialization to the same sex role, differences in the construction of black masculinity, or Latina femininity, or middle-aged gay masculinity, or Midwestern older white femininity, etc., would all be effaced. Sex role theory is unable to account for the differences *among* men or *among* women because it always begins from the normative prescriptions of sex *roles,* rather than the experiences of men and women themselves. (Remember that the differences among men and among women—not the differences between women and men—provide most of the variations in attitudes, traits, and behavior we observe.)

A second problem with sex role theory is that the separate tanks into which males and females are sorted look similar to each other. When we say that boys become masculine and girls become feminine in roughly similar ways, we posit a false equivalence between the two. If we ignore the power differential between the two tanks, then both privilege and oppression disappear. "Men don't have power," writes pop therapist Warren Farrell, "men and women have roles."[32] Despite what men and women may *feel* about their situation, men as a group have power in our society over women as a group. In addition, some men—privileged by virtue of race, class, ethnicity, sexuality, etc.— have power over other men. Any adequate explanation of gender must not only account for gender difference but also for male domination. Theories of sex roles are inadequate to this task.[33]

This theoretical inadequacy stems from the sorting process in the first place. Sex role theorists see boys and girls sorted into those two separate categories. But what we know about being a man has everything to do with what it means to be a woman; and what we know about being a woman has everything to do with what it means to be a man. Constructions of gender are *relational*—we understand what it means to be a man or a woman in relation to the dominant models as well as to one another. And those who are marginalized by race, class, ethnicity, age, sexuality, and the like also measure their gender identities against those of the dominant group.

Finally, sex role theory assumes that only individuals are gendered, that gendered individuals occupy gender-neutral positions and inhabit gender-neutral institutions. But gender is more than an attribute of individuals; gender organizes and constitutes the field in which those individuals move. The institutions of our lives—families, workplaces, schools—are themselves gendered institutions, organized to reproduce the differences and the inequalities between women and men. If one wants to understand the lives of people in any situation, the French philosopher Jean-Paul Sartre once wrote, one "must inquire first into the situation surrounding [them]."[34] Theorists of sex roles and androgyny help us move beyond strictly psychological analyses of gender. But the inability to theorize difference, power, relationality, and the institutional dimension of gender means that we will need to build other elements into the discussion. Sociological explanations of gender begin from these principles.

INEQUALITY AND DIFFERENCE

The Social Construction of Gender Relations

*Society is a masked ball, where every one hides his real charac-
ter, and reveals it by hiding.*

—RALPH WALDO EMERSON
"WORSHIP" (1860)

My self . . . is a dramatic ensemble.

—PAUL KLEE

In one of its most thoughtful definitions, C. Wright Mills defined sociology as the in-
tersection of biography and history. In his view, the goal of a sociological perspective
would be to locate an individual in both time and space, to provide the social and historical contexts in which a person constructs his or her identity. In that sense, sociology's bedrock assumption, upon which its analyses of structures and institutions rest,
is that individuals shape their lives within both historical and social contexts. We do
not do so simply because we are biologically programmed to act in certain ways, nor
because we have inevitable human tasks to solve as we age. Rather, we respond to the
world we encounter, shaping, modifying, and creating our identities through those encounters with other people and within social institutions.

   Thus, sociology takes as its starting points many of the themes raised in earlier
chapters. Sociological perspectives on gender assume the variability of gendered identities that anthropological research has explored, the biological "imperatives" toward
gender identity and differentiation (though sociology locates the source of these imperatives less in our bodies and more in our environments), and the psychological imperatives toward both autonomy and connection that modern society requires of individuals in the modern world. To a sociologist, both our biographies (identities) and
history (evolving social structures) are gendered.

   Like other social sciences, sociology begins with a critique of biological determinism. Instead of observing our experiences as the expressions of inborn, interplanetary differences, the social sciences examine the variations among men and among

women, as well as the differences between them. The social sciences thus begin with the explicitly social origin of our patterns of development.

Our lives depend on social interaction. Literally, it seems. In the thirteenth century, Frederick II, Emperor of the Holy Roman Empire, decided to perform an experiment to see if he could discover the "natural language of man." What language would we speak if no one taught us language? He selected some newborn babies, and decreed that no one speak to them. The babies were suckled and nursed and bathed as usual, but speech and songs and lullabies were strictly prohibited. All the babies died. And you've probably heard those stories of "feral children"—babies who were abandoned and raised by animals became suspicious of people and could not be socialized to live in society after age six or so. In all the stories, the children died young, as did virtually all the "isolates," those little children who are locked away in closets and basements by sadistic or insane parents.[1] What do such stories tell us? True or apocryphal, they suggest that biology alone—that is, our anatomical composition—doesn't determine our development as we might have thought. We need to interact, to be socialized, to be part of society. It is that interaction, not our bodies, that makes us who we are.

Often, the first time we hear that gender is socially constructed, we take it to mean that we are, as individuals, not responsible for what we do. "'Society' made me like this," we might say. "It's not my fault." (This is often the flip side of the other response one often hears: "In America an individual can do anything he or she wants to do," or "It's a free country and everyone is entitled to their [sic] own opinion.") Both of these rhetorical strategies—what I call reflexive passivity and impulsive hyperindividualism—are devices that we use to deflect individual accountability and responsibility. They are both, therefore, misreadings of the sociological mandate. When we say that gender identity is socially constructed, what we do mean is that our identities are a fluid assemblage of the meanings and behaviors that we construct from the values, images, and prescriptions we find in the world around us. Our gendered identities are both voluntary—we choose to become who we are—and coerced—we are pressured, forced, sanctioned, and often physically beaten into submission to some rules. We neither make up the rules as we go along, nor do we fit casually and without struggle into preassigned roles.

For some of us, becoming adult men and women in our society is a smooth and almost effortless drifting into behaviors and attitudes that feel as familiar to us as our skin. And for others of us, becoming masculine or feminine is an interminable torture, a nightmare in which we must brutally suppress some parts of ourselves to please others—or, simply, to survive. For most of us, though, the experience falls somewhere in between: There are parts we love and wouldn't part with, and other parts where we feel we've been forced to exaggerate one side at the expense of others. It's the task of the sociological perspective to specify the ways in which our own experiences, our interactions with others, and the institutions combine to shape our sense of who we are. Biology provides the raw materials, while society and history provide the context, the instruction manual, that we follow to construct our identities.

In the first chapter, I identified the four elements of a social constructionist perspective on gender. Definitions of masculinity and femininity vary, first, from culture to culture, and, second, in any one culture over historical time. Thus, social constructionists rely on the work of anthropologists and historians to identify the commonalities and the differences in the meanings of masculinity and femininity from one culture to another, and to describe how those differences change over time.

Third, gender definitions also vary over the course of a person's life. The issues confronting women when they are younger—their marketability in both the workplace and the marriage market, for example—will often be very different from the issues they face at menopause or retirement. And the issues confronting a young man about proving himself and achieving what he calls success, and the social institutions in which he will attempt to enact those experiences, will change throughout his life. For example, men often report a "softening," the development of greater interest in caregiving and nurturing when they become grandfathers than when they became fathers—often to the puzzlement and distress of their sons. But in their sixties and seventies, when their children are having children, these men do not feel the same pressures to perform, to leave a mark, to prove themselves. Their battles are over, and they can relax and enjoy the fruits of their efforts. Thus, we rely on developmental psychologists to specify the normative "tasks" that any individual must successfully accomplish as he or she matures and develops, and we also need scholars in the humanities to explore the symbolic record that such men and women leave us as evidence of their experiences.

Finally, definitions of masculinity and femininity will vary within any one culture at any one time—by race, class, ethnicity, age, sexuality, education, region of the country, etc. You'll recall that it seemed obvious that an older gay black man in Chicago would have a different idea of what it meant to be a man than a heterosexual white teenager in rural Iowa.

Social constructionism thus builds on the other social and behavioral sciences, adding specific dimensions to the exploration of gender. What sociology contributes are the elements that the social psychology of sex roles cannot explain adequately: difference, power, and the institutional dimensions of gender. To explain difference, social constructionism offers an analysis of the plurality of gender definitions; to explain power, it emphasizes the ways in which some definitions become normative through the struggles of different groups for power—including the power to define. Finally, to explain the institutional dimension, social constructionism moves beyond socialization of gendered individuals who occupy gender-neutral sites, to the study of the interplay between gendered individuals and gendered institutions.

BEYOND SEX ROLE THEORY

As we saw in the last chapter, social psychologists located the process of acquisition of gender identity in the developmental patterns of individuals in their families and in early childhood interaction. Specifically, sex role theorists explored the ways in which individuals come to be gendered, and the ways in which they negotiate their ways toward some sense of internal consistency and coherence, despite contradictory role definitions. Still, however, the emphasis is on the gendering of individuals, and occasionally on the inconsistent cultural blueprints with which those individuals must contend. Sociological understandings of gender begin, historically, with a critique of sex-role theory, with sociologists arguing that such theory is inadequate to fully understand the complexities of gender as a social institution. Sociologists have identified four significant problems with sex role theory—problems that require its modification.

First, the use of the idea of role has the curious effect of actually minimizing the importance of gender. Role theory uses drama as a metaphor—we learn our roles through socialization and then perform them for others. But to speak of a gender role makes it sound almost too theatrical, and thus too easily changeable. Gender, as Helena Lopata and Barrie Thorne write, "is not a role in the same sense that being a teacher, sister, or friend is a role. Gender, like race or age, is deeper, less changeable, and infuses the more specific roles one plays; thus, a female teacher differs from a male teacher in important sociological respects (e.g., she is likely to receive less pay, status and credibility)." *To make gender a role like any other role is to diminish its power in structuring our lives.*[2]

Second, sex role theory posits singular normative definitions of masculinity and femininity. If the meanings of masculinity and femininity vary across cultures, over historical time, among men within any one culture, and over the life course, we cannot speak of masculinity or femininity as though each was a constant, singular, universal essence. Personally, when I read what social psychologists wrote about the "male sex role" I always wondered whom they were writing about. "Who, me?" I thought. Is there really only *one* male sex role and only one female sex role?

One of the key themes about gender identity is the ways in which other differences—race, class, ethnicity, sexuality, age, region—all inform, shape, and modify our definitions of gender. To speak of one male or one female sex role is to compress the enormous variety of our culture's ideals into one, and to risk ignoring the other factors that shape our identities. In fact, in those early studies of sex roles, social psychologists did just that, suggesting that, for example black men or women, or gay men or lesbians evidenced either "too much" or "too little" adherence to their appropriate sex role. In that way, homosexuals or people of color were seen as expressing sex role problems; since their sex roles differed from the normative, it was they who had the problem. (As we saw earlier, the most sophisticated sex role theorists understand that such normative definitions are internally contradictory, but they still mistake the normative for the "normal.")

By positing this false universalism, sex role theory assumes what needs to be explained—how the normative definition is established and reproduced—and explains away all the differences among men and among women. Sex role theory cannot fully accommodate these differences among men or among women. A more satisfying investigation must take into account these different definitions of masculinity and femininity constructed and expressed by different groups of men and women. Thus, we speak of *masculinities* and *femininities*. What's more, sociologists see the differences among masculinities or femininities as expressing exactly the opposite relationship than do sex role theorists. Sex role theorists, if they can accommodate differences at all, see these differences as aberrations, as the failure to conform with the normal sex role. Sociologists, on the other hand, believe that the differences among definitions of masculinity or femininity are themselves the outcome of the ways in which those groups interact with their environments. Thus, sociologists contend that one cannot understand the differences in masculinity or femininity based on race or ethnicity without first looking at the ways in which institutional and interpersonal racial inequality structures the ways in which members of those groups actively construct their identities. Sex role theorists might say, for example, that black men, lesbians, or older Latinas experience discrimination because their definitions of masculinity and femininity are "different" from the norm. To a sociologist, that's only half right. A sociologist would add that these groups develop different definitions of masculinity and femininity in active engagement with a social environment in which they are discriminated against. Thus, their differences are more the product of discrimination than its cause.

This leads to a third arena in which sociologists challenge sex role theory. Gender is not only plural, it also relational. A related problem with sex role theory is that it posits two separate spheres, as if sex role differentiation were more a matter of sorting a herd of cattle into two appropriate pens for branding. Boys get herded into the masculine corral, girls the feminine. But such a static model also suggests that the two corrals have virtually nothing to do with one another. "The result of using the role framework is an abstract view of the *differences* between the sexes and their situations, not a concrete one of the *relations* between them."[3] But what surveys indicate is that men construct their ideas of what it means to be men *in constant reference* to definitions of femininity. What it means to be a man is to be unlike a woman; indeed, social psychologists have emphasized that while different groups of men may disagree about other traits and their significance in gender definitions, the "antifemininity" component of masculinity is perhaps the single dominant and universal characteristic.

Fourth, because gender is plural and relational, it is also situational. What it means to be a man or a woman varies in different contexts. Those different institutional contexts demand and produce different forms of masculinity and femininity. "Boys may be boys," cleverly comments feminist legal theorist Deborah Rhode, "but they express that identity differently in fraternity parties than in job interviews with a female manager."[4] Gender is thus not a property of individuals, some "thing" one has, but a specific set of behaviors that are produced in specific social situations. And thus gender changes as the situation changes.

Sex role theory cannot adequately account for either the differences among women and men, their different definitions of masculinity and femininity in different situations, without implicitly assuming some theory of deviance. Nor can it express the relational character of those definitions. In addition, sex role theory cannot fully account for the power relationships between women and men, and among different groups of women and different groups of men. Thus, the fourth and perhaps most significant problem in sex role theory is that it *depoliticizes* gender, making gender a set of individual attributes and not an aspect of social structure. "The notion of 'role' focuses attention more on individuals than on social structure, and implies that 'the female role' and 'the male role' are complementary (i.e. separate or different but equal)," write sociologists Judith Stacey and Barrie Thorne. "The terms are depoliticizing; they strip experience from its historical and political context and neglect questions of power and conflict."[5]

But how can one speak of gender without speaking of power? As I pointed out in chapter 1, a pluralistic and relational theory of gender cannot pretend that all masculinities and femininities are created equal. All American women and all American men must also contend with a singular vision of both masculinity and femininity, specific definitions that are held up as models against which we all measure ourselves.

These are what sociologist R. W. Connell calls the "hegemonic" definition of masculinity and the "emphasized" version of femininity. These are normative constructions, the ones against which others are measured and, almost invariably, found wanting. (Connell's trenchant critique of sex role theory, therefore, hinges on his contention that sex role psychologists do not challenge but in fact reproduce the hegemonic version as the "normal" one.) The hegemonic definition is a "particular variety of masculinity to which others—among them young and effeminate as well as homosexual men—are subordinated."[6] We thus come to know what it means to be a man or a woman in American culture by setting our definitions in opposition to a set of "others"—racial minorities, sexual minorities, etc. One of the most fruitful areas of research in sociology today is trying to specify exactly how these hegemonic versions are established, and how different groups negotiate their ways through problematized definitions.

Sex role theory proved inadequate to explore the variations in gender definitions, which requires adequately theorizing of the variations *within* the category men or women. Such theorizing makes it possible to see the relationships between and among men, or between and among women as structured relationships as well. Tension about gender was earlier theorized by sex role theory as a tension between an individual and the expectations that were established by the sex role—that is, between the individual and an abstract set of expectations.

This leads to the fifth and final problem with sex role theory—its inadequacy in comprehending the dynamics of change. Movements for social change, such as feminism or gay liberation, become movements to expand role definitions, and to change role expectations. Their goal is to expand role options for individual women and men, whose lives are constrained by stereotypes. But social and political movements are not only about expanding the opportunities for individuals to break free of the constraints of inhibiting sex roles, to allow their "true" selves to emerge; they are about the redistribution of power in society. They demand the reallocation of resources, and an end to forms of inequality that are embedded in social institutions as well as sex role stereotypes. Only a perspective that begins with an analysis of power can adequately understand those social movements. A social constructionist approach seeks to be more concrete, specifying tension and conflict not between individuals and expectations, but between and among groups of people within social institutions. Thus, social constructionism is inevitably about power.

What's wrong with sex role theory can, finally, be understood by analogy. Why is it, do you suppose, no reputable scholars today use the terms *race roles* or *class roles* to describe the observable aggregate differences between members of different races or different classes? Are such "race roles" specific behavioral and attitudinal characteristics that are socialized into all members of different races? Hardly. Not only would such a term flatten all the distinctions and differences among members of the same race, but it would also ignore the ways in which the behaviors of different races—to the extent that they might be seen as different in the first place—are the products of racial inequality and oppression, and not the external expression of some inner essence.

The positions of women and blacks have much in common, as sociologist Helen Hacker pointed out in her ground-breaking article "Women as a Minority Group," which was written nearly a half-century ago. Hacker argued that systematic structural inequality produces a "culture of self-hatred" among the target group. And yet we do not speak of "race roles." Such an idea would be absurd, because (1) the differences within each race are far greater than the differences between races; (2) what it means to be white or black is always constructed in relationship to the other; (3) those definitions make no sense outside the context of the racially based power that white people, as a group, maintain over people of color, as a group. Movements for racial equality are about more than expanding role options for people of color.

Ultimately, to use role theory to explain race or gender is a form of blaming the victim. If our gendered behaviors "stem from fundamental personality differences, socialized early in life," suggests psychologist David Tresemer, then responsibility must lie at our own feet. This is what R. Stephen Warner and his colleagues call the "Sambo theory of oppression"—"the victims internalize the maladaptive set of values of the oppressive system. Thus behavior that appears incompetent, deferential, and self-degrading is assumed to reflect the crippled capabilities of the personality."[7] In this world view, social change must be left to the future, when a more egalitarian form of childhood socialization can produce children better able to function according to hegemonic standards. Social change comes about when the oppressed learn better the ways of their oppressors. If they refuse, and no progress is made—well, whose fault is that?

A NOTE ABOUT POWER

One of the central themes of this book is that gender is about difference and also about inequality, about power. At the level of gender relations, gender is about the power that men as a group have over women as a group, and it is also about the power that some men have over other men (or that some women have over other women). It is impossible to explain gender without adequately understanding power—not because power is the consequence of gender difference, but because power is what produces those gender differences in the first place.

To say that gender is a power relation—the power of men over women and the power of some men or women over other men or women—is among the more controversial arguments of the social constructionist perspective. In fact, the question of power is among the most controversial elements in all explanations of gender. Yet it is central; all theories of gender must explain both difference and domination. While other theories explain male domination as the result of sex differences, social constructionism explains differences as the result of domination.

Yet a discussion about power invariably makes men, in particular, uncomfortable or defensive. How many times have we heard a man say, when confronted with women's anger at gender-based inequality and discrimination, "Hey, don't blame me! I never raped anyone!" (This is analogous to white people's defensive response denying that one's family ever owned or continues to own slaves, when confronted with the contemporary reality of racial oppression.) When challenged by the idea that the gender order means that men have power over women, men often respond with astonishment. "What do you mean, men have all the power? What are you talking about? I have no power at all. I'm completely powerless. My wife bosses me around, my children boss me around, my boss bosses me around. I have no power at all!" Most men, it seems, do not feel powerful.

Here, in a sense, is where feminism has failed to resonate for many men. Much of feminist theory of gender-based power derived from a symmetry between the structure of gender relations and women's individual experiences. Women, as a group, were not *in* power. That much was evident to anyone who cared to observe a corporate board, a university board of trustees, or a legislative body at any level anywhere in the world. Nor, individually, did women *feel* powerful. In fact, they felt constrained by gender inequality into stereotypic activities that prevented them from feeling comfortable, safe, and competent. So women were neither in power nor did they feel powerful.

That symmetry breaks down when we try to apply it to men. For although men may be *in* power everywhere one cares to look, individual men are not "in power," and they do not feel powerful. Men often feel themselves to be equally constrained by a system of stereotypic conventions that leave them unable to live the lives to which they believe they are entitled. Men as a group are in power (when compared with women), but do not feel powerful. The feeling of powerlessness is one reason why so many men believe that they are the victims of reverse discrimination and oppose affirmative action. Or why some men's movement leaders comb through the world's cultures for myths and rituals to enable men to claim the power they want but do not feel they have. Or even why many yuppies took to wearing "power ties" while they munched their "power lunches" during the 1980s and early 1990s—as if power were a fashion accessory for those who felt powerless.

Pop psychologist Warren Farrell called male power a "myth," since men and women have complementary roles, and equally defamatory stereotypes of "sex object" and "success object." Farrell often uses the analogy of the chauffeur to illustrate his case. The chauffeur is in the driver's seat. He knows where he's going. He's wearing the uniform. You'd think, therefore, that he is in power. But from his perspective, someone else is giving the orders; he's not powerful at all. This analogy does have some limited value: Individual men are not powerful, at least none but a small handful of individual men. But what if we ask one question of our chauffeur, and try to shift the frame just a little. What if we ask him: What is the gender of the person who *is* giving the orders? (The lion's share of riders in chauffeur-driven limousines are, after all, upper-class white men.) When we shift from the analysis of the individual's experience to a different context, the relations between and among men emerge also as relations of power—power based on class, race, ethnicity, sexuality, age, and the like. "It is particular groups of men, not men in general, who are oppressed within patriarchal sexual relations, and whose situations are related in different ways to the overall logic of the subordination of women to men."[8]

Like gender, power is not the property of individuals—a possession that one has or does not have—but a property of group life, of social life. Power *is*. It can neither be willed away nor ignored. Here is how the philosopher Hannah Arendt put it:

> Power corresponds to the human ability not just to act but to act in concert. Power is never the property of an individual; it belongs to a group and remains in existence only so long as the group keeps together. When we say of somebody that he is "in power" we

actually refer to his being empowered by a certain number of people to act in their name. The moment the group, from which the power originated to begin with . . . disappears, "his power" also vanishes.[9]

To a sociologist, power is not an attitude or a possession; it's not really a "thing" at all. It cannot be "given up" like an ideology that's been outgrown. Power creates as well as destroys. It is deeply woven into the fabric of our lives—it is the warp of our interactions and the weft of our institutions. And it is so deeply woven into our lives that it is most invisible to those who are most empowered.

GENDER AS AN INSTITUTION

My argument that power is the property of a group, not an individual, is related to my argument that gender is as much a property of institutions as it is part of our individual identities. One of the more significant sociological points of departure from sex role theory concerns the institutional level of analysis. As we've seen, sex role theory holds that gender is a property of individuals—that gendered people acquire their gender identity and move outward, into society, to populate gender-neutral institutions. To a sociologist, however, those institutions are themselves gendered. Institutions create gendered normative standards, express a gendered institutional logic, and are major factors in the reproduction of gender inequality. The gendered identity of individuals shapes those gendered institutions, and the gendered institutions express and reproduce the inequalities that compose gender identity.

To illustrate this, let us undertake a short thought experiment. To start with, let's assume that (1) men are more violent than women (whether biologically derived or socialized, this is easily measurable by rates of violent crime); that (2) men occupy virtually all the positions of political power in the world (again, easily measurable by looking at all political institutions); and that (3) there is a significant risk of violence and war at any moment.

Now, imagine that when you awaken tomorrow morning, all of those power positions in all those political institutions—every president and prime minister, every mayor and governor, every state, federal or local official, every member of every house of representatives and every parliament around the world—was a woman. Do you think the world would be any safer from the risk of violence and war? Do you think you'd sleep better that night?

Biological determinists and psychologists of sex roles would probably answer "yes." Whether from fundamental biological differences in levels of testosterone, brain chemistries, or evolutionary imperatives, a biological perspective would probably conclude that since females are less violent and aggressive than men, the world would be safer. (It is ironic, then, that the same people who believe these biological differences are also among the least likely to support female candidates for political office.) And those who observe that different socialization produces women who are more likely to avoid hierarchy and competition and search instead for peaceful solutions by another gendered value system would also breathe a collective sigh of relief.

"But," I hear some of you saying, "what about the women who have already *been* heads of state. What about Golda Meir, Indira Ghandi, and Margaret Thatcher? They're not exactly poster girls for a pacific ethic of care, are they?"

Indeed, not. And part of the reason that they were so unladylike in political office is that the office itself demands a certain type of behavior, independent of the gender of the person who holds it. Often it seems that no matter who occupies those positions, he—or she—can do little to transform them.

This observation is the beginning of a sociological perspective—the recognition that the institutions themselves express a logic—a dynamic—that reproduces gender relations between women and men and the gender order of hierarchy and power. Men *and* women have to express certain traits to occupy a political office, and his or her failure to do so will make the officeholder seem ineffective and incompetent. (These criteria apply to men also, as anyone who witnessed the gendered criticisms launched against Jimmy Carter for being frightened by a swimming rabbit or for his failure to invade Iran during the hostage crisis in 1979–1980 can testify.)

To argue that institutions are gendered is *only* the other half of the story. It's as simplistic to argue that the individuals who occupy those positions are genderless as it is to argue that the positions they occupy are gender neutral. Gendered individuals occupy a place within gendered institutions. And thus it is quite likely that if all the positions were filled with the gender that has been raised to seek peaceful negotiations instead of the gender that is accustomed to drawing lines in the sand, the gendered mandates of those institutions would be affected, modified, and moderately transformed. In short, if all those positions were filled with women, we might sleep more peacefully at night—at least a little bit more peacefully.

Another example will illustrate this in a different way. In chapter 2, I introduced the work of Barbara McClintock, the Nobel Prize–winning research cytogeneticist. McClintock came upon her remarkable discovery of the behavior of molecules by a very different route than that used by her male colleagues. While earlier models had always assumed a hierarchically ordered relationship, McClintock, using what she called "feminine methods," and relying on her "feeling for the organism," discovered that instead of each cell being ruled by a "master molecule," cells were driven by a complex interaction among molecules. In this case, the gender of the person collided with the gendered logic of scientific inquiry to generate a revolutionary—and Nobel Prize–winning—insight.[10]

To say, then, that gender is socially constructed requires that we locate individual identity within a historically and socially specific and equally gendered place and time, and that we situate the individual within the complex matrix of our lives, our bodies, and our social and cultural environments. A sociological perspective examines the ways in which gendered individuals interact with other gendered individuals in gendered institutions. As such, sociology examines the interplay of those two forces—identities and structures—through the prisms of socially created difference and domination.

Gender revolves around these themes—identity, interaction, institution—in the production of gender difference and the reproduction of gender inequality. These themes are quite complex and the relationships between and among them are also complex. These are the processes and experiences that form core elements of our personalities, our interactions with others, and the institutions that shape our lives. These experiences are shaped by our societies, and we return the favor, helping to reshape our societies. We are gendered people living in gendered societies.

A social constructionist perspective however goes one step farther than even this. Not only do gendered individuals negotiate their identities within gendered institutions, but also those institutions produce the very differences we assume are the properties of individuals. Thus, "the extent to which women and men do different tasks, play widely disparate concrete social roles, strongly influences the extent to which the two sexes develop and/or are expected to manifest widely disparate personal behaviors and characteristics." Different structured experiences produce the gender differences that we often attribute to people.[11]

Let me illustrate this phenomenon, first with a mundane example and then with a more analytically complex one. At the most mundane level, think about public restrooms. In a clever essay on the "arrangement between the sexes," the late sociologist Erving Goffman playfully suggested the ways in which these public institutions produce the very gender differences they are supposed to reflect. Though men and women are "somewhat similar in the question of waste products and their elimination," Goffman observes, in public, men and women use sex-segregated restrooms, clearly marked "gentlemen" and "ladies." These rooms have very different spatial arrangements, such as urinals for men and more elaborate "vanity tables" and other grooming facilities for women. We think of these as justifiably "separate but equal."

But in the privacy of our own homes, we use the same bathrooms, and feel no need for separate space. What is more, virtually no private homes have urinals for men, and few have separate and private vanity tables for women. (And of course, in some cultures, these functions are performed publicly, with no privacy at all.) Had these needs been biologically based, Goffman asks, why are they so different in public and in private? The answer, of course, is that they are not biologically based at all:

> The *functioning* of sex differentiated organs is involved, but there is nothing in this functioning that biologically recommends segregation; *that* arrangement is a totally cultural matter. . . . Toilet segregation is presented as a natural consequence of the difference between the sex-classes when in fact it is a means of honoring, if not producing, this difference.[12]

In other words, by using separate facilities, we "become" the gentlemen and ladies who are supposed to use those separate facilities. The physical separation of men and women creates the justification for separating them—not the other way around.

At the less mundane, but certainly no less important level, take the example of the workplace. In her now-classic work, *Men and Women of the Corporation*, Rosabeth Moss Kanter demonstrated that the differences in men's and women's behaviors in organizations had far less to do with their characteristics as individuals, than it had to do with the structure of the organization. Organizational positions "carry characteristic images of the kinds of people that should occupy them," she argued, and those who do occupy them, whether women or men, exhibited those necessary behaviors. Though the criteria for evaluation of job performance, promotion, and effectiveness seem to be gender neutral, they are, in fact, deeply gendered. "While organizations were being defined as sex-neutral machines," she writes, "masculine principles were dominating their authority structures." Once again, masculinity—the norm—was invisible.[13]

In a series of insightful essays, sociologist Joan Acker has expanded on Kanter's early insights, and specified the interplay of structure and gender. It is through our experiences in the workplace, Acker maintains, that the differences between women and men are reproduced and by which the inequality between women and men is legitimated. Institutions are like factories, and what they produce is gender difference. The overall effect of this is the reproduction of the gender order as a whole. Thus, an institutional level cannot be left out of any explanation of gender—because institutions are fundamentally involved in both gender difference and gender domination. "Gender is not an addition to ongoing processes, conceived as gender neutral" she argues. "Rather, it is an integral part of those processes."[14]

Institutions accomplish the creation of gender difference and the reproduction of the gender order, Acker argues, through several "gendered processes." These gendered processes mean that "advantage and disadvantage, exploitation and control, action and emotion, meaning and identity, are patterned through and in terms of a distinction between male and female, masculine and feminine." She observes five of these processes:

1. the production of gender divisions—the ways in which "ordinary organizational practices produce the gender patterning of jobs, wages, and hierarchies, power and subordination." In the very organization of work, gender divisions are produced and reinforced, and hierarchies maintained—often despite the intentions of well-meaning managers and supervisors.
2. the construction of symbols and images "that explain, express, reinforce, or sometimes oppose those divisions." Gender images, such as advertisements, reproduce the gendering of positions so that the image of a successful manager or business executive is almost always an image of a well-dressed, powerful man.
3. the interactions between individuals—women and men, women and women, men and men, in all the forms and patterns that express dominance and submission. For example, conversations between supervisors and subordinates typically involve power dynamics, such as interruptions, sentence completion, and setting the topic for conversation, which, given the gendered positions within the organization will reproduce observable conversational gender differences.
4. the internal mental work of individuals "as they consciously construct their understandings of the organization's gendered structure of work and opportunity and the demands for gender-appropriate behaviors and attitudes." This might include patterns of dress, speech, and general presentation of self.
5. the ongoing logic of organizations themselves—how the seemingly gender-neutral theories of organizational dynamics, bureaucracy, and organizational criteria for evaluation and advancement are actually very gendered criteria masquerading as "objective" and gender neutral.[15]

As we've seen, sex role theory assumed that gendered individuals enter gender-neutral sites, thus maintaining the invisibility of gender-as-hierarchy, and specifically the invisible masculine organizational logic. On the other hand, many organizational theories assume that genderless "people" occupy those gender-neutral sites. The problem is that such genderless people are assumed to be able to devote themselves single-mindedly to their jobs, have no children or family responsibilities, and may even have familial supports for such single-minded workplace devotion. Thus, the genderless job holder turns out to be gendered as a man. Once again, the invisibility of masculinity as the unexamined norm turns out to reproduce the power differences between women and men.

One or two more examples should suffice. Many doctors complete college by age twenty-one or twenty-two, medical school between twenty-five and twenty-seven, and then endure three more years of internship and residency, during which time they are occasionally on call for long stretches of time, sometimes, even two or three days straight. They thus complete their residencies by their late twenties or early thirties. Such a program is designed for a male doctor—one who is not pressured by the ticking of a biological clock, for whom the birth of children will not disrupt these time demands, and who may even have someone at home taking care of the children while he sleeps at the hospital. No wonder women in medical school—who number nearly one-half of all medical students today—began to complain that they were not able to balance pregnancy and motherhood with their medical training. (The real wonder is that the male medical school students had not noticed this problem earlier!)

Similarly, lawyers just out of law school who take jobs with large corporate law firms are expected to bill up to fifty to sixty hours per week—a process that probably requires working between eighty and ninety hours per week. Assuming at least six hours of sleep per night, a one-hour round-trip commute, and one half-day of rest, these young lawyers are going to have a total of about seventeen hours per week to eat, cook, clean their houses, talk with and/or make love with their spouse (or date if they're single), and spend time with their children. Without that half-day off on the weekend, they have about one hour per day for everything else. Failure to submit to this regime places a lawyer on a "Mommy track" or a "Daddy track," which means that everyone will think well of you for being such an involved parent, but that you are certain never to be promoted to partner, to join all the rest of the lawyers who made such sacrifices for their careers.

Or, finally, take academic tenure. In a typical academic career, a scholar completes a Ph.D. about six to seven years after the BA, or roughly by one's early thirties. Then he or she begins a career as an assistant professor and has six more years to earn tenure and promotion. This is usually the most intense academic work period of a scholar's life—he or she works night and day to publish enough scholarly research and prepare and teach their courses. The early thirties are also the most likely child-bearing years for professional women. The academic tenure clock is thus timed to a man's rhythms—and not just any man, but one who has a wife or other family supports to relieve him of family obligations as he works to establish his credentials. Remember the adage "publish or perish?" Often, to academics struggling to make tenure, it feels as though publishing requires that family life perish.

Observing the institutional dimension also offers the possibility to observe adjustment and readjustment within institutions as they are challenged. Sometimes, their boundaries prove more permeable than originally expected. For example, what happens when the boundaries between work and home become permeable, when women leave the home and enter the gendered workplace? Judith Gerson and Kathy Peiss suggest that boundaries "*within* the workplace (e.g., occupational segregation) and inter-actional micro-level boundaries assume increased significance in defining the subordi-nate position of women." Thus, occupational segregation can reproduce gender dif-ference *and* gender inequality by assigning women to secondary statuses within organizations. For those women who enter nontraditional positions, though, micro-level boundary maintenance would come into play—"the persistence of informal group behavior among men (e.g., after-work socializing, the uses of male humor, modes of corporate attire)—act to define insiders and outsiders, thus maintaining gender-based distinctions."[16]

Embedded in organizational structures that are gendered, subject to gendered or-ganizational processes, and evaluated by gendered criteria, then, the differences be-tween women and men appear to be the differences solely between gendered individ-uals. When gender boundaries seem permeable, other dynamics and processes can reproduce the gender order. When women do not meet these criteria (or, perhaps more accurately, when the criteria do not meet women's specific needs), we see a gender-segregated workforce and wage, hiring, and promotional disparities as the "natural" outcomes of already-present differences between women and men. It is in this way that those differences are generated and the inequalities between women and men are le-gitimated and reproduced.

(One should, of course, note that it is through these same processes that the "dif-ferences" between working-class and professional men, between whites and people of color, and between heterosexuals and homosexuals are also produced, and the in-equalities based on class or race or sexuality are legitimated and reproduced. Making gender visible in these organizational processes ought not to blind us to the complex interactions with other patterns of difference and principles of inequality. Just as a male pattern becomes the unexamined norm, so too does a white, heterosexual, and middle-class pattern become the unexamined norm against which others' experiences and performances are evaluated.)

The idea of organizational gender neutrality, then, is the vehicle by which the gen-der order is reproduced. "The theory and practice of gender neutrality," writes Acker, "covers up, obscures, the underlying gender structure, allowing practices that perpet-uate it to continue even as efforts to reduce gender inequality are also under way."[17] Organizations reflect and produce gender differences; gendered institutions also re-produce the gender order by which men are privileged over women and some men— white, middle-class, heterosexual—are privileged over other men.

"DOING GENDER"

There remains one more element in the sociological explanation of gender. According to sex role theory, we acquire our gender identity through socialization, and afterward, we are socialized to behave in masculine or feminine ways. It is thus the task of society to make sure that the men act in the masculine manner, and that the women act in the fem-inine manner. Our identity is fixed, permanent, and—now—inherent in our personali-ties. We can no more cease being men or women than we can cease being human.

In an important contribution to the social constructionist perspective, sociologists Candace West and Don Zimmerman argued that gender was less a component of identity—fixed, static—that we take with us into our interactions, but rather the product *of* those interactions. They argued that "a person's gender is not simply an aspect of what one is, but, more fundamentally, it is something that one *does,* and does recurrently, in interaction with others." We are constantly "doing" gender, performing the activities and exhibiting the traits that are prescribed for us.[18]

If our sex role identity were inherent, West and Zimmerman might ask, in what does it inhere? What are the criteria by which we sort people into those sex roles to begin with? Typically, our answer returns us to biology, and, more specifically, to the primary sex characteristics that we believe determine which gender one will become. Biological sex—externally manifested genitalia—becomes socialized gender role. Those with male genitalia are classified in one way; those with female genitalia are classified in another way. These two sexes become different genders, which are assumed to have different personalities and require different institutional and social arrangements to accommodate their natural—and now, socially acquired—differences.

Most of the time, we carry around these types of commonsense understandings. We see primary sex characteristics (those present at birth) as far more decisive than secondary sex characteristics (those that develop at puberty) for the assignment of gender role identity. But how do we know? When we see someone on the street, it is their *secondary* sex characteristics that we observe—breast development, facial hair, musculature. Even more that that, it is the behavioral presentation of self—how they dress, move, talk—that signals for us whether that someone is a man or a woman. It would be a strange world, indeed, if we had constantly to ask to see someone's genitals to make sure they were who they appeared to be!

One method that sociologists developed to interrogate this assumption has been to imagine that primary and secondary sex characteristics did not match. In many cases, "intersexed" infants, or hermaphrodites—whose primary sex characteristics cannot be easily discerned visually—have their genitals surgically reconstructed, depending upon the size of the penis, and not on the presence or absence of Y chromosomes. To these surgeons "chromosomes are less relevant in determining gender than penis size." Therefore, to be labeled "male" does not necessarily depend upon having one Y and one X chromosome, nor upon the production of sperm, "but by the aesthetic condition of having an appropriately sized penis." The surgeons assume that no "male" would want to live as a man with such minute genitalia, and so they "correct" what will undoubtedly be perceived as a problem. (These surgically constructed females go on to live their lives as women.). It would appear then that size really does matter—at least to the doctors![19]

In a brilliantly disconcerting study, *Gender: An Ethnomethololological Approach,* Suzanne Kessler and Wendy McKenna proposed two images in which primary and secondary sex characteristics did not match. (See figures 5.1 and 5.2.) Which one is the "man" and which is the "woman"? How can you tell? If you base your decision on primary sex characteristics—the genitals—you would have to conclude that many of the people with whom you interact in daily life might be hiding their "true" selves. But, if you base your decision on what you see "above the waist," which is more visible in

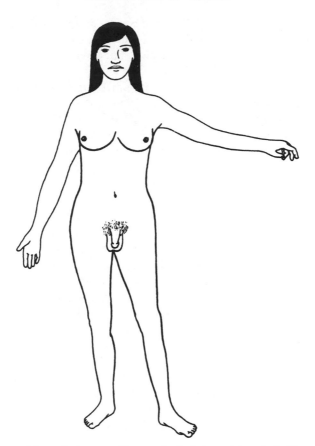

Figure 5.1. Figure with penis, breasts, hips, no body hair, and long hair. From *Gender: An Ethnomethodological Approach* by Kessler and McKenna. Copyright © 1985 by University of Chicago Press. Reprinted by permission of John Wiley & Sons, Inc.

daily life, you would have to conclude that many people may actually be a different sex from that which they appear to be.

Looking at those images, one might be tempted to dismiss this as the stuff of fantasy. After all, in real life, people's genitals match their secondary sex characteristics, and we are always easily able to tell the difference, right? Well, maybe not always. Recall the consternation in the popular film *The Crying Game,* when it was revealed, to both the audience and the film's protagonist simultaneously, that Dil, the woman he was in love with, was actually a man. And remember everyone's reaction when Dustin Hoffman revealed that Emily Kimberly was in fact Edward Kimberly in *Tootsie;* or the Broadway play *M Butterfly,* which was about a man who lived with a woman for more than thirty years *without ever realizing that he was actually a man.* And think of the commotion and confusion about Marilyn Manson in recent years. And what about the consternation and disgust expressed by men who pay cross-dressing prostitutes for oral sex and then find out that "she" is actually "he." Such confusion is often the ba-

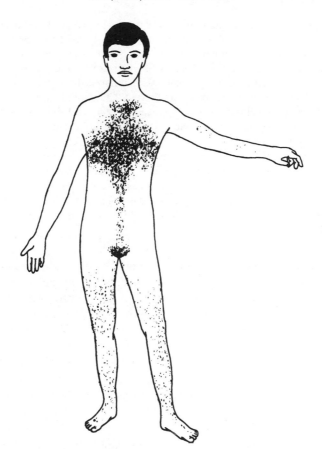

Figure 5.2. Figure with vulva, no breasts, no hips, body hair, and short hair. From *Gender: An Ethnomethodological Approach* by Kessler and McKenna. Copyright © 1985 by University of Chicago Press. Reprinted by permission of John Wiley & Sons, Inc.

sis for comedy. Knowing whether someone is male or female is far more important to the observer than it often is to the observed, as fans of the television program *Saturday Night Live* will recall with the ambiguous character, "Pat." People who interacted with Pat were constantly trying to trick him/her into revealing what he/she "really" was, while Pat nonchalantly answered their questions and eluded every rhetorical trap.

Of course, these are all media creations and in real life, "passing" is far more difficult and far less common. But one reason we enjoy such a parade of ambiguous characters is because gender certainty is so important to us. Without it, we feel as if we have lost our social bearings in the world, and are threatened with a kind of "gender vertigo," in which the dualistic conceptions that we believe are the foundations of our social reality turn out to be more fluid than we believed or hoped.[20] It's as though our notions of gender are anchored in quicksand. One sociologist reported how she became disturbed by the sexual ambiguity of a computer salesperson:

The person who answered my questions was truly a salesperson. I could not categorize him/her as a woman or a man. What did I look for? (1) Facial hair: She/he was smooth skinned, but some men have little or no facial hair. (This varies by race, Native Americans and Blacks often have none.) (2) Breasts; She/he was wearing a loose shirt that hung from his/her shoulders. And, as many women who suffered through a 1950s adolescence know to their shame, women are often flat-chested. (3) Shoulders: His/hers were small and round for a man, broad for a woman. (4) Hands: Long and slender fingers, knuckles a bit large for a woman, small for a man. (5) Voice: Middle range, unexpressive for a woman, not at all the exaggerated tones some gay males affect. (6) His/her treatment of me: Gave off no signs that would let me know if I were of the same or different sex as this person. There were not even any signs that he/she knew his/her sex would be difficult to categorize and I wondered about this even as I did my best to hide these questions so I would not embarrass him/her while we talked of computer paper. I left still not knowing the sex of my salesperson, and was disturbed by that unanswered question (child of my culture that I am).[21]

Transvestites and cross-dressers reveal the artifice of gender. Gender is a performance, a form of drag, by which, through the successful manipulation of props, signs, symbols, behaviors, and emotions, we attempt to convince others of our successful acquisition of masculinity or femininity. Or by which we play with the conventions of successful gender acquisition, as in the antics of pro basketball player Dennis Rodman.

By contrast, transgendered people who have had genital reconstructive surgery often reinstate anatomy as the chief signifier of gender identity, as if a man could not be a "real" woman as long as he possessed a penis, or a woman could not be a "real" man as long as she did not possess one. Often transgendered people—or transsexuals—enact an exaggerated set of gendered traits of their newly reconstructed biological sex. Male-to-female transsexuals often become hyperfeminine, prissy, and passive; female-to-male transsexuals may become assertively and aggressively masculine.

Cross-dressers know better, or rather, know different: As "social constructionsists," they know that successfully being a man or a woman simply means convincing others that you are what you appear to be. Just ask Ru Paul, who seems to float almost effortlessly between the two. (I say "seems" advisedly, since it probably takes "him" as long to accomplish the male presentation of self as it does to accomplish the female.) Or ask Alison Laing, a husband and a father, who spends about 80 percent of his time dressed in women's clothes and 20 percent dressed as a man. "We don't have to live in gender boxes," he says.[22]

Most of us find the walls of those boxes enormously comforting. We learn gender performance early in childhood, and it remains with us virtually all our lives. When our gender identities are threatened, we will often retreat to exaggerated displays of hyper-masculinity or exaggerated femininity. And when our sense of others' gender identity is disrupted or dislodged, we can become anxious, even violent. "We're so invested in being men or women that if you fall outside that easy definition of what a man or woman is, a lot of people see you as some kind of monster," commented Susan Stryker, who is a male-to-female transsexual. Many transsexuals are murdered or attacked every year.[23]

The fascinating case of "Agnes" reported by Harold Garfinkel also demonstrates these themes. Agnes was first encountered in the late 1950s by a psychiatrist, Robert Stoller, and by Garfinkel, a sociologist. Though Agnes appeared in every way to be a very feminine woman, she also had a penis, which she regarded as a biological mistake. Agnes "knew" she was a woman, and acted (and demanded to be treated) as a woman. "I have always been a girl," she proclaimed to her interviewers, and regarded her early childhood socialization as a relentless trauma of being forced to participate in activities for boys, like sports. Since genitals were not "the essential signs of her femininity," Agnes instead referred to her prominent breasts and her lifelong sense that she was, in fact, female. "Her self-described feminine feelings, behavior, choices of companions, and the like were never portrayed as matters of decision or choice but were treated as *given* as a natural fact," writes Garfinkel. (Revealingly, Garfinkel refers to Agnes, as I have, with a feminine pronoun, although biologically Agnes possessed male genitalia.)[24]

Understanding how we do gender, then, requires that we make visible the performative elements of identity, and also the audience for those performances. It also opens up unimaginable possibilities for social change; as Suzanne Kessler points out in her study of "intersexed people" (hermaphrodites):

> If authenticity for gender rests not in a discoverable nature but in someone else's proclamation, then the power to proclaim something else is available. If physicians recognized that implicit in their management of gender is the notion that finally, and always, people construct gender as well as the social systems that are grounded in gender-based concepts, the possibilities for real societal transformations would be unlimited.[25]

Kessler's gender utopianism does raise an important issue in the sociological perspective. In saying that we "do" gender we are saying that gender is not only something that is done to us. We create and re-create our own gendered identities within the contexts of our interactions with others and within the institutions we inhabit.

A Sociology of Rape

In previous chapters, we've illustrated theoretical perspectives by observing how each perspective deals with one specifically gendered phenomenon—rape. We've seen, for example, how some evolutionary biologists explain rape as an evolutionary reproductive strategy for "losers" who are unable to pass on their genetic inheritance by old-fashioned seduction. (It is therefore evolutionary biologists, not mainstream feminists who insist that rape and sex are the same thing!) And we've seen how anthropologists undermine such biological arguments, suggesting instead that rape varies dramatically from one culture to another, and what causes the differences between rape-prone and rape-free societies is the status of women. Where women are valued and honored, rape rates are exceptionally low. Where women are degraded and devalued, rape rates are high.

Psychologists enable us to differentiate between rapists and non-rapists by understanding the psychodynamic processes that lead an individual man to such aberrant behavior. Whether because of childhood trauma, unresolved anger at his mother, a sense of inadequate gender identity, rapists are characterized by their deviance from the norm. "Rape is always a symptom of some psychological dysfunction, either temporary and transient, or chronic and repetitive." In the popular view, rapists are "sick individuals."[26]

As we have seen, the sociological perspective builds upon these other perspectives. But it offers a radical departure from them, as well. Rape is particularly illustrative because it is something that is performed almost exclusively by one gender—men—although it can be and is done to both men and women. Thus, it is particularly useful for teasing out the dynamics of both difference (since only men do it) and dominance (since its primary function is the domination of either women or men). Instead of seeing a collection of sick individuals, sociologists look at how ordinary, how normal, rapists can be—and then at the culture that legitimates their behaviors. Sociology also assesses the processes and dynamics that force all women to confront the possibility of sexual victimization—a process that reproduces both gender division and gender inequality.

Sociological studies of rapists have found that many are married or have steady, regular partners. Studies of gang rape reveal an even more "typical" guy who sees himself simply as going along with his friends. Rapists see their actions in terms that express power differentials between women and men. They see what they do to women as their "right," a sense of entitlement to women's bodies. And they often see their behavior in light of their relationship with other men. For example, the members of Spur Posse, a group of teenage boys in southern California accused of numerous acts of date and acquaintance rape, kept score of their "conquests" using athletes' uniform numbers—which only the other boys could understand. And during wartime, the rape of vanquished women becomes a form of communication between the victor and the loser, and women's bodies are the "spoils of war."

While rape is an act of aggression by an individual man, or a group of men, it is also a social problem women, as a group, face. Women may deal with rape as individuals—by changing their outfits, their patterns of walking and talking, their willingness to go to certain places at certain times—but rape affects all women. Rape is a form of "sexual terrorism," writes legal theorist Carol Sheffield, a "system of constant reminders to women that we are vulnerable and targets solely by virtue of our gender. The knowledge that such things can and do happen serves to keep all women in the psychological condition of being aware that they are potential victims."[27]

To the sociologist, then, rape thus expresses both a structure of relations and an individual event. At the individual level, it is the action of a man (or group of men) against a woman. It is sustained by a cultural apparatus that interprets it as legitimate and justified. It keeps women in a position of vulnerability as potential targets. In this way, rape reproduces both gender difference (women as vulnerable and dependent upon men for protection, women afraid to dare to enter male spaces such as the street for fear of victimization) and gender inequality.[28]

TOWARD AN EXPLANATION OF THE SOCIAL CONSTRUCTION OF GENDER RELATIONS

So, how shall we think about gender from a sociological perspective? The elements of a definition seem clear enough. We shall explore three related levels—(1) identity; (2) interaction: (3) institution—and, of course, the interactions among them, in order to explain the related phenomena—gender difference and gender inequality.

First, we understand that gender is not a "thing" that one possesses, but a set of activities that one *does*. When we do gender, we do it in front of other people; it is validated and legitimated by the evaluations of others. Gender is less a property of the individual than it is a product of our interactions with others. West and Zimmerman call gender a "managed property," which is "contrived with respect to the fact that others will judge and respond to us in particular ways." Women and men are distinct social groups, constituted in "concrete, historically changing—and generally unequal—social relationships." What the great British historian E. P. Thompson once wrote about class applies equally to gender. Gender "is a relationship, not a thing"—and like all relationships we are active in its construction. We do not simply inherit a male or female sex role, but we actively—interactively—constantly define and redefine what it means to be men or women in our daily encounters with one another. Gender is something one *does,* not something one *has.*[29]

Second, we understand that we do gender in every interaction, in every situation, in every institution in which we find ourselves. Gender is a situated accomplishment, as much an aspect of interaction as it is of identity. As Messerschmidt puts it, "[G]ender is a situated accomplishment in which we produce forms of behavior seen by others in the same immediate situation as masculine or feminine." Gender is what we bring to these interactions and what is produced in them as well.[30]

Nor do we do gender in a genderless vacuum, but, rather, in a gendered world, in gendered institutions. Our social world is a built on systemic, structural inequality based on gender; social life reproduces both gender difference and gender inequality. We need to think of masculinity and femininity "not as a single object with its own history, but as being constantly constructed within the history of an evolving social structure." As Katherine Pyke defines it, gender is:

> an emergent property of situated interaction rather than a role or attribute. Deeply held and typically nonconscious beliefs about men's and women's essential natures shape how gender is accomplished in everyday interactions. Because those beliefs are molded by existing macrostructural power relations, the culturally appropriate ways of producing gender favor men's interests over those of women. In this manner, gendered power relations are reproduced.[31]

In short, sociology is uniquely equipped to understand both what is really different between women and men, and what is not really different but only seems to be, as well as the ways in which gender difference is the product of—and not the cause of—gender inequality. We are gendered people living gendered lives in a gendered society—but we do actually live on the same planet. (In fact it may be that only on this planet would such differences make a difference.)

In the remainder of this book, we'll look at some of the institutions that create gender difference and reproduce gender inequality—families, schools, workplaces—and observe some of the ways in which those differences and that inequality are expressed through our interactions with one another—in love, sex, friendship, and violence.

PART 2

GENDERED IDENTITIES, GENDERED INSTITUTIONS

CHAPTER   6

THE GENDERED FAMILY

Nobody has ever before asked the nuclear family to live all by itself in a box the way we do. With no relatives, no support, we've put it in an impossible situation.

—MARGARET MEAD

I don't like nostalgia unless it's mine.

—LOU REED

A decade ago, in 1992, then–vice president Dan Quayle ignited a public debate about the family simply by attacking a fictional character on a television show. Murphy Brown's decision to become a single mother, he charged, "mock[ed] the importance of fathers," and presented single parenthood as "just another lifestyle choice." Forty-one million Americans watched Murphy's rhetorical revenge. In the September 21, 1992, broadcast of the show, she chastised Quayle's "painfully unfair" comments, reminding him, and America, that "families come in all shapes and sizes."

But the flap didn't end there. A year later, a magazine article proclaimed that "Dan Quayle Was Right," and suddenly, America was arguing about what became known as "family values." Some shouted that the family was "in crisis"—falling apart because of high rates of divorce, teen pregnancies, single parenthood, latchkey children being raised by strangers, and gay men and lesbians demanding the right to marry and have or adopt children. To them, the "traditional" nuclear family of the 1950s, of *Leave It to Beaver* and other sitcoms of the period—defined by one of its defenders as "a legal lifelong sexually exclusive, heterosexual monogamous marriage, based on affection and companionship, in which there is a sharp division of labor with the female as full time housewife and the male as primary provider and ultimate authority"—was fast disappearing under the double-barreled assault of a permissive society and a welfare state. Scores of punitive policy initiatives were designed to shore up this besieged institution and restore this version of the family, including laws that would restrict divorce, repress women's right to choose, reiterate a heterosexual norm in family life, and recast marriage from a legal contract to a sacred "covenant."[1]

Others, though, celebrated these new and diverse familial permutations, arguing that they confirm the strength of the American family. To the celebrants of family diversity, family problems were caused by the pretense that 1950s sitcom model remains both universal and universally desirable. *Leave It to Beaver* was not the only model of family happiness; American families were more like *The Jeffersons* and *The Brady Bunch*. In fact, those same punitive policy initiatives exacerbated the very family problems they were designed to correct, and thereby restricted the equality of women and children. If the right wing's version of family values were to be implemented, journalist Katha Pollitt argues,

> [W]e'd have to bring back the whole 19th century: restore the cult of virginity and the double standard, ban birth control, restrict divorce, kick women out of decent jobs, force unwed pregnant women to put their babies up for adoption on pain of social death, make out of wedlock children legal nonpersons.

This unlikely (and thoroughly nasty) scenario suggests that we'd better get used to the differences in the ways we choose to live and design policies to support and encourage all forms of the family.[2]

Both sides of the debate have some merit. The data on the crisis of the family seem overwhelming: Marriage rates have consistently declined; only two-thirds of American women aged thirty-five to forty-four were legally married in 1998; the marriage rate that year (8.3 per 1,000) was the lowest in forty years. Cohabitation (both prior to marriage and in lieu of marriage) has increased dramatically in the past two decades, from 1.1 million in 1977 to nearly 5 million in 1997. Nearly 40 percent of first marriages end in divorce and 60 percent of those marriages involve children. One-third of all births are to unmarried people (1.3 million in 1999). Among whites, the proportion of births to unmarried women went from 5 percent in 1964–1969 to 26 percent in 1998; among black women, the proportion rose from 35 percent to 69 percent. Thirty-six percent of children live without their biological fathers. And children who are raised by only one parent are more likely to be poor, commit a crime, drop out of school, have lower grades, and have emotional problems.[3]

Though the family feels like one of the most fragile of social institutions, it is, in fact, perhaps the most resilient. American families have changed dramatically over the course of our history, and the family form continues to adapt to changing circumstances. There is, however, only modest evidence that the family is in decline or decay. Marriage remains quite popular, with more than nine in ten Americans taking the plunge. The proportion of women who remain single all their lives is actually lower today than it was at the turn of the century. That almost one-half of all marriages in the United States are remarriages indicates both the increasing numbers of divorces and the continued belief in the institution of marriage. More men than ever are identifying themselves as fathers, and there are more single fathers raising children than ever before as well. And virtually everyone wants to get married—including gay men and lesbians, whose campaigns for the right to marry are currently on the political agenda (and are, ironically, opposed by the very people who want to "defend" marriage).[4]

If the nuclear family is not exactly in crisis, then what is all the noise about? Some part of the family values debate rests on what we might call "misplaced nostalgia"—a romanticized notion that the family form of the 1950s (the era of many of the debaters' adolescence) is a timeless trope that all family forms ought to emulate. In the 1960s, anthropologist Raymond Birdwhistell labeled this "the sentimental model" when he described the way people in rural Kentucky talked about or "remembered" their families—which, as he pointed out, bore little resemblance to the families in which they actually lived. Often our descriptions of the family conform more to this mythic model than to our actual experiences. When transformed into public policy, this blurred and ahistorical vision is often accompanied by a hearing disorder that seeks to block out the unpleasant sounds of modernity—the cacophonous chorus of different groups of people in a democracy, the hum of the workplace toward which both women and men are drawn, the din of television and rock or rap music, the moans of the sexual revolution.

Much of the family values debate is a displaced quarrel with feminism, which is often wrongly blamed or wrongly credited with what may be the single greatest transformation of American society in the twentieth century—the entry of women into the workplace. This process long antedates modern feminism, although the attack on the "feminine mystique" launched by the women's movement in the 1960s gave working women a political peg upon which to hang their aspirations and longings.

Finally, much of the debate about the crisis of the family is based on a misreading of history. Although we think of the family as the "private" sphere, a warm respite from the cold competitive world of the economic and political life, the family has never been a world apart. The modern family was built upon a wide foundation of economic and political supports; it is today sustained by an infrastructure that includes public funding for roads, schools, and home buying, and the legal arrangements of marriage and divorce. The workplace and family are deeply interconnected; the "family wage" organizes family life as well as economic life, expressing an idealized view of what the family is and should be. This public component of the private sphere is often invisible in current debates about the family, in part because it is so deeply ingrained in our historical development. The current "crisis" dates back to the beginning of the twentieth century, but the origins of the current dilemma lie much farther back in our nation's past.

A Brief History of the American Family

From the start, American families were the beneficiaries of dramatic changes in family morality that swept Europe and the colonies in the mid-eighteenth century. Though paternal authority was still the core of the "well-ordered family," a new morality of "affective individualism" led to an ideal of warmer and more intimate relationships between husbands and wives and between parents and children. In a "surge of sentiment," men and women were encouraged to marry on the basis of mutual affection; marriage was regarded as the "union of individuals" rather than as the "union of two lineages." Husbands became less brutal to their wives—there was a decline in wife beating and in men insisting on their conjugal "rights"—and parents less harsh toward their children, measured by a decline in corporal punishment.[5]

American women had greater freedom than their European counterparts. Without dowries to tie them economically to their families, and with the right to own property in their own names after marriage, American women had an easier time both marrying and remarrying. Thus, the eighteenth- and early-nineteenth-century American family looked less like a miniature monarchy and more a "little commonwealth" in which husbands, wives, and children "worked together as participants in common enterprise." There was far less differentiation between "his" and "her" spheres: Women and men both worked in and around their homes; women produced many of the things needed for the family; and men worked to a rhythm of family time, not industrial time. Just as women and men were involved in the worlds of work, fathers and mothers were both involved in child rearing; historian John Demos writes of an "active, encompassing fatherhood, woven into the whole fabric of domestic and productive life." In fact, at the dawn of the nineteenth century child-rearing manuals were written to fathers, not mothers, and children were largely raised by their same-sex parent in an informal but common sex-segregated pattern.[6]

In the first decades of the nineteenth century, however, this world was transformed. By the middle of the century, a gap between work and home grew dramatically, both in reality and in ideology to create the separation of spheres. Family life "was wrenched apart from the world of work," and the workplace and the home clearly demarcated as *his* and *hers*. In 1849, Alfred Lord Tennyson expressed this separation of spheres in a poem, "The Princess":

Man for the field and woman for the hearth:
Man for the sword and for the needle she:
Man with the head and woman with the heart:
Man to command and woman to obey;
All else confusion.[7]

Men experienced this separation in two ways. Paid work shifted from home and farm to mill and factory, shop and office. Men now marched to a different beat as the day's rhythm shifted to the incessant pounding of industry. Second, men's share of the work around the home was gradually industrialized and eliminated as such tasks as fuel gathering, leather working, and grain processing shifted to the external world. This further "liberated" men to exit their homes and leave the rearing of both sons and daughters to their wives.

If men were liberated, women's position was as exalted in popular literature as it was potentially imprisoning in reality. In popular literature, from the nation's pulpits and in high art, women's work was reconceptualized, not as "work" at all, but rather as a God-given mission. While some home-based work was eliminated, such as spinning and weaving, much of women's sphere remained intact; they still cooked meals and baked bread, even if their husbands no longer grew and milled the grain or butchered the meat they cooked. Housecleaning and child rearing were increasingly seen as "women's work."

Though men's and women's spheres were symmetrical and complementary, they were not equal. As Catherine Beecher and Harriet Beecher Stowe wrote in their celebrated book, *The American Woman's Home* (1869):

When the family is instituted by marriage, it is man who is head and chief magistrate by the force of his physical power and requirement of the chief responsibility; not less is he so according to the Christian law, by which, when differences arise, the husband has the deciding control, and the wife is to obey.[8]

Many historians argue that this new ideology actually represented a historical decline in women's status. Historian Gerda Lerner, for example, points out that there were fewer female storekeepers and businesswomen in the 1830s than there had been in the 1780s. "Women were," she argues, "excluded from the new democracy." Democracy meant mobility—geographic, social, economic—and women were "imprisoned" in the home by the new ideology of feminine domesticity. Little wonder women's sphere needed the ideological buttressing of rhapsodic poetry and religious sermons to keep it in place. But men's "liberation" from the home was also partly illusory, for they were also in exile from it. As early as the 1820s and 1830s, critics were complaining that men spent too little time at home. "Paternal neglect at the present time is one of the most abundant sources of domestic sorrow," wrote the Rev. John S. C. Abbott in *Parents Magazine* in 1842. The father, "eager in the pursuit of business, toils early and late, and finds no time to fulfill . . . duties to his children." Theodore Dwight attempted to persuade men to resume their responsibilities at home in *The Father's Book* (1834), one of the nation's first advice books for men.[9]

The family had now become the "haven in a heartless world" that the great French writer Alexis de Tocqueville observed when he visited the United States in the early 1830s. "Shorn of its productive functions, the family now specialized in child-rearing and emotional solace, providing a much-needed sanctuary in a world organized around the impersonal principles of the market."[10]

Of course, this ideology and reality of the separation of spheres in mid-nineteenth-century America was largely white and middle class; but it was imposed on others as the norm, as the "American" family form. Working-class women and women of color continued to work outside the home, while the men shared housework and child care more readily out of economic necessity if not because of ideological commitment. Cast "primarily as workers rather than as members of family groups, [minority] women labored to maintain, sustain, stabilize and reproduce their families while working in both the public (productive) and private (reproductive) spheres."[11]

Having been relegated to women, the family's importance also declined, its integration into the community attenuated. As if to compensate for this shift, the family's symbolic importance increased. Events that had been casually organized were routinized as family events; community celebrations became household celebrations. "The Family" as site of sentimentalized romantic longing was an invention of the nineteenth century, as families tried to shore up what they were in fact losing. Historian John Gillis writes:

> When men had worked at home, mealtimes had seldom been private, or even very regular. Holidays had revolved around community festivals and visiting rather than home-cooked meals and private family celebrations. Leisurely dinner hours, Sunday family time, and nuclear family togetherness on holidays such as Christmas were invented during the mid-nineteenth century.[12]

The rapid industrialization of the American economy in the decades following the Civil War only reinforced earlier trends. By 1890, only about 2 percent of married women were employed outside the home. And probably just as few men were working inside it. As motherhood came to be seen as women's sole "calling," the importance of fatherhood declined. "The suburban husband and father is almost entirely a Sunday institution," one writer in *Harper's Bazaar* put it in 1900. Articles with titles like "It's Time Father got Back in the Family" appeared with some regularity in popular magazines. "Poor father has been left out in the cold," observed Progressive reformer Jane Addams in 1911. "He doesn't get much recognition. It would be a good thing if he had a day that would mean recognition of him." (This noble idea had to wait another sixty-one years to be implemented.)[13]

Turn-of-the-century commentators fretted about the crisis of the family. The divorce rate had been steadily climbing since soldiers returned from the Civil War—from 7,000 in 1860 to 56,000 in 1900 and 100,000 in 1914. In 1916, one in every four marriages in San Francisco ended in divorce; in Los Angeles the number was one in five, and, in the more traditional and Catholic Chicago, one in seven. A 1914 survey of women graduates of Barnard, Bryn Mawr, Cornell, Mount Holyoke, Radcliffe, Smith, Vassar, Wellesley, and Wells colleges showed that fewer than 40 percent had married. Of Harvard graduates during the 1870s, almost one-third between the ages of forty and fifty were still single. "In fifty years, there will be no such thing as marriage," predicted the esteemed Harvard psychologist John Watson at the dawn of the new century.[14]

The crisis of the family was so pressing that President Theodore Roosevelt convened the first White House Conference on Children in 1909. Roosevelt believed that men needed to be encouraged to become more active fathers and that white, native-born women needed encouragement to have more children, lest white people commit what he called "race suicide." And he also believed that poverty, especially the poverty of widowed mothers, was the primary problem in the lives of children, and that it was the government's obligation to help. Roosevelt advocated giving money to single mothers who had been certified as capable of providing decent care to their children if only they had a little more cash in their pocketbooks.[15]

The separation of spheres provided the foundation for a virtual perpetual crisis of the family throughout the twentieth century. Women's efforts to leave the home—to go to college, enter the labor force, join unions, attend professional schools—were met with significant resistance, and men's interest in returning home waxed and waned through the 1940s. World War II disrupted this pattern, as women entered the labor force in dramatic numbers. But the postwar economic boom, which was fueled by massive government expenditure in highway and school construction and the GI Bill that made single-family suburban home ownership a reality for an increasing number of American families, also stabilized this aberrant family form: the nuclear family of June and Ward Cleaver and their children Wally and the Beaver.[16]

This massive infusion of public expenditures to shore up the nuclear family ideal—breadwinner husband, housewife mother, and their children—was accompanied by a dramatic increase in marriage rates and a sharp decline in the ages of first marriage. While today's marriage rates and marriage ages are in keeping with the rest of the twentieth century, the era 1945–1960 stands out as dramatically different, as "young men and women . . . reacting against the hardships and separations of depression and war . . . married unusually early." In 1867, there were 9.6 marriages per 1,000 people in the United States; a century later, the number was 9.7. In 1946, by contrast, the number hit an all-time high of 14.2. Thus, the 1950s pattern of family life—characterized by high rates of marriage, high fertility, and low and stable rates of divorce—which many continue to regard as an ideal—"was the product of a convergence of an unusual series of historical, demographic and economic circumstances unlikely to return again" in the words of two leading family historians.[17]

As soon as this new family form emerged it was declared to be natural—that is, both biologically inevitable and morally appropriate. The effort to reinforce it became a constant hum in the nation's ears. "The effort to reinforce traditional norms seemed almost frantic," writes historian William Chafe, "as though in reality something very different was taking place." In academia, the structural-functionalist school of social science gave it legitimacy, arguing that the isolated suburban nuclear family, with distinct separation of spheres, served the needs of both children and society. The family system required both expressive (female) and instrumental (male) components to function appropriately, wrote sociologist Talcott Parsons, and this could only be accomplished in a family in which the housewife mother maintained the home for her breadwinner husband who worked outside it. Here's how another sociologist described this domestic paradise in 1955:

> Father helps mother with the dishes. He sets the table. He makes formula for the baby. Mother can supplement the income of the family by working outside. Nevertheless, the American male, by definition, *must* "provide" for his family. He is *responsible* for the support of his wife and children. His primary area of performance is the occupational role, in which his status fundamentally inheres; and his *primary* function in the family is to supply an "income," to be the "breadwinner." There is simply something wrong with the American adult male who doesn't have a "job."
>
> American women, on the other hand, tend to hold jobs *before* they are married and to quit when "the day" comes; or to continue in jobs of a lower status than their husbands. And not only is the mother the focus of emotional support for the American middle class child, but much more exclusively so than in most societies. . . . The cult of the warm, giving "Mom" stands in contrast to the "capable," "competent," "go-getting" male. The more expressive type of male, as a matter of fact, is regarded as "effeminate," and has too much fat on the inner side of his thigh.[18]

A generation of middle-class men tried to toe the line of bland conformity as suburban breadwinners; here was the corporate clone of countless satires, the "man in the gray flannel suit" who drove his late-model car down to the suburban train station to catch the same train every morning—with every other man in the neighborhood. And a generation of women cooked and cleaned, dusted and mopped, washed and ironed, toiling to meet ever-increasing standards of cleanliness.

For many parents and children of the baby boom, this family form worked well. Suburban life was safer and simpler than the crowded cities from which many fifties families fled, and family life gave postwar men a secure anchor in an increasingly insecure corporate world. The home front centered on the kids' homework and a plethora of hobbies and leisure time pursuits, from hiking and camping, to concerts and theatre, sailing and photography. Middle-class Americans took family vacations, hung out together in family rooms, and purchased family-sized packages of prepared foods— when they weren't practicing gourmet French cooking. They walked together to the local library or movie theatre. Some husbands doted on their wife-companions, and together they built lives more stable, comfortable, child-centered, and companionable—divorce being a last resort—than anything their own parents had ever envisioned. Listen, for example, to poet Archibald MacLeish's loving praise of the wife he credits with securing his vision of marital bliss:

> In all that becomes a woman
> Her words and her ways are beautiful
> Love's lovely duty
> The well-swept room . . .

and, he concludes

> The greatest and richest good—
> My own life to live in—
> This she has given me
> If giver could.

To be sure, MacLeish's vision of domestic bliss rested on the unwavering commitment to separate spheres and male primacy (she gives him his life to live, but he does not give her hers). We might like to hear her side of the story. Yet, still, "[t]hose ideas and images, like religious language and imagery, still have the power to move us in complex ways," wrote the friend who recently sent me MacLeish's poem as a reminder of that era. "When we encounter them—this evolution of romantic love into domestic peace, love, and tranquility—even the most cynical and liberated among us catch our breath and wonder if something irreplaceable has been lost." If contemporary promoters of family values are overly nostalgic about this romanticized family form, their critics are often equally one-sided in their dismissal of it.[19]

The veneer of domestic bliss only partially concealed an increasing restlessness on the part of both husbands and wives (not to mention their children, for whom the 1960s would provide many creative [and not so creative] outlets for their discontent). Many women and men felt frustrated and unhappy with this supposedly "natural" family form. Some fathers felt alienated from their families, and especially from their children. Though they watched Ward Cleaver, Jim Anderson, and other devoted dads on television sitcoms, a large number of middle-class American men were better fathers in theory than in practice; they talked more about spending more time with their children than they actually did. Full-time housewifery and motherhood were "something new and historically unprecedented," and wives, laboring under the "senseless tyranny of spotless shirts and immaculate floors," swallowed their growing resentment as the world passed them by. In his 1957 panorama of American culture, *America as a Civilization,* historian Max Lerner discussed the "ordeal" of the modern woman, arguing that "the unhappy wife has become a characteristic culture type."[20]

Such unhappiness also fueled an increasingly politicized anger. In 1963, Betty Friedan's feminist call to arms, *The Feminine Mystique,* rang like a tocsin across those neatly manicured suburban lawns and campus quadrangles. Calling the suburban home a "comfortable concentration camp," she declared that real life lay outside worrying about dishpan hands and diaper rash. Beatniks, playboys, and juvenile delinquents presented three alternatives to the suburban breadwinner. And the era's popular music exposed the ironies of such "well-respected men" and their wives, gulping vast quantities of "mother's little helper."[21]

In fact, no sooner was it fully established and acknowledged, than this "traditional" family began to crack under the enormous weight put upon it. The family was supposed to be the sole source of comfort and pleasure in an increasingly cold bureaucratic world; the marital union was the single most important and sustaining bond of intimacy and friendship that a person could have. Gone were the more "traditional" supports of community networks, civic participation, and extended kinship ties—now the family was supposed to provide for all psychological and emotional needs.

It was almost too much to bear; the "traditional" family was an anachronism from the moment of its birth. In the 1960s, fewer than one-half (43 percent) of American families conformed to the traditional single-earner model; one-fourth (23 percent) were dual-earner couples. Yet nearly nine out of ten (88 percent) white children under the age of eighteen lived with both parents, and 9 percent lived with one parent, and 3 percent with neither parent. Among black families, two-thirds (67 percent) lived with both parents and one-fifth lived in mother-only households.

The family of the 1970s and early 1980s was actually stronger and more resilient because of its increasing diversity of form. In the early 1970s, Theodore Caplow and a team of sociologists returned to Middletown (Muncie, Indiana) fifty years after the landmark historical study of small-town America conducted by Robert and Helen Lynd. They found the family in better shape than it had been in the 1920s. Much of the credit was due to economic and social conditions—better pay, more leisure time, improved housing. Parents spent more time with their children than they had a half-century earlier. More flexible gender roles, women's increased opportunities, and increased knowledge about birth control and sexuality had markedly enhanced husbands' relationships with their wives.[22]

But since the early 1980s, the family has indeed been in trouble, partly because of the dramatic withdrawal of public supports. Decreased and depressed wages, especially for men, decreased leisure time, decreased funding for public housing, greater needs for both parents to work, and the return to earlier restrictions on access to birth control and to abortion have all led to dramatic declines in the quality of family life. Many of the problems associated with the family are really problems that are attendant upon economic downturn. In 1970, 15 percent of all children under age eighteen were living in families defined as "poor"; today that number is closer to one-fourth.[23]

For middle-class families the erosion of leisure time and the increasing demands of work have added strain to already attenuated family relationships. The "5 O'Clock Dad" of the 1950s family has become "an endangered species." More than 10 percent of men with children under six years old work more than sixty hours a week, and 25 percent more work between fifty and sixty hours. (Fewer than 8 percent of women with children that young work such long hours.) Ever resilient and responsive to the progressive erosion of the family foundation, American families have responded with a host of changes and modifications—as well as a host of prophets and pundits promoting false solutions.[24]

Since the 1960s, the age of first marriage has crept steadily upward, increasing by three years for both women (twenty-four) and men (twenty-six). The numbers of children has steadily declined as couples have delayed child bearing so that both women and men could attend college and establish themselves in the labor force. Today only half of American children live in nuclear families with both parents. One-fifth live in step families, and one-fourth live in single-parent homes. The number of single parents has increased about 6 percent a year. While single parents living with their children counted for only 13 percent of all families in 1970; they represented more than one-fourth (29 percent) of all families by 1991, and 23 percent of all families in which the children are eighteen or under. Fathers currently head 14 percent of all single-head households with children. These percentages are the highest among industrial nations.[25]

The number of people who have not married by age 30 has increased from 11 percent for women and 19 percent for men in 1970 to 31 percent of women and 45 percent of men. The numbers of women ages twenty-five to forty-four who had never married in 1950 were 9 percent for women of color and 10 percent for white women; by 1979, those numbers were 23 percent for women of color and 10 percent for white women. Cohabitation is increasingly common, and not simply as a phenomenon among college students and young people. (In fact, most cohabitors have never attended college and represent the least educated sector of society; cohabitation is replacing early marriage among poor and working-class people.) And 40 percent of all cohabiting households include children.[26]

At the same time, divorce rates have soared. There were only about 2 divorces per 1,000 married women ages fifteen and older in 1860, and about four in 1900, there are more than twenty today. Nearly one-half of all marriages begun in 1980 and 1990 will end in divorce. These divorce rates are the highest in the industrial world. Most divorces occur after only a few years of marriage. As a result, it might be fair to say that the family is less the "haven in a heartless world" of nostalgic sentimentalism and more like a "shock absorber" of contradictory pressures from the world outside it. The "traditional" family—male breadwinner, housewife mother—is the norm in about one household in ten, while dual-earner families and other family forms (including single-parent households and gay and lesbian families) comprise about 40 percent each.[27]

A recent article in *Newsweek* asserted that "the American family does not exist." Rather, the article suggested, "we are creating many American families, of diverse styles and shapes. . . . We have fathers working while mothers keep house; fathers and mothers working away from home; single parents; second marriages . . . childless couples; unmarried couples with and without children; gay and lesbian parents." Such family diversity is well illustrated by one prominent contemporary political figure: a white middle-class Southern boy, born into a single-parent family, raised by his mother alone, who divorced his first wife, has never paid alimony or child support, has no contact with his children, and has a lesbian sister who is starting her own family. Who could such a model of diversity be? It's Newt Gingrich, once the Speaker of the House of Representatives—and—Mr. Family Values.[28]

As the family has changed, so too have our ideas about it. Family sociologist Scott Coltrane writes that "support for separate spheres and the automatic dominance of men has weakened dramatically in the past few decades, though a substantial minority of Americans still clings to the so-called traditional view." Consider one or two examples: In the mid-1970s, one man being interviewed by sociologist Lillian Rubin said that "[i]f a man with a wife and kids needs a job, no woman ought to be able to take it away from him." Few men today would express such a sense of entitlement to those jobs as to consider them "his" property. In 1977, two-thirds of Americans agreed with the statement that "it is much better for everyone involved if the man is the achiever outside the home and the woman takes care of the home and family." Twenty years later, fewer than two out of five (38 percent) agreed with it, and fewer than 30 percent of all baby boomers agreed. In 1977, more than half agreed with the statement that "it is more important for the wife to help her husband's career than to have one herself." By 1985 slightly over one-third (36 percent) agreed, and by 1991 29 percent did. Today the number is closer to one-fourth.[29]

These sentiments are echoed around the world. In a recent international Gallup Poll, fewer than half of those questioned agreed that the "traditional" male breadwinner/ female housewife model was desirable in the United States (48 percent), Chile (49 percent), France (46 percent), and Japan (46 percent). In only one country, Hungary, did a majority agree (66 percent); while several countries found less than one-third of the population supporting this family structure, including Spain (27 percent), India (28 percent), Germany (28 percent), and Taiwan (26 percent).

The "traditional" family, a normative ideal when it was invented, has never been the reality for all American families. And it is even less so today. It represents the last outpost of traditional gender relations—gender differences created through gender inequality—that are being challenged in every observable arena. Families are gendered institutions; they reproduce gender differences and gender inequalities among adults and children alike. Families raise children as gendered actors, and remind parents to perform appropriate gender behaviors. It is no wonder, then, that each specific aspect of family life—marriage, child rearing, housework, divorce—expresses the differences and the inequalities of gender.

GENDERED MARRIAGE

Consider, for a moment, how we think about marriage. A woman devises some clever scheme to "trap" a man. When she's successful, her friends all celebrate the upcoming nuptials with delighted anticipation at a bridal shower. Women celebrate their weddings—they have finally "landed" a man. Their future is secure. By contrast, men "mourn" their upcoming nuptials. They've been trapped, and the future that stretches out before them is now heavy with responsibilities laid upon them by the "old ball and chain," the smiling warden of their personal prison. The bachelor party, traditionally held the night before the wedding, exudes a mournful, elegiac quality underneath it's raucous exterior, as the groom goes out with his male friends for his "last night of freedom," a night that often consists of smoking fat cigars, getting rip-roaring drunk, and watching porn movies, and/or hiring lap dancers or prostitutes.

If you believed this cultural definition of marriage—something she wants and he has to be coerced or tricked into—you would think that marriage benefited women, that it was "their" domain. Yet according to much social science research, you would be mistaken. In the early 1970s, sociologist Jessie Bernard identified two distinct marriages, "his" and "hers." And, she argued, "his is better than hers." Marriage benefits men. All psychological measures of indices of happiness and depression suggest that married men are much happier than unmarried men, while unmarried women are somewhat happier than married women. (The greatest difference is between married and unmarried men.) A greater proportion of men than women eventually marry; husbands report being more satisfied than wives with their marriages; husbands live longer and enjoy better health benefits than unmarried men, as well as better health than women; and, fewer men than women try to get out of marriage by initiating divorce. After divorce, men remarry much more quickly than women, and widowers die sooner after the death of a spouse than widows. Married men earn more than single men. And single men are less likely to be employed, tend to have lower incomes than married men, and are more prone to crime and drug use.[30]

All this suggests that marriage is a better deal for men than it is for women. And how could it be otherwise? Given the traditional division of labor in the family (she works, he doesn't) and the nontraditional division of labor outside the family (he works, and she probably does, too), the husband who works outside the home receives the emotional and social and sexual services that he needs to feel comfortable in the world. His wife, who (probably) works as well, also works at home providing all those creature comforts—and receives precious few of them in return. As *New York Times* writer Natalie Angier summed up this research, "marriage is pretty good for the goose much of the time, but golden for the gander practically all of the time."[31]

To be sure, marriage also benefits women, and is therefore positive for both. According to sociologist Linda Waite, married people have more sex more often than unmarried people, and enjoy it more. Married people have longer life expectancies and fewer health problems, lower levels of risky behavior, suicide, depression, and other psychological problems. And married people save more.

Some of these benefits are explained by other factors that have little, if anything, to do with the matrimonial state. For example, married men's higher incomes seems to come from the unequal politics of housework (the wife's doing the housework frees the married man to work longer hours), and the fact that married couples save more has more to do with women in the labor force than it does with being married. And the fact that the benefits of marriage fall far more readily toward men would suggest that marriage increases, not diminishes, gender inequality. Women and men are unequal going into their marriages, and marriage only exacerbates this inequality, by benefiting men more than women.[32]

In recent years, some of the subjective measures of marital happiness have declined for both women and men. The sharp reversal of young men's economic prospects—the declining wages of white men in the Reagan era and since—combined with the increased tension in work-family negotiations, changing attitudes about child care and housework, and the absence of governmental provision of a structural foundation of adequate health care, child care, and family friendly workplace policies have all led to increased strains on marriage. Can the family continue to absorb the shock, as these forces buffet an institution that is at once so enduring and so fragile?

GENDERED PARENTS, GENDERING CHILDREN

Another cause of the decline in marital happiness is, surprisingly, children. Children tend to put a damper on marital bliss. Couples who remain childless report higher levels of marital satisfaction than do those with children. They're better educated, more likely to live in cities, and the wives are more committed to their careers. They have more savings and investments, of course, and are more apt to buy an expensive home in their fifties. Marital happiness sinks with the arrival of the first baby, plunges even farther when the first child hits school age, and drops again when he or she hits the teenage years. Husbands begin to feel better about their marriages once their children turn eighteen, but wives don't feel better about their marriages until after the children leave home, according to Mary Bebin, a sociologist at Arizona State University.[33] Yet having and raising children is one of the major purposes of the family, its raison d'être. If one of the chief purposes of the family is to maintain both gender inequality and gender difference between the parents, then its other chief purpose is to ensure that those gendered identities are imparted to the next generation. It is in the family that the seeds of gender difference are first planted, that we first understand that being a man or a woman, a boy or a girl, has different, and unequal, meanings.

Gender socialization begins at birth and continues throughout our lives. How do parents influence gender differences in their children? Parents possess a set of gender-specific ideas of what their children need; that is, they were themselves socialized to some belief in what girls and boys of various ages are like. Through college courses and textbooks, the popular press, child-rearing manuals, "old wives' tales" admonitions from friends and relatives, reports from other parents, and adages (such as "What are little girls made of? Sugar and spice and everything nice" and "What are little boys made of? Frogs and snails and puppy dogs' tails"), they have developed not only the construct *child*, but also constructs *boy child* and *girl child*, and they attach different expectations to them.

Parents also have hopes and desires for what kinds of adults their children will be, what types of roles they will play (however vaguely defined), and ideas about what adult "personality" characteristics are most valuable for effectively playing those roles. In addition, parents observe what they perceive as "typical behavior" of girls and boys their own child's age. Throughout childhood, gender difference and gender inequality are created and reinforced through play, the media, and the schools.

Gender typing begins even before the child is born. Prior to the widespread use of amniocentesis (a medical technique that can be used to detect genetic defects as well as the gender of the fetus), parents spent hours speculating about the sex of the as-yet-unborn child, often making guesses based upon the amount of kicking and other intrauterine behavior. Relatives and friends contributed opinions whether the baby was "high" or "low," and making such comments as, "With that much activity, it must be a boy!" In those cases where amniocentisis is not used and in those countries where these medical developments are not available, parents still spend time speculating about the sex of their child.

Announcing the child's birth announces its gender—typically a card that says, "It's a Boy!" or "It's a Girl!" on the front. Before you know anything else about the baby, you know its sex. It's only when you open the card that you know his or her name, other vital characteristics, and often, who the parents are! The amused remarks of visitors during the first days echo the same gendered sentiments. While some people may feel that gender stereotyping is inappropriate, in a majority of cases boys are still greeted with such comments as, "Who knows, some day he may be president," or, "With that size he'll grow up to be a football player," and girls are more likely to elicit such comments as, "She's beautiful; she'll really knock the boys out when she grows up!" or, "It won't be too long before she's a mother too."

During infancy, expectations about how each gender ought to be treated lead to different behaviors by parents and other adults. A large body of research has yielded findings about this issue that I can only briefly summarize. During the first six months of life, mothers tend to look at and talk to girl infants more than to boy infants, and mothers tend to respond to girls' crying more immediately than they do to boys'. In fact, these behaviors tend to be greater for girls over the first two years of life. Boys, on the other hand, receive more touching, holding, rocking, and kissing than do girls in the first few months, but the situation is reversed by age six months. By one year, female infants are allowed and encouraged to spend significantly more time than males in touching and staying in close proximity to their mothers. The girls are encouraged to move away at later ages, but never as much as boys are. Parents' interest in building autonomy or independence seems to explain this difference. As a result of gender stereotypes, mothers believe that boys rather than girls should be independent and encourage them to explore and master their world. Many mothers start to wean their sons from physical contact with themselves at an earlier age. And parents, in general, are more restrictive with their daughters and create more limits on their acceptable behavior from a very early age.

Parents' early treatment of their infant is usually not a deliberate effort to teach the child a "proper" gender role, but rather reflects the fact that the parents themselves accept the general societal roles for men and women. Though no longer universal, it is still the case that often sons are treated as though they are "naturally" sturdy and active; they are played with more roughly, and greeted with smiles and other indications of pleasure when they respond appropriately. And girls are still thought to be more delicate and gentle, and sweetness and cooperation are likely to elicit parental approval.

Other adults reinforce these different parental behaviors. Researchers have found that people interact with infants based more on their assumptions about what is appropriate for the gender than on the characteristics of the child itself. For example, subjects in one experiment consistently gave gender-specific toys (dolls for girls, hammers for boys) to infants who, they were told, were either girls or boys. They described the babies, whose sex they did not know, with highly gendered adjectives—"strong" and "big" for boys and "soft" and "pretty" for girls. (Obviously, in this kind of experiment, the subjects were as likely to be right as they were to be wrong, and so they were describing the infants more in terms of information received *about* them than any direct observation of them.) One experiment showed a videotape of a nine-month-old's reaction to a jack-in-the-box, a doll, a teddy bear, and a buzzer. Half the observers were told the child was a boy; the other half were told it was a girl. When asked about the child's expressions of anger, fear, and pleasure the observers saw different emotions when the child played with the jack-in-the box. The child's reaction was agitated, and then the child cried. Those who thought the child was a boy thought "he" was angry; those who thought the child was a girl thought "she" was afraid.[34]

As the child moves from the infant to the toddler stage, somewhere around age two, research shows that gender typing increases. Boys are told, "Boys don't cling to their mothers," and, "Big boys don't cry." Boys' independence, aggression, and suppression of emotion are rewarded, and failure to comply brings increasing disapproval. Girls are encouraged to express emotions and control aggression, and they are given more opportunities to be dependent; crying is tolerated longer than among boys.

The toys children play with are designed to be sold as girls' toys or boys' toys. Girls are given dolls and doll houses; boys get trucks and building blocks, and are told that they are "sissies" if they want to play with girls' toys. These labels come originally from adults, for it has been noted that, at age two-and-a-half, many boys prefer dolls and doll houses; they are urged away from them because parents consider them to be girls' toys. Parental responses are quickly absorbed by the children, who shortly thereafter display quite different toy and game preferences. Advertisements, salespeople, and other agents of socialization all reinforce these cues from parents, and children pick up cues all around themselves. These toys are also seen as embodying certain emotional traits that are consistent with men or women. Lott argues that toys for girls encourage dependency on others, while toys for boys stress independence and problem solving.[35]

From a very early age, physical appearance is tied to social definitions of masculinity and femininity. Girls are rewarded for their looks and for appearing attractive, while boys are more frequently rewarded for physical performance. These differences continue well into adolescence. Girls are taught to capitalize on good looks, cuteness, and coyness, and learn to look in mirrors and seek reflections of themselves from others. Boys discover that athletic ability and performance are what count for males.

The earliest interaction with other children is an arena where children express and utilize the gender expectations that they have picked up from parents and the world around them. Researchers have found that after only one year in school, children tend to discriminate in their choices of playmates, choosing those of their own sex and excluding those of the opposite sex. Psychologists Eleanor Maccoby and Carol Jacklin's research indicates that children, regardless of gender, prefer to play with other children like themselves. Their study of two-to-three-year-old children raises interesting questions. Jacklin and Maccoby took pairs of children (some were same-sex pairs and others were cross-sex pairs), dressed them alike, and had them play together. Observers were unable to tell if the children were boys or girls, or if the pairs were same or cross-sex. (Of course, the children were able to tell.) The results indicated that the same-sex pairs played more peacefully and steadily together than did the cross-sex pairs.[36]

Most experimental research suggests that boys and girls begin very early to develop two gender cultures that are dramatically different. Though they do not begin their lives in sex-segregated play worlds, children increasingly play with members of their own sex. In these sex-segregated play worlds, boys learn the prototypes of behaviors that will be expected of them as men, including those behaviors that characterize the sexual expectations of adult men. At the same time, girls learn prototypes of the behaviors that will be expected of them as women, also including sexual expectations. Boy's play is more rough-and-tumble and competitive, designed to permit some boys to win and others to lose. Boys attempt to influence the direction of the play with direct demands; girls use more subtle and indirect methods to try to influence each other. Boys play to achieve dominance; girls play to make sure everyone has a good time.[37]

In their play worlds, boys and girls accomplish their gender identities in different ways. Girls are often "banned" from some sports and allowed to play others only under simpler rules (e.g., touch or flag football). Even when they play the same sports, boys and girls do not play them together. When asked why they didn't, they replied, almost amused, with statements such as, "Don't you know, boys don't play with girls," as if the adults were strange not to already know that.

In general, boys tend to acquire masculinity as much by avoiding anything feminine as by imitating men directly. By contrast, girls' activities and identities seem to be more directly modeled on imitation than on repudiation or avoidance of masculinity. On the surface, this observation echoes Freud's idea that for boys, separation from mother entails a life-long repudiation of femininity as the mechanism by which the boy establishes his autonomy; for girls, the project is to root one's identity in identification with the mother, thereby reinforcing the concreteness of the identification. But this may be a result of the materials from which children construct their gender identities rather than the result of some innate drive. For example, think about the kinds of images boys and girls see in comic books and television shows. Think about the kinds of role playing that boys and girls do. Boys will role play mythic heroes (cowboys, Indians, soldiers, superheroes, Ninja Turtles), while girls often role play mothers, nurses, and teachers. That is, boys learn that their future vistas are limitless, playing at identities that defy conventional limits; girls learn that their future worlds are bounded by concrete social constraints. Though this has changed significantly in recent years, it has changed far more for girls than for boys. Girls now play soccer and fantasize about becoming Xena or Buffy the Vampire Slayer, who are clearly stronger and sexier than any of the men they routinely conquer.

Early gender distinctions are far from absolute, but the direction of change has tended to go in only one way. Some girls are "tomboys," and may be allowed to play in informal neighborhood games when extra players are needed. But it is only in recent years that formal organized sports leagues, such as in soccer and softball, have been opened to girls. For boys, the opportunities to play at girls' games are rare; the label sissy is more negative than the label tomboy. Girls have more "boy toys" than boys have "girl toys." There is a series of "boy things" that are all right for girls to do, but, by and large, there is no transfer the other way.

This asymmetry in crossing over to the other gender's play style also indicates the way that masculinity is far more rigid a role construction than femininity, and how that rigidity is also part of the coercive mechanisms of gender role socialization. Gender is not simply the expression of what is "right" and "appropriate"; rather, our cultural definitions of what is right and appropriate are derived from the ways in which adults see things, and in part, depend upon who it is that makes up the rules in the first place. Children's play both expresses and anticipates the inequality that informs gender relations in adulthood.[38]

Boys and girls both understand the inequality between women and men, and understand, too, that their less-than-equal status gives girls a bit more latitude in the types of cross-sex (gender-inappropriate) behavior they may exhibit. Girls think they'd be better off as boys, and many of them declare that they would rather be boys than girls. By contrast, boys tend to see being girls as a fate worse than death. "If I were a girl," one third grader said, "everybody would be better than me, because boys are better than girls."

Statements like this make us wince because they reveal how deeply connected are gender difference and gender inequality, and how the former serves as the justification for the latter. This little boy, like millions of other little boys, has come to understand that his status in the world depends upon his ability to distance himself from femininity. By exaggerating gender difference, he both assures and reassures himself of his higher status. It is largely through the routine daily events of family life that children learn what it means to be boys or girls, and it is through those same events that gender inequality is reproduced between grown up women and men. Children's interactions "are not preparation for life," sociologist Barrie Thorne concludes. "They are life itself."[39]

The Gendered Politics of Housework and Child Care

We are living through a historic fundamental transformation of family life. Perhaps the greatest single shock the family has had to absorb has been the entry of women into the workplace. This is, perhaps, the most profound and dramatic social change in American society in the last century, rippling outward to transform every other social institution. That women now work outside the home as a matter of course, of economic necessity, and of ambition and will has dramatically altered the life of the modern family. Some would like to turn back the clock to the rather unusual and short-lived family form that emerged in the 1950s, and reassert it as the norm. Such a vision is unlikely to be embraced by most men, let alone most women, who today work outside the home because they want to and because they have to—and because it's good for them, good for their husbands, and good for their children.

Working mothers report higher levels of self-esteem and are less depressed than full-time housewives. Yet they also report lower levels of marital satisfaction than do their husbands, who are happier than the husbands of traditional housewives. Why would this be so? In part, because women's workload actually increases at home, while the men benefit by having almost the same amount of work done for them at home and having their standard of living buttressed by an additional income.[40]

So women today are working more but enjoying family life less. Perhaps one reason women are so tired and unhappy is that they remain responsible for what sociologist Arlie Hochschild has called "the second shift," the housework and child care that every family must do to function properly. The movement of women from the home to the workplace has not been accompanied by a comparable movement of men back into the home. The transformation of American life promised by women's entry into the labor force is a "stalled revolution," a revolution that depends, now, on changes in men's attitudes and behaviors.

In 1970, a young feminist writer described what she saw as "the politics of housework." In the spirit of the feminist slogan "the personal is political," Pat Mainardi argued that the separation of spheres that defined the traditional family and made housework "women's work" was a reflection of male domination, not the expression of some feminine biological predisposition toward laundry or dishwashing. Women did housework and child care because they *had* to, she argued, not because they *wanted* to, or because of some genetic master plan. And men didn't do housework because they could get out of it.[41]

Few people actually *like* doing housework. "A woman's work is never done, and happy she whose strength holds out to the end of the [sun's] rays," wrote Martha Moore Ballard in her diary in 1795. Nearly a century later, Mary Hallock Foote wrote: "I am daily dropped in little pieces and passed around and devoured and expected to be whole again next day and all days and I am never *alone* for a single minute." And in 1881, Helen Campbell wrote that spring housecleaning was "a terror to every one, and above all to gentlemen, who resent it from beginning to end." Perhaps Emily Dickinson said it best (using the passive voice). " 'House' is being 'cleaned,' " she wrote. "I prefer pestilence." (Of course, she wasn't the one cleaning it; Bridget and her other servants simply disturbed her peace.)[42]

Dozens of studies have assessed the changing patterns of housework, child care, and the different amounts of investments in family life. Who does what? How do people decide? Are men doing more now than they used to? Can they be encouraged/asked/cajoled/forced to do more? One statistic about family involvement is revealing of a larger pattern. Most studies, as you will see, suggest how little men's participation in family life has changed. In one respect, though, it has changed dramatically and completely. Thirty years ago, virtually no fathers were present at the births of their children; today more than 90 percent are present in the delivery room. If men *want* to change their involvement in the family, there is evidence that they are capable of doing so quickly and relatively easily.[43]

When it comes to other areas of family involvement, though, such as housework, the evidence reveals little change. Virtually all researchers have come to the same conclusion: men's participation in family work has been "surprisingly resistant to change." One study of 489 married couples found that men share household responsibility "only occasionally." Another found the percentage of men who fully share housework to be about one-fifth. (But the one-fifth who do share housework were the happiest couples in the study.) The percentage of housework men do compared to women decreases as men grow older; this may, in part, be because the changes in men's household participation occurred relatively recently, and older men grew up expecting to do little to none.[44]

And what men do is dramatically different from what women do. It's as if our houses were divided into discrete "zones"—his and hers—and husbands and wives had their own sphere of responsibility. "His" domain is outdoors—the yard, the driveway—or an outdoor space moved indoors, such as the basement, garage, trash receptacles, and den; "her" domain is always indoors—the kitchen, laundry room, bedrooms, and bathroom. (If she moves outdoors, it is often with an "indoor" element—hanging laundry, tending the garden.) These two domains demand different types of activities. In one study, women and men were asked to list all the different things they do around the house. The total number of items on each list was roughly equivalent. But when the specific tasks were examined, the men listed items such as "wash the car" and

"mow the lawn," while the women listed "cook the meals" and "make the beds." As
Arlie Hochschild explains:

> Even when couples share more equitably in the work at home, women do two-thirds of the
> daily jobs at home, like cooking and cleaning up—jobs that fix them into a rigid routine.
> Most women cook dinner and most men change the oil in the family car. But, as one mother
> pointed out, dinner needs to be prepared every evening around six o'clock, whereas the car
> oil needs to be changed every six months, any day around that time, any time that day.[45]

What's more, men tend to see their participation in housework *in relation* to their wives'
housework; women tend to see their work as necessary for family maintenance. That's
why men use terms like "pitch in" or "help out" to describe the time they spend in
housework—as if the work was their wives' to do. "When men do the dishes it's called
helping," Anna Quindlen, op-ed writer for the *New York Times* observed wryly. "When
women do dishes, that's called life."[46]

It is true that men's share of housework has increased significantly; "husbands of
working wives are spending more time in the family than in the past." In 1924, 10 percent of working-class women said their husbands spent "no time" doing housework;
today that percentage is less than 2 percent. Between the mid-1960s and the mid-1970s,
men's housework increased from 104 to 130 minutes a day, while women's decreased
from 7.4 to 6.8 hours a day. In another survey of 4,500 married dual career couples
between the ages of twenty-five and forty-four, 15 percent of the men admitted that
they performed less than one hour of housework per week. The median amount for
men was about five hours a week; for women it was about twenty hours. Men reported
that they did 10 percent of the housework in 1970, and 20 percent in 1990—which,
depending upon how you look at it, represents double the percentage in only twenty
years, or, still, only one-fifth the amount that needs to be done.[47]

Although men report that they currently do between one-fifth and one-fourth of
all domestic labor, there is some evidence that asking people how much housework
they do leads to rather large inaccuracies, for people often report how much they think
they ought to be doing, not how much they actually do. Both women and men overreport the amount of housework they do—men overreport by about 150 percent, more
than double the overreporting by women (68 percent). Interestingly, more privileged
husbands with egalitarian gender attitudes tended to overreport at a higher rate than
more traditional husbands, who probably believed that they should not be doing so
much housework. Less-privileged "supermoms" were more likely to overreport their
housework than more privileged working mothers, because only such inflated hours
could justify their staying at home. The overreporting by men was so significant that
the researchers doubt "that husbands have increased their supply of domestic labor to
the household in the past 25 years."[48]

Other survey methodologies have yielded results that make me confident that
men's participation in housework has increased somewhat over the past quarter-
century, though probably not as much as men themselves might claim. When couples
were asked to keep accurate records of how much time they spent doing which household tasks, men still put in significantly less than their wives. The most recent study
using time diaries found that men were doing sixteen hours of housework per week—

up from twelve hours in 1965. (This is four times the amount of housework that Japanese men do, but only two-thirds of the housework that Swedish men do.) Men's increased participation has not been a steady progressive rise; rather, it increased from 1965 to 1985, and has leveled off since.[49]

In fact, the major findings of these recent studies is not that men are doing more housework but that less housework is being done—by anyone. In 1965, women did forty hours a week; now they do twenty-seven, so the total amount of time that men and women spend doing housework has decreased from fifty-two hours to forty-three hours per week. And marriage tends to exacerbate the differences between women and men. It turns out that men reduce their housework when they form a couple, and increase it when they leave; women increase their time spent in housework when they form a couple, and reduce it when they leave.[50]

Housework turns out to fluctuate a lot by timing, season, and marital status, and among different groups of men. Not all men are doing more housework; or, rather, some men are doing more of it than others. Men's changing experience of family life depends on age, race, class, and level of education. Younger men, for example, are doing far more around the house than their fathers did—though their wives still do a lot more. A poll of women younger than thirty in *Ladies Home Journal* in May 1997 found that 76 percent said they do most of the laundry; 73 percent do most of the cooking; 70 percent do most of the housecleaning; 67 percent do most of the grocery shopping; and 56 percent pay most of the bills. In Canada, the numbers are similar: 77 percent of women prepare meals on an average day, compared with 29 percent of the men, and 54 percent of the women clean up after meals, compared with 15 percent of the men.[51]

Though we tend to think that sharing housework is the product of progressive, liberal, well-educated families, the data suggest another picture entirely. In every single subcategory (meal preparation, dishes, cleaning, shopping, washing, outdoor work, auto repair and maintenance, and bill paying) black men do significantly more housework than white men. In more than one-fourth of all black families, men do more than 40 percent of the housework, that is, men's "share" of housework comes closer to an equal share. In white families, only 16 percent of the men do that much. And blue-collar fathers—municipal and service workers, policemen, firefighters, maintenance workers—are twice as likely (42 percent) as those in professional, managerial, or technical jobs (20 percent) to care for their children while their wives work. This difference comes less from ideological commitments and more from an "informal flex time," a split shift arrangement with one's spouse, which is negotiated by about one-fourth of all workers in the United States, and one-third of all workers with children under age five.[52]

The presence of children increases the gender gap. Mothers spend far more time with children than fathers do, especially when the children are infants, when families report "very low levels of paternal engagement." Mothers spend 50 percent more time with kindergarten–fourth grade children than do fathers. Men's share of child care increases as the children get older, both requiring a different type of engagement and also perhaps offering more "fun" for dad. But when researchers asked about how much time each parent spends *alone* with the children, fathers averaged only 5.5 hours a week, mothers averaged closer to 20 (19.5) hours a week—a 350 percent difference. When they have children, men tend to spend longer hours at work, in part because they have to earn more to support their children, and in part because they either want to, or because they simply are able to. Their wives, of course, spend less time at work, thus exaggerating the gender gaps both at work and at home. "The gender gap is present even with no children," notes sociologist Beth Ann Shelton, "but it is exacerbated by the presence of children in the household."[53]

Children learn the gender expectations that their parents teach them. One 1991 study found that daughters of women working full-time did more than ten hours a week of housework; sons did less than three hours a week. A recent study found that one of the best predictors of men's participation in child care was whether or not their fathers did housework and child care. One consultant who runs workshops called Grateful Dad found a more seasonal fluctuation in men's participation around the house. While pundits fished around for possible explanations, he had a more parsimonious answer: Football season was over.[54] Such research makes me think that the appropriate response to the feminist-inspired Take Our Daughters to Work Day—during which parents take their daughters to their workplaces to demystify it and to show them that they, too, can have ambition—would be a National Son Day, a Sunday afternoon when fathers would teach their sons how to wash the dishes, do the laundry, make the beds, and vacuum the floors—provided, of course, that the fathers know how to do such things!

Yet there is some evidence of change in men's participation in child care. The major pull toward increasing men's participation in domestic work is as fathers, not as husbands. Men seem to maintain the contradictory ideas that they want to shield and protect their wives from life's unpleasantness, while they steadfastly refuse to perform a task as degrading as washing out the toilet. According to demographer Martha Farnsworthe Riche, "The great lesson of the past 15 to 20 years is that men don't care if the house is clean and neat, by and large." Or, as one wife noted, wearily, "I do my half, I do half of [my husband's] half, and the rest doesn't get done."[55]

But when it comes to being fathers, men are evidently willing to do more. A poll in *Newsweek* magazine found that 55 percent of fathers say that being a parent is more important to them than it was to their fathers, and 70 percent say they spend more time with their children than their fathers spent with them. A 1995 survey sponsored by Families and Work Institute found that 21 percent of the 460 men surveyed said that they would prefer to be home caring for their families if they had enough money to live comfortably. (This is actually a fairly low percentage, since the amount these men believed they needed in order to live comfortably was more than $200,000.)[56]

And they've had some support in becoming more active fathers. Dr. Benjamin Spock's multi-decade best-selling book *Babies and Child Care* noted (and perhaps even encouraged) the shift in thinking about father's involvement. In the first edition, Dr. Spock suggested that men could be somewhat involved in child care:

> Some fathers have been brought up to think that the care of babies and children is the mother's job entirely. This is the wrong idea. You can be a warm father and a real man at the same time. . . . Of course I don't mean that the father has to give just as many bottles or change just as many diapers as the mother. But it's fine for him to do these things occasionally. He might make the formula on Sunday.

In its most recent current edition (1998), however, Dr. Spock records the shifts his work has helped to bring about:

> Men, especially the husbands of women with outside jobs, have been participating increasingly in all aspects of home and child care. There is no reason why fathers shouldn't be able to do these jobs as well as mothers. . . . But the benefit may be lost if this work is done as a favor to the wife, since that implies that raising the child is not really the father's work but that he's merely being extraordinarily generous.[57]

Still, American men's participation in child care lags behind the rates of participation in other industrial countries. In Australia, Canada, and the Netherlands, men's rates are about double the rates in the United States, while in Britain the rates were about 40 percent higher. Former congresswoman Pat Schroeder used to tell a revealing story from her own life. Just after her first election, her husband explained to a journalist from *Redbook* that, in the future, it would be he who would be taking the children to the pediatrician. When she read the interview, Schroeder immediately telephoned her husband and said, "For $500, what is the name of the children's pediatrician?" He responded, somewhat sheepishly, that what he had meant was that he would be *willing* to take the children, if she asked him to.[58]

This anecdote is telling in another way. Men consistently report that they would *like* to spend more time with their children and families, *if they only could.* "No man, on his deathbed, ever regretted spending too much time with his family," is the way Senator Paul Tsongas put it when he left the senate. Many men say they want to do more, but demands of work continue to get in their way. Others fear being seen by their colleagues and bosses as less committed to their careers, and of being placed on a "daddy track" from which there will be no advancement. Still others continually bump up against inflexible ideas of what it means to be a man. "The person whom I damaged most by being away when [my children] were growing up was me," observed one man sadly. "I let my nurturing impulse dry up."

For some men (and women) these desires are spilling over into action. In a study sponsored by the Dupont corporation, 47 percent of managerial women and 41 percent of managerial men had told their supervisors that they would not be available for relocation; 32 percent of women and 19 percent of men had told their bosses that they would not take a job that required extensive travel; and 7 percent of the women and 11 percent of the men had already turned down a promotion they had been offered. To want to spend more time with the family is an old and tired male lament; to actually sacrifice career ambitions to do so is a new development, a most visible way to walk one's talk.[59]

Men often say that they want to be involved fathers and to spend more quality time with their children. But rarely are they willing to make such sacrifices in order to do it. The payoffs, however, when they do, can turn out to be great. Men who do more housework are also better fathers. And men who have closer relationships with their children report greater marital satisfaction and better health. They feel less stress (if you can believe that!) and less pressure to be successful, powerful, and competitive. They also live longer, causing the normally staid British financial magazine *The Economist* to quip, "Change a nappy, by God, and put years on your life." "When males take full responsibility for child care," sociologist Barbara Risman points out, "they develop intimate and affectionate relationships with their children." Nurturing their children is good for men's health. And, of course, increased family involvement by men benefits women, freeing them from the obligations of the second shift. And that enhances gender equality: recall that anthropologists found consistently that women's economic and political status is highest in those cultures in which men do more domestic work.[60]

To increase men's participation in housework and child care will require a combination of micro-level and macro-level supports. Individually, men have to *want* to do more, and they will also need support from their wives and from their male friends, coworkers, and colleagues. They'll need to know *how* to do it, as well, learning the set of skills that, taken together and performed regularly, constitute nurturing and caring—cooking, cleaning, laundry. "Unless fathers do a greater share of the work at home, mothers will remain disadvantaged in working outside the home. Mothers can't win unless fathers change, too."[61]

Working couples will also need to have structural, macrolevel supports, such as family friendly workplace policies, paid parental leave, and adequate health care. The United States is one of the few countries in the world without a national policy of paid maternity leave; some Nordic countries include additional paternity leave as well. Nearly every Western European country has a child allowance—a payment to families for each child they have, regardless of income or whether the mother is employed or not. And corporations have not stepped into the institutional breach created by such governmental indifference to the plight of working parents. Only 8 percent of American workers have any child care benefits provided by their employers. Corporate and governmental policies to promote the health and well-being of working families is a tall order, to be sure, but leaving individual family members to sort it out for themselves guarantees that little will change. The "failure to invest in children can lead to economic inefficiency, loss of productivity, shortages in needed skills, high health care costs, growing prison costs, and a nation that will be less safe, less caring, and less free."[62]

Perhaps the most interesting trend is the gradual separation of housework and child care over the last decade. While mothers and fathers are spending from four to six hours *more* per week with their children, women have dramatically decreased the amount of housework they do, and men have not exactly jumped in to fill the void. "Either the house is clean or I see my kids," is how one female doctor in Milwaukee put it. Evidently, choosing between housework and child care is easier than choosing between career or family.[63]

That women continue to perform the lion's share of the second shift puts enormous strains on marriage. Balancing work and family pulls working women in different directions, and either way they move, they are bound to feel guilty and frustrated. Even Karen Hughes, President George W. Bush's senior counselor and the architect of his policies, decided to return to Texas and her family because she couldn't have it all. One high-level executive, who recently quit her job, confessed that she "had as much going my way as any working mother could have. And I was absolutely flat-out. All I managed to do were the kids and my job. I could have continued to do this indefinitely, but I would have been a shell of myself."[64]

THE "CONSTRUCTED PROBLEMS"
OF CONTEMPORARY FAMILY LIFE

Obviously, a woman or a man who feels like a "shell of myself" cannot provide a strong foundation on which to build a family, with a vibrant marriage and healthy children who are nourished physically and emotionally. Yet, increasingly, that's how parents feel, and their relationships with each other and with their children suffer as a result. Without a concerted national policy to assist working women and men to balance work and family obligations, we continue to put such enormous strains on two sets of bonds, between husbands and wives and between parents and children, and virtually guarantee that the "crisis" of the family will continue. And we will also continue to face a series of "constructed problems"—problems that stem from the strain felt by individual families as they negotiate the increased pressures of sustaining dual-career couples and dividing housework and child care in the absence of help from the outside.

In the 1950s, the government stepped in where once the community and extended kinship networks had sustained family life, and created an infrastructure (schools, hospitals, roads, and suburban homes) that supported and sustained family life. Today, we expect families to accomplish far more—expect them, for example, to support children often beyond high school and college and to provide for virtually all of an adult's emotional needs—on far less. It is from this widening chasm between what we expect from our families and what support we offer them that several "constructed problems" emerge. These problems are also the result of gender inequality—both its persistence and the efforts by women to remedy it. Only when we develop a sustained national effort—both individually and politically—to reduce the gender inequality in both the home and the workplace, will these constructed problems begin to ease.

The "Problem" of Day Care

Take, for example, the "problem" of day care. Many American are reluctant to place their children in day care, the government has no national funding for day care centers, and employers contribute about 1 percent of the total spent on child care. There is virtually no quality care available for infants and toddlers, and the costs of private care are staggering to parents at all income levels. Yet the most common conclusion from the research on the impact of day care on children's development is that there are no negative psychological, intellectual, developmental, or emotional consequences to being in day care. In fact, there is some evidence that quality child care has positive effects on children's curiosity, their ability to share, create friendships, and become ready for school. What's more, a 1996 National Institutes of Health study found that children's attachment to their mothers is not affected by whether or not they are in day care, what age they enter, or how may hours they spend there.[65]

So there really is a "problem" with day care—despite its positive effects, there's not enough of it, it's not affordable, and the government and our employers don't seem to care very much about our children. But that is not the "problem" we are asked to worry about. Almost daily, we seem to be bombarded with headlines that remind us of negative consequences, including child sexual abuse at day care centers. The implication of such terrifying stories is that if these children were home with their mothers, where they "belong," such terrible things would not be happening to them. The "problem" of day care turns out to be a debate about whether or not women should be working outside the home. "Having a nanny read you a story isn't the same as having your mother do so," writes William R. Mattox, a senior writer for the conservative Family Research Council. "A mother's worth cannot be reduced to the cost of what a paid substitute might command. To suggest that it can is like saying that the value of a woman making love to her husband is equal to the going rate for prostitutes in the area."[66]

To ask whether or not women should work outside the home is, of course, to ask the wrong question. For one thing, it poses a class-based contradiction, since we encourage poor women to leave the home and go to work, and middle-class women to leave the workplace and return home. The landmark Welfare Reform legislation of 1996 requires that welfare recipients start working within two years of going on welfare. "It is difficult to argue that poor mothers should find jobs but that middle class mothers should stay home," writes family researcher Andrew Cherlin. And when they can find jobs, working-class and middle-class women are simply not going to stop working.[67]

Nor is there any reason that they should, since there is no evidence whatsoever that mothers working outside the home adversely affects children. In fact, most of the evidence indicates that both direct and indirect benefits accrue to children of working mothers. Such children tend to have expanded role models, more egalitarian gender role attitudes, and more positive attitudes toward women and women's employment. Daughters of employed women are more likely to be employed, and in jobs similar to those of their mothers, than daughters of nonemployed women. Moreover, adolescent children of working mothers assume more responsibility around the home, which increases their self-esteem.[68]

Working outside the home also increases women's self-esteem and sense of personal efficacy and well-being, so working mothers tend to be happier in their marriages—which makes divorce less likely. One study found that the happier wives were in their jobs, the happier they were in their marriages. In a four-year study sponsored by the National Institute for Mental Health, Rosalind Barnet observed three hundred dual-career families, and found that the women were neither depressed nor stressed out, but said they had good marriages and good relationships with their children. Another survey of more than eight hundred two-career couples found similar results.[69]

Not only *will* women continue to work outside the home, but they *should* work outside the home, argues Joan Peters. "If they do not, they cannot preserve their identities or raise children" who are able to be both independent and family-oriented. But, "women can do so successfully only if men take half the responsibility for child care." Again, the "solution" turns out to be social and political. Only one-third of all employees in large and mid-size U.S. companies can even receive unpaid parental leave. Both nationally and in each family, the solution turns out to be greater gender equality—not women working less outside the home, but men working more inside it.[70]

The "Problem" of "Babies Having Babies"

The problem of day care is related to the problem of "babies having babies"—the increasing fertility of teenage women. Despite the dramatic decline in overall fertility in the United States, one segment of the population has witnessed a rise in fertility rates—teenagers. About 1 million teen pregnancies occur in the United States each year. The United States currently has the highest rate of births to teenage mothers of all industrial nations—double that of the next highest country, the United Kingdom (which includes all of Ireland in its tabulation). Often the problem of teenage motherhood is a mask for what is really bothering its critics—women's sexual agency. Some concern stems from a disguised critique of feminism, which enables women to explore a healthy and safer sexuality. Efforts to stop teen motherhood have included, for example, increasing restrictions on access to birth control, and even birth control *information,* and restrictions on abortion, including parental consent and waiting periods.

Take, for example, the statistics on rates of teenage motherhood. In the mid-1950s, only about one-fourth (27 percent) of all girls had sexual intercourse by age eighteen; in 1988, 56 percent of girls and 73 percent of boys had sexual intercourse by age eighteen. In 1991, the rate of adolescent childbearing—births to teen mothers per one thousand girls—was 62.1, the highest rate since 1971, which was the year before abortion was legalized. This accounts for 9 percent of all births in the nation. Two-thirds of these young women were unmarried, compared with 1960, when only 15 percent were unmarried.[71]

Such numbers can be "read" in several ways. For some, it illustrates a calamitous increase in teen motherhood, attributable to wanton teenage sexuality and rampant immorality, an erosion of respect for the institution of marriage, and the growing crisis of fatherlessness. But for others, it illustrates the erosion of access to adequate birth control information, the steady attacks on women's right to choose that restrict women's access to abortion and other means of birth control, and the increased freedom of young people from their parents' insistence on "shotgun weddings."

On these questions, the research is unanimous: Restricting access to information about birth control, access to birth control, and access to abortion have no bearing on rates of sexual activity. In fact, virtually all studies of the effect of sex education indicate a *decrease* in rates of sexual activity, greater sexual selectivity, and higher rates of safer sex practices. Young people will continue to become sexually active in their mid-teens, whether or not they have access to birth control or information about it. In fact, restricting access is the surest way to encourage unwanted pregnancy. No wonder the highest rates of teen pregnancy occurred before abortion was legal.

The crisis of babies having babies is also a way to blame women for men's irresponsibility. Politically, we are saying to young women that if they are going to dance (become sexually active) they will have to pay the piper (bear the consequences of unwanted pregnancies). But if, as we also know, it takes two to tango, perhaps the solution to the crisis of young motherhood lies both in increasing the abilities of these young women to become responsible (adequate health care, birth control information, and access to birth control) and in fostering a more responsible young manhood. In fact, casting the crisis as "babies having babies" masks another serious problem—young girls' sexual victimization by men. Most of the fathers of babies born to teenage mothers are *not* themselves teenagers, but are adult men whose predatory sexual behavior goes unnoticed when the problem is cast in this way.

Occasionally, the problem of babies having babies is merged into the problem of unwed parenthood in general. Out-of-wedlock births in America have increased 600 percent in the past three decades, from 5 percent of all births in 1960 to about one-third today. Out-of-wedlock births to black parents have increased from 22 percent in 1960 to almost 70 percent today. Doomsayers abound. David Blankenhorn, a conservative policy pundit, claims that the United States is moving toward "a post-marriage society" in which marriage is no longer a dominant institution. Again, one can attribute this to the increased freedom of both women and men from shotgun weddings, which certainly kept the number of out-of-wedlock births down. And, Andrew Cherlin points out that much of this increase is not to single mothers or welfare cheats, but to cohabiting white mothers. That is, most of the births are to people in commited relationships, who just don't happen to be married.[72]

But this controversy also illustrates the way family life and public policy are intimately connected. The percentage of out-of-wedlock births in the Nordic countries—Sweden, Norway, Denmark—is significantly higher than the rate in the United States. But there, with adequate child care, universal health care, and access to free education, the "need" of children to be born to married parents—access to parental health care programs, for example—is eliminated by a concerted policy of state spending to ensure the health and well-being of its citizens. So women and men marry when they want the additional sanctioning of religious authority, not because they need to be married for economic reasons.

The "Problem" of Fatherlessness

The question of men's responsibility also surfaces in the debates about fatherlessness. In recent years, commentators have noticed that fathers are not around, having left their children either through divorce or cavalier indifference. Recent works such as David Blankenhorn's *Fatherless America* or David Popenoe's *Life Without Father* have credited absent fathers with causing myriad social problems, ranging from juvenile delinquency, crime, and violence to unemployment. We read, for example, that 70 percent of all juveniles in state reform institutions come from fatherless homes. This bodes especially ill for young boys, because without a father, we are told, these young boys will grow up without a secure foundation in their manhood: "In families where the father is absent, the mother faces an impossible task: she cannot raise a boy into a man. He must bond with a man as he grows up," writes psychologist Frank Pittman. It is a mistake to believe that "a mother is able to show a male child how to be a man." "Boys raised by traditionally masculine fathers generally do not commit crimes," adds David Blankenhorn. "Fatherless boys commit crimes." In a home without a father, Robert Bly writes somewhat more poetically, "the demons have full permission to rage." This has consequences for both the fathers and the boys, creating in one moment two sets of unattached and unconstrained males roaming around the streets. "Every society must be wary of the unattached male," family researcher David Popenoe reminds us, "for he is universally the cause of numerous social ills."[73]

It is true that more children of both sexes are being raised in single-parent homes, and that the "single parent" doing that child raising is more often than not a woman. Whereas just over one in ten (11 percent) children were being raised by unmarried mothers in 1970, nearly one-fourth (24 percent) are being raised that way as of 1996. More than one in four (26 percent) of all birth are to single women. But the number of single fathers has increased from about 393,000 in 1970 (10 percent of all single parents raising children) to more than 2 million today (20 percent of single parents raising children)—without much appreciable decrease in raging demons.[74]

It's also true that the other side of the "feminization of poverty" coin is the "masculinization of irresponsibility"—the refusal of fathers to provide economically for their children. What is less certain, however, is the impact of fathers on the myriad social problems with which their absence seems to be correlated. Involvement by nonresident fathers does provide some benefits to children, and consistently predicts higher academic achievement—which argues for maintaining fathers' connection to their children. And although fatherlessness may be correlated with high crime rates, that does not mean that fatherlessness *caused* the criminality. In fact, it might just be the other way around. To be sure, high crime rates and fatherlessness are indeed correlated. But it turns out that they are *both* products of a larger and more overwhelming problem: poverty.[75]

The National Academy of Sciences reports that the single best predictor of violent crime is not fatherlessness but "personal and neighborhood income." And, it turns out, fatherlessness also varies with income; the higher the income bracket, the more likely the father is home—which suggests that the crisis of fatherlessness is actually a crisis of poverty. In his impressive ethnographic research on street gangs in Los Angeles, Martin Sanchez-Jankowski found "as many gang members from homes where the nuclear family was intact as there were from families where the father was absent" and "as many members who claimed close relationships with their families as those who denied them." Clearly, something other than the mere presence or absence of a father is at work here.[76]

Occasionally public policy actually discourages fathers from maintaining contact with their children after separation or divorce. Or for paying child support in the first place. If a poor man pays child support to the state government, the state typically keeps the money to pay itself back for welfare payments paid to its children, on the logic that poor children might otherwise double-dip. But as a result, the mother and children see no tangible evidence of the father's efforts to support his children. So, he might decide to give them money directly, under the table, which tangibly supports them, but does nothing to offset his allocated payments, so the state may still have his wages garnished, arrest him, or otherwise penalize him. (Only Wisconsin allows the father's payments to go directly to the family without a reduction in welfare benefits— a policy that motivates fathers to pay and reduces the amount of time that mothers stay on welfare.)[77]

The confusion of correlation and causation also reveals a deeper confusion of consequence and cause. Fatherlessness may be a consequence of those larger, deeper, more structural forces that drive fathers from the home and keep them away—such as unemployment or increased workplace demands to maintain a standard of living. Pundits often attempt to transform the problem of fatherlessness into another excuse to blame feminism, and specifically women working outside the home. They yearn for a traditional nuclear family, with traditional gender inequality. For example, David Popenoe writes nostalgically about the family form of the 1950s—"heterosexual, monogamous, life-long marriage in which there is a sharp division of labor, with the female as the full-time housewife and the male as primary provider and ultimate authority"—

without pausing to underscore that such a family form was also dramatically unequal when viewed from a gender perspective. Such a vision substitutes form for content, apparently under the impression that if only the family conformed to a specific form, then the content of family life would dramatically improve.[78]

The "Problem" of Divorce

It's hard to deny that divorce *is* a real problem. The divorce rate in the United States is astonishingly high, around half of all marriages—considerably higher than in other industrialized countries, more than double the rates in Germany and France, and nearly double the rate in Sweden and Britain—countries where individuals remain supported by national health care and children specifically benefit from adequate access to education and health care, while their custodial parents receive regular governmental stipends. (These, of course, ameliorate the harsh economic impact of divorce.) According to the Census Bureau, the number of divorced people had more than quadrupled from 4.3 million in 1970 to 19.3 million in 1997. This represents 10 percent of all adults aged eighteen or over, up from 3 percent in 1970.[79]

Divorce may be a serious social problem—but not exactly for the reasons that many political commentators claim it is. First, these high divorce rates are not shattering the family. Rates of marital dissolution are roughly the same as they have been for a very long time. Looked at historically, high rates of divorce are merely accomplishing by conscious action what higher mortality rates had accomplished in earlier period. As historian Lawrence Stone put it, "the median duration of marriage today is almost exactly the same as it was 100 years ago. Divorce, in short, now acts as a functional substitute for death: both are means of terminating marriage at a premature stage." (Of course, he adds, the psychological effects are not the same.)[80] Nor does the number of divorces necessarily indicate a loss of faith in marriage. Ninety-five percent of men and 94 percent of women between the ages of forty-five and fifty-four have been married. In fact, writes sociologist Constance Ahrons, author of *The Good Divorce,* "we like marriage so much that many of us will do it two, three, or more times." Remarriages now comprise about one-half of all marriages every year.[81]

The problem with divorce is more accurately linked to the constructed problem of fatherlessness and the real problem of gender inequality. Divorce reform was promoted, after all, by women who, at the turn of the last century, sought to provide legal recourse to those who wanted to escape marriages that were desperately unhappy, and others brutally, even violently oppressive. The option of divorce loosened the marital knot to keep it from choking women. Like birth control and abortion, both of which have also generated heated debates, divorce undermined men's power over women and reduced gender inequality in the family.

Although liberalized divorce laws may have reduced gender inequality within marriage, they seem neither to have reduced it entirely nor reduced it after the marriage is dissolved. One recent study found that three of four women listed pathological behaviors by male partners (adultery, violence, substance abuse, abandonment) as their reason for divorce. Just as there are "his" and "her" marriages, there are also "his" and "her" divorces because divorce affects wives and husbands differently. Divorce exaggerates gender differences in the marriage, exacerbating gender inequality. In the mid-

1980s, family researcher Leonore Weitzman calculated that following divorce, the woman's income drops a precipitous 73 percent, while her ex-husband's income increases 42 percent. In recent years, these data have been revised as overly dramatic, but no research suggests that the economic and social statuses of women and men after divorce are equivalent, and researchers still agree that women's resources decline somewhat more than men's. (Men's income goes down if their wives had careers.) As sociologist Paul Amato writes, "[T]he greater the inequality between men and women in a given society, the more detrimental the impact of divorce on women."[82]

Divorce has different impacts on women and on men. Many divorced fathers "lose almost all contact with their children over time," writes David Popenoe. "They withdraw from their children's lives." More than half of all divorced fathers have no contact with their children; even one-third of the noncustodial fathers who have written visitation provisions have not seen their children in the past year. Noncustodial mothers, however, rarely lose contact with their children after divorce, maintaining family connections over employment possibilities and new relationships. In addition, divorced men exhibit increased symptoms of psychological and emotional distress. Divorce seems to affect women more adversely in material and financial terms and men more adversely in emotional and psychological terms.[83]

What predicts continued paternal involvement in their children's lives after a divorce is the quality of the relationship between the ex-spouses prior to the divorce. And ironically, it also appears that is the men who were more involved with their children prior to the divorce who are most likely to disappear after it, while those who were relatively uninvolved prior to divorce tended to remain more active with their children afterward. In part, as Edward Kruk observes, this counterintuitive difference stems from the less-involved fathers also being more "traditional" in their outlooks, which would increase their sense of commitment to family life even after divorce; while more "liberal" men were more likely to see themselves as "free" from family responsibilities.[84]

The debate about divorce in contemporary America often has less to do with the divorcing couple and far more to do with the anticipated outcome on children. In a widely publicized study, psychologist Judith Wallerstein found that a significant number of children "suffer long-term, perhaps permanent detrimental effects from divorce," while other children repress these effects, only to have them emerge years later. Children, she argues, lose the "scaffolding" upon which they construct their development. "When that structure collapses," they write, "the children's world is temporarily without supports. And children, with a vastly compressed sense of time, do not know that the chaos is temporary." Ten years after divorce, Wallerstein found a significant number still adrift, troubled, and achieving less than expected. Many were having trouble establishing and sustaining relationships of their own. Twenty-five years after divorce, those problems have not disappeared—in fact, they may be exacerbated. "When people decide to divorce, it has a short-term and long-term traumatic effect upon the children that makes their subsequent life journey more difficult," she writes. A lousy marriage, she now concludes, beats a good divorce. And a "good enough" marriage will dramatically enhance children's lives.[85]

While such dire warnings as Wallerstein's have claimed countless magazine covers and public discussion, there is far less social science in her work than at first meets the eye. After following sixty-one families in an affluent California suburb, she concluded that about one-half the women and two-thirds of the men carried serious emotional problems through to adulthood, including the inability to form cohesive relationships, distrust of the opposite sex, and associated problems. But Wallerstein had no control group, even of similarly affluent white families. So how do we know that the divorce was the cause of these later emotional problems? What's more, about one-third of the original children were not interviewed for this survey—are they the ones who adjusted successfully and moved on with their lives? We cannot know. And finally, and most damning, the original participants in the study were recruited through a promise of free therapy for divorcing couples who were having a difficult time of it. Wallerstein herself tells us (in the first volume, though she fails to mention this in subsequent volumes) that most of them were having serious psychological problems *to begin with*. Only one-third were functioning adequately; half the fathers and close to half the mothers were "moderately disturbed or frequently incapacitated by disabling neuroses or addictions." She goes on:

> Here were the chronically depressed, sometimes suicidal individuals, the men and women with severe neurotic difficulties or with handicaps in relating to another person, or those with long-standing problems in controlling their rage or sexual impulses.

Hardly the sort of nationally representative sample that would provide convincing evidence. What Wallerstein has found is that the children of divorcing seriously psychologically impaired parents will have some difficulties themselves down the road.[86]

Most research on divorce finds that following the initial emotional upset that affects nearly all children, over the long term, "most children settle down and return to a normal process of maturation." Another recent book found that about three-fourths of children of divorce are "coping reasonably well and functioning in the normal range." Most children recover from the stress of divorce and show few adverse signs a few years later if they have adequate psychological supports and economic resources.[87]

No one doubts that divorce is difficult for children, or that being raised by two parents is probably better than being raised by one. For starters, with two parents, each is less likely to be tired and overworked. This makes higher levels and higher quality parent-children interaction more likely. And there is little doubt that, all else being equal, two people raising children together, whatever the parents' sexual orientation, is better for the children than one. The debate really concerns what we mean by "all else being equal." If we compare, for example, the educational achievement scores, sense of well-being, or levels of psychological and emotional adjustment of children who are raised in intact families and those raised in single-parent, post-divorce families, we find that those in single parent families manifest lower levels of well-being, self-esteem, educational attainment, and adjustment than those in two-parent homes.

But such comparisons are misdirected, for they compare two types of families—divorced and intact—as if they were equivalent. Divorce is not a remedy for marriage; it is a remedy for a *bad* marriage. And when researchers compare the outcomes for children between being raised in a post-divorce family versus being raised in an intact—*but unhappy*—family, the evidence is clear. The consequences of divorce on children depend on the level of marital conflict prior to the divorce. One study found that children in divorced families did, indeed, feel lonely, bored, and rejected more often than those in intact families—but that children in unhappily married families felt the highest levels of neglect and humiliation.[88]

A longitudinal study begun in 1968 by psychologists Jeanne and Jack Block tracked a group of three-year-olds for several years. When the children were fourteen, the Blocks looked back at their data, and found that some of the children whose parents would eventually divorce, especially the boys, were observed to be more aggressive and impulsive, and more likely to be in conflict with their parents. Although, as sociologist Arlene Skolnick observes, it is impossible to discern whether parental conflict led to problems for these children, or vice versa, it is clear that "these children's problems did not result from the divorce itself." Another British study tracking sevnteen thousand families, also found that children's problems long antedate divorce and that problems among young children can, in fact, be a good predictor of eventual divorce.[89]

The most systematic research on these issues has been undertaken by family sociologists Paul Amato and Alan Booth and their colleagues. Amato and Booth found the single best predictor of a child's happiness and well-being to be the quality of the parents' marriage. Those children who grow up in homes where parental conflict is high and a divorce ensues do as well as those who grow up in happily married, intact homes. What's more, parents who are jealous, moody, inclined to fly off the handle, critical, and prone to dominate their spouse have a far worse effect on their children's eventual marriages than whether or not the parents are divorced. Further, they found that in high-conflict families, children have higher levels of well-being if their parents divorced than if they stayed together; while in low-conflict families, children have higher levels of well-being if their parents stayed together than if they divorced. Divorce, Amato and Booth conclude, "is beneficial for children when it removes them from a high conflict marriage. But, like marriage, divorce ought not be entered into casually or without thought, because the consequences can be deleterious "when it removes them from a low-conflict marriage."[90]

The preponderance of research echoes these themes. Levels of family conflict are far more important in the lives of children than whether or not families stay together. Most research has found that "frequent marital and family conflict in so-called intact families is detrimental to children's physical health, and that divorce may, in fact, insulate some children and adolescents from prolonged exposure to health-threatening family interactions." And it turns out that parent-child relations prior to marriage are the key determinant of whether the divorce is psychologically catastrophic. Content, it would appear, is more important than form.[91]

But this may be yet another case of mistaking correlation for causation. While it may be true that children from divorced families experience more severe problems than children in intact families, it may be that *both* the divorces and the problems are caused by something else—the greater marital conflict. A longitudinal study found that children in families that eventually divorce manifest problems long before the actual divorce. The authors argue that many of the consequences attributed to divorce may, in fact, derive from the marital conflict and family stress that precede a divorce, rather than from the divorce itself. Blaming the problems of children on their parents' divorce "is a bit like stating that cancer is caused by chemotherapy," argues the president of the Family and Divorce Mediation Council of Greater New York. "Neither divorce nor chemotherapy is a step people hope to have to take in their lives, but each may be the healthiest option in a given situation." Americans seem to agree. A 1990 Gallup Poll found that 70 percent of Americans agreed that "when husbands and wives with young children are not getting along," they should "separate rather than raise the children in a hostile atmosphere." Less than one-fourth (24 percent) said that such a couple should "stay together for the sake of the children."[92]

The solution that some propose to the problem of divorce is, of course, simple: make divorce harder to obtain. The state of Louisiana has instituted "covenant marriages," which, unlike the contractual legal marriage, demand that couples take literally and seriously the provision of " 'til death do us part." Several other states are now considering such a distinction. Yet most family researchers agree that such a triumph of form over content—making divorce harder to get without changing the content of the marriage—would "exacerbate the bitterness and conflict that are associated with the *worst* outcomes of divorce for kids."[93]

Divorce is a serious undertaking, and not to be undertaken casually. But it is a "necessary 'safety-valve' for children (and parents) in high conflict households." From the standpoint of the children, "an end to an unhappy marriage is probably preferable to living in a household characterized by tension and acrimony," while forcing unhappy families to stay together would have the most deleterious outcomes for children, as well as for the adults. Following divorce, most families "adjust," and some even "thrive." Divorce might better be seen as a social indicator that something is wrong not with one-half of all marriages, taken individually, but with the institution of marriage, that the foundation upon which marriage rests cannot sustain and support one-half of all the marriages that take place—without some serious efforts on the part of policy makers. Family therapist Betty Carter pointed out that if any other social institution were failing more than half the people who entered it, we would demand that the institution change to fit people's new needs, not the other way around.[94]

The "Problem" of Child Custody

Whether or not divorce has simply accomplished by social policy what high mortality rates used to accomplish "naturally," there is one significant difference between the two methods to dissolve a marriage. With a divorce often comes the problem of child custody. Prior to the Industrial Revolution, children were seen as an economic "good," and courts utilized an economic means test to determine who would receive custody, and custody was regularly and routinely given to fathers. In the early years of the twentieth century, though, children came to be seen as a luxury, and so a new test, based on care and nurture, was used to determine custody arrangements—a policy that favored mothers. Today, the "best interest of the child" is the criterion employed to provide the foundation for custody decisions, although in practice, the best interests of the child are presumed to be better served by staying with the mother not the father, since the presumption is that mothers provide better child care—especially for young children—than do fathers.

Such a policy makes a certain amount of sense, since women perform most of the tasks that provide the care and nurture that children most need. And yet, in the late 1970s, 63 percent of fathers who requested custody received it, a significant increase from the 35 percent and 37 percent who requested and received it in 1968 and 1972 respectively. In a recent study of one thousand divorces in two California counties, psychologist Eleanor Maccoby and law professor Robert Mnookin found that a majority of mothers and fathers wanted joint legal custody, while those that didn't preferred that they, and not their spouses, be given custody. Nearly 82 percent of mothers and 56 percent of fathers requested the custody arrangement they wanted, while 6.7 percent of women and 9.8 percent of men requested more than they wanted and 11.5 percent of women and 34.1 percent of men requested less than they wanted. This suggests that "gender still matters" in what parents ask for and what they do to get it. That mothers were more likely to act on their desires by filing for a specific request also indicates that men need to ask for more up front to avoid feeling bitter later.[95]

Maccoby and Mnookin's research is notable for another finding. Children living with mothers generally did as well as children living with fathers; "the welfare of kids following a divorce did not depend a lot on who got custody," Maccoby told a journalist, "but rather on how the household was managed and how the parents cooperated." But one consequence of current custody arrangements is paternal withdrawal. Whether this is because the father is bereft to be kept from regular contact with his children or because once the marital bond is severed experiences a euphoria of "freedom" and considers himself to have escaped from a conflict-ridden family situation, it appears that many men "see parenting and marriage as part of the same bargain—a package deal," write sociologists Frank Furstenberg and Andrew Cherlin. "It is as if they stop being fathers as soon as the marriage is over." In one nationally representative sample of eleven-to-sixteen-year-old children living with their mothers, almost half had not seen their fathers in the previous twelve months. Nearly half of all divorced fathers in the United States pay no child support; in Europe the comparable number is about one-fourth.[96]

Paternal withdrawal, it turns out, actually affects the father-daughter relationship most significantly, even more than the much-touted father-son relationship, whereas the mother-daughter relationship seems to be the most resilient to divorce and custody disputes. This may surprise those who believe that the father-son bond is the most fragile and most hard-hit by postdivorce fatherlessness, but it illustrates how frequently daughters are ignored in that literature, and how both boys and girls benefit from paternal responsibility and continued presence in their children's lives.[97]

In recent years, postdivorce fatherhood has become a political issue, as "father's rights" organizations have sprouted up, declaring men to be the victims of inequality in custody decisions. It is true that most court decisions grant custody to the mother, based on the "best interest of the child" standard. Father's rights groups challenge this assumption, and claim that, invariably, joint custody is preferable for children. Sometimes, it appears that their rhetoric substitutes these aggrieved fathers' vindictiveness against ex-wives, or their bewilderment at the entire divorce proceeding, for the "best interests" of children, but it also appear to be the case that all things being equal, joint physical and legal custody ought to be the norm in custody decisions. Here, of course, "all things being equal" means that there is no discernible danger to the child of sexual or physical abuse; that the parents can manage to contain their own postdivorce conflict and prevent the children from becoming pawns in a parental power struggle; and that the parents agree to equally support the children financially and emotionally. Such arrangements may be more difficult for parents than for children, who often report "a sense of being loved by both parents," as well as "feeling strongly attached to two psychological parents, in contrast to feeling close to just one primary parent." Contrary to some popular opinion, joint custody "does not create uncertainty or confusion," and seems to benefit children, who say they are more satisfied with the arrangement than those in single-custody homes and consider having two homes advantageous.[98]

We know, too, that joint custody will benefit men, who will, by maintaining a legal connection to their children, be far more likely to continue to share financial responsibilities for their development. What's more, joint custody may relieve the deep sense of loss, disengagement, and depression often experienced by men who are cut loose from continued involvement with their families. On the other hand, mandated joint legal custody may not be so good for women. Feminist legal theorist Martha Fineman argues that mandated joint legal custody may appear to be gender neutral, but gender "neutrality" in one arena in an overall system of gender inequality may perpetuate gender discrimination, much the way the abandonment of affirmative action sounds race or gender neutral, but actually favors white males over others by the withdrawal of explicit challenge to historical discrimination. As Fineman writes:

> What may have started out as a system which, focusing on the child's need for care, gave women a preference *solely* because they had usually been the child's primary caretaker, is evolving into a system which, by devaluing the content or necessity of such care, gives men more than an equal chance to gain the custody of their children after divorce if they choose to have it, because biologically equal parents are considered as equal in expressive regards. Nonnurturing factors assume importance which often favor men.[99]

Perhaps the most judicious system of child custody will be one that recognizes the difference in "inputs" between fathers and mothers in the actual experiences of the children—time spent in child care, level of parental involvement in child development—while at the same time presuming that both parents are capable of and interested in (absent any evidence to the contrary) continued committed and involved relationships with their children. Men's increased involvement in predivorce child care ought to be reflected in custody arrangements, as should women's continuing to shoulder the overwhelming majority of such care, despite their commitments to work. Fathers' "rights" following divorce will come more readily if the fathers have recognized their responsibilities during the marriage.[100]

The "Problem" of Gay and Lesbian Families

Another recent constructed problem is that of gay and lesbian families. It's ironic that the same political commentators who fret about the decline of the family are the very people who would prevent gay men and lesbians from creating them. But the problems of gay families—marriage, child rearing—are actually less about families, and more about the legal status of homosexuals. As soon as the Hawaii state Supreme Court indicated the likelihood that it would recognize gay and lesbian marriages in 1997, for example, several states rescinded their adherence to the "full faith and credit" clause of the U.S. Constitution, the provision that requires one state to recognize contracts concluded in another states, such as marriage, voting, education, or driving. Soon thereafter, the U.S. Congress passed the Defense of Marriage Act, as if the institution of marriage were under attack by those who seek to enter it. It is expressly legal for gay men and lesbians to adopt children in only ten states and the District of Columbia (Alaska, California, Minnesota, Oregon, Washington, Massachusetts, New Jersey, New York, Pennsylvania, and Vermont).[101]

One reason that many gay and lesbians couples want to marry is because so many benefits accrue to married couples—benefits that heterosexual couples often take for granted. These include the right to inherit from a spouse who dies without a will; the right to consult with doctors and make crucial medical decisions if the partner is incapacitated; the right of residency of a foreign spouse; the right to Social Security benefits; the right to include a spouse on one's health plan; the right to visit a spouse in a government institution such as a prison or hospital; and the right to immunity from having to testify against one's spouse in a legal proceeding.[102]

It is true that gay male relationships are more fragile than heterosexual relationships and that gay men are more "promiscuous" (i.e., have a greater number of different sexual partners) than heterosexuals, though neither of these statements is true of lesbians. Some of the reasons for this disparity can be found in masculine gender socialization, which discourages men from commitment to domestic life in the first place; exclusion from formal, legal marriage, which cements heterosexual relationships and increases the couple's likelihood of staying together despite disagreement; lack of children, who are often the reason that heterosexual couples continue to work on their relationships; and social disapproval and institutionalized homophobia, which can destabilize any couple. "It is paradoxical that mainstream America perceives gays and lesbians as unable to maintain long term relationships while at the same time denying them the very institutions that stabilize such relationships" argued Craig Dean, executive director of the Marriage Rights Fund.[103]

Marriage is more than a legal right, more than a relationship. It is an institution, the bedrock institution of our ideal of the family. Without the right to marry, it is codified into law that gay relationships are less valuable, less important, than heterosexual ones. Such a devaluation leads to the very promiscuity that is used as the rationale for denying the right to marry in the first place.

In many cases, gay and lesbian couples provide a model of family life. For one thing, gay and lesbian couples are "less likely to fall into patterns of inequality" that define heterosexual marriages. By bringing together two people of the same gender, gender inequality is neutralized and gender difference eliminated. Compared with heterosexual couples, gay and lesbian couples are more likely to share housework; lesbian couples are the most egalitarian of all couple arrangements.[104] And, it turns out, gay men and lesbians often make excellent parents. In the late 1960s, one woman lamented her position, not as a lesbian, but as a non-parent:

> One of my mother's big disappointments was the fact that there would be no grandchildren. I love both of my parents a great deal, and I would do almost anything for their happiness, but I couldn't do that. I think I was saddened too, when . . . I knew that I wasn't ever going to have children. And I would like to have some . . . for myself.[105]

Just as heterosexual women once felt they were forced to choose between having a career and having a family, many gay men and lesbians felt forced to choose between acknowledging their sexuality and having a family. And just as women today are unwilling to make that choice, wanting to "have it all," so too are gays and lesbians, who have decided that their homosexuality ought not to disqualify them as good parents. In 1976, there were between 300,000 and 500,000 gay and lesbian parents; today there are an estimated 1.5 to 5 million lesbian mothers, and between 1 and 3 million gay fathers. Currently, between 8 and 13 million children (about 5 percent of all children in the United States) are being raised by at least one gay parent.[106]

None of the fears of gay parenting has materialized. There is no evidence that gay fathers or lesbian mothers exert any special negative influence on child development or that they sexually abuse their children. In fact, the few studies that have been conducted show that "the outcomes for children in these families tend to be better than average." For example, when fathers come out to their children, even if they are not raising the children themselves, it tends to relieve family stress and strengthen the bond between father and child. The research on lesbian mothers suggests that their children, both boys and girls, have similar patterns of gender identity development to children of heterosexual parents at comparable ages, and display no differences in intelligence or adjustment. "Quality of mothering" rather than sexual orientation is the crucial determinant of children's development.[107] As the fifteen-year-old daughter of a lesbian mother put it:

> I think I am more open-minded than if I had straight parents. Sometimes kids at school make a big deal out of being gay. They say it's stupid and stuff like that. But they don't really know, because they aren't around it. I don't say anything to them, but I know they are wrong. I get kind of mad, because they don't know what they are talking about.

This statement echoed a recent New Jersey court decision, which found that children in gay and lesbian families

> emerge better equipped to search out their own standards of right and wrong, better able to perceive that the majority is not always correct in its moral judgments, and better able to understand the importance of conforming their beliefs to the requirements of reason and tested knowledge, not the constraints of currently popular sentiments or prejudice.

Such sentiments, as family sociologist Judith Stacey pointed out, might well "serve as child-rearing ideals for a democracy."[108]

A recent meta-analysis of social science studies of gay and lesbian parenting suggests that children of these parents are more accepting of homosexuality, and may be more likely to indicate a willingness to consider homosexual relationships themselves, although they are no more likely to identify themselves as "gay" than children of heterosexual parents. More interestingly however are the *gender* consequences, as opposed to the sexual ones: daughters of lesbian and gay parents are more assertive, confident, and ambitious, while sons are less conforming to traditional notions of masculine aggression and domination, and more fluid in their gender identities.[109]

In fact, many mental health professionals have suggested that the secrecy and shame surrounding a parent's homosexuality are probably more detrimental to the child's well-being than the homosexuality itself. As psychologist Don Clark puts it: "It is more important for the gay person not to hide gay identity from offspring, because they are too close to keep in ignorance. To hide is to give yourself the message that you are ashamed and that there is some cause for shame. To hide it is likely to give them the same message,. And it is not such a good feeling to have a parent who is ashamed." And when secrecy surrounds the mothers' lesbianism, serious communication problems can result, and children in this situation were perceived by themselves and their mothers to be moody, depressed, and withdrawn. The mothers did not realize that the secrecy or silence surrounding their lesbian orientation was related to their daughters' psychological problems.[110]

Although some opposition to gay marriage has come from within the gay and lesbian community itself, where some have expressed fears that the desire for marriage is a repudiation of a more radical vision of gay liberation, the case for gay marriage and family finds increasing support both inside and outside the gay community.

The Real Problem of Family Violence

For too many Americans—children and parents alike—the family bears only a passing resemblance to the "haven in a heartless world" of nostalgic myth. Far from shielding their members from the cold and violent world outside its doors, the family *is* that cold and violent world. Violence tears at the fabric of the family. While I will discuss some forms of family violence, particularly the violence between women and men, in a later chapter (see chapter 11), here I want to discuss violence between parents and children, as well as violence among children. Family violence is remarkably gendered, reproducing and reinforcing gender inequality. The overwhelming amount of family violence is perpetrated by males—husbands beating wives, fathers hitting children, or sons hitting their parents, boys hitting their brothers or their sisters. "The actual or implicit threat of physical coercion is one of many factors underlying male dominance in the family," writes sociologist Murray Straus.[111]

Violence against children by parents is among the most controversial type of family violence. Although widespread support exists for corporal punishment—more than three-fourths of Americans believe that it is all right for a parent to spank a child—that support disappears when such violent behaviors by parents against children becomes systematic or extreme. Most Americans have hit their children, and most children have been hit by their parents. But the costs may outweigh the obvious benefits of immediate compliance from the child. Spanking is associated with several negative behaviors in children, including aggression, antisocial behavior and mental health problems. The American Academy of Pediatrics has taken an official stand against spanking.[112]

While the most common forms of parental violence against children are spanking or slapping, one in five parents have hit their child with an object, almost 10 percent have kicked, bit, or hit their children with their fist, and almost one in twenty families have experienced a parent beating up a child. And although mothers as well as fathers commit this violence, they are not equivalent. In one study, Bergman and his colleagues found that men are over ten times more likely to inflict serious harm on their children, and that every perpetrator of the death of a child in this limited sample was either a father or a father surrogate.[113]

The most evident consequence of parental violence against children is observed in the behaviors of children. Children see that violence is a legitimate way to resolve disputes, and learn to use it themselves. Violence against siblings is ubiquitous in American families. As Straus writes:

> Violence between siblings often reflects what children see their parents doing to each other, as well as what the child experiences in the form of discipline. Children of non-violent parents also tend to use non-violent methods to deal with their siblings and later with their spouses and children. If violence, like charity, begins at home, so does non-violence.[114]

(Parents wondering how to discourage violence among their children might begin by resisting the temptation to hit them, and settling marital problems without resorting to violence.)

The long-term consequences of parental violence against children are also evident. The greater the corporal punishment experienced by the child, the greater the probability that the child will hit a spouse as an adult. And the likelihood is also higher that children hit by their parents will strike back. Child-to-parent violence is also serious; nearly one in ten (9 percent) of all parents of children aged between ten and seventeen are victims of violence perpetrated by their own children. Mothers are more likely to be victims of such violence, especially in the more severe cases.

The antecedent causes of children hitting their parents, and especially their mothers, are directly related to the severity of the violence experienced by the child and the severity of the spousal violence the child observes. Children see their mothers hit by their fathers, and they "learn that mothers are an appropriate and acceptable target for intrafamily violence," writes sociologist Richard Gelles. Nowhere is the gender inequality of the family more evident than when a young boy hits his mother because he has learned by watching his father that violence against women is acceptable behavior for a boy coming into manhood.[115]

THE FAMILY OF THE FUTURE

Perhaps the most consistent finding to emerge from the literature on divorce, custody, and sexual orientation is that the form of the family—intact, divorced, single parent, lesbian or gay—matters far less for children than its content. A home filled with love and support, where parents spend both quality time and quantity time with their children and with each other is the strongest predictor of future physical, emotional, and psychological health of both the children and their parents. Family sociologist Arlene Skolnick writes that the most reliable studies "find that family structure—the number of parents in the home or the fact of divorce—is not in itself the critical factor in children's well-being. In both intact and other families, what children need most is a warm, concerned relationship with at least one parent."[116]

For example, a recent longitudinal study followed 126 Harvard undergraduates since their student days in the 1950s. Thirty-five years later, 116 of them were reevaluated. Of these, 25 percent who rated their parents as loving and caring had developed major illnesses, while 87 percent of those who had rated their parents as uncaring had experienced at least one serious health problem. (The researchers controlled for other potential causes, such as family history of illness, parental death or divorce, smoking habits, and marital experiences.) Men who had a low perception of the parental care and love that they received as children had a far greater risk of becoming ill in midlife.[117]

The crisis of the family appears less a crisis of form than a series of challenges to its content. It is true that both marital happiness and children's well-being have both declined over the past two decades. But it seems equally true that, as David Demo writes, "the negative consequences attributed to divorce, single-parent family structure and maternal unemployment have been greatly exaggerated." As a gendered institution, the family rests on assumptions about gender difference and the reality of gender inequality at both interpersonal and structural levels. At the structural level, gender inequality is maintained by governmental indifference to the plight of working families—from inadequate child care and parental leave provisions to a failure to support and sustain different types of families, in which children may grow up sensing that their lives are not as valuable and worthwhile as those of others.[118]

Family friendly workplace policies would enable and encourage families to balance their working lives and their family commitments. In the United States, slightly more than one-third of workers at companies with more than one hundred employees get unpaid maternity leave and, although 83 percent of all working men say that they feel the need to share the responsibilities of parenting, only 18 percent of such corporations actually offer parental leave to men, and only 9 percent of all companies do. Compare this with Sweden or Norway, for example, where couples are offered one full year of paid parental leave at 80 percent of their salary. Norway and Sweden have even instituted what they call "daddy days," when fathers can take parental leave after the mother has returned to work, to ensure that the fathers have a special time to spend with their children. In these countries, even grandparents get financial support to take time away from work to spend with their new grandchildren! These sorts of policies proclaim that a nation loves and cherishes its children so much that it is willing to use its resources to foster and facilitate that love. To me, *that's* "family values."[119]

Yet despite our claims to be a society that values the next generation, American governmental policy actually makes effective parenting more difficult for rich and poor alike. Inadequate funding for education, inadequate health care for children and adults, inadequate corporate policies regarding parental leave, and "family unfriendly" workplaces—with inflexible hours, rigid time schedules, and lack of on-site child care facilities—place too great a burden on already fragile and strained marital bonds and bonds between children and their parents. "We're trying to do what women want of us, what children want of us, but we're not willing to transform the workplace," notes an anthropologist who studies men's lives in several different cultures.[120]

The family as a gendered institution also depends on interpersonal relationships among family members, on the gendered division of household labor that reproduces male domination in society. Gender inequality is expressed in the different amounts of housework and child care performed by men and by the different trajectories of men's and women's lives following divorce. It is maintained too often by the real or implicit threat of violence.

In my opinion, gender equality in the family does not require a large "dose of androgyny," nor do I prescribe, as does sociologist Andrew Greeley, that "men become more like women." Just as it is possible for women to enter the workplace without becoming "masculinized," it is also possible for men to return home from their long exile without becoming "feminized." If present trends continue, it seems inevitable that men will be doing an increasing amount of what used to be called "women's work" inside the home, just as women are doing an increasingly amount of what used to be called "men's work" outside it. One can easily accommodate changes in one's activities without transforming one's identity or self-image.[121]

It was in the nineteenth century that the ideology of the separation of spheres was invented and imposed, "imprisoning" women in the home and "exiling" men from it. In the latter half of the twentieth century, the structural foundations of that ideology eroded, and it came under increasing ideological attack. My prediction is that the twenty-first century will witness a "re-integration of spheres," in which home and work will become increasingly similar, and men and women will be more active participants in both spheres. We should "insist on a closer integration between people's professional lives and their domestic lives," writes social critic Christopher Lasch. "Instead of acquiescing in the family's subordination to the workplace, [we] should seek to remodel the workplace around the needs of the family . . ." And on the home front, an increasing number of people are "telecommuting" to work, traveling from bedroom to home office, and using computers, fax machines, modems, and telephone lines to conduct paid work, while they cook for their children and clean the house during breaks.[122]

The most dramatic shift in family life in the twenty-first century will surely be the changing roles of men, just as the most dramatic demographic shift in the workplace in the twentieth century was the entry of women. Family sociologist Scott Coltrane predicts that as wives are employed for longer hours, identify more with their jobs, and provide a larger share of family income, men will do increasing amounts of housework. What's more, he argues, as "fathers become more involved in baby care, they will begin to take more responsibility for routine child care, and a significant minority will move beyond the role of household helper." In the workplace, men will increasingly identify as fathers, just as within the home, women have increasingly identified as workers.[123]

When men and women fully share housework and the raising of children, gender inequality in the family will gradually decrease, and the gender stereotypes and gender differences that were presumed to be the source of that inequality will also gradually begin to dissolve. After all, as we learn from anthropologists, those societies in which men take a larger role in child care are those in which women's status tends to be highest. Plus, a society in which women and men share parenting will be a society in which they are also equally active in the labor force. A change in the private sphere will bring about dramatic changes in the public sphere.

Think, for a moment, about the implications of shared parenting and housework, about the full impact of the reintegration of spheres. A child who experiences love and nurturing from his or her father and mother will come to see that nurturing is something that *adults* do, not something that women do and men may or may not do, depending on whether there's a good game on the television. So all children, both boys and girls, will expect to be nurturing when they become adults. Similarly, a child will also see that working is also something that *adults* do, not something that men do and women may or may not do, depending on whether their husband "allows" it, or whether they're raising children. In this sense, shared parenting might be a crucial step in "degendering" the two most highly gendered experiences we have, the two experiences that Freud himself identified as the most crucial elements of healthy adult life: love and work.

Robert Frost wrote these oft-quoted lines:

Home is the place where, when you go there
they have to take you in.

Our families are places in which we are both constrained by duty and obligation, and inspired by love, respect, and honor. Love, we've found, can abide in traditional families, in single-parent families, and in gay and lesbian families. It can sustain children in intact families or after divorce. What matters is the content of the family, not its form. Love can abide, nourish and sustain—wherever it lives, and in whatever form.

CHAPTER 7

THE GENDERED
CLASSROOM

The Higher Education of Women is one of the great world battle-cries for freedom; for right against might. It is the cry of the oppressed slave. It is the assertion of absolute equality.

—HENRY FOWLE DURANT
PRESIDENT, WELLESLEY COLLEGE
"THE SPIRIT OF THE COLLEGE" (1877)

"Math class is tough" were the first four words Barbie ever spoke. When Mattel introduced the talking Barbie in 1992, a new group of her nearly 800 million owners heard more than a teenager's complaint—even if that teenager was the buxom blond bombshell whose feet were designed to fit into high heels. They heard the way gender inequality and gender differences are reproduced.[1]

The interplanetary theory of gender tells us that boys and girls are fundamentally and categorically different, that boys excel in science and math, play violently in the playground, and shout out in class; girls, on the other hand, sit quietly, speak softly, play gingerly, and excel in French and in literature. At the same time, of course, we sit in the same classroom, read the same books, listen to the same teachers, and are supposedly graded by the same criteria.

But are we having the same experience in those classes? Not exactly. Our gendering experiences begin even before we get to school. By the time we enter our first classroom, we are learning more than our ABCs, more than spelling, math, and science, more than physics and literature. We learn—and teach one another—what it means to be men and women. And we see it all around us in our schools—who teaches us, what they teach us, how they teach us, and how the schools are organized as institutions. Schools are like old-fashioned factories, and what they produce is gendered individuals. Both in the official curriculum—textbooks and the like—and in the parallel, "hidden curriculum" of our informal interactions with both teachers and other students, we become gendered. This is reinforced in the parallel curriculum presented by the mass media. And the message students get—from both the content and the form of education—is that women and men are different and unequal, and that the inequality comes from those differences, and that, therefore, such inequality is justified. Consider, though, the opposite position—that the differences we observe are the *products,* not the cause, of gender inequality. As law professor Deborah Rhode writes, "What schools teach and tolerate reinforces inequalities that persist well beyond childhood."[2]

• 159 •

TRADITIONAL EDUCATION FOR MANHOOD

Since the eighteenth century in America, education was reserved for upper-class boys and men. We've seen earlier how opponents of women's equality used biological arguments to maintain gender exclusion—how, for example, they argued that higher education for women would result in "monstrous brains and puny bodies" with "flowing thought and constipated bowels," because it would violate the "plan" their bodies held for them. Harvard professor Edward Clarke cited cases of "pale, weak, neuralgic, dyspeptic, hysterical, menorraghic, dysmenorrhoeic" educated women with "arrested development of the reproductive system."[3]

Many of the Victorian opponents of women's education believed that women could not withstand and would not wish to subject themselves to the rigors of higher education. By contrast, some opponents of coeducation also believed that bringing women and men together would have disastrous effects on both sexes. Since the "minds of men and women are radically different," wrote one editorialist in the U. C. Berkeley *Daily Californian* in the 1890s, they must be taught separately. When the University of Michigan first debated coeducation in 1858, its president opposed it because "[m]en will lose as women advance, we shall have a community of defeminated women and demasculated men." A local paper applauded the trustees' decision, arguing that to educate women would "unwoman the woman and unman the man."[4]

Some worried that educating women and men together would "emasculate" the collegiate curriculum, watering it down by forcing the inclusion of subjects and temperaments better omitted, slowing down the pace, or otherwise reducing standards that would allow women to keep up. In his influential treatise on adolescence, the great psychologist G. Stanley Hall warned against coeducation because it "harms girls by assimilating them to boys' ways and work and robbing them of their sense of feminine character," while it harms boys "by feminizing them when they need to be working off their brute animal element." By making boys and girls more alike, he warned, coeducation would "dilute" the mysterious attraction of the opposite sex—that is, coeducation would cause homosexuality. (Of course, Hall could not yet have previewed Alfred Kinsey's studies of human sexuality, which found that most homosexual experimentation among males occurred precisely in those single-sex institutions—all-male schools, summer camps, Boy Scouts, the military, and prisons—that Hall believed would be palliatives against homosexuality.)

Of course, there were also strong supporters of women's education, such as the founders and first presidents of historically women's colleges, such as Matthew Vassar and Milo Jewett (Vassar), Henry Durant (Wellesley), and L. Clark Seelye (Smith). Durant went as far as to argue that the real meaning of women's education was "revolt"—"against the slavery in which women are held by the customs of society—the broken health, the aimless lives, the subordinate position, the helpless dependence, the dishonesties and shams of so-called education."[5]

Women's physical weakness and helpless dependency were thus *consequences* of gender inequality, not their cause. The great British physician Henry Maudsley elaborated this more sociological explanation for women's difference in 1874:

There are other reasons which go to make up the languid young-ladyhood of the American girl. Her childhood is denied the happy out-door sports of her brothers. There is a resolute shutting out of everything like a noisy romp; the active games and all happy, boisterous play, by field or roadside, are not *proper* to her! She is cased in a cramping dress, so heavy and inconvenient that no boy could wear it for a day without falling into gloomy views of life. All this martyrdom to propriety and fashion tells upon strength and symmetry, and the girl reaches womanhood a wreck. That she reaches it at all, under these suffering and bleached out conditions, is due to her superior elasticity to resist a method of education which would have killed off all the boys years before. . . . There are abundant statistics to prove that hard study is the discipline and tonic most girls need to supplant the too great sentimentality and useless day dreams fostered by fashionable idleness, and provocative of "nerves" melancholy, and inanition generally, and, so far as these statistics can, that the women-graduates of these colleges make as healthy and happy wives and mothers as though they had never solved a mathematical problem, nor translated Aristotle.[6]

Official policies promoting coeducation did not deter its male opponents. In 1900, the University of Rochester promised to open the door to women—if women could raise enough money to construct new dormitories and facilities. When they did—after Susan B. Anthony sold her life insurance policy to make it past the final monetary hurdle—and women tried to enter the classrooms, male students responded by stamping their feet, physically blocking classroom doors, and jeering at them whenever they appeared on campus. The administration responded by physically segregating the women in a separate, but clearly less-than-equal, college of their own. The collegiate classroom they had struggled so hard to enter did not exist so much to train them intellectually as it was to ensure social obedience to gender difference. They had entered another gendered classroom.

THE GENDERED CLASSROOM

The formal educational gendering process begins the moment we enter school, and continues throughout our educational lives. In nursery schools and kindergarten classes, we often find the heavy blocks, trucks, airplanes, and carpentry tools in one place, and the dolls and homemaking equipment in another. While they may be officially "open" to anyone for play, the areas are often sex-segregated by invisible but real boundaries. In the elementary school years, the informal play during out-of-school hours involves different sports, different rules, and different playground activities.

The nursery school where I taught in the late 1970s was divided into three zones. Indoors was a place for quiet play, and there were shelves of books, a small sandbox with cups and saucers, a quiet room, and a set of easels for painting. Immediately outside the building was the "near yard," which included two larger sandboxes with several larger pots and pans arrayed around them and an area marked off for foot-games such as hopscotch. Beyond this lay the "far yard" which included jungle gyms, a large unenclosed sandbox, and other gross motor skills activities.

In the morning, the three-year-old girls would come into school quietly, place their coats neatly in their open locker, and walk slowly and uncertainly into the inside room.

There they would look for a friend, and sit quietly looking at books, talking, or playing at the interior sandbox while they adjusted to a new day at school. The boys would race in, throw their coats into their lockers (missing half the time), and dash outside, grab a truck, and run to the far yard, shouting all the way.

All the boys, that is, except Brad. Brad was a quiet and thoughtful three-year-old, kind and considerate, and one of the brightest students I ever taught—at any age! Each morning, Brad would walk in and head right for the easels, where he would spend his entire day happily painting. Some days he would go into full-scale production, producing painting after painting; on other days he would paint for a while, and then stare dreamily outside at the trees.

When his parents saw me—the new male teacher—they were thrilled. "You *must* get Brad to go out to the far yard!" they pleaded with me, a look of terror in their eyes. "Please," Brad's mother repeated, softly. "Please."

One didn't need a Ph.D. in elementary education to understand what was so terrifying to Brad's parents. The specter of homosexuality hung in the air. Brad was not acting like the other boys, and his gender nonconformity was seen as a signal of his future sexual orientation. I tried to reassure his parents that Brad seemed genuinely happy painting, and that he was very good at it, but they were not satisfied until I also promised that I would encourage Brad to play with trucks. They were certain that the nursery school could produce a masculine—and heterosexual—son. (Brad, I think, was hoping that they'd leave him alone and let him become an artist. As for me, I would occasionally come over to the easel where Brad was painting and ask if he wanted to come with me to the far yard. Invariably, he'd smile broadly and decline, and return to his art.)

While there are some signs of change, this nursery school experience is reproduced in every classroom in every town and city in America, every day. Boys and girls learn—and teach each other—what are the appropriate behaviors and experiences for boys and girls, and make sure that everyone acts according to plan. What's less visible is the ways the teachers and curriculum overtly and subtly reinforce not only gender difference, but the inequalities that go along with, and even produce that difference.

The classroom setting reproduces gender inequality. "From elementary school through higher education, female students receive less active instruction, both in the quantity and in the quality of teacher time and attention," note education professors Myra and David Sadker, summarizing the research in their important book, *Failing at Fairness*. Many teachers perceive boys as active, capable of expressing anger, quarrelsome, punitive, alibi-building, and exhibitionistic, and they perceive girls as affectionate, obedient, responsive, and tenacious. When boys "put girls down," as they often do at that age, teachers (female usually) often say and do nothing to correct them, thus encouraging their notion of superiority. Many teachers assume that girls are likely to "love" reading and "hate" mathematics and sciences, and they expect the opposite of boys.[7]

Teachers call on boys more often and spend more time with them. They ask boys more challenging questions than they do girls, and wait longer for boys to answer. They urge boys to try harder, constantly telling boys that they can "do it." One study found that in all ten of the college classrooms observed, boys were more active, regardless of the gender of the teacher, though a female teacher increased girls' participation significantly. The report sponsored by the American Association of University Women summarized these studies when it concluded that whether "one is looking at preschool classrooms or university lecture halls . . . research spanning the past twenty years consistently reveals that males receive more teacher attention than do females." Part of the reason for this is that boys demand more attention, and part of the reason is that teachers also treat boys and girls differently. When the Sadkers were researching their book, they asked teachers why they paid more attention to the boys. The teachers told them things like: "Because boys needs it more" and "Boys have trouble reading, writing, doing math. They can't even sit still."[8]

Here's a particularly evocative example from *Failing at Fairness*, a book that documents the myriad ways in which gender inequality permeates the classroom. One fifth grade classroom they observed was having a particularly noisy and rambunctious discussion about who was the best president in American history. "Just a minute," the teacher told the class. "There are too many of us here to all shout out at once. I want you to raise your hands, and then I'll call on you. If you shout out, I'll pick somebody else." This restored order for a moment. Then one boy enthusiastically called out:

> STEPHEN: I think Lincoln was the best president. He held the country together during the war.
> TEACHER: A lot of historians would agree with you.
> MIKE (seeing that nothing happened to Stephen, calls out): I don't. Lincoln was okay, but my Dad liked Reagan. He always said Reagan was a great president.
> DAVID (calling out): Reagan? Are you kidding?
> TEACHER: Who do you think our best president was, Dave?
> DAVID: FDR. He saved us from the Depression.
> MAX (calling out): I don't think it's right to pick one best president. There were a lot of good ones.
> TEACHER: That's interesting.
> KIMBERLY (Calling out): I don't think that presidents today are as good as the ones we used to have.
> TEACHER: Okay, Kimberly. But you forgot the rule. You're supposed to raise your hand.[9]

Journalist Peggy Orenstein observed another junior high school class, where boys "yelled out or snapped the fingers of their raised hands when they wanted to speak, [while the] girls seemed to recede from class proceedings." As one girl told her "Boys never care if they're wrong."[10]

WHAT CHILDREN SEE

One reason the boys don't seem to care if they're wrong is because it's virtually always their faces they see illustrated in the content of the courses. They know they can make mistakes, because they will continue to be centrally reflected in course content. Early in the school years, children learn to read, thus opening a new source of influence. And they begin to observe the content of other media—television, films, or cartoons.

Do these materials counter sex typing? Until recently, studies of children's books and anthologies consistently reported traditional sex differences and pro-male biases. Females have been vastly underrepresented in pictures, in titles, and as main characters, and often are completely absent. In addition, female characters have usually been cast in insignificant or secondary roles. Their activities have been limited to loving, watching, or helping, while males engaged in adventuring and solving problems. Women were not given jobs or professions; motherhood was presented as a full-time, lifetime job. The son in the family wore trousers and the daughter wore a skirt; he was active, she was passive. In biographies, women are often portrayed as dependent. For example, Marie Curie is depicted as a helpmate to her husband, rather than as the brilliant scientist and Nobel Prize winner that she was.[11]

In elementary school books, the gender bias has been consistent. In 1972, Leonore Weitzman and her colleagues surveyed winners of the Caldecott Award for the best children's books for the years 1967 to 1971. Since then, the research has been updated twice, most recently in 1987, and the researchers now find that though females are more visible in the books, their portrayal still reveals gender biases. Females are still depicted in passive and submissive positions, whereas males are shown as active and independent. Even in these more recent books, they conclude:

> Not only does Jane express no career goals, but there is no model to provide any ambition. One woman in the entire twenty books has an occupation outside the home and she works at the Blue Tile Diner. How can we expect Dick to express tender emotions without shame when only two adult males in this collection have anything resembling tender emotions and one of them is a mouse.[12]

In 1975, the U.S. Department of Health, Education and Welfare surveyed 134 texts and readers from sixteen different publishers, looking at the pictures, stories, and language used to describe male and female characters. "Boy-centered" stories outnumbered "girl-centered" stories by a five to two ratio; there were three times as many adult male characters as there were adult female characters; six times as many biographies of men as of women; and four times as many male fairy tales as female. Recalling her American history classes, one scholar recently remembered a strange biological anomaly—"a nation with only founding fathers."[13]

Of course, some changes have occurred over the past quarter-century. In children's books today, girls and women are far more likely than before to be depicted as the main character, and far less likely to be depicted as passive, without ambition or career goals. But gender stereotypes still prevail: girls are still depicted as more interested in domestic life than boys are. In fact, the major change in all media images—books, television, and movies—has been that women are no longer cast as helpless domestic helpmates. There has been no comparable change in the depiction of men or boys in children's books, no movement of men toward more nurturing and caring behaviors. As in real life, women in our storybooks have left home and gone off to work, but men still have enormous trouble coming back home.[14]

As in children's books, so too in the other media that enter our lives. What children learn in school is reinforced at home, not only in our families, but also in our entertainment. Television, movies, MTV videos—all reiterate gender stereotypes. Television takes vast chunks of its time to deliver entertainment and commercial messages to younger children, as well as to those in school. There are programs for preschoolers in the morning, for school children when they have returned home, and for all children every Saturday morning. For many children this is one of their largest commitments of waking time; for parents, it often serves as a built-in baby sitter.

The presentation of gender roles on children's television shows has been, at least until recently, quite similar to that of children's readers, the playground, and the schools. Boys are the centerpiece of a story; they do things and occupy the valued roles. Girls serve as backdrop, are helpful and caring, and occupy the less-valued roles. Even *Sesame Street,* hailed as a breakthrough in enjoyable educational programming, presents far more male characters than female. Commercials for children on Saturday morning usually depict boys driving cars or playing with trucks, and girls playing with dolls. There has been some pressure to eliminate gender stereotyping in both commercials and show content, but television shows are linked into a gender-stereotyped system. Toy manufacturers sell gender-linked toys, parents buy them, and writers often take their stories from existing materials (including the toys that are for sale, such as G.I. Joe and the Ninja Turtles) for children.

Television commercials are especially powerful, perhaps even more powerful than the shows themselves, because they are expressly designed to persuade. Commercials also link gender roles with the significant adult roles that the young will be playing in the future. The authoritative voices advising you what to buy are nearly all men's voices, which indicates to children who the experts are. Similarly, gender stereotypes are attached to consumption, one of the most valued activities in U.S. society. By linking material benefits to gender roles, the commercials teach a powerful lesson—if you consume this product, this is the kind of man or woman you can be.

Beyond the children's hours, we find the same shifts we observed in children's books. In the 1970s, the TV airwaves were stocked with cartoon-like people in evening programs that showed women as less visible and helpless, usually indoors, and constantly serving the needs of others; men, by contrast, were engaged in physical activities (such as climbing trees) and as the rescuers, leaders, actors, often outdoors. Even the characters in more contemporary shows, which show single or divorced women, are careful to watch their morals and make sure they marry for love. When a hard choice is made, love or children always come first. These shows offer us women who appear to be a kind of "Mary Poppins"—whether single *(Mary Tyler Moore),* divorced *(Alice),* or widowed *(Golden Girls).* The 1950s protoypical female character, Lucy, spent most of her time devising strategies to get out of the house and into the workplace— preferably acting, singing, or dancing in Ricky's nightclub revue. Other women in the 1960s and early 1970s, resorted to magic (Samantha, Jeannie) to support their ambitious husbands, while Alice Cramden, like some others, found that by staying home they really were the authority figure.

By the 1970s, a new female character appeared, personified by Mary Tyler Moore. Single and sexual, Mary Richards was also a go-getter on the job, and quite unwilling to sacrifice career for family life. She wanted it all. Her character opened the door for a parade of women who were less subservient to men (Rhoda and Cagney and Lacey) and more assertive in the workplace as well as at home (Roseanne) and not even especially "nice" (Murphy Brown). Today women appear to be nearly at home in the workplace as they are at home, and virtually all prime-time dramas include female doctors, lawyers, judges, and cops.

These changes in women's real and media-depicted lives have not been matched with parallel shifts in the depiction (or the realities) of men's lives. Men still seem to troop off to work, as ambitious and motivated as ever. Gone are the days when men found themselves as devoted dads like Jim Anderson or Ward Cleaver, whose careers rarely tugged at their time. When men return home, they usually are the butt of humor—from Ralph Cramden's bluster and Ozzie Nelson's domestic patriarch-as-layabout loafer in the 1950s and 60s, to Homer Simpson's and Tim Allen's inability to rule the roost and Dan Conner's utter lack of interest in it. To be sure, there are exceptions, such as Bill Cosby as successful career man and loving father, and who now plays a genial retiree. But most men do most of the nurturing and caring in the public sphere, in the workplace, the way Mark Greene did on *ER* or Bobby Donnell does on *The Practice*.

In the representation of women and men, then, television images generally mirror American ambivalence about change. Women can leave the home, but will encounter problems in sustaining a satisfying family life; men cannot find a way back into domestic life without being emasculated. Thus, in our real lives and on TV, gender difference and gender inequality are mutually reinforcing ideologies. Yet there are some encouraging fissures in the structure as well as moments of reform and resistance to traditional notions of gender difference.

Television, films, and other media also habituate viewers, young and old, to a culture that accepts and expects violence. In the nation's most through investigation of violence on television, The National Television Violence Study, four teams of researchers systematically examined TV violence. They found that violence is ubiquitous (61 percent of all shows contained some violence), and that typically it is perpetuated by a white male, who goes unpunished and shows little remorse. The violence is typically justified, although nearly one-half (43 percent) presented it in a humorous way. Consistently, "the serious and long-lasting consequences of violence are frequently ignored."[15]

Media presentations do not have immediate effects on the gender behavior of children. Although the media influence the ideas about gender that children have, children also negotiate a real world of people who do not fit these stereotypes. Media representations become just one more element in a child's process of organizing his or her own ideas of gender, part of his or her "concept formation" about gender. Nor do these media presentations have the dramatic and immediate effects that media critics often ascribe to them, since most of human learning is a steady accumulation of information, attitudes, and ways of responding rather than a sudden revelation or recognition. The media simply provide another push toward accepting current arrangements as if they were natural, right, and preordained.

GENDER DIVERGENCE IN ADOLESCENCE

The combination of exclusion from the curriculum, gender stereotypes in the media, and the often invisible discrimination in the classroom itself results in a divergence between girls and boys by adolescence. Though in elementary school girls have somewhat higher self-esteem and higher achievement levels than young boys, girls' self-esteem plummets in junior high school. Girls' IQs fall by about thirteen points; boys' IQs fall about three points. Girls find out that they are more valued for their appearance than for their talents. One young girl, Ashley Reiter, a winner of the Westinghouse Talent Competition for her project of mathematical modeling, remembered the day she won her first math contest, which coincided with her first pair of contact lenses. When she showed up at school the next day, triumphant about her victory, "[e]veryone talked about how pretty I looked," she recalled. "Nobody said a word about the math competition." Another college-age woman remembered that in high school people were "always surprised to learn I have a 4.0 and I'm a National Merit Finalist. Their image of me is 'that *blond* girl who used to go out with Scott.' Why can't they understand there's more to me?" Is it any wonder that, in one survey, adolescent girls were about half as likely as boys to cite their talents as "the thing I like most about myself," but about twice as likely as the boys to cite some aspect of their appearance? Or, as feminist literary critic Carolyn Heilbrun puts it, that girls sacrifice "truth on the altar of niceness."[16]

As a result, girls experience their adolescence in school in dramatically different ways from boys. Eating disorders, such as anorexia and bulimia, are significant problems from junior high school through college, and the evidence is that their frequency is increasing—and at increasingly younger ages. One in ten teenage girls becomes pregnant each year. Although most of the fathers of those babies are over twenty-one, those fathers who are still students are likely to stay in school; the mother is likely to drop out and stay out.

The "chilly classroom climate" for girls also takes place within a sexually "hostile environment." In recent years, sexual harassment has become a significant problem in more than our workplaces; it's also a problem in our classrooms. In 1980, the nation's first survey of sexual harassment in schools, conducted by the Massachusetts State Department of Education, found widespread sexual harassment of girls. A 1986 Minnesota survey of predominantly white and middle-class juniors and seniors in vocational schools found that between one-third and three-fifths of the girls had experienced sexual harassment.

Lawsuits followed, and finally the issue began to get the attention it deserved. In 1991, nineteen-year-old Katy Lyle was awarded $15,000 to settle a lawsuit she brought against her Duluth, Minnesota, school district, because school officials failed to remove explicit graffiti about her from the walls of the boys' bathrooms, even after her parents complained several times. The next year, Tawnya Brawdy was awarded $20,000 from her Petaluma, California, junior high school, which took no action to stop boys from making obscene sounds and gestures about her breasts. (Tawnya had reached puberty early and developed large breasts at a young age. The boys' behavior made her life so miserable that she could not eat, sleep, or function in class.) That same year, the U.S. Supreme Court unanimously sided with a young girl, Christine Franklin, in her case against the Gwinnett County, Georgia, school board, and awarded her $6 million in damages resulting from a violation of Title IX.

By the spring of the next year, 1993, almost half of all the sexual harassment cases then being investigated by the U.S. Department of Education's Office of Civil Rights involved elementary and secondary schools. And it continues to plague our nation's schools. As I write, the Supreme Court has just heard another case in which a young girl, subject to sexual harassment by another student, has held the school board liable. In this case, *(Davis v. Monroe County Board of Education),* a mother sued the school board because she claimed her ten-year-old daughter suffered a constant "barrage of sexual harassment and abuse" from one of her classmates while her teachers and other school officials ignored it. According to a study commissioned by the American Association of University Women, nearly four-fifths of girls (78 percent) and more than two-thirds of boys (68 percent) have been subjected to harassment. In both cases, it's almost invariably other boys who are the perpetrators. As Bernice Sadler put it:

> Sexual persecution starts at a very early age. In some elementary schools there is skirt flip-up day; in others girls refuse to wear clothes with elastic waistbands because the boys pull down their slacks and skirts. In junior high schools boys tape mirrors to the tops of their shoes so they can look up girls' dresses. Groups of boys in some high schools claim tables near the line where food is purchased. Whenever a female students walks by, they hold up a card with a number on it: one for an unattractive girl and ten for a superstar. In other schools there is "Grab a Piece of Ass Week" or lists circulate, such as "The Twenty Sluttiest Girls in School."[17]

In the infamous case of Spur Posse, a group of relatively affluent young boys in southern California simply took these messages a little farther than most. In 1993, a large group of young women and girls—one as young as ten!—came forward to claim that members of Spur Posse had sexually assaulted and raped them. Members of the group apparently competed with one another to see who could have sex with the most girls. They kept an elaborate coded score of their exploits by referring to various athletes' names as a way of signifying the number of conquests. (The name "Spur Posse" was a reference to the San Antonio Spurs, the guys' favorite pro basketball team.) Thus a "Reggie Jackson" would refer to forty-four, the number on his jersey, while "David Robinson" would signify fifty different conquests. In this way, the boys could publicly compete with one another without the young women understanding that they were simply the vehicles for homosocial competition.

When some of these young women accused the boys of assault and rape, many residents of their affluent suburb were shocked. The boys' mothers, particularly, were horrified when they heard that their fifteen-year-old sons had had sex with forty-four or fifty girls. A few expressed outrage. But the boys' fathers seemed to glow with pride. "That's my boy," declared the dads in chorus. "Nothing my boy did was anything any red-blooded American boy wouldn't do at his age," gloated one father. "My dad used to brag to his friends," one Posse member confessed on a TV talk show. And we wonder where the kids get it from?[18]

WHAT ABOUT THE BOYS?

Given these dramatically divergent patterns, you might think that the systematic demolition of girls' self-esteem, the denigration of their abilities, and the demotion of their status would yield positive effects for young boys, that boys would rise as the girls declined. But that isn't what happens. In the elementary grades, boys are more likely to be sent to child psychologists by about four to one, and far more likely to be diagnosed with dyslexia and Attention Deficit Disorder (ADD) than are girls. Beginning in elementary school, and continuing throughout their schooling, boys receive poorer report cards; they are far more likely to repeat a grade. Nine times more boys than girls are diagnosed as hyperactive; boys represent 58 percent of those in special education classes for the mentally retarded, 71 percent of the learning disabled, and 80 percent of the emotionally disturbed. Nearly three-fourths of all school suspensions are of boys. By adolescence, boys are more likely to drop out, flunk out, and act out in class. Their self-esteem also drops during adolescence—not, admittedly, as much as girls' self-esteem, but it does drop.[19]

These data are often used to suggest that boys, not girls, are the new victims of significant gender discrimination in schools. After all, what happens to boys in schools? They have to sit quietly, take naps, raise their hands, be obedient—all of which does extraordinary violence to their "natural" testosterone-inspired rambunctious playfulness. "Schools for the most part are run by women for girls. To take a high spirited second or third grade boy and expect him to behave like a girl in school is asking too much," comments Christina Hoff Sommers, author of *The War Against Boys*. The effect of education is "pathologizing boyhood." "On average, boys are physically more restless and more impulsive (than girls)," comments school consultant Michael Thompson. "We need to acknowledge boys' physical needs, and meet them." While we've been paying all this attention to girls' experiences—raising their self-esteem, enabling them to take science and math, deploring and preventing harassment and bullying—we've ignored the boys. "What about the boys?" asks the backlash chorus.[20]

Make no mistake: Boys' needs do merit our serious attention. We've already observed the consequences of ignoring them. But the classroom is hardly the feminizing environment that critics charged at the turn of the last century as well as today. In my classroom, women students dress in flannel shirts, blue jeans and T-shirts, leather bomber jackets and athletic shoes. They call each other "guys" constantly, even if the group is entirely composed of women. The classroom, like the workplace, is a public sphere institution, and when women enter the public sphere, they often have to dress and act "masculine" in order to be taken seriously as competent and capable. (I will detail this workplace process in the next chapter.) A recent advertising campaign for Polo by Ralph Lauren children's clothing pictured young girls, aged about five or six, in Oxford button-down shirts, blazers, and neckties. Who is being feminized and who is being masculinized?

As we've seen, there is little evidence that boys' aggression is biologically based. Rather, we understand that the negative consequences of boys' aggression are largely the social byproduct of exaggerating otherwise healthy and pleasurable boisterous and rambunctious play. And it is exaggerated by boys so that they may better fit in with other boys; they overconform to the expectations of their peers. Instead of uncritically celebrating "boy culture," we might inquire instead into the experience when boys cease being boys themselves, and begin to posture and parade their masculinity before the evaluative eyes of other boys.

At that moment we might find a psychological "disconnect," equivalent to that observed by Carol Gilligan with young girls. Gilligan and her associates described the way that assertive, confident, and proud young girls "lose their voices" when they hit adolescence. It is the first full-fledged confrontation with gender inequality that produces the growing gender gap in adolescence.[21] By contrast, boys become more confident, even beyond their abilities, just as girls grow less confident. Gender inequality means that just at the moment that girls lose their voices, boys *find* one—but it is the inauthentic voice of bravado, of constant posturing, of foolish risk taking and gratuitous violence. According to psychologist William Pollack boys learn that they are supposed to be in power, and thus begin to act like it. "Although girls' voices have been disempowered, boys' voices are strident and full of bravado," he observes. "But their voices are disconnected from their genuine feelings." Thus, he argues, the way we bring boys up leads them to put on a "mask of masculinity," a posture, a front. They "ruffle in a manly pose," as the poet William Butler Yeats put it, "for all their timid heart."[22]

That girls "lose their voice" means that girls are more likely to undervalue their abilities, especially in the more traditionally "masculine" educational arenas such as math and science, and the more traditionally masculine employment arenas such as medicine, the military, or architecture. Only the most able and most secure women take such courses or pursue those career paths. Thus, their numbers tend to be few, and their grades high. Boys, however, possessed of this false voice of bravado (and many facing strong family pressure to enter traditionally masculine arenas) are likely to *overvalue* their abilities, to remain in programs though they are less qualified and capable of succeeding.

This difference, and not some putative discrimination against boys, is the reason that girls' mean test scores in math and science are now, on average, approaching those of boys. Too many boys who overvalue their abilities remain in difficult math and science courses longer than they should; they pull the boys' mean scores down. By contrast, the few girls whose abilities and self-esteem are sufficient to enable them to "trespass" into a male domain skew female data upward.

A parallel process is at work in the humanities and social sciences. Girls mean test scores in English and foreign languages, for example, also outpace boys. But this not the result of "reverse discrimination," but because the boys bump up against the norms of masculinity. Boys regard English as a "feminine" subject. Pioneering research in Australia by Wayne Martino and his colleagues found that boys are uninterested in English because of what it might say about their (inauthentic) masculine pose. "Reading is lame, sitting down and looking at words is pathetic," commented one boy. "Most guys who like English are faggots," commented another. The traditional liberal arts curriculum is seen as feminizing; as Catharine Stimpson recently put it sarcastically, "[R]eal men don't speak French."[23]

Boys tend to hate English and foreign languages for the same reasons that girls love it. In English, they observe, there are no hard and fast rules, but rather one expresses one's opinion about the topic and everyone's opinion is equally valued. "The answer can be a variety of things, you're never really wrong," observed one boy. "It's not like maths and science where there is one set answer to everything." Another boy noted:

> I find English hard. It's because there are no set rules for reading texts. . . . English isn't like maths where you have rules on how to do things and where there are right and wrong answers. In English you have to write down how you feel and that's what I don't like.

Compare this to the comments of girls in the same study:

> I feel motivated to study English because . . . you have freedom in English—unlike subjects such as maths and science—and your view isn't necessarily wrong. There is no definite right or wrong answer and you have the freedom to say what you feel is right without it being rejected as a wrong answer.[24]

It is not the school experience that "feminizes" boys, but rather the ideology of traditional masculinity that keeps boys from wanting to succeed. "The work you do here is girls' work," one boy commented to a researcher. "It's not real work." Added another, "When I go to my class and they [other boys] bunk off, they will say to me I'm a goody goody." Such comments echo the consistent findings of social scientists since James Coleman's path-breaking 1961 study that identified the "hidden curriculum" among adolescents in which good-looking and athletic boys were consistently more highly rated by their peers than were good students.[25]

Gender disparities are also evident on college campuses. Women now constitute the majority of students on college campuses, passing men in 1982, so that in eight years women will earn 58 percent of bachelor's degrees in U.S. colleges; and there are three women for every two men at the nation's community colleges. One reporter, obviously a terrible statistics student, tells us that if present trends continue, "the graduation line in 2068 will be all females." (That's like saying that if the enrollment of black students at Ole Miss was one in 1964, twenty-four in 1968, and four hundred in 1988, that by 1994 there would have been no white students there.) Women now outnumber men in the social and behavioral sciences by about three to one, and they've invaded such traditionally male bastions as engineering, where they now make up about 20 percent of all students, and biology and business, where the genders are virtually on par.[26]

But the numbers cited by these critics just don't add up. For one thing, more *people* are going to college than ever before. In 1960, 54 percent of boys and 38 percent of girls went directly to college; today the numbers are 64 percent of boys and 70 percent of girls. And while some college presidents fret that to increase male enrollments they'll be forced to lower standards (which is, incidentally, exactly the opposite of what they worried about twenty-five years ago when they all went coeducational), no one seems to find gender disparities going the other way all that upsetting. Of the top colleges and universities in the nation, only Stanford sports a fifty-fifty gender balance. Harvard and Amherst enroll 56 percent men, Princeton and Chicago 54 percent men, Duke and Berkeley 52 percent, and Yale 51 percent. And that doesn't even begin to approach the gender disparities at Cal Tech (65 percent male, 35 percent female) or MIT (62 percent male, 38 percent female). Nor does anyone seem driven to distraction about the gender disparities in nursing, social work, or education, traditionally far lower paid occupations than those professions where men still predominate (engineering and computer sciences).

Much of the great gender difference we hear touted is actually what sociologist Cynthia Fuchs Epstein calls a "deceptive distinction," a difference that appears to be about gender but is actually about something else—in this case, class or race. The shortage of male college students is also actually a shortage of *nonwhite* males. The gender gap between college-age white males and white females is rather small, 51 percent women to 49 percent men. But only 37 percent of black college students are male, and 63 percent female, and 45 percent of Hispanic students are male, compared with 55 percent female.

Those who suggest that feminist-inspired reforms have been to the detriment of boys seem to believe that gender relations are a zero-sum game, and that if girls and women gain, boys and men lose. But the reforms that have been initiated to benefit girls in class—individualized instruction, attention to different learning pathways, new initiatives, classroom configurations, teacher training, and more collaborative team-building efforts—have been to the benefit of boys as well, as such methods would also target boys' specific experiences.

And the efforts to make the classroom safer, more hospitable to girls have also redounded to boys' benefit. Take, for example, classroom decorum. In 1940, the top disciplinary problems identified by high school teachers were (in order): talking out of turn, chewing gum, making noise, running in the hall, cutting in line, dress code violations, and littering. In 1990, the top disciplinary problems were (again, in order): drug abuse, alcohol abuse, pregnancy, suicide, rape, robbery, and assault.[27] Challenging stereotypes, decreased tolerance for school violence and bullying enables both boys and girls to feel safer at school. Those who would simply throw up their hands in resignation and sigh that "boys will be boys," would have you believe that nothing can or should be done to make those classrooms safer. To my mind, those four words, "boys will be boys," may be the most depressing words in educational policy circles today.[28]

The "battle of the sexes" is not a zero-sum game—whether it is played out in our schools, our workplaces, or our bedrooms. Both women *and* men, girls *and* boys will benefit from real gender equality in the schools. "Every step in the advancement of woman has benefited our own sex no less than it has elevated her," was how an editorial in the Amherst College campus newspaper, *The Amherst Student,* put it when the school first debated coeducation at the turn of the twentieth century.[29]

THE SCHOOL AS GENDERED WORKPLACE

Just as historically women and girls were excluded from the classroom as students, so too were women excluded from the profession of teaching. Remember Ichabod Crane in Washington Irving's "The Legend of Sleepy Hollow"? In the eighteenth and nineteenth centuries, teaching had been seen as a respectable profession for a man. But the mid- to late-nineteenth-century gender ideology of the "separation of spheres" meant that women were pushed out of other arenas of work, and they soon began to see elementary education as a way they could fulfill both their career aspirations and also their domestic functions of maternal nurturance.

This coincided conveniently with the expansion of public elementary school education, and especially the age segregation of students. (Remember that in the sixteenth to the eighteenth centuries, the educational norm was the one-room schoolhouse in which all ages were schooled together.) By segregating students into age categories, women's specific appropriateness with the younger students became apparent. Besides, administrators could pay these women teachers much lower salaries than they paid men. As a result, elementary education became "feminized." This meant that the occupational prestige and salaries of teachers dropped, discouraging men from entering the field and ensuring that it would become even more populated by women. Teaching was "women's work." But not, of course, school administration, which has remained largely a masculine arena. Thus, the school came to resemble every other social institution in American society.

The frightful consequences were much debated at the turn of the twentieth century. Some warned of the "invasion" of women teachers as if it were the "Invasion of the Boy Snatchers." One of the founders of American psychology, J. McKeen Cattell, worried about this "vast horde of female teachers" to whom boys were exposed. This had serious consequences; a boy taught by a woman, one admiral believed, would "render violence to nature," causing "a feminized manhood, emotional, illogical, noncombative." Another worried that "the boy in America is not being brought up to punch another boy's head or to stand having his own punched in a healthy and proper manner."[30]

In these first years of the twenty-first century, women still hold most of the primary education positions, and virtually all positions in pre-kindergarten and special education. In 1994, 72.5 percent of all public and private school teachers were women and six of every ten women teachers were in the elementary grades. The number of women teachers decreases as students progress through the educational ranks. Most male teachers wind up in secondary and postsecondary educational positions, whereas most female teachers end up in elementary grades.[31]

Sex composition of the labor force is related to its salary structure. It is virtually axiomatic that the greater the proportion of women in the field, the lower the salary. Within the educational field, women continue to earn less money than men doing the same jobs. The average female pre-kindergarten teacher in 1980 earned $8,390, while her male counterpart earned $14,912. (Data since then are consistent.) Ninety-seven percent of all pre-kindergarten teachers are women. As one progresses through the educational system the salary discrepancies become even more pronounced, in part because raises are based on years of experience, and women take more time off for childbearing.

Change has been more evident in higher education. A study in 1975 found that four out of five college teachers were men; by 1989 about one-third of all college teachers were women. But the implications of such evidence are not necessarily that gender equity is even close to having been achieved. When ranked by quality of school, women made up less than 10 percent of the faculty at high prestige colleges, but nearly 25 percent at community colleges. More than two-thirds of women teach at two and four year colleges; men are equally divided between research universities and all other institutions. And the "uneven distribution of the sexes within academia," noted by sociologist Martin Trow in 1975, continues. Men continue to dominate in sciences, where teaching loads are lower and the number of research and teaching assistants is highest. For example, women make up 45 percent of all lecturers, 35 percent of all assistant professors, 25 percent of all associate professors, and about 10 percent of all professors in the sciences and engineering. By contrast, women dominate in the semi-professions (nursing, social work, education) and those fields that require significant classroom contact, such as languages.[32]

And that's not all. The slight trickling down of salary increases among college teachers have also been soaked up mainly by men. Between 1970 and 1980, female salaries increased 66 percent; men's salaries increased 70 percent. In 1970, women were making 84 percent of men's salaries; but in 1980, they were making only 70 percent. Today, women at all ranks receive lower salaries than do men at the same rank, in the same field, in the same department.

Women also dominate the ranks of the most populous arena of college teaching—adjunct lecturers and instructors. Part-time instructors, victims of both an educational glut and covert gender discrimination, currently teach about one-half of all college classes, yet they are paid by the course, even if hired on yearly contracts, with neither health nor retirement benefits, and with paltry salaries. Well over half of them are women. Men are dramatically overrepresented at the top of the educational pyramid. In 1972, fewer than 3 percent of all top-level college and university administrators were women, and the typical relationship held that the more women administrators, the lower the prestige of the school. (This was modified, but only slightly, at the historically all-women colleges.) Only in the late 1990s, as women assumed the presidencies at Duke, University of Pennsylvania, Princeton, and SUNY at Stony Brook—as well as presidencies at historically women's colleges, such as Vassar, Smith, Wellesley, and Bryn Mawr—did this equation begin to break down.

THE GENDER OF EDUCATION TODAY

One might think that after so many years of educational reform, and especially attention to the differences between girls and boys, that things would be getting better. But the National Assessment of Educational Progress found that the gender differences for thirteen-year-olds actually increased in all the sciences except biology, as boy's skills improved and girls' skills declined. One educator sadly concluded that it is still true today that "[c]oeducational schools are male-dominated and male-controlled institutions."[33]

Simple enumeration of equality may not be the answer. One teacher told journalist Peggy Orenstein that after learning that teachers paid more attention to boys than to girls, she explained to the class that henceforth she was going to call on both sexes exactly equally, and to make sure she did, she would hold the attendance roster in her hand. What happened next surprised her. "After two days the boys blew up," she told Orenstein. "They started complaining and saying that I was calling on the girls more than them. I showed them it wasn't true and they had to back down. I kept on doing it, but for the boys, equality was hard to get used to; they perceived it as a big loss."[34]

(Of course, equality is virtually always seen as a loss by the privileged group. If a teacher gives exactly equal time to heterosexuality and to homosexuality, to people of color as to white people, to women and to men, he or she is invariably going to be criticized as being biased in favor of the minority group. When one is used to being the center of attention all the time, being out of the limelight for a moment or even an hour can feel like complete rejection.)

So, what is the answer? A return to single-sex schools? Some educators have thought so. In the early 1970s, as virtually all previously all-male colleges and many previously all-female colleges became coeducational, several studies indicated that single-sex colleges still held significant benefits. A study by Elizabeth Tidball in 1973 looked at the educational backgrounds of women listed in *Who's Who of American Women* and concluded that women's colleges with large numbers of women faculty provided the most beneficial environment for educating women.[35]

Although it is true that most of the women listed in those volumes from the 1960s and before had gone to Vassar, Radcliffe, Bryn Mawr, Smith, and the other Seven Sister colleges, Tidball's study had several serious flaws. Her data came from the 1960s, before any formerly all-male Ivy League and other prestigious all-male schools were opened to women, and the actual number of women in the study was so small as to defy efforts at generalization. Second, there were far more women's colleges at the time—nearly three hundred in 1960, compared with just eighty-four in 1990. Third, many of the women listed in *Who's Who* were there because of the accomplishments of their fathers or their husbands; that is, they were not accomplished in their own right, but only in their connection to a man—which couldn't have been the result of attending an all-women's college. (For example, until the 1980s, most women who were in the U.S. Senate, House of Representatives, or were governors of states were the daughters or widows of men who had held those offices.)[36]

Perhaps the most glaring error in the Tidball research was that she assumed that it was attendance at the single-sex college that led to wealth and fame. However, most of the women who attended such prestigious colleges were *already* wealthy and had likely gone to single-sex boarding schools (or at least private preparatory schools). What Tidball had inadvertently measured was not the effect of single-sex schools on women's achievement, but the correlation between social class and attendance at all-female colleges. Here was a reported gender difference that turned out not to be a gender difference at all. Class turned out to be the far better predictor of women's achievement than whether their college was single-sex or coeducational. Subsequent research found that coeducational colleges produced a higher percentage of women earning bachelor's degrees in the sciences, engineering, and mathematics.[37]

There was, additionally, some evidence that men's achievement was improved by attending a single-sex college. Again, many of these supposed gains in achievement vanished when social class and boys' secondary school experiences were added to the equation. In fact, when one discusses gender equality, the outcome of attending an all-male college, according to sociologist David Riesman was "usually unfortunate. Stag undergraduate institutions are prone to a kind of excess." While Jencks and Riesman "do not find the arguments against women's colleges as persuasive as the arguments against men's colleges," they conclude:

> The all male-college would be relatively easy to defend if it emerged from a world in which women were established as fully equal to men. But it does not. It is therefore likely to be a witting or unwitting device for preserving tacit assumptions of male superiority—assumptions for which women must eventually pay. So, indeed, must men . . . [who] pay a price for arrogance vis-a-vis women. Since they almost always commit a part of their lives into a woman's hands anyway, their tendency to crush these women means crushing

a part of themselves. This may not hurt them as much as it hurts the woman involved, but it does cost something. Thus while we are not against segregation of the sexes under all circumstances, we are against it when it helps preserve sexual arrogance.[38]

In short, what women often learn at all-women's colleges is that they can do anything that men can do. By contrast, what men learn is that they (women) cannot do what they (the men) do. In this way, women's colleges may constitute a challenge to gender inequality, while men's colleges reproduce that inequality.

Consider an analogy with race here. One might justify the continued existence of historically all-black colleges on the grounds that such schools challenge racist ideas that black students cannot achieve academically, and provide a place where black students are free of everyday racism and thus free to become serious students. But one would have a more difficult time justifying maintaining an all-white college, which would, by its existence, reproduce racist inequality. Such a place would be more like David Duke University than Duke University. Returning to gender, as psychologist Carol Tavris concludes, "there is a legitimate place for all-women's schools if they give young women a stronger shot at achieving self-confidence, intellectual security, and professional competence in the workplace." On the other hand, since coeducation is based "on the premise that there are few genuine differences between men and women, and that people should be educated as individuals, rather than as members of a gender," the question is "not whether to become coeducational, but rather when and how to undertake the process."[39]

Single-sex education for women often perpetuates detrimental attitudes and stereotypes about women, that "by nature or situation girls and young women cannot become successful or learn well in coeducational institutions."[40] Even when supported by feminist women, the idea that women cannot compete equally with men in the same arena, that they need "special" treatment, signals an abandonment of hope, the inability or unwillingness to make the creation of equal and safe schools a national priority. "Since we cannot do that," we seem to be telling girls, "we'll do the next best thing— separate you from those nasty boys who will only make your lives a living hell."[41]

In some cases, making one's life a living hell was sort of the pedagogical point. Virginia Military Institute and The Citadel, both state-supported military-style institutions, fought women's entry because, they claimed, their "adversative" educational methodology—cadets are regimented and uniformed, heads are shaved, privacy is entirely removed, and stress is intentionally induced by incessant drilling, merciless harassment, and rigid discipline—is only effective for males. Women, the school claimed, were "not capable of the ferocity requisite to make the program work." They are "physically weaker . . . more emotional, and cannot take stress as well as men." If admitted, VMI averred, female cadets would "break down crying" and suffer "psychological trauma" from the rigors of the system.[42] While males "tend to need an environment of adversativeness or ritual combat in which the teacher is a disciplinarian and a worthy competitor," females "tend to thrive in a cooperative atmosphere in which the teacher is emotionally connected with the students," was the way The Citadel's lawyers put it.[43]

The Citadel also argued that women's entry would destroy the mystical bonding experience among the male cadets. One of The Citadel's expert witnesses, Major General Josiah Bunting III (a VMI graduate who is now superintendent at VMI), suggested that women would be "a toxic kind of virus" that would destroy The Citadel. "Adolescent males benefit from being able to focus exclusively on the task at hand, without the intrusion of any sexual tension," he claimed.[44]

Instead of women's entry, VMI and The Citadel proposed funding women's "leadership" training at nearby private all-female colleges. Such programs were not to be "separate but equal"—the fiction maintained by segregated schools to maintain segregation that was ruled unconstitutional in 1954—but, as VMI protested, "distinct but superior," since their educational methodologies would be tuned to the needs of males and females respectively. The Supreme Court saw through this charade, and overwhelmingly determined that these women's programs would be but a "pale shadow" of VMI; women were admitted in 1997.

In reality, the "rigors" of the adversative system are attractive to only a small number of men to begin with, and probably to an even smaller number of women. In Fall 2002, twenty-four women cadets enrolled at VMI. There has also been a 70 percent increase in applications from men.

Such proposals to maintain sex segregation in education also seem to be based on faulty understandings of the differences between women and men, the belief in an unbridgeable chasm between "them" and "us" based on different styles of learning, qualities of mind, structures of brains, and ways of knowing, talking, or caring. John Dewey, perhaps America's greatest theorist of education, and a fierce supporter of women's equal rights, was infuriated at the contempt for women suggested by such programs. Dewey scoffed at "'female botany,' 'female algebra,' and for all I know a 'female multiplication table,'" he wrote in 1911. "Upon no subject has there been so much dogmatic assertion based on so little scientific evidence, as upon male and female types of mind." Coeducation, Dewey argued, was beneficial to women, opening up opportunities previously unattainable. Girls, he suggested, became less manipulative, and acquired "greater self-reliance and a desire to win approval by deserving it instead of by 'working' others. Their narrowness of judgment, depending on the enforced narrowness of outlook, is overcome; their ultra-feminine weaknesses are toned up." What's more, Dewey claimed, coeducation is beneficial to men. "Boys learn gentleness, unselfishness, courtesy; their natural vigor finds helpful channels of expression instead of wasting itself in lawless boisterousness," he wrote.[45] Another educational reformer, Thomas Wentworth Higginson, also opposed single-sex schools. "Sooner or later, I am persuaded, the human race will look upon all these separate collegiate institutions as most American travelers now look at the vast monastic establishments of Southern Europe; with respect for the pious motives of their founders, but with wonder that such a mistake should ever have been made."[46] While Higginson predicted correctly for the collegiate level—there are today only three all-male colleges and less than half the number of all-female colleges than there were forty years ago—there are also some efforts to revive the single-sex ideal, at both the collegiate and the secondary levels.

TOWARD GENDER EQUALITY IN SCHOOLS

Many school districts are today experimenting with single-sex schools, or single sex classrooms, especially to teach math and science to girls. There have been notable experiments with single-sex schools for black boys in Detroit and Newark, and for black girls in New York City to teach math and science. In Detroit, for example, city officials tried to respond to a crisis in the black community: of 24,000 males enrolled in the Detroit public schools, only 30 percent had grade point averages better than 2.0; boys were suspended three times more often than girls; 60 percent of the drug offenses were committed by eighth and ninth grade dropouts. The city of Detroit proposed an all-male academy to offer boys "self-esteem, rites of passage, role model interaction and academic improvement." While these goals were worthy, many parents objected that the project was ignoring the needs of girls, and, faced with likely lawsuits and public opposition, the city officials withdrew the plan. Similar programs were canceled or withdrawn in Philadelphia and Miami, though one is still in operation in Baltimore. President Bush has also advocated some forms of single sex schools.[47]

The evidence to support such innovations is inconsistent and discouraging. In a sense, such schools propose a "racial" or "gender" remedy for a problem of "class"—since *children,* both boys and girls, would no doubt thrive in schools with lot of resources, small classes, and fabulously trained teachers. In addition, much of the celebrated "need" for positive role models and the excoriation of black men for abandoning their families takes no account of the economic uncertainties that black males face, nor of the economic pressures that tear families apart. Economic hope for a real future would probably go a lot farther in keeping families together and keeping boys in school and off the streets.[48]

And for girls? At the new Young Women's Leadership School in Harlem, 160 middle school girls are doing somewhat better than their counterparts at coeducational schools. Ninety percent of them scored at or above grade level on math tests; 63 percent read at or above grade level (compared with 51 percent and 44 percent respectively, for the rest of New York City). And their attendance rates exceed city averages by 3 percent. "Our intention is to give inner-city kids a choice which in the past has only been reserved for the wealthy and parochial school children," said Ann Rubenstein Tisch, one of the school's founders.[49]

But that school is currently being opposed legally by the American Civil Liberties Union and by the National Organization for Women on the grounds that it discriminates against boys. And the claims of benefits are being challenged empirically by a recent study by the American Association of University Women, which found that while many girls report that they feel single-sex classrooms are more conducive to learning, they also show no significant gains in achievement in math and science. Another researcher found some significant differences between coeducational and single-sex classes—but only in Catholic schools, not in private single-sex schools, and only for girls. A third researcher noted that the advantages of one or the other type of school are nonexistent for middle-class and otherwise advantaged students, but found some positive outcomes for black or Hispanic girls from low socioeconomic homes. "Separating by sex is not the answer to inequities in the schools," noted Maggie Ford, president of the AAUW Educational Foundation. And Kenneth Clark, the pioneering African American educator, was equally unequivocal. "I can't believe that we're actually regressing like this. Why are we still talking about segregating and stigmatizing black males?" he asked. He should know: His research provided the empirical argument against "separate but equal" schools in the U.S. Supreme Court's landmark *Brown v. Board of Education* civil rights decision in 1954.[50]

The findings of the only systematic study of a pilot program for single-sex schools in California reported rather depressing results. Traditional gender stereotypes remained in full effect; in fact, such schools actually perpetuated stereotypes that girls were good and boys were bad, which should prompt some reconsideration from those who want to "rescue" boys from meddling feminists. In the end, after three years, five of the six school districts closed their single-sex academies.[51]

Another arena in which gender inequality in education is today being challenged is in extracurricular activities, especially sports. Here, girls once received the clear message that their place was on the sidelines, cheering for the boys, whose programs received the lion's share of funding. The passage of amendments to the Education Act of 1972 contained Title IX, which abolished sex discrimination in public schools and has since been taken to mandate that women's sports be funded equally with men's (excluding football, which is extraordinarily expensive for schools to fund, and which virtually no women are able to play). Since then, girls' participation in interscholastic sports has soared from 300,000 to over 2 million, and the involvement of college-age women has expanded by more than 600 percent.[52]

Predictably, this clear and unequivocal success has been met with loud and vociferous criticism that adequate enforcement of Title IX programs has rendered males the "second sex" of college sports, the new victims of reverse discrimination, since a number of men's teams have been cut to achieve the proportionality mandated by Title IX. Such short-sighted criticism fails to note several important ways in which equality in sports is good for both women and men. By maintaining a zero-sum approach, for example, they miss the ways in which both male and female sports programs are utterly disfigured by the salaries paid to male coaches in big-revenue college sports. When many college football and basketball coaches earn salaries—not including endorsement bonuses from athletic footwear companies—that are often ten times higher than the salary of their college's president, then clearly revenues for college sports need not mandate the cutting of a men's team, but the reallocation of funds throughout the entire athletic program. Simple fairness would dictate that girls and boys have equal opportunities to participate in sports, as in the rest of their lives, and the dramatic success of Title IX demonstrates that when such opportunities are offered, women take them. Besides, what could be of more benefit to a guy than a woman who is strong and capable and appreciates the physicality of her own body?[53]

Across the country, state governments are mandating gender equity programs for elementary and secondary education. These programs are designed to reduce the obstacles that continue to stand in the way of girls' *as well as boys'* achievement—the harassment and bullying from other boys, and the brutal enforcement of rigid stereotypes of masculine and feminine behavior by both teachers and classmates. For the same assumptions—that males and females are so fundamentally different that we could not possibly learn equally and together—plague both boys and girls. Gender inequality in education produces the gender differences we assume, with deleterious consequences for both genders; it impairs both boys' and girls' efforts to find their voices, discipline their minds, and prepare themselves for their futures.

THE GENDERED WORKPLACE

Well, Son, I'll tell you:
Life for me ain't been no crystal stair.
It had tacks in it,
And splinters,
And boards all torn up,
And places with no carpet on the floor—
Bare.

—LANGSTON HUGHES
"MOTHER TO SON"

Freud once wrote that the two great tasks for all human beings were "to work and to love." And it is certainly true that people have always worked—to satisfy their basic material needs for food, clothing, and shelter, to provide for children and loved ones, to participate in community life, as well as to satisfy more culturally and historically specific desires to leave a mark on the world and to move up the social ladder. So it shouldn't surprise us that virtually every society has developed a division of labor, a way of dividing the tasks that must be done in order for the society as a whole to survive. And since gender, as we have seen, is a system of both classification and identity and a structure of power relations, it shouldn't surprise us that virtually every society has a gendered division of labor. There are very few tasks, in very few societies, that are not allocated by gender. This doesn't necessarily imply that the tasks assigned to one gender are less or more significant to the life of the community than the other's. One might use a variety of criteria to assign tasks, and one might determine the relative values of each in a variety of ways. Valuing women's work over men's work, or vice versa, is not inevitable; it is an artifact of cultural relationships.

All this hardly comes as a surprise. But what might surprise contemporary American readers is that the gendered division of labor that many have called "traditional," the separation of the world into two distinct spheres—the public domain of work, business, politics, and culture, and the private world of the home, domestic life, and child care—is a relatively new phenomenon in American society. The doctrine of separate spheres was not firmly established until the decades just before the Civil War, and even then it was honored as much in the breach as in its fulfillment. Women have always worked outside the home for both economic and personal reasons—though they have had to fight to do so. The so-called traditional system of dads who head out to work every morning, leaving mom to stay at home with the children, a full-time housewife and mother, was an invention of the 1950s—and part of a larger ideological effort to facilitate the reentry of American men back into the workplace and domestic life after World War II, and to legitimate the return of women from the workplace and back into the home.

What might surprise us is that this universal gendered division of labor tells us virtually nothing about the relative values given to the work women and men do. And, interestingly, it turns out that in societies in which women's work is less valued—that is, in more traditional societies in which women's legal status is lower—women do *more* work than the men do, up to 35 percent more in terms of time. (see figure 8.1)

The Changing Gender Composition of the Labor Force

Perhaps the most significant change in the relationship of gender and work is numerical—the enormous shift in the gender composition of the labor force. In the twentieth century, women have entered every area of the labor force, and in unprecedented numbers. The impact has been enormous. In my classes I often illustrate this phenomenon by asking the women who intend to have full-time careers or jobs outside the home to raise their hands. Without exception, all two hundred or so women do. Then I ask them to keep their hands raised if their mothers have or had a full-time job or career outside the home for at least eight years without interruption. About one-half put their hands down. Then I ask them to still keep their hands raised if their grandmothers had a full-time job or career outside the home for at least eight uninterrupted years. Perhaps now two or three hands remain raised. In the class, one can clearly see the differences in women's working lives over just three generations.

What would happen if I posed the same question to the men in the class? "How many men expect to have full-time careers, outside the home, when they graduate from college?" The very question sounds ridiculous. *Of course* they expect to have careers, as did their fathers, grandfathers, and great-grandfathers. They'd never put their hands down, unless a distant relative was unemployed or we reach back to the 1930s Great Depression.

This experiment illustrates in miniature the dramatic change in the composition of the labor force. The percentage of both women and men entering the labor force increased throughout the twentieth century, but women's rate of increase far outpaced men's. The percentage of women working has risen from 20.6 percent in 1900 to more than 60 percent in 2000 (men's rates were 85 percent and 74 percent respectively). Marriage and children have slowed that entry, but the trajectory is still the same. Only 6 percent of married women worked outside the home in 1900; 61 percent do so today. And while only 12 percent of married women with children under six years old were working outside the home as recently as 1950, nearly two-thirds were doing so less than forty years later.

This dramatic increase in labor force participation has been true for all races and ethnicities. (Black women's rates [64 percent] are slightly higher than white women's [60 percent], and Hispanic women's rates are slightly lower [56 percent] than both

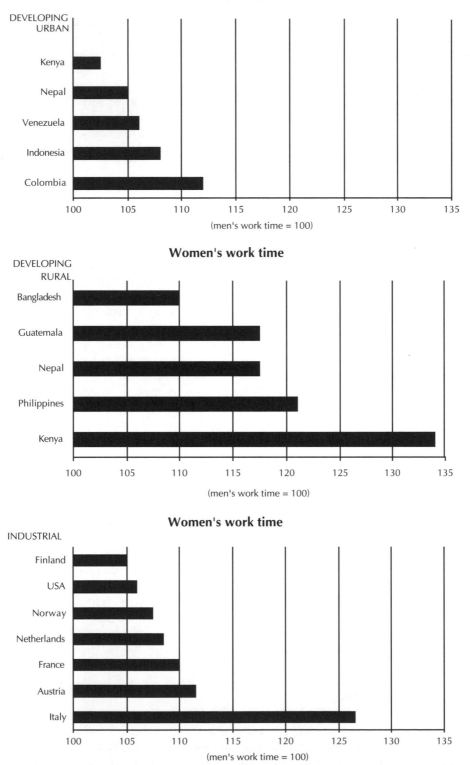

Figure 8.1. Women work more hours than men. From United Nations, *Human Development Report 1995* (Oxford University Press, 1995). Reprinted by permission of publisher.

Percentage of each group in labor force

Figure 8.2. Labor force participation of women. From *The First Measured Century* by Theodore Caplow, Louis Hicks and Ben J. Wattenberg.

black and white women. Among men, however, Hispanic men have the highest rates [79 percent] compared with white men [74 percent] and black men [66 percent.][1] Even since 1970, the increase in women's participation has been dramatic. In the next decade, 80 percent of all new entrants into the labor force will be women, minorities, and immigrants. Among married women, the data are actually more startling. In 1900, only 4 percent of married women were working, and by 1960, only 18.6 percent of married women with young children were working. This number has tripled since 1960, so that today, nearly 60 percent of all married women with children under six years old are in the labor force.[2]

Women's entry into the labor force has taken place at every level, from low-paid clerical and sales work through all the major professions. In 1962, women represented less than 1 percent of all engineers, 6 percent of all doctors, and 19 percent of all university professors. By 1990, women made up over 7 percent of all engineers, one-fifth of all doctors, and almost two-fifths of all university professors. From 1970 to 1995, women's share of doctoral degrees jumped from 25 percent to 44 percent among whites and from 39 percent to 55 percent among blacks. "The increasing representation of women among the ranks of managers in organizations," writes sociologist Jerry Jacobs, "is perhaps the most dramatic shift in the sex composition of an occupation since clerical work became a female dominated field in the late 19th century."[3]

We've come a long way, indeed from the mid-nineteenth century, when a young Mary Taylor wrote to her friend Charlotte Brontë that "there are no means for a woman to live in England, but by teaching, sewing, or washing. The last is the best, the best paid, the least unhealthy and the most free." These changes have rippled through the rest of society, gradually changing the relationship of the family to the workplace. Gone forever is the male breadwinner who supports a family on his income alone. What was the norm at the turn of the century now constitutes less than 5 percent of all families. Forget the Cleavers, the Andersons, and the Nelsons. Forget the Cramdens and the Nortons. And forget even Lucy, whose every scheme to enter the work world, from the bakery to Ricky's nightclub act, ended in disaster. Today, the norm is the dual-earner couple. And yet we don't seem to get it. The *Workplace 2000* report issued during the Reagan administration, for example, admitted that "most current policies were designed for a society in which men worked and women stayed home."[4]

THE PERSISTENCE OF GENDER IDEOLOGIES

Such statements acknowledge that while the realities of home and workplace have changed, our ideas about them have lagged far behind. Many American still believe in the "traditional" male breadwinner/female housewife model even if our own lives no longer reflect it—much like the way we say we believe in the individual small shop-keeper, the Mom and Pop grocery on Main Street, as the cornerstone of American business—even as we shop almost exclusively at Wal-Mart, The Gap, Sam's Clubs, and shopping malls. Our adherence to gender ideologies that no longer fit the world we live in has dramatic consequences for women and men, both at work and at home.

Since the early nineteenth century, the workplace has been seen as a masculine arena, where men could test and prove their manhood against other men in the dog-eat-dog marketplace. Working enabled men to confirm their manhood as breadwin-ners and family providers. The workplace was a site of "homosocial reproduction"—a place where men created themselves as men. As psychiatrist Willard Gaylin writes:

> [N]othing is more important to a man's pride, self-respect, status, and manhood than work. Nothing. Sexual impotence, like sudden loss of ambulation or physical strength, may shat-ter his self-confidence. But . . . pride is built on work and achievement, and the success that accrues from that work. Yet today men often seem confused and contradictory in their attitudes about work.[5]

Gaylin captures a contradiction at the heart of men's relationship to the workplace: On the one hand, it is the most significant place where men prove manhood and confirm identity, and on the other hand, all that breadwinning and providing does not neces-sarily make men happy. "I have never met a man—among my patients or friends," Gaylin writes, "who in his heart of hearts considers himself a success."[6]

The nineteenth-century ideal of the self-made man, and the prospect of unlim-ited upward mobility for those who worked hard enough, placed men on a treadmill of work, sacrifice, and responsibility. If a man could rise as high as his dreams and discipline could take him, he could also fall just as far. A 1974 Yankelovitch survey found that about 80 percent of American men were unhappy in their jobs. Another study found that 74 percent of men said they would choose a slower career track to spend more time with their families. "No man on his deathbed ever said he wished he had spent less time with his family and more time at the office," as the familiar cliché had it.

Yet why would men be unhappy in an arena whose homosociality they struggle so hard to maintain? Part of the reason has to do with what happens in the workplace. Given the demands of corporate or factory life, men rarely, if ever, experience any ability to discuss their inner lives, their feelings, their needs. The workplace becomes a treadmill, a place to fit in, not to stand out. A place where a man sacrifices himself on the altar of family responsibility. Perhaps one of the most poignant expressions of this dilemma comes in Arthur Miller's elegiac play *Death of a Salesman,* when Willy Loman's sons confront their own futures in the workplace. First Biff looks down that road:

> Well, I spent six or seven years after high school trying to work myself up. Shipping clerk, salesman, business of one kind or another. And it's a measly manner of existence. To get on that subway on the hot mornings in summer. To devote your whole life to keep stock, of making phone calls, or selling or buying. To suffer fifty weeks of the year for the sake of a two-week vacation, when all you really desire is to be outdoors, with your shirt off. And always to have to get ahead of the next fella. And still—that's how you build a future.

Then his brother, Happy, responds with his vision of that future:

> All I can do now is wait for the merchandise manager to die. And suppose I get to be merchandise manager? He's a good friend of mine, and he just built a terrific estate on Long Island. And he lived there about two months and sold it, and now he's building another one. He can't enjoy it once it's finished. And I know that's just what I would do. I don't know what the hell I'm workin' for.[7]

Many men say they lose sight of what they're working for. Men often feel that they are supposed to be tough, aggressive, competitive—the "king of the hill," the boss, his "own man," on "top of the heap." We measure masculinity by the size of a man's paycheck. Asked why he worked so hard, one man told an interviewer:

> I don't know . . . I really hate to be a failure. I always wanted to be on top of whatever I was doing. It depends on the particular picture but I like to be on top, either chairman of the committee or president of an association or whatever.[8]

Most men, of course, are neither at the top of the hierarchy nor likely to get there. Raised to believe that there are no limits, they bump constantly into those limits and have no one to blame except themselves. Men, as the saying goes, are "unsexed by failure": They cease to be seen as real men.

Women, on the other hand, are "unsexed by success." To be competent, aggressive, and ambitious in the workplace may be both gender confirming and gender conforming for men, but they are gender *non*conforming, and thus gender disconfirming for women, undermining her sense of herself as feminine. Geri Richmond, a chemist, describes how she constantly battled between being "feminine" and being a scientist. A high school cheerleader and chemistry whiz, she gradually shed all the trappings of traditional femininity in graduate school in order to fit in—she threw out her dresses, nail polish, makeup, high-heeled shoes. She even tossed out her hand lotion, out of fear that its scent would evoke femininity.[9]

In the all-male workplace, women's role was to "lubricate" the male-male interactions. Women performed what sociologist Arlie Hochschild called "emotion work," making sure that the all-male arena was well oiled and functioning smoothly. So, for example, women performed jobs such as stewardess, office manager, cocktail waitress, and cheerleader to make sure the male-male interactions went smoothly—and remained unmistakably heterosexual.[10]

If woman had no "real" role in the workplace, what did she do there? The traditional idea was that women worked either because they *had* to—because they were single, working class, and/or the sole economic support for their children or themselves— or for the extra pocket money ("play money") that they, as middle-class consumers, wanted for their extra little trifles. This often made working women apologetic for working at all. "If the world were perfect," it pushed them to say, "we would stay home with our children, which is after all, where we belong and where we would rather be." But such a position belies women's actual experience. Women work, the political columnist Katha Pollitt writes, "because we enjoy our jobs, our salaries, the prospect of a more interesting and secure future than we would have with rusted skills, less seniority, less experience."[11]

The combination of the persistence of traditional gender ideologies and changes in economic and social realities makes today's workplace a particularly contentious arena for working out gender issues. On the one hand, women face persistent discrimination based on their gender: they are paid less, promoted less, and assigned to specific jobs despite their qualifications and motivations; and they are made to feel unwelcome, like intruders into an all-male preserve. On the other hand, men say they are bewildered and angered by the changes in workplace policy that make them feel like they are "walking on eggshells," fearful of making any kind of remark to a woman lest they be hauled into court for sexual harassment.

The structural backdrop to this current workplace wariness and corporate confusion is one of the highest levels of workplace gender inequality in the industrial world. That the United States manifests this gender inequality may contradict American assumptions about freedom and equality of opportunity, but it is not so terribly surprising since we also have among the highest general levels of income inequality in general in the industrial world. According to a study commissioned by the Paris-based Organization for Economic Cooperation and Development, the difference between the best-paid 10 percent and the lowest-paid 10 percent of all working Americans is wider than in any other industrialized nation. During the economic boom of the 1980s, the top 1 percent of the income pyramid received about 60 percent of all the economic gains of the decade. The next 19 percent received another 25 percent, so that, in all, 85 percent of all economic gains of the decade went to the top one-fifth of the economic hierarchy. The bottom fifth of Americans actually lost 9 percent and the next fifth above them lost 1 percent. So much for "trickle down" economics! For the bottom 80 percent of Americans, the peak earning year in the last three decades was 1973—that is, their annual incomes have since then either remained flat or declined. According to the Congressional Budget Office, mean family income, in fact, has remained absolutely flat. Measured in constant dollars, mean family income in 1973 was $35,474; in 1990 it was $35,353.

Remember, also, this is average *family* income—and the greatest single change in the labor force is the increasing presence of women. So this means that men's incomes have actually declined over the past quarter-century. A thirty-year-old man in 1949 saw his real earnings rise by 63 percent by the time he turned forty. In 1973, that same thirty-year-old man would have seen his real income *fall* by 1 percent by his fortieth birthday. These economic indicators are particularly important as the general context for gender inequality, because they suggest that the majority of male workers have felt increasingly squeezed in the past two decades, working longer and harder to make ends meet, while experiencing a decline in income. This increased economic pressure, coupled with increased economic precariousness caused by downsizing, corporate lay-offs, and market volatility, has kept American men anxious about their previously un-challenged position as providers and breadwinners.

THE PERSISTENCE OF GENDER DISCRIMINATION IN THE WORKPLACE

For many years, the chief obstacle facing women who sought to enter the labor force was sex discrimination. Discrimination occurs when we treat people unequally because of personal characteristics that are not related to the job. Discrimination can be when we treat people who are similar in different ways, or when we treat people who are different in similar ways. For example, women and African Americans are seen, legally, as "similar" in all functionally relevant aspects relating to employment, housing, or ed-ucation. Therefore, to exclude one race or gender from housing, educational opportu-nities, or employment would be a form of discrimination. On the other hand, people with certain physical disabilities are seen as legally *different,* and thus deserving of an-tidiscrimination protection. Treating them "the same" as able-bodied people—failing to provide wheelchair accessible facilities, for example—is therefore also a form of discrimination.

In gender discrimination in the workplace, employers have historically referred to a variety of characteristics about women in order to exclude them, for instance, women didn't really want to work; they didn't need the money; they have different aptitudes and interests. It was assumed that women either couldn't do a job, or, if they could, they would neither want to nor need to do it. What these arguments share is a belief that the differences between women and men are decisive, and that these differences are the source of women's and men's different experiences. Such arguments also pro-vided the pretense for justifying race discrimination in employment and education, at least until 1954, when the Supreme Court ruled in *Brown v. Board of Education of Topeka* that there were no compelling differences between blacks and whites that could serve as a qualification for equal access to employment or education. Today, the court holds race cases to what it calls "strict scrutiny," meaning that discrimination on the basis of race is always legally suspect, and there are no legal grounds for racial discrimination. It is discrimination to treat those who are alike—blacks and whites—as if they are different.

This is not completely true, however, when it comes to gender. In its cases in volving gender discrimination, the Supreme Court has granted only "intermediate scrutiny." Discrimination on the basis of gender is permissible, but only under the most exceptional of circumstances. The basis for the discrimination may not rely on any stereotypic ideas about the differences between women and men, and there must be a "bona fide occupational qualification"—that is, the discrimination must be based on some occupational requirement that either only men or only women could perform. In federal cases, the discrimination must also be "substantially related to an important governmental interest"—that is, it must serve some larger goal of the government.

Consider, for example, the case of a nine-year-old girl who applies to work as a lifeguard at the beach. Denying her the job would not be a case of either gender or age discrimination, because one would equally deny it to a nine-year-old boy, since age is a functionally relevant category for the performance of the job. But it is extraordinarily difficult to demonstrate in court that the requirements of any particular job are such that only women or only men could possibly perform them.

One such case involved a woman who applied for a job with Trans World Airlines. During her interview, she was asked about her marital status, her plans regarding pregnancy, her relationship with another TWA employee, the number of children she had, whether they were legitimate, and her child care arrangements. In fact, that was *all* she was asked at her first interview. She was not hired. The courts found that she had been treated differently based on gender, and thus had been discriminated against. Can we even imagine the interviewers asking a male applicant those kinds of questions?

Most legal cases involving workplace discrimination have involved women bringing suit to enter formerly all-male workplaces. One interesting recent case, however, explored the other side of the coin. The Hooters restaurant chain was sued by several men who sought employment as waiters in restaurants in Illinois and Maryland. Historically, Hooters only hired "voluptuous" women to work as their "scantily-clad" bartenders and food servers. The male plaintiffs, and their lawyers, argued that such a policy violates equal employment statutes. Hooters countered that its restaurants provide "vicarious sexual recreation," and that "female sexuality is a bona fide occupation," citing other all-female occupations such as Playboy Bunnies and the Rockettes. Hooters' waitresses "serve Buffalo wings with a side order of sex appeal," was the way one newspaper columnist put it. Company spokesman Mike McNeil claimed that Hooters doesn't sell food; it sells sex appeal—and "to have female sex appeal, you have to be female." (The EEOC quietly dropped its own investigation, saying it had better cases to pursue.) Eventually, the case was settled out of court, with Hooters paying $3.75 million to the men and their attorneys, and adding a few men to their staff as bartenders—but not as waiters.[12]

SEX SEGREGATION

Outright gender discrimination is extremely difficult to justify. But far more subtle and pervasive mechanisms maintain gender inequality. Perhaps the most ubiquitous of these is sex segregation. Sex segregation, writes sociologist Barbara Reskin, "refers to women's and men's concentration in different occupations, industries, jobs, and levels in workplace hierarchies." Thus, sex segregation becomes, itself, a "sexual division of paid labor in which men and women do different tasks, or the same tasks under different names or at different times and places." Different occupations are seen as more appropriate for one gender or the other, and thus women and men are guided, pushed, or occasionally shoved into specific positions.[13]

In fact, sex segregation in the workplace is so pervasive that it appears to be the natural order of things, the simple expression of women's and men's natural predispositions. In that sense, it's more subtle than some garment factories in Bangladesh, where male and female workers actually work on different floors to ensure no contact between them. In the United States, it *appears* to be the result of our "natural" differences; but, as we have seen before, these differences are themselves the consequence of segregation. Today, fewer than 10 percent of all Americans have a co-worker or a colleague of the other sex who does the same job, for the same employer, in the same location, on the same shift. Though almost equal numbers of women and men go off to work every morning, we do not go together to the same place, nor do we have the same jobs. In fact, of the nearly 66 million women in the labor force in the United States, 30 percent worked in just ten of the 503 "occupations" listed by the U.S. Census. Or, to put it another way, more than 52 percent of all women or all men would have to change their jobs for the occupational distribution to be completely integrated.[14]

Sex segregation starts early and continues throughout our work lives. And it has significant consequences for incomes and experiences. I frequently ask my students how many of them worked as babysitters when they were younger. Typically, at least two-thirds of the women say they have, and occasionally one or two men say they have. How much did they earn? They average about four to five dollars an hour, typically earning twenty dollars for an afternoon or evening. When I ask how many of them have earned extra money by mowing lawns or shoveling snow, though, the gender division is reversed. Most of the men, but only an occasional woman, said they had those jobs, and typically earned about twenty or twenty-five dollars per house— or about one hunderd dollars a day. And while it is true that shoveling snow or mowing lawns require far more physical exertion than babysitting, babysitting also requires specific social, mental, and nurturing skills, caring and feeding, and the ability to respond quickly in a crisis. And in most societies, ours included, it is hardly the menial physical laborerers who are paid the most (think of the difference between corporate executives and professional lawn mowers). In fact, when grown-ups do these jobs— professional baby nurse or lawn maintenance—their incomes are roughly similar. What determines the differences in wages for these two after-school occupations has far less to do with the intrinsic properties of the jobs and far more to do with the gender of who performs them. That we see the disparities as having to do with something other than gender is exactly the way in which occupational sex segregation obscures gender discrimination.

The impact of sex segregation on income remains just as profound as the differences between babysitting and snow shoveling for the rest of our lives. Job segregation by sex is the single largest cause of the pay gap between the sexes. Consider that in 1995, while women represented 46 percent of all workers in the civilian labor force (more than 57 million women), they were only 13.4 percent of all dentists, 8.4 percent of all engineers, 26.2 percent of all lawyers and judges, 11 percent of all police and detectives, 5 percent of firefighters, 8.9 percent of all precision, production, crafts, and repair workers, and 24.4 percent of all physicians. On the other hand, women were also 98.5 percent of all secretaries, 93.1 percent of all nurses, 96.8 percent of all child care workers, 88.4 percent of all telephone operators, 74.7 percent of all teachers (excluding college and university), 82.9 percent of all data entry keyboard operators. Almost one-half of all female employees today work in occupations that are more than 75 percent female.[15]

Explanations of sex segregation often rely on the qualities of male and female job seekers. Because of differential socialization, women and men are likely to seek different kinds of jobs for different reasons. However, socialization alone is not sufficient as an explanation. "Socialization cannot explain why a sex-segregated labor market emerged, why each sex is allocated to particular types of occupations, and why the sex typing of occupations changes in particular ways over time." Instead, we need to think of sex segregation as the outcome of several factors—"on the differential socialization of young men and women, sex-typed tracking in the educational system, and sex-linked social control at the workplace, at the hiring stage and beyond."[16]

If sex segregation were simply the product of socialized differences between women and men, we should expect that professions would have roughly comparable gender distributions in other cities or countries. But they do not. For example, in New York City, there are only twenty-five women out of 11,500 firefighters, or .03 percent of the force. In Minneapolis, 17 percent of the fire fighters are women. Or take dentists. In the United States, dentistry is a heavily male-dominated profession; in Europe, most dentists are female. In Russia, about half of all doctors are women, and have been for some time. Assuming that European and Russian women and men are roughly similar to North Americans, you would expect the gender composition of dentistry or medicine to be similar.

This leads to another consequence of sex segregation: wage differentials. Professions that are male dominated tend to have higher wages; professions that are female dominated tend to have lower wages. And though one might be tempted to explain this by the characteristics of the job, it turns out that the gender composition of the position is actually a better predictor. Again, take dentists. In the United States, dentistry sits near the top of the income pyramid. In Europe, the income level of dentists is about average. This difference has nothing to do with the practice of dentistry, which is, one assumes, fairly comparable. The wage difference is entirely the result of the gender of the person who does the job. There is nothing inherent in the job that makes it more "suitable" for women or for men.

One of the easiest ways to see the impact of sex segregation on wages is to watch what happens when a particular occupation begins to change its gender composition. For example, clerical work was once considered a highly skilled occupation, in which a virtually all-male labor force was paid reasonably well. (One is reminded, of course, of the exception to this rule, the innocent and virtuous Bob Cratchit in Charles Dickens's *A Christmas Carol*.) In the early part of the twentieth century, in both Britain and the United States, though, the gender distribution began to change, and by the middle of the century, most clerical workers were female. As a result, clerical work was reevaluated as less demanding of skill and less valuable to the organization; thus, workers' wages fell. As sociologist Samuel Cohn notes, this is a result, not a cause, of the changing gender composition of the workforce.[17]

Veterinary medicine, also, had long been a male-dominated field. In the late 1960s, only about 5 percent of veterinary students were women. Today that number is closer to 70 percent and the percentage of female veterinarians has more than doubled since 1991, while the number of male veterinarians has declined by 15 percent. And their incomes have followed the changing gender composition. In the 1970s, when males dominated the field, veterinarians' incomes were right behind those of physicians; today veterinarians average about $70,000 to $80,000 a year, while physicians average closer to double that figure. "Vets are people with medical degrees without the medical income," commented one veterinary epidemiologist.[18]

The exact opposite process took place with computer programmers. In the 1940s, women were hired as keypunch operators, the precursor to computer programmer, because the job seemed to resemble clerical work. In fact, however, computer programming "demanded complex skills in abstract logic, mathematics, electrical circuitry and machinery, all of which," sociologist Katharine Donato observed, "women used to perform in their work" without much problem. However, once programming was recognized as "intellectually demanding," it became attractive to men, who began to enter the field, and thus drove wages up considerably.[19]

The relationship between gender composition and prestige (and wages) has long been in evidence. In the 1920s, the feminist writer Charlotte Perkins Gilman found it

amusing to see how rapidly the attitude toward a given occupation changed as it changed hands. For instance, two of the oldest occupations of women, the world over, were that of helping other women to bring babies into the world and that of laying out the dead. Women sat at the gates of life, at both ends, for countless generations. Yet as soon as the obstetrician found one large source of income in his highly specialized services, and the undertaker found another in his, these occupations became "man's work"; a "woman doctor" was shrunk from even by women, and a "woman undertaker" seemed ridiculous.[20]

(It is interesting that women have returned to obstetrics, but undertaking remains virtually all male.)

The sex of the worker is also vitally important in determining wages. Women and men are paid not to do the same work, but different work, and they are evaluated on different standards. As William Bielby and James Baron write, "[M]en's jobs are rewarded according to their standing within the hierarchy of men's work, and women's jobs are rewarded according to their standing within the hierarchy of women's work. The legitimacy of this system is easy to sustain in a segregated workplace." Stated simply, "women's occupations pay less at least partly *because* women do them."[21]

Legal remedies for sex stereotyping of occupations have yielded mixed results. In a 1971 case, *Diaz v. Pan American World Airways,* the U.S. Court of Appeals for the Fifth Circuit ruled that men could not be denied employment as flight attendants on the grounds that passengers expected and preferred women in this position. In 1996, you will recall from the last chapter, the Supreme Court ruled that women could not be denied the educational opportunity offered to men at the Virginia Military Institute, despite the school's arguments that women would not want such an "adversative" education, nor would they be able successfully to withstand the physical rigors of the program.

A recent lawsuit against Wal Mart, the world's largest chain of retail stores, illustrates the problem of sex segregation. While 72 percent of Wal-Mart's hourly sales employees are women, they represent less than one-third of the company's managers (compared with 56 percent at their competitors), according to the lawsuit filed on behalf of nearly three-quarters of a million women. A lawsuit against Home Depot in the 1990s alleging similar sex segregation, was settled out of court for $65 million (plus $22.5 million in lawyers' fees).[22]

Perhaps the most widely cited case in sex segregation was the case of *EEOC v. Sears*, a case brought by the Equal Employment Opportunity Commission against the giant chain of retail stores. The EEOC had found that Sears had routinely shuttled women and men into different sales positions, resulting in massive wage disparities between the two. Women were pushed into over-the-counter retail positions, largely in clothing, jewelry, and household goods, where commissions tended to be low and workers received straight salary for their work. Men, on the other hand, tended to concentrate in high-end consumer goods, such as refrigerators and televisions, which offered high commissions.

Sears argued that this sex-based division of retail sales resulted from individual choice on the part of its male and female labor forces. Differential socialization, they suggested, led women and men to pursue different career paths. Women, Sears claimed, were less interested in the more demanding, intensely competitive, and time-consuming higher-end commission sales positions, and were interested in those that offered them more flexibility, while the men were more interested in those pressure-filled, high-paying positions. Women, Sears argued, were more relationship-centered and less competitive.

The EEOC, by contrast, argued that although Sears did not intend to discriminate, such outcomes were the result of gender-based discrimination. The case did not pit the interests or motivations of all men against those of all women, but rather included only those women who were already in the labor force, who, one assumed, had similar motivations to those of men in the labor force. Just because it is true, argues historian Alice Kessler-Harris, who was an expert witness for the EEOC, that there are average differences between women and men in their motivations does not mean that every single member of the group "men" or "women" are identical to every other member, and that some would not seek the opportunities afforded to the other group. To discriminate against individuals on the basis of average between-group differences ignores the differences *within* each group, differences that often turn out to be greater than the differences between the groups.

Such behavior, of course, relies on stereotypes, and should be prohibited under the law. Stereotypes assume that all members of a group share characteristics that, possibly, some members of the group share—and even, occasionally, most members share. Logically, stereotypes fall into a compositional fallacy—assuming that what is true of some is true for all. So it would be illogical to assert that just because all members of category A are also members of category B, therefore all members of category B are members of category A. You know nothing, for example, about the relative size of these categories: all As can be Bs, and yet all Bs may not be As. Thus, in the classic formulation of the compositional fallacy one might say that "all members of the Mafia are Italian, but all Italians are not members of the Mafia," or that "all humans are animals, but not all animals are human."

In the Sears case, the U.S. Supreme Court upheld Sears's acquittal on sex discrimination charges, in part because they said that no single individual woman had stepped forward and declared that she had sought to enter high-commission sales or had been refused because of these stereotypes. (Often legal cases seem to need a concrete plaintiff because the courts are less convinced by aggregate statistical disparities if no individual has been harmed.) And the Court found that gender differences did play a role, that "since difference was real and fundamental, it could explain statistical variations in Sears hiring." Yes. And it probably also explains the differences in salary.[23]

INCOME DISCRIMINATION: THE WAGE GAP

Another major consequence of the combination of sex segregation and the persistence of archaic gender ideologies is income discrimination. At both the aggregate level and the individual level—whether we average all incomes or look at the specific individuals' wages for the jobs they do—women earn less than men. This wage difference begins early in our lives—even before we begin working. A 1995 *Wall Street Journal* report observed that elementary school girls receive smaller allowances and are asked to do more chores than boys are.[24]

Income inequality often remains invisible precisely because of sex segregation— what appears to us simply as paying people doing different *jobs* is actually a way of paying different *genders* differently for doing roughly the same jobs with the same skill levels. As long as it appears that it is the attribute of the job, and not of the gender of the person doing the job, income inequality remains invisible to us. In 1999, the median annual income for men working full-time was $37,057. For women it was $27,194, about 73 percent of men's annual income. On average, working women bring home $192 a week less than men. To illustrate the extent of this wage inequality, every year the president proclaims a date in early April "National Pay Inequity Awareness Day." Why then? "Because the average woman in a full-time job would need to work for a full year and then until early April of the next year to match what the average man earned the year before."[25]

The National Committee on Pay Equity estimated that in 1996 alone, working women lost almost $100 million due to wage inequality. Over the course of her lifetime, the average working woman will lose about $420,000. And the gender gap in income is made more complex by both race and educational level. Black and Hispanic men earn less than white men, and black men earn only slightly more than white women. Black and Hispanic women earn significantly less than white men or white women, and black women earn slightly more than Hispanic men.

What is, perhaps, most astonishing is how consistent this wage gap has been. In biblical times, female workers were valued at thirty pieces of silver, while men were valued at fifty, or 40 percent more. In the United States, this wage difference has remained relatively constant for the past 150 years! Since the Civil War, women's wages have fluctuated between one-half and two-thirds of men's wages. And in the second half of the twentieth century, women's annual incomes have ranged only between 56.6 percent and 72 percent of men's. Although the wage gap has closed somewhat in the 1980s and early 1990s, reaching 77 percent at its peak in 1993, there appears to have been some recent backsliding. In late 1997, women's annual income was slightly less than 75 percent of men's. In fact, part of the reason for the apparent closing of the wage gap was not that women's incomes rose so significantly, but that men's incomes fell.[26]

The wage gap varies with the level of education. College-educated women earn 29 percent less than college-educated men; in fact, college-educated women earn about the same as non-college-educated men. And the gap varies with age, actually increasing throughout women's lives. The reason for this is simple: Women and men enter the labor force at more comparable starting salaries; women aged 15–24 earn 93 percent as much as their male counterparts. But as they continue their careers, gender discrimination in promotion and raises adds to the differences in income, so that women aged 55–59 earn only 62 percent as much as men. A report from the General Accounting Office found that the difference in salaries between male and female managers actually grew by as much as twenty-one cents for every dollar earned between 1995 and 2000.[27]

Another reason for this increasing wage gap as people age has to do with the different experiences of women and men in the labor force. When men enter the labor force, they enter for good, while women occasionally take time out for childbearing and parental leave. This has a calamitous effect on women's wages, and fuels the growing gap across the life span. In fact, women who drop out of the labor force have lower real wages when they come back to work than they had when they left. Two sociologists recently calculated that each child costs a woman 7 percent in wages.[28]

Within any occupation, women tend to be concentrated at the bottom of the pay scale. Across all industries, women make up nearly one-half the workers, but only 12 percent of the managers. Sociologist Judith Lorber described the reason that female physicians earn less than men. "The fault may not lie in their psyches or female roles, but in the system of professional patronage and sponsorship which tracked them out of their prestigious specialties and 'inner fraternities' of American medical institutions by not recommending them for the better internships, residencies, and hospital staff positions, and by not referring patients," she writes.[29]

How have women coped with this income inequality? In the 1860s, one woman came up with a rather novel solution:

> I was almost at the end of my rope. I had no money and a woman's wages were not enough to keep me alive. I looked around and saw men getting more money, and more work, and more money for the same kind of work. I decided to become a man. It was simple. I just put on men's clothing and applied for a man's job. I got good money for those times, so I stuck to it.[30]

Novel, yes, but not exactly practical for an entire gender! So women have pressed for equal wages—in their unions, professional associations, and in every arena in which they have worked. In 1963, Congress passed the Equal Pay Act and established the Equal Employment Opportunity Commission to monitor discrimination by race and by gender. To date, the EEOC has heard thousands of cases, among them, a 1986 case in which The Bethlehem Steel Corporation was found to be paying women workers about $200 a month less than men doing the same clerical work. (In a settlement out of court, the company paid each of the 104 female plaintiffs $3,000.) In a widely discussed 1992 case, a female assistant metropolitan editor at *The New York Times* earned between $6,675 and $12,511 less than male co-workers doing the same job. What's more, she earned $2,435 less than the male editor she replaced; and $7,126 less than the man who replaced her when she quit in disgust.

Women thus face a double bind in their efforts to achieve workplace equality. On the one hand, traditional gender ideologies prevented them from entering those occupations that paid well; they have been pushed into other less well-paying sectors of the economy. On the other hand, when they enter those well-paying fields, they are prevented from moving up. This is what is known as the "glass ceiling."

THE "GLASS CEILING"

One consequence of sex segregation is discrimination against women in promotion. Women face the twin barriers of the "glass ceiling" and the "sticky floor," which combine to keep them stuck at the bottom and unable to reach the top. The sticky floor keeps women trapped in low wage positions, with little opportunity for upward mobility. The glass ceiling consists of "those artificial barriers, based on attitudinal or organizational bias, that prevent qualified individuals from advancing upward within their organization into management level positions."[31]

A recent court case provides examples of both phenomena, and a graphic illustration of how traditional gender stereotypes continue to work against women. Eight women brought suit against the Publix Super Markets, Inc., a large chain of groceries with more than 700 stores throughout the South. One of the plaintiffs said that she was stuck in a cashier's job and was denied a transfer or promotion to stocking shelves because, as a male supervisor told her, women were not capable of holding supervisory positions. Another woman employee was denied a promotion on the grounds that she was not the head of her household—despite the fact that she was raising her three children alone! In February 1997, Publix agreed to pay $81.5 million to settle the case.

The glass ceiling keeps women from being promoted equally with men. Women hold only 7 percent of all corporate board seats. Between 95 percent and 97 percent of all senior managers are men. Of the 4,012 highest paid directors, officers, or corporate CEOs in America, only nineteen—less than one-half of one percent—were women. And the glass ceiling's effects are multiplied when race is brought into the equation. In 1970, between 1 percent and 3 percent of all senior management positions in all Fortune 500 companies were held by women and minorities; in 1990, only 5 percent were held by women and minorities. In 1988, 72 percent of all managers in companies with more than one hunderd employees were white men; 23 percent were white women; 3 percent were black men, and 2 percent were black women.

Business Week surveyed 3,664 business school graduates in 1990 and found that a woman with an MBA from one of the top business schools earned an average of $54,749 in her first year after graduation, while a man from a similar program earned $61,400. This 12 percent gap actually widened as these business graduates progressed. A 1993 study of the Stanford University Business School class of 1982 found that only ten years after graduation, 16 percent of the male graduates were CEOs, chairmen, or presidents of companies, compared with only 2 percent of the women.

Again, these different trajectories have virtually nothing to do with the ambitions or aspirations of the men and women who occupy these positions. For two years, an economist followed five female and five male trainees in a large Swedish multinational corporation (with six thousand employees). All came from similar backgrounds, had similar education, and had similar goals and ambitions. All ten aspired to top management positions. After their training, they all still were similar. At the end of the time, all the men and none of the women had entered the top management group.

The glass ceiling occurs under a variety of circumstances. Corporate management may be either unable or unwilling to establish policies and practices that are effective mechanisms to promote workplace diversity. The company may not have adequate job evaluation criteria that allow for comparable worth criteria, or they may rely on traditional gender stereotypes in evaluation. Limited family-friendly workplace policies will also inhibit women's ability to rise.

Perhaps the most important element that reinforces the glass ceiling is the informal effort by men to restore or retain the all-male atmosphere of the corporate hierarchy. Equal opportunities for advancement would disrupt the casual friendliness and informality of the homosocial world at the top—the fact that those with whom one interacts share similar basic values and assumptions. "What's important is comfort, chemistry, relationships and collaborations," one manager explained. "That's what makes a shop work. When we find minorities and women who think like we do, we snatch them up." One British study of female MBAs, for example, found that by far the "most significant" and "most resistant" barrier to women's advancement was the " 'men's club' network."[32]

Perhaps the most celebrated case involving a corporate glass ceiling was the 1989 Supreme Court decision in *Hopkins v. Price Waterhouse*. A woman, Ann Hopkins, was denied promotion to partnership in one of the nation's largest and most prestigious accounting firms. Although she had brought more business into the company than any of the men who were promoted, she was perceived as abrasive and demanding. Opponents of her promotion said she was "macho" and that she "overcompensated for being a woman" and that she would benefit from "a course at charm school." One of her supporters told her that she might make partner if she could learn to "walk more femininely, talk more femininely, dress more femininely, wear makeup, have her hair styled, and wear jewelry." The court awarded her $400,000 in back pay and fees, and required that she be promoted to partner.

The Hopkins case provides a perfect illustration of the ways in which traditional gender stereotypes also impede women's progress. Had Ms. Hopkins *been* more traditionally feminine, she would never have been the aggressive and ambitious success that she became. Thus, either way, women lose. Either they are too aggressive, in which case they are seen as mannish, "ball-busting bitches," or they are too ladylike, and as a result are passed over as being too passive, sweet, and not ambitious enough.

In 1991, Congress passed the Civil Rights Act, which established a Glass Ceiling Commission whose goal it was to eliminate "artificial barriers based on attitudinal or organizational bias." These barriers included relying on word-of-mouth to fill upper level positions (the "old boys' network"), and suggested that a system of monetary compensations be instituted for word-of-mouth referrals of qualified women and minorities. Some companies have already instituted their own policies designed to enable women to break through the glass ceiling in all three areas where women experience it—hiring, promotion, and retention. These tend to be among the more forward-looking companies. For example, in 1992, Reebok International initiated a diversity program in hiring practices by developing effective college recruitment policies and internships for women and minorities. In two years, the company tripled its minority employment to 15 percent of its U.S. workforce, and increased the number of women to more than 50 percent. The Bank of Montreal targeted promotion, and between 1991 and 1993 the bank increased the percentage of women at the executive level from 29 percent to 54 percent. The bank also initiated a program that specified targets for promoting and retaining women and minorities, and developed a series of gender awareness workshops for senior management. Finally, in 1993–1994, Lotus, the international software company, tried to increase retention of capable women and minorities who were leaving the company because they felt they did not get either the information they needed to be effective or the opportunities they expected. The company offered incentives to managers who reduced turnover and initiated disincentives for managers whose staff showed higher turnover rates. Turnover of women fell from 21 percent to 16 percent, and among African Americans from 25.5 percent to 20.5 percent.

The glass ceiling has different impacts on men, depending upon your political persuasion. Writer Warren Farrell argues that all the attention to the ways women are held back from promotion by the glass ceiling hides the fact that it is *men* who are the victims of sex discrimination in the workplace. Men, Farrell argues, are the victims of the "glass cellar"—stuck in the most hazardous and dangerous occupations. In fact, Farrell argues, of the 250 occupations ranked by the *Jobs Related Almanac*, the twenty-five worst jobs (such as truck driver, roofer, boilermaker, construction worker, welder, and football player) were almost all male. Over 90 percent of all occupational deaths happen to men. All the hazardous occupations are virtually all-male—including firefighting (99 percent), logging (98 percent), trucking (98 percent), and construction (97 percent)—while the "safest" occupations are those held by women, including secretary (99 percent female) and receptionist (97 percent).[33]

He has a point: Many of the jobs that men take *are* hazardous—and made more so unnecessarily by an ideology of masculinity that demands that men remain stoic and uncomplaining in the face of danger. Thus, on dangerous construction sites or off-shore oil rigs, men frequently shun safety precautions, such as safety helmets, as suitable, perhaps, for sissies or wimps, but not for "real" men. But the conclusion that men are discriminated against, and not women, flies in the face of both evidence and reason. For the jobs that are the most exclusively male are also those whose members have fought most fiercely against the entry of women in the first place. And they're far better paid than the jobs that are almost exclusively female. For example, the nation's fire departments have been especially resistant to women joining their "fraternal order," doing so only under court order and often welcoming women with a significant amount of harassment. It would be odd to propose that this is the result of discrimination against men, or to blame women for not entering those occupations from which they have been excluded by men's resistance.

THE PROBLEM OF TOKENS

What really does happen when women enter "men's" occupations and men enter "women's" occupations? In both cases, they experience tokenism. But their experiences as tokens are often very different. Tokens are those people who are admitted into an organization but who are recognizably different from the large majority of the members of the organization. But tokens are more than simple the members of a numerical minority: Tokens are accepted not *despite* their minority status but *because* of it. They are actively discouraged from recruiting others like themselves, and become eager to fit in and become part of the organizational mainstream. Typically, tokens may even become more strongly wedded to organizational norms than members of the numerical majority.

According to Rosabeth Moss Kanter, whose pioneering work, *Men and Women of the Corporation,* first analyzed the problem, tokenism heightens the boundaries between groups rather than dismantling them, as the contrast between the token and the majority is exaggerated to become the sole difference. Tokens, Kanter writes, are thus "often treated as representative of their category, as symbols rather than as individuals."[34] The token is always in the spotlight—everyone notices him or her, but only because he or she is different. Tokens are rarely seen as similar to others in the group. Thus, tokens have a double experience of visibility—they are *hyper*-visible as members of their "category," but they are completely *invisible* as individuals.

Think about a situation where you were virtually the only "something" in a group. It could be that you were the only man or woman, the only white person or person of color, the only gay or straight person in a group. How did you feel when someone would turn to you and say, "So, how do white people feel about this issue?" or, "What do women say about this?" At that moment you ceased to be an individual and were seen only as a representative of the group. Chances are you responded by saying something like, "I don't know. I'm not all women or all white people. You'd have to take a survey." If you can imagine that experience of hypervisibility and invisibility all the time in your workplace, you'll begin to have an idea what tokenism feels like.

Simultaneous hypervisibility and invisibility have serious consequences. "The token does not have to work hard to have her presence noticed, but she does have to work hard to have her achievements noticed," Kanter writes. The token is often forced to choose between the two—"trying to limit visibility—and being overlooked—or taking advantage of the publicity—and being labeled a 'troublemaker.'" This can take an enormous emotional and psychological toll:

> Tokenism is stressful; the burdens carried by tokens in the management of social relations take a toll in psychological stress, even if the token succeeds in work performance. Unsatisfactory social relationships, miserable self-imagery, frustrations from contradictory demands, inhibition of self-expression, feelings of inadequacy and self-hatred, all have been suggested as consequences of tokenism.[35]

Kanter argued that her theory of tokenism held regardless of whether the tokens were male or female. Subsequent research has suggested dramatically different experiences when women are the tokens in a largely male work world, and when men are the tokens in a largely female occupation.[36] Men entering mostly female occupations have the opposite experience from women. They don't bump up against a glass ceiling; instead, they ride on what sociologist Christine Williams calls the "glass escalator," having a much easier time being promoted than even women do. Williams conducted interviews with seventy-six men and twenty-three women in four occupations—nursing, librarianship, elementary education, and social work. She found that men experienced positive discrimination when entering those fields; several people noted a clear preference for hiring men. And men were promoted to managerial positions more rapidly and frequently, thus making men overrepresented in the managerial ranks. Men who do women's work, it appears, may earn less than men who work in predominantly male occupations, but they earn more and are promoted faster than women in the same occupation.[37]

Men did experience some negative effects, especially in their dealings with the public. For example, male nurses face a common stereotype that they are gay. Male librarians faced images of themselves as "wimpy" and asexual; male social workers were seen as "feminine" or "passive." One male librarian found that he had difficulty establishing enough credibility so that the public would accept him as the children's "storyteller." Ironically, though, Williams found that these negative stereotypes of men doing "women's work" actually added to the glass escalator effect, "by pressuring men to move *out* of the most female-identified areas, and *up* to those regarded as more legitimate and prestigious for men."[38]

Williams concluded that men "take their gender privilege with them when they enter predominantly female occupations: this translates as an advantage in spite of their numerical rarity." Men, it seems, win either way. When women are tokens, men retain their numerical superiority and are able to maintain their gender privilege by restricting a woman's entry, promotion, and experiences in the workplace. When men are tokens, they are welcomed into the profession, and use their gender privilege to rise quickly in the hierarchy. "Regardless of the problems that might exist," writes Alfred Kadushin, "it is clear and undeniable that there is a considerable advantage in being a member of the male minority in any female profession."[39]

Such a statement goes a long way toward explaining why men continue to resist workplace equality. After all, men have a pretty good deal with things as they are; as economist Heidi Hartmann writes:

> Low wages keep women dependent on men because they encourage women to marry. Married women must perform domestic chores for their husbands. Men benefit, then, from both higher wages and the domestic division of labor. This domestic division of labor, in turn, acts to weaken women's position in the labor market. Thus, the hierarchical domestic division of labor is perpetuated by the labor market, and vice versa.[40]

Workplace inequality is not only a good deal for men, it is also often invisible to them. Inequality is almost always invisible to those who benefit from it—in fact, that's one of the chief benefits! What is certainly not a level playing field is *experienced* as level, which leads men to feel entitled to keep things just as they are. Let me give you one example. I recently appeared on a television talk show opposite three "angry white males" who felt that they had been the victims of workplace discrimination. The show's title, no doubt to entice a large potential audience, was "A Black Woman Stole My Job." These men all complained that they had been the victims of "reverse discrimination," since, they believed, they had lost a job possibility to a woman who was less qualified than they.

In my comments to these "angry white men," I invited them to consider one word in the show's title—the word "my." What did that word mean? Did they feel that those jobs were actually "theirs," that they were entitled to them, and that when some "other" person—black, female—got the job, that person was really taking "their" job? But by what right is that his job? By convention, perhaps, by a historical legacy of discrimination, certainly. Of course, a more accurate title for the show should have been "A Black Woman Got A Job" or ". . . Got *The* Job." But "his" job? Competing equally for rewards that we used to receive simply by virtue of our race or our sex actually feels like discrimination. Equality will always feel uncomfortable for those who once benefited from inequality.

Another reason that men resist the gender-integrated workplace is that men say they would be distracted by women. A headline in the *Wall Street Journal* in 1991 announced that "Women as Colleagues Can Turn Men Off." The 1995 report of the Department of Labor's Glass Ceiling Commission quoted one male executive who said "What's important is comfort, chemistry, . . . and collaborations." Many white men, he continued, "don't like the competition and they don't like the tension" of working alongside female colleagues. That the presence of women would distract men from the tasks at hand, or disturb the fragile yet necessary bonding among males was also the argument made by men in the military and at military schools such as VMI and The Citadel.[41]

Except, as we've seen, it's not necessarily true. There are many situations in which women and men work side by side without there being any "distractions." Doctors and nurses, managers and secretaries don't seem to have much problem with distraction. It's not the presence or absence of women that seems to be distracting—it's the presence of women *as equals* that that men are really worrying about.

SEXUAL HARASSMENT

Sexual harassment is one of the chief ways that men resist gender equality in the workplace. The nation's current preoccupation with sexual harassment is fueled by several different trends—the increased reporting by women of their experiences at work or in school, the re-labeling of behaviors that men used to take for granted, the increasing pressure that men face in the workplace, and the increasing willingness of the legal system to assign blame—costly blame—for this practice. Sexual harassment was first identified as a form of sex discrimination and litigated in the late 1970s. Feminist lawyer Catharine MacKinnon argued that sexual harassment was a violation of Title VII of the 1964 Civil Rights Act, which makes it "an unlawful employment practice for an employer . . . to discriminate against any individual with respect to his compensation, terms, conditions, or privileges of employment, because of such individual's race, color, religion, sex, or national origin." Sexual harassment, MacKinnon argued, violated this law because it discriminated against women on the basis of their sex, and, what's more, sexual harassment created a hostile environment for working women.[42] By 1982, the U.S. Court of Appeals for the Eleventh Circuit declared:

> Sexual harassment which creates a hostile or offensive environment for members of one sex is every bit the arbitrary barrier to sexual equality at the workplace that racial harassment is to racial equality. Sure, a requirement that a man or woman run a gauntlet of sexual abuse in return for the privilege of being allowed to work and make a living can be as demeaning and disconcerting as the harshest of racial epithets.[43]

But it was not until 1991 that the extent of the problem, and its effects on women in the workplace began to be fully recognized. In October of that year, Anita Hill declared that she had been sexually harassed by Clarence Thomas when she worked for him at the EEOC, and suddenly the entire nation sat transfixed before their television sets as his confirmation hearings to the U.S. Supreme Court took a dramatically different turn. Hill alleged that she had been subject to unwanted sexual advances, vile pornographic attempts at humor, and constant descriptions of Thomas's sexual prowess—even after she had made it clear that she was not interested in dating her boss.

At the time, the Senate Judiciary Committee treated Hill as if she were the criminal, accusing her of harboring desires for Thomas, insinuating that she was "a woman scorned," and implying that she was being duped by liberals who sought to derail the nomination. And, at the time, the nation split about evenly on the question of whom they believed, Thomas or Hill. The media declared in unison that the committee's harsh and suspicious treatment of Hill would have a "chilling effect" on American women, who would be less likely to come forward and describe the harassment that they had experienced.

A chilling effect? Have the media ever been more wrong? In the ensuing decade there has been more of a national thaw—as thousands of women described what they had earlier kept as shameful personal secrets. The number of sexual harassment cases has more than doubled since 1991. Suddenly the nation had a name for what had been happening for decades to women in the workplace. In homes across the nation women were telling their husbands, their children, their parents, their friends of what had happened to them. By 1997, well over 80 percent of Americans had come to realize that Anita Hill had been telling the truth all along.

Since that time, sexual harassment has become a major issue in America. The EEOC handles about five thousand complaints of sexual harassment per year. Between 50 percent and 85 percent of working women will experience some form of sexual harassment during their career. In a 1981 study of female federal employees, 12 percent reported mild harassment (suggestive gestures or remarks, pressure for dates), 29 percent reported severe harassment (touching, fondling, pressure for sex, menacing letters or phone calls), and 1 percent were raped on the job. A 1989 study of almost a thousand female attorneys found that 60 percent had experienced sexual harassment; 13 percent had been the victim of rape, attempted rape, or assault. Only 7 percent of those attorneys reported the incident to their firm. A 1997 study of two thousand attorneys at twelve of the largest law firms found that 43 percent had experienced sexual teasing, jokes, remarks, or questions; 29 percent had experienced suggestive looks or gestures; and 26 percent had experienced deliberate touching, pinching, leaning over, or cornering—all within the past year alone.[44]

And it's not just lawyers and other professionals. In fact, the number of cases filed with the EEOC more than doubled between 1990 and 1995, from about 7,500 in 1990 to about 15,500 in 1995 and again in 1996—and the majority of those cases were from women in blue-collar jobs. Women were far more likely to experience sexual harassment in traditionally male-only jobs such as mining, construction, transportation, or manufacturing than they were in professional and white-collar jobs. Clearly, when women try to "cross over" into male-dominated jobs, they are seen as invaders, and sexual harassment is a way to keep them out.[45]

Sexual harassment takes many forms, from sexual assault to mocking innuendo. Typically, it takes one of two forms. In the most obvious, *quid pro quo* version, a trade or barter of sexual contact for a reward or the avoidance of punishment. This is the sex-for-grades model of teacher-student interaction, or the "sleep with me and you'll get promoted" or "don't sleep with me and you'll get fired" workplace scenario. Thus, for example, did former U.S. Senator Robert Packwood end his congressional career—after nearly a dozen former female staffers accused him of unwanted kissing, fondling, attempts at sexual contact, and inappropriate remarks during his otherwise distinguished twenty-seven-year career. (Though Paula Jones claimed that then-governor Clinton committed this form of sexual harassment, the judge found no merit to her case because there was no evidence that her career had been adversely affected by the sexual come-on.)

The second form is far murkier, and is understood as the creation of a "hostile environment," one in which women feel compromised, threatened, or unsafe. Women in medical schools, for example, described sexual harassment as taking several different forms, including being ignored, left behind during rounds, and not invited to assist during medical procedures. Consistently, female medical students reported being subject to jokes or pranks, hearing women's bodies being mocked during anatomy classes, and finding pornography shuffled into anatomy slides during lectures. Some law students recall "ladies' days," when women were actually called on in class.

One of the more interesting recent sexual harassment cases involved the Mitsubishi Motor Corporation. In December 1994, twenty-nine women working at the car company's plant in Normal, Illinois, filed a lawsuit alleging sexual harassment, claiming that their male co-workers routinely groped and grabbed at them. Some women had to agree to have sex in order to obtain jobs. Drawings of breasts, genitals, and sex acts were labeled with the names of women workers, and attached to the cars' fenders as they passed down the assembly line. After an investigation, the EEOC filed its own suit against the company in April 1996, on behalf of more than 280 women employees. A little over a year later, after a critical review of the company's policies and procedures by former Labor Secretary Lynn Martin, the company settled its suit with twenty-seven of the twenty-nine original plaintiffs for $9.5 million, and began to implement broad changes in its corporate management.[46]

Whether sexual harassment is manifest as *quid pro quo* or hostile environment, it is rarely about sexual attraction between employees. Men accused of harassment are seldom men who are simply awkward at asking women out for dates, or men who are unusually lustful. Sexual harassment is, in fact, just the opposite. It is about making workers feel unwelcome in the workplace, about reminding them that they do not belong because the workplace is men's space. As legal scholar Deborah Rhode writes, it is a "strategy of dominance and exclusion—a way of keeping women in their places and out of men's."[47]

Think, for example, of sexual harassment on the street. Imagine a man making a rude, offensive comment to a woman as she walks by. "Hey, baby," he shouts, "nice tits!" or, "You look good enough to eat!" If you were to ask this man about his comment, he might shrug off the issue by saying he was just trying to meet women, or to indicate sexual interest. But what if we were to take these men at their words? Imagine what would happen if that woman who is being harassed were to turn around and say, "Who me? Great. Dinner at eight?" Or if she had met his crude remarks with some crudeness of her own. What would that man do now?

It's clear that these remarks are not meant to attract women, but, rather, to repel them and send them scurrying away, reminded that the streets belong to men and that women who dare to walk on them alone, or who show up in bars alone, are defying an unwritten ordinance. Such remarks are rude reminders of male entitlement, an unwritten and often unconscious sense that the public arena belongs to "us," and that interlopers, female invaders, will be reminded that they don't really belong.

Until recently, the workplace has been such a male space, a homosocial preserve. But that world has vanished forever. It is now virtually impossible for a man to go through his entire working life without having a female colleague, co-worker, or boss. Women have entered the former boys' clubs—the streets, the corporate boardroom, the hallowed halls of learning—and they are not going away, as much as some men might wish them to. Just when men's breadwinner status is threatened by economic downsizing and corporate restructuring, women appear on the scene and become easy targets for men's anger. *This* is the context in which we must consider the question of sexual harassment, its gendered political economy so to speak. Sexual harassment in the workplace is a distorted effort to put women back in their place, to remind them that they are not equal to men in the workplace, that they are, still, after all their gains, just women, even if they are in the workplace. "Harassment is a way for a man to make a woman vulnerable," says Dr. John Gottman, a psychologist at the University of Washington.

And it works. Harrassed women report increased stress, irritability, eating and sleeping disorders, and absenteeism. Often, as one researcher writes, they feel humiliated and helpless, and describe the "daily barrage of sexual interplay in the office as psychological rape." Harassment occurs most frequently in the most recently integrated workplaces, like the surgical operating theater, firefighting, and investment banking, where women are new and in the minority. "Men see women as invading a masculine environment," says Dr. Louise Fitzgerald, a University of Illinois psychologist. "These are guys whose sexual harassment has nothing whatever to do with sex. They're trying to scare women off a male preserve."[48]

One other thing that sexual harassment is typically *not* about, is one person telling the truth and the other person lying. Sexual harassment cases are difficult and confusing precisely because there are often many truths. "His" truth might be what appears to him as an innocent indication of sexual interest or harmless joking with the "boys in the office" (even if those "boys" happen to include women). He may experience sexual innuendo or references to pornography as harmless fun, what the workplace was supposed to be like for men. He works there, therefore he's entitled to treat the workplace as an extension of the locker room. "Her" truth may be that his seemingly innocent remarks cause stress, anxiety about promotion, firing, and sexual pressure.

The law about sexual harassment has reflected these two truths. Until *Ellison v. Brady,* a 1991 Circuit Court case, the legal standard of harassment was whether a "reasonable person" would see the behavior as harassment. But in that case, the court suggested that the reasonable *person* meant a reasonable man, and that men and women might well see the situation differently. Harassers often "do not realize that their conduct creates a hostile working environment," the court found, but "the victim of sexual harassment should not be punished for the conduct of the harasser." Thus, the court established a "reasonable *woman* standard," because, as the court opinion stated, "a sex-blind reasonable person standard tends to be male-biased and tends to systematically ignore the experiences of women."

This case changed all the rules, since the intention of the harasser is no longer the standard against which the crime is measured—it's the effect on the victim. And this change has, predictably, caused a significant amount of defensiveness and confusion among American men. After all, the rules have been changed. What used to be routine behavior for men in the workplace is now called sexual harassment. "Clarence Thomas didn't do anything wrong, that any American male hasn't done," commented Dale Whitcomb, a thirty-two-year-old machinist during the Thomas confirmation hearings. Two-thirds of the men surveyed said they would be complimented if they were propositioned by a woman at work, giving some idea about how men have misperceived the problem.

At the societal level, sexual harassment stymies women's equality. And it is costly. Both private and public sectors lose millions because of absenteeism, reduced productivity, and high turnover of female employees. One study from *Working Woman* magazine indicated that the top 150 of the *Fortune* 500 companies lose $6.7 million *per year* due to sexual harassment. The United States Merit Systems Protection Board reports that absenteeism, job turnover, and lost productivity because of sexual harassment cost the government an estimated minimum of $189 million a year. Corporate executives and partners in large law firms tell us they are terrified about massive lawsuits from charges of sexual harassment.[49]

Men are also harmed by sexual harassment. Certainly, male supervisors and employers are hurt when sexual harassment makes women less productive. With increased absenteeism, higher rates of turnover, and greater job-related stress, women will not perform to the best of their abilities. Some men may find such compromised performance a relief—competing with women as equals and losing may be too great a blow to fragile male egos—but supervisors cannot afford to have women working at less than their best without it eventually also affecting their own performance evaluations. Supervisors and employers should want *all* their employees to feel safe and comfortable so that they may perform to the maximum of their abilities. As individuals, men's ability to form positive and productive relationships with equal colleagues in the workplace is undermined by sexual harassment. So long as sexual harassment is a daily occurrence and women are afraid of their superiors in the workplace, innocent men's cordial and courteous behaviors may also be misinterpreted.

And finally, men can be harmed by sexual harassment from other men. In March 1998, the U.S. Supreme Court ruled that men can be the victims of sexual harassment from other men, even when all the men involved are heterosexual. Sexual harassment, then, has been expanded to include men who are not traditionally "masculine" and are therefore punished for it by other men, as well as women, who are harassed when they act "too" masculine, or when they don't act masculine "enough." And people still believe that the workplace isn't gendered!

REMEDIES FOR WORKPLACE INEQUALITY

Despite all the arguments about gender difference that presume we are from different planets, the fact is that comparable percentages of women and men are in the workplace, and for the same reasons. Yet the workplace remains a decidedly unequal arena, plagued by persistent sex segregation, wage inequality, sex discrimination, and sexual harassment. These inequalities exaggerate and even create the differences we think we observe. How can the workplace become a more equal arena, a place in which women *and* men can earn a living to support themselves and their families and experience the satisfaction of efficacy and competence?

One arena of change is the application of existing law. A good beginning might be full compliance with the 1963 Pay Equity Act, which prohibits employers from paying different wages to men and women who are doing the same or essentially the same work, or Title VII of the 1964 Civil Rights Act, which guarantees the absence of discrimination based on race, sex, or national origin. To date, thirty states have undertaken some form of pay equity reform and about $527 million has been disbursed by twenty state governments to correct wage discrimination.

But a simple strategy of pay equity would be unlikely to make wages more equal, since, as we have seen, wage inequality depends on sex segregation for its legitimacy (and its invisibility). Comparable worth programs require that "dissimilar work of equivalent value to the employer be paid the same wages." Thus, comparable worth programs require a systematic review of jobs, ordering them on criteria of complexity and skills required so that they can be compared and thus wages allocated on a more gender equal basis. Some social scientists have devised the Gender Neutral Job Comparison System to measure jobs more accurately; the system also factors into its equations such traditionally invisible (and traditional "female") skills such as emotional labor or undesirable working conditions.[50]

Comparable worth programs have become necessary because sex segregation is so intimately tied to wage inequality. But such policies have generated significant opposition, largely based on misperceptions of what the idea entails. For example, some argue that it is impossible to determine the worth of jobs, despite the fact that nearly two-thirds of all companies already utilize job evaluations. Others say it will interfere with the normal operations of the labor market—as if the labor market set wages to begin with, and not bureaucracies, union officials, and managers relying on gender stereotypes. (If the labor market operated perfectly, there would be no wage discrimination, would there?) Others argue that it opens a door for a paternalist government to set wage levels, or that it would bankrupt employers forced to pay women higher wages. But each firm could set its wage levels based on skill, not sex. And besides, women earning higher wages would have increased consumer purchasing power, which would help the economy, not hurt it.[51]

Comparable worth and pay equity schemes are not, of course, without their problems. They might have a remedial effect of evening out women's and men's wages at lower levels, for example, but they would also preserve the gap between lower levels and upper-level management jobs, since both pay equity and comparable worth preserve "the idea that some jobs are worth more than others." What's more, they mute the effect of persistent gender stereotypes in the evaluations of positions, so that some men would be able to continue to resist gender equality by embedding it in performance evaluations.[52]

Workplace equality also requires interventionist strategies in hiring and promotion. Although in recent years the trend has been for the United States to abandon affirmative action policies, such policies have been enormously effective in leveling the playing field even a little bit. (Could that be why there's so much opposition? After all, as political commentator Michael Kinsley notes, affirmative action is one of the few policies that "gives white men whining rights in the vicimization bazaar, just like minorities and women." One reason well-meaning Americans say they oppose affirmative action is that members of minority groups would find it demeaning to accept positions strictly on the grounds that they are members of an underrepresented group, despite the fact that few women or minorities actually are hired or promoted for that reason alone. Anyway, it's probably more demeaning to be *denied* a position or a promotion because of membership in that group. When Barbara Babcock, an assistant attorney general in the Carter administration, was asked how she felt about getting her position because she was a woman, she replied, "It's better than not getting your job because you're a woman."[53]

Another remedy will be the elimination of the "mommy track"—a new and subtle way that workplace gender inequality is reproduced. The mommy track refers to the ways in which workplace discrimination transmutes itself into discrimination against those workers who happen to take time off to get pregnant, bear children, and raise them. Though it is illegal to discriminate against women because of pregnancy, women are often forced off the fast track onto the mommy track because of what appear to be the demands of the positions they occupy. Young attorneys, for example, must bill a certain number of hours per week; failing to do so will result in their being denied partnerships. A woman thus faces a double bind: to the extent that she is a good mother, she cannot rise in the corporate world; to the extent that she rises in the corporate world, she is seen as a bad mother.[54]

The most obvious set of remedies fall under the general heading of "family friendly workplace policies"—that collection of reforms, including on-site child care, flexible working hours, and parental leave, that allow parents some flexibility in balancing work and family life. *The National Report on Work and Family* reported in December 1997 that these were among the most significant criteria in helping companies to retain qualified and well-trained personnel.

In the end, workplace equality will require significant ideological and structural change—both in the way we work and in the way we live. We still inherit such outmoded ideas about what motivates us to work, and what skills we bring when we get there. John Gray's recent book *Mars and Venus in the Workplace* rehearsed his stereotypes about how men and women approach their work so differently, so that men "retreat to a cave" when they have a problem to work out by themselves, while women "demonstrate sharing, cooperation, and collaboration." Except that such interplanetary styles depend at least as much on the problem to be solved as the gender of the person solving it. To make men feel more comfortable, Gray recommends that we take photos of male workers alongside their achievements and ask about their favorite football teams—ideas that Lucy Kellaway, a writer for the *Financial Times*, found "ill conceived, outdated and bizarre."[55]

Structural change is equally important as replacing tired old clichés. As sociologists Ronnie Steinberg and A. Cook write:

> Equal employment requires more than guaranteeing the right to equal access, the right to equal opportunity for promotion, or the right to equal pay for equal, or even comparable worth. Additionally, it warrants a broader policy orientation encompassing social welfare laws that assume equality within the family; widespread use of alternative work arrangements that accommodate the complexities of family life within two-earner families; and a rejuvenated union movement, with female leadership more active at work sites in defending the rights of women workers. Social welfare laws, family policy, and government services must create incentives toward a more equal division of responsibilities for family and household tasks between men and women. Increasing child care facilities, as well as maintaining programs to care for the elderly, would help alleviate some of the more pressing demands made on adults in families. . . . This also means that tax policy, social security laws, and pension programs must be amended to make government incentives to family life consistent with a family structure in which husbands and wives are equal partners.[56]

Another sociologist, Karen Oppenheim Mason, writes that gender inequality in the workplace is likely to remain "unless major revisions occur in our ideology of gender and the division of labor between the sexes." Ultimately, she concludes, "job segregation is just a part of the generally separate (and unequal) lives that women and men in our society lead, and, unless the overall separateness is ended, the separateness within the occupational system is unlikely to end either."[57]

But it will be worth it. Workplace equality will enable both women *and* men to experience more fulfilling lives—both in the workplace and outside of it.

TOWARD A BALANCE OF WORK AND FAMILY

Despite enormous and persistent gender inequality in the workplace, women are there to stay. Women work for the same reasons that men work—to support themselves and their families, to experience the sense of accomplishment, efficacy, and competence that comes from succeeding in the workplace. Both men and women work because they want to and because they have to. The social and economic realities of most American families' lives these days is that both partners are working, which means that both are struggling to balance work and family life.

Several different kinds of policy reforms have been proposed to make the workplace more "family friendly"—to enable working men and women to effect that balancing act. These reforms generally revolve around three issues: on-site child care, flexible working hours, and parental leave. By making the workplace more family friendly, by implementing these three policy reforms, the workplace would, we think, be transformed from Ebenezer Scrooge's accounting firm into the set from the hit film *9 to 5*. Suddenly, overnight, when the evil boss was gone, the workplace was transformed. Green plants were everywhere. The women's desks had photographs of their children, while their children played in playpens right behind them. And, of course, productivity shot up so high that the corporate CEO decided to maintain these changes permanently.

But in the United States, we continue to think of these reforms as *women's* issues. It is women who campaign for them, and women who say they want them. One recent best-selling book put all the pressure on women to accommodate themselves to the virtual impossibility of balancing work and family. Sylvia Hewlett found startlingly high percentages of childlessness among high-achieving women, and argued, "[T]he brutal demands of ambitious careers, the asymmetries of male-female relationships and the difficulties of bearing children late in life conspire to crowd out the possibility of having children." Childlessness becomes, as she puts it, a "creeping non-choice," and she urges women to be "intentional" about family life—grabbing a husband and having babies in your twenties, and putting the career on the back burner.[58]

Hewlett's solutions may appear overly voluntaristic, assuming that individual women need to make individual choices, rather than structural changes to the workplace itself, but they do have a ring of truth to them—because they are half right. The research does suggest that having children does stymie women's career ascendancy, and putting one's career first may hinder one's ability to have children.[59] But in both of these halves of the equation there is a variable missing: men. Women's career chances are stymied and their maternity is eclipsed *only if the men in their lives don't change.*

But on-site child care, flex time, and parental leave are not women's issues, they're *parents'* issues, and to the extent that men identify as parents, they are reforms that men ought to want as well. Politically, women probably cannot get the kinds of reforms they need without men's support; personally, men cannot have the lives they say they want without supporting these reforms. Women have already become what we might call "private careerists"—people who are willing to claim their workplace ambitions in the private domain of their homes and families, willing to reorganize the shape, the size, and the timing of their family lives to try and balance both. Now we need a "public fatherhood" to complement that—men who are publicly committed, in their workplaces, to reorganize their career trajectories to accommodate their family responsibilities and commitments. Private careerism needs a public fatherhood.

Which was, you may recall, the trap that British Prime Minister Tony Blair fell into when he and his wife were expecting the birth of their son in 2000. Could he take the parental leave that he and his government had fought to institute? Did he dare? Of course, his wife Cherie, a high-prestige lawyer who earns three times what Blair earns as prime minister and is the family breadwinner, took all of her allotted thirteen weeks of unpaid parental leave. Could Blair take a week off?

The answer was "almost." Public opinion was split: overwhelmingly (72 percent) Britons supported the idea of men taking parental leave, but more than half (57 percent) thought Blair shouldn't use it. His wife urged him to follow the example of the

Finnish prime minister who had just taken six whole days off when his daughter was born. In the end, he took two days off, and worked from home.[60]

It's celebrated cases such as this that make clear the problems we will continue to have in balacing work and family. These are both structural and attitudinal. The United States is one of only six countries that have no legal requirement for paid maternity leave—let along paternity leave. And in order for women to be able to balance family and work, they will need government support—real family values—and changes in the attitudes of men.[61]

Balancing work and family will enable women to live the lives they say they want to live. Working mothers are happier and more productive, both as mothers and as workers, than full-time mothers, notes psychologist Faye Crosby. Another psychologist, Joan Peters, writes that "mothers *should* work outside the home. If they do not, they cannot preserve their identities or raise children to have both independent and family lives." But to do so will require a dramatic change in the lives of American men. Men will need to take on their share of housework and child care—not merely to "pitch in" or "help out." Balancing work and family will also enable American men to live the lives they say they want to live. As one man recently put it:

> It's amazing. I grew up thinking a man was someone who was gone most of the time, then showed up and ordered people around and, aside from that, never said a word. I don't want my sons to have to deal with that kind of situation or to think that's how the world is.[62]

With more men like him—and a generation of women who refuse to remain second-class citizens in the workplace—his sons and his daughters may come to know a very different world.

P
A
R
T

3

GENDERED
INTERACTIONS

CHAPTER 9

GENDERED INTIMACIES

Friendship and Love

"Man's love is of man's life a thing apart," wrote the legendary British Romantic poet George Gordon, Lord Byron, "'Tis woman's whole existence." Presumably, this was because men like him had other, far more important things to occupy their time—such as poetry, politics, and sexual conquest. A century and a half later, novelist Doris Lessing commented that she'd never met a man who would destroy his work for a love affair—and she never met a woman who wouldn't.

Byron's and Lessing's statements underscore how unconsciously our most intimate relationships are shaped by gender, how women and men have different experiences and different expectations in our friendships, in love, and in sex. Like the family, sex and love are also organized by gender, which may not come as much of a surprise. After all, how often have we heard a woman complain that her husband or partner doesn't express his feelings? How often have we heard men wonder what their wives are doing talking on the phone all the time? And how often do we hear of men saying that their extramarital affair was 'just sex," as if sex could be separated from emotions? How often do we hear women say that?

Part of the intergalactic theory of gender—that women and men come from different planets—emphasizes these differences between women and men. We hear that it is our celestial or biological natures that decree that women be the emotionally adept communications experts and men the clumsy unemotional clods. And yet, the gender differences in intimate relationships often don't turn out to be the ones we expected; nor are the differences as great as commonsense assumptions predict. While it is true that men and women often have different ways of liking, loving, and lusting, these differences are neither as great as predicted, nor do they always go in the directions that common sense would lead us to expect. Moreover, the differences we observe in the contemporary United States did not always exist, nor are they present in other cultures. In this and the next chapter, I'll explore the gender of intimacy by examining friendship and love, and sexuality. (I've already discussed the gender of marriage and the family, so I'll confine myself here to nonmarital relationships.) What we'll see is that the gendering of intimate life—of friendship, love, and sex—is the result of several historical and social developments.

THE GENDER OF FRIENDSHIP

In fact, women were not always considered the emotional experts. As Byron's maxim suggests, historically it was men's "way of loving" that was considered superior. From

Greek and Roman myths to Renaissance balladry, men's friendships were celebrated as the highest expression of the noblest virtues—bravery, loyalty, heroism, duty—which only men were thought to possess. Think of Orestes and Pylades, Hercules and Hylas, David and Jonathan, Roland and Oliver, Achilles and Patroclus.

For the Greeks, friendship was even more noble than marital love, or the eroticized idealization of the young boy by the older man. As described by Plato and Aristotle, friendship occurred only between peers, and transcended sexuality. Only men could develop the emotional depth and connections that could cement a friendship. And our own literature affords us no shortage of such friendships—from Huck Finn and Tom Sawyer, Wyatt Earp and Doc Holliday, Butch Cassidy and the Sundance Kid, the Lone Ranger and Tonto, to Kirk and Spock, and Murtaugh and Riggs. Walt Whitman constantly celebrated "the dear love of man for his comrade, the attraction of friend to friend."

A virtual parade of literary figures commented on men's capacity for friendships and women's inability to form deep and lasting friendships, attributed largely to her lack of strong emotions about anything. The sixteenth-century French moralist Michel Montaigne's classic essay "On Friendship" described his relationship with his best friend in a language that most of us would use to describe our spouse (Montaigne wrote little about his wife and children). Friends, for instance, were "souls that mingle and blend with each other so completely that they efface the seam that joined them." In a 1960 essay on the topic, the British man of letters C. S. Lewis treated friendship as if it were entirely a masculine domain. "Only men," wrote Jeremy Taylor in his *Discourse on Friendship,* were "capable of all those excellencies by which men can oblige the world."[1]

Many women agreed. For example, the eighteenth-century British feminist and writer Mary Wollstonecraft believed that while "the most holy bond of society is friendship," it was men, not women who were most adept at it. And Simone de Beauvoir, whose book *The Second Sex* is one of modern feminism's groundbreaking works, commented that "women's feelings rarely rise to genuine friendship."[2]

Why were men's friendships considered deep and lasting, and women's fleetingly emotional? In a controversial study, anthropologist Lionel Tiger argued that the gender division of labor in hunting and gathering societies led to deeper and more durable friendships among men. Hunting and warfare, the domains of male activity, required deep and enduring bonds among men for survival, and thus close male friendships became a biologically based human adaptation. Women's friendships, however pleasant, were not "necessary" in an evolutionary sense.[3]

In this century, however, we've witnessed a dramatic transformation in the gendered division of emotional labor. Since the early 1970s, studies of friendship have taken a decidedly different turn, fueled in part by two related events. On the one hand, feminism began to celebrate women's experiences not as a problem but as a source of solidarity among women. Women's greater experiences of intimacy and emotional expressiveness were seen not as a liability but as an asset in a culture that increasingly elevated the expression of feelings as a positive goal. And it was not just women who were suddenly celebrating exactly what Tiger and others had claimed women lacked—the capacity for the deep and intimate bonds of friendship. A new generation of male psychologists and advocates of "men's liberation" were critical of the traditional male sex role as a debilitating barrier to emotional intimacy. It was *women's* experiences in friendships, and women's virtues—emotional expressiveness, dependency, nurturing, intimacy—that were now desirable.

And it was *men* who were said to be missing something—a capacity for intimacy, skills at nurturing. One psychologist derided "the inexpressive male," and sociologist Mirra Komorovsky explored men's "trained incapacity to share." Another psychologist claimed that men's routine avoidance of self-disclosure was dangerous to their emotional and even physical health, while another explored the very few social skills that men have developed to cement close intimate friendships. No wonder that psychologist Joseph Pleck spoke for many male liberationists when he observed that men's emotional relationships are "weak and often absent."[4]

Psychologist Robert Lewis examined four "barriers" to emotional intimacy among men: (1) competition, which inhibits the ability to form friendships and also minimizes the ability to share vulnerabilities and weaknesses; (2) the false need to be "in control," which forbids self-disclosure and openness; (3) homophobia, which inhibits displays of affection and tenderness toward other men; (4) lack of skills and positive role models for male intimacy. Men, he argued, learn to avoid appearing weak and vulnerable in order to maintain a competitive edge.[5]

In contemporary society, we have reversed the historical notion of friendship. Most women, according to surveys, believe that women's friendships are decidedly better than men's because they involve personal concern, intimate sharing, and more emotional exchange, while men's friendships were seen (by the same women) as more likely to involve work, sports, business, and other impersonal activities. By contrast, men, when asked the same question about which gender's friendships were better, responded that they hadn't really given the matter much thought. In a widely cited study, psychologist Daniel Levinson concluded that for men, friendship was noticeable, largely, by its "absence"; as he writes:

> As a tentative generalization, we would say that close friendship with a man or woman is rarely experienced by American men. The distinction between a friend and acquaintance is often blurred. A man may have a wide social network in which he has amicable "friendly" relationships with many men and perhaps a few women. In general, however, most men do not have an intimate male friend of the kind that they recall fondly from boyhood or youth. Many men have had casual dating relationships with women, and perhaps a few complex love-sex relationships, but most men have not had an intimate non-sexual friendship with a woman.[6]

Before we continue, ask yourself how you felt as you read the statement above. Does it describe your experiences? Or does it reveal that the definitions of friendship, love, and intimacy have been transformed from glorifying their more "masculine" components at the expense of "feminine" ones, to the reverse? One sociologist has criticized what she calls the "feminization of love," so that now intimacy is defined by "feminine" norms, which favor gender differences over similarities, reinforce traditional gender stereotypes, and render invisible or problematic men's ways of creating and sustaining intimacy.[7]

GENDER DIFFERENCES IN FRIENDSHIP:
REAL AND IMAGINED

Most of the research on gender differences in friendship turns out to reinforce existing stereotypes of women as emotionally expressive and men as inexpressive and either incapable or uninterested in nurturing. There's even some evidence that brain differences account for friendship differences. A recent study found that while men respond to stress with the now-famous "fight or flight" response, women look to friends or allies as a source of emotional sustenance in a response labeled "tend and befriend." The researchers believe that this is because men respond to stress by releasing testosterone, which causes the fight or flight response, while women release oxytocin, which produces a calming effect and a desire for closeness. (I suspect men's response may have less to do with testosterone and more to do with norms of masculinity that turn every stressful encounter into a demonstration of masculine prowess; women's tending and befriending may also be a rational sizing up of the situation and a need for allies to even the odds.)[8] In another psychological experiment, Sharon Brehm reversed the genders of two stereotypically gendered friendship events, to reveal how different, and "odd" they would sound:

> Jim and Henry were good close friends. Often, they would stay up half the night talking about love and life and how they felt about everything and everyone. In times of trouble, each was always there for the other to lean on. When they experienced any conflicts in their romantic relationships with women, they'd immediately be on the phone to each other, asking advice and getting consolation. They felt they knew everything about each other.
>
> Sally and Betty were good close friends. Often, they would stay up half the night playing chess or tinkering with Sally's old car, which was constantly breaking down. In times of trouble, they'd always help each other out. Sally would loan Betty money, or Betty would give Sally a ride home from work whenever their best efforts had failed to revive Sally's beloved 1960 Chevy. They went everywhere together—to the bars, to play basketball, to the latest sci-fi movie. They felt they were the best of buddies.[9]

It does sound strange, of course. But does it mean that men have shallower, less emotionally demanding and rewarding friendships than women, or that women and men achieve the same ends via different means?

Some psychologists found few differences in what women and men say they desire in a friend. Mayta Caldwell and Letitia Peplau, for example, studied college students' friendships and found that while both women and men desire intimacy and closeness, have roughly the same number of close and casual friends, and spent about the same amount of time with their friends, they often have different ways of expressing and achieving intimacy with them. Men were almost twice as likely to say they preferred "doing some activity" with their best friend, and looked for friends who liked "to do the same things" as they did. Women, by contrast, were more likely to choose someone "who feels the same way about things" as a friend, and "just talking" as their preferred mode of interaction. Sociologist Beth Hess found that women were twice as likely to talk about personal issues with their friends.[10]

Other researchers don't believe the men's responses—no matter what they say. Men may "*perceive* that they are being open and trusting," write sociologists Lynne Davidson and Lucille Duberman, "even though they report little investment in the personal and relational levels of the friendship." Despite the findings that both women and men say they disclose equal amounts of personal information, and that they are completely open and trusting of their best friends, the authors conclude that women actually disclose more to their friends. For example, they describe one man who said of his best friend, "We are pretty open with each other, I guess. Mostly we talk about sex, horses, guns, and the army." From this, they conclude that these friends do not disclose their feelings. Yet the authors do not probe beneath this response, to uncover, possibly, the way that talking about sex (like sexual fears, questions, or inadequacies) or the army (and the intense emotions of terror, exhilaration, and shame it evokes) does not require just as deep a level of trust as women's friendships.[11]

Not all research that finds gender differences in friendship turns a deaf ear to the voices of half its informants. In a revealing portrait of the role of friendship in our lives, Lillian Rubin interviewed more than three hundred women and men, and found startling differences in both the number and the depth of friendships. "At every life stage between twenty-five and fifty-five, women have more friendships, as distinct from collegial relationships or workmates, than men," she writes, "and the differences in the content and quality of their friendships are marked and unmistakable." Generally, she writes, "women's friendships with each other rest on shared intimacies, self-revelation, nurturance, and emotional support." By contrast, she argues, men's friendships are characterized by shared activities, and conversations center on work, sports, or expertise— "whether about how to fix a leak in the roof or which of the new wine releases is worthy of celebrating." Three-fourths of the women Rubin interviewed could identify a best friend, while more than two-thirds of the men could not. Even when a man could identify a best friend, Rubin found that "the two usually shared little about the interior of their lives and feelings." If we understand intimacy to be based on both verbal and nonverbal sharing of thoughts and feelings so that the intimate understands the inner life of the other, then men's friendships are, Rubin concludes, "emotionally impoverished."[12]

Other research corroborates some of her findings. Women were far more likely to share their feelings with their friends than were men; engage in face-to-face interactions instead of men's preferred side-to-side style; and discuss a wider array of issues than men did. Women's friendships seem to be more person oriented; men's more activity oriented. Women's friendships appear to be more "holistic," and men's are more "segmented." Women may say they have fewer friends, one study found, but those they have are more intimate.[13]

These differences are reinforced by technological developments. Take, for example, the telephone. For women, the telephone serves as the chief form of relationship maintenance, making it possible to sustain friendships over long distances and with increased time pressures. However, for men, the telephone is a poor substitute for the shared activities that sustain men's friendships. Men tend to use the telephone far less to sustain intimacy. "I'm not friends the way she's friends," one man told sociologist Karen Walker. "I don't work on them. I don't pick the phone up and call people and say 'how are you?' " And another man compared his friendships with those of his partner:

It's not like Lois, the woman I live with, and the women in her group. They're real buddies; they call each other up and talk for hours; they do things together all the time. We just never got that close, that's all.[14]

Even after a long day in a workplace where she talks on the phone constantly as a receptionist or secretary, a woman is far more likely to call her friends at night.

Without such relationship maintenance, men's friendships experience greater attrition than women's over time. "Over the years, the pain of men's loneliness, the weakening of their male ties, the gradually accumulating disillusionment with male friends, the guilt at their own betrayals of others, are just ignored. Partly it is a result of resignation. We lower our expectations. The older we get, the more we accept our essential friendlessness with men."[15]

In general, gender differences in friendships tend to be exactly what common-sense observation and talk-show pseudo-revelations would suggest. Men are more reserved in their emotional patterns, and less likely to disclose personal feelings, lest they risk being vulnerable to other men; women tend to be comparatively more open and disclosing. But that is part of the problem. These differences make it appear that men and women come from different planets, when often the differences have nothing whatever to do with gender and everything to do with *other* factors in our lives—such as our workplace experiences, our marital status, our age, race, ethnicity, and sexual orientation. Those factors may tell us more about which gender differences are "real" and which are really symptomatic of something else.

Of course, at the same time, we should be careful not to overstate the case. As one psychologist warns:

> There is, of course, a danger here of "reifying" gender differences by underplaying the other factors which shape people's friendships. . . . [I]n order to analyse friendship satisfactorily it is necessary to examine the range of social and economic factors that pattern an individual's immediate social environment, rather than focusing solely on any particular one. . . . [F]riendship is certainly influenced by gender, but exactly in what way depends on the interaction there is with the other factors that collectively shape the personal space for sociability that people have.[16]

In fact, it turns out that there is "much more similarity than dissimilarity in the manner in which women and men conduct their friendships," writes psychologist Paul Wright, in a review of the existing literature of gender differences. While it is true, he notes, that women are "somewhat more likely to emphasize personalism, self-disclosure, and supportiveness" and men are "somewhat more likely to emphasize external interest and mutually involving activities," these differences "are not great, and in many case, they are so obscure that they are hard to demonstrate." What's more, what differences there are tend to diminish markedly and virtually disappear "as the strength and duration of the friendship increases."[17]

For example, when women and men choose a best friend, they look for the same virtues—communication, intimacy, and trust. And the majority of us—75 percent of women and 65 percent of men—choose someone of the same sex as our best friend. Even when we're not looking for a "best friend," women and men tend to look for similar things in a potential friend. Both women and men select the same indicators of intimacy. In fact, Wall and her colleagues' study of fifty-eight middle-class men revealed a pattern—stressing confidentiality and trust over simply the pleasure of one's company—that was more consistent with middle-class British women than middle-class

British men. This really isn't much of a surprise; we all—women and men—know what we are *supposed* to want and value in a friend.[18]

But apparently what we do in our friendships turns out to be not nearly as different as we might have thought. Differences in self-disclosure turn out to be very small. Men's friendships seem to be based on "continuity, perceived support and dependability, shared understandings, and perceived compatibility," qualities based on shared perceptions rather than constant, sustained interaction to maintain them. Yet men's friendships also center on "self-revelation and self-discovery, having fun together, intermingled lives, and assumed significance"—as did women's.[19]

In sum, most studies that measure interpersonal skills, friendship styles, or self-disclosure, find few, if any, significant differences between women and men when it comes to friendship. What is more, since "feminine" expressions of intimacy now define the criteria for evaluation, men's styles of intimacy may become invisible. It is not that men do not express intimacy, but that they do it in different ways. Psychologist Scott Swain argues that men do express intimacy "by exchanging favors, engaging in competitive action, joking, touching, sharing accomplishments and including one another in activities." It's often covert, embedded in activities, rather than direct. One man Swain interviewed put it this way:

> I think that the men characteristics [sic] would be the whole thing, would just be the whole thing about being a man. You know, you go out and play sports with your brothers, and have a good time with them. You just . . . you're doing that. And there are some things that you can experience, as far as emotional, [with] your best friends that are men . . . you experience both. And that's what makes it do good is that. With most of the girls you're not going to go out and drink beer and have fun with them. Well, you can, but it's different. I mean it's like a different kind of emotion. It's like with the guys you can have all of it.[20]

And what about those "differences" in friendship styles, like using the telephone? Perhaps it is true that women use the telephone more to sustain friendships, but that may be because men see the telephone as impersonal, and they see friendship as a relief from having to do business over the phone. In other words, gender might not be the only variable in predicting phone use in friendships. Barbara Bank reports that men are just as likely to defend their friends, to ask for help when needed and to go out of their way to help their friends as are the women she studied. What's more, women are just as capable of developing friendships that incorporate traditionally "masculine" friendship virtues—trust, loyalty, obligation—as are men, and it is these qualities that often lead women to value friendship highly in their social worlds.[21]

Perhaps it's the combination of gender with other factors that best predicts our friendship patterns. For example, some of the studies that found gender differences compared working men with housewife women. But surely whether one works outside the home or not dramatically affects both the quality and the quantity of our friendships. "The combination of the inflexible demands of the workplace and the cultural expectations associated with familial roles are at least as powerful as determinants of the nature of men's social ties, as are whatever socially acquired capacities and preferences men might possess," writes sociologist Ted Cohen. Those who work outside the home, satisfy their intimacy needs in the family and thus seek friendship to meet needs for sociability. This is true of both women *and* men who work outside the home. By contrast, those who stay at home with children need friends to fulfill intimacy needs as well, because children, no matter how much we love them, are not capable of sustaining intimate relationships of mutual self-disclosure with their parents (nor would we want them to). Since those who remain at home with children tend to be women, these people have "less space in their lives for leisure and less opportunity for engaging in sociable relationships than most men."[22]

WHAT ELSE AFFECTS OUR FRIENDSHIPS?

Sociologists who explore the impact of race, ethnicity, age, class, or sexuality on social life suggest that factors other than gender may complicate the convenient gendering of friendship. Racism, for example, directly affects black men and women's experiences of friendships. For example, impassivity and inexpressiveness for men may be an adaptive strategy to "disguise painful emotions such as shame and sadness influenced by frustrations encountered with mainstream society." On the other hand, black men exhibit significant emotional expressiveness, often designed to release anger and resentment toward the existing social structure. (Thus the expressive styles of black men, which whites come to assume are part of black culture, are in fact adaptive strategies to deal with the outrage and injustice of racism and economic inequality.) "For Black men in this society," writes journalist Martin Simmons "the world is a hostile, dangerous place—a jungle." Friendship is a survival strategy: "Me and him against the world."[23]

Class also shapes black men's emotional experiences. Working-class black male friendships are often self-disclosing and close, in part due to a shared political ideology. Yet upwardly mobile black men have fewer friends, and those they have are less intimate, than their working-class counterparts, in part because they have accepted traditional definitions of masculinity. While such celebration may be a useful rhetorical strategy of resistance to racism, it may have negative consequences for male-female relationships and for the men themselves. Shanette Harris suggests that the very strategies embraced by black men to "promote African American male empowerment and survival" may also lead to such maladaptive behaviors as gang membership, and fewer economic opportunities than might have accrued via adopting traditional masculine behaviors. She suggests that the definition of masculinity must be "redefined to exclude themes of domination and superiority."[24]

Age and marital status also affect friendship patterns. Unmarried men are more likely to maintain close and intimate friendships with both women and other men than are married men, for example. And the dynamics of the friendships themselves tend to erase gender differences. For example, when the duration and closeness of friendships are controlled, women do not exhibit the face-to-face style and men the side-by-side style that researchers found. Women and men are equally as likely to be self-revealing in face-to-face interactions with close long-time friends.[25]

When we sift through the conflicting evidence, some gender differences in friendships do assert themselves with a certain insistence. And most of them concern sexuality—whether avoiding it with same-sex friends, or confronting it with cross-sex friends. With cross-sex friends, sexual attraction almost always complicates matters. "Men can't be friends with women," Harry tells Sally in the famous movie. "Sex always gets in the way."

Harry was half right. Sex does show up in cross-sex friendship among heterosexual women and men. Inevitably. But men and women *can* still be friends. It's just more work. Virtually all the men and women Rubin interviewed described sexual tension in their cross-sex friendships, which made stability and trust in the relationship more fragile. "Once a relationship becomes sexual, I'm inclined to give too much away," says one woman, explaining why she didn't want the confuse the two. Another woman explained the contradiction in her life:

> I'd like to have friendships with men, but I don't seem to be able to pull it off very well. If you get sexually involved, it ruins whatever friendship was possible, and if you don't, there's all that gaminess that goes on. In my experience, it's a problem whatever you do or . . . don't do.
>
> I used to be friends with this guy who never made any kind of a sexual overture, and I didn't exactly love that either. It made me feel unattractive and undesirable. It wasn't even so much that I wanted to go to bed with him, but I wanted him to want to.[26]

When we say someone is "just a friend," we're usually lowering them on the cosmic hierarchy of importance. But it's equally true that we believe friendship to be purer, and more lasting than sexual relationships. In our world, lovers may come and go, but friends are supposed to be there forever. That's why we also often find ourselves saying that we don't want to "ruin" the friendship by making it sexual. This contradiction—the ranking of lover over friend in the statement "just a friend" versus the ranking of friend over lover in our desire not to "ruin" the friendship—also may work itself out in gendered ways, though in exactly the opposite of the ways we typically expect women and men to behave. After all, it is typically women, not men, who try to keep the love of a friend and the sexual attraction of a lover separate, and it's men who seek to connect sex and love.

Since emotional disclosure equals vulnerability and dependency, and those feelings accompany sexual relationships with women, most men reported that they were less comfortable disclosing their true feelings to a close male friend than to a woman friend. To be emotionally open and vulnerable with another man raises the second significant gender difference in friendship—the impact of homophobia. Homophobia is one of the central organizing principles of same-sex friendships for men, and virtually nonexistent for women. Homophobia is more than simply the irrational fear and hatred of gay people; it is also the fear that one might be misperceived as gay by others. Think of all the things that you do to make sure no one gets the "wrong idea" about you—from how you walk and talk, to how you dress and act, to how you interact with your friends.

For men, friendship itself may be seen as a problem to be explained. Needing, caring about, being emotionally vulnerable and open to another man are acts of nonconformity to traditional notions of masculinity. As one sociologist put it:

> The very basic assumption friends must make about one another is that each is going beyond a mere presentation of self in compliance with "social dictates." Inevitably, this makes

friendship a somewhat deviant relationship because the surest test of personal disclosure is a violation of the rules of public propriety.[27]

Thus, to even raise the question of male friendships is to raise the "specter" of homosexuality. In the opening pages of his book on male friendships, Stuart Miller writes that the first person he sought to interview, a philosophy professor, said to him, "Male friendship. You mean you're going to write about homosexuality?" The next interviewee, this time a science professor, brought up the same issues. "You must be careful. You know, of course, that people will think you're writing about homosexuality." "Everywhere I have gone," Miller reports, "there has been the same misconception. The bizarre necessity to explain, at the beginning, that my subject is not homosexuality." And Lillian Rubin found that "association of friendship with homosexuality is so common among men."[28]

Homophobia inhibits men's and women's experience of physical closeness. In one famous experiment from the early 1970s, high school girls behaved as close friends had behaved in the nineteenth century. They held hands, they hugged each other, sat with their arms around the other, and kissed on the cheek when they parted. They were instructed to make sure that they did not give any impression that such behavior was sexual. And yet, despite this, their peers interpreted their behavior as indication that they were lesbian, and their friends ostracized them. For men, also, homophobia restricts expressions of intimacy. One man explained why he would feel weird if he hugged his best friend:

> The guys are more rugged and things, and it wouldn't be rugged to hug another man. That's not a masculine act, where it could be, you know, there's nothing unmasculine about it. But somebody might not see it as masculine and you don't want somebody else to think that you're not, you know—masculine or, . . . but you still don't want to be outcast. Nobody I think wants to be outcast.[29]

Several of my male students recently observed that when they go to the movies with a male friend, they always try to leave a seat empty between them, "so it doesn't seem like we're there, you know, 'together,'" as one of them put it.

For men or women who are, "you know, together"—that is, for lesbians and gay men—cross-sex and same-sex friendships often have different styles. In a 1994 survey, Peter Nardi and Drury Sherrod found significant similarities in the same-sex friendship patterns of gay men and lesbians. Both value close, intimate friendships, define intimacy in similar ways, and behave similarly with their friends. Two differences stood out to the researchers—how they dealt with conflict and sexuality within their friendships. Gay men, for example, are far more likely to sexualize their same-sex friendships than are lesbians. "Like their straight sisters, lesbians can have intensely intimate and satisfying relationships with each other without any sexual involvement," writes Lillian Rubin. While it may overstate the case to claim, as Rubin does, that asexual gay male friendships are "rare," such gender differences between lesbians and gay men underscore that gender, not sexual orientation, is often the key determinant of our intimate experiences. For gay men, it may be that sex is less significant, rather than that friendship is more significant.[30]

Gay men, after all, also report far more cross-sex friendships than do lesbians, who report few, if any, male friends. Yet lesbians have far more friendships with heterosexual women than gay men have with heterosexual men. Lesbians' friendships tend to be entirely among women—straight or gay. Gay men, by contrast, find their friends among straight women and other gay men. "Lesbians apparently feel they have more in common with straight women than with either gay or straight men," writes one commentator.[31]

Of course, they do. Gender is the one of the key determinants in their social lives. And yet gay men and lesbians also share one important theme in the construction of their friendships. While heterosexuals clearly distinguish between friends and family, many gay men and lesbians fuse the two, both out of necessity (being exiled from their families when they come out) and choice. "A person has so many close friends," comments a gay male character in Wendy Wasserstein's Pulitzer Prize–winning play *The Heidi Chronicles*. "And in our lives, our friends are our families."[32]

THE HISTORICAL "GENDERING" OF INTIMATE LIFE

These three major differences—the different experience of sexual tension in cross-sex friendships, the impact of homophobia, and the gendered differences in friendship patterns among gay men and lesbians—require some explanation. Lionel Tiger, for example, had stressed evolutionary prehistoric demands of hunting and warfare as the reasons why men's friendships appeared to him to be so much deeper than women's. Contemporary research has no shortage of reasons why women's friendships are deeper and more intimate than men's. Many of these reasons, though, turn out to be tautologies in which gender is both the dependent and independent variable. Women's and men's friendships patterns differ because women and men are different. Men are more instrumental and task-oriented, women more expressive and empathic. And thus their friendships are described with the same language. Such explanations don't explain very much.

Some writers offer psychoanalytic explanations. For example, scholars such as Lillian Rubin and Nancy Chodorow, who are both sociologists and psychologists, argue, as Rubin puts it, that "the traditional structure of parenting comes together with the developmental tasks of childhood and the cultural mandates about masculinity and femininity to create differences in the psychological structures of women and men." Our experiences of friendship, love, and intimacy are the result of the different developmental tasks of young boys and young girls as they struggle to achieve a sense of self and identity. The young boy must separate from his mother—the source of love, nurturance, and connection—and establish his independence. He learns to downplay the centrality of those experiences, because they will tend, he thinks, to emasculate him. Thus, emotional intimacy often negates or diminishes sexual excitement for men. For girls, by contrast, continued connection with their mothers ensures a continuity of emotionality, love, and nurturance: in fact, it becomes the foundation for women's experience of sexual intimacy, rather than its negation. As a result, separation and individuation are more difficult for women; connection and intimacy more difficult for men. This constellation permits women "to be more closely in touch with both their attachment and dependency needs than men are."[33] (See chapter Four for a fuller discussion of this process.)

While such explanations seem right, they take little notice of the dramatic variations in gender development and friendship styles in other cultures. In some societies, for example, boys must still undergo rigorous ritual separation from their mothers; and yet they, and not women, are still seen as having the deeper interior emotional lives and the more intimate and expressive friendships. For example, anthropologist Robert Brain documents several societies in Africa, South America, and Oceania in which men develop enormously close male friendships, ritually binding themselves together as "lifetime comrades, blood brothers, or even symbolic 'spouses.'"[34]

Psychoanalytic explanations take us part of the way, but even they must be inserted into the larger-scale historical transformation of which they are a part. The notions that boys and girls have such dramatically different developmental tasks is, itself, a product of the social, economic, and cultural transformation of European and American societies at the turn of the century. That transformation had several components, which transformed the meaning and experience of friendship, love, and sexuality. Both Rubin and Chodorow recognize this. "Society and personality live in a continuing reciprocal relationship with each other," Rubin writes. "The search for personal change without efforts to change the institutions within which we live and grow will, therefore, be met with only limited reward."[35]

Rapid industrialization severed the connection between home and work. Now, men left their homes and went to work in factories or offices, places where expressions of vulnerability or openness might give a potential competitor an economic advantage. Men "learned" to be instrumental in their relationships with other men; in their friendships, men have come to "seek not intimacy but companionship, not disclosure but commitment." The male romantic friendship, so celebrated in myths and legend, was, in America a historical artifact.[36]

Simultaneously, the separation of spheres also left women as the domestic experts: Women became increasingly adept at emotional expression just as men were abandoning that expressive style. Separate spheres implied more than the spatial separation of home and workplace; it divided the mental and social world into two complementary halves. Men expressed the traits and emotions associated with the workplace—competitiveness, individual achievement, instrumental rationality—while women cultivated the softer domestic virtues of love, nurture, and compassion.

The cultural equation of femininity with emotional intimacy exaggerated gender differences in friendships, love, and sexuality. These differences, then, were the *result* of the broad social and economic changes, not their cause; the exclusion of women from the workplace was the single most important differentiating experience. That is, again, a case where gender inequality produced the very differences that then legitimated the inequalities. And, ideologically, the triumph of autonomy as the highest goal of individual development, along with the ascendant ideal of companionate marriage—marriage based on the free choice of two people who devote themselves emotionally only to each other—reinforced the growing gender gap in emotional expressiveness. When we began to marry for love, we fused sexual passion and deep friendship—for the first time in history. (Remember how the Greeks had kept those three completely separate.)

Finally, the birth of the modern homosexual had enormous implications for the construction of gendered ways of loving. French philosopher Michel Foucault argued that "the disappearance of friendship as a social institution, and the declaration of homosexuality as a social/political/medical problem, are the same process." Prior to the turn of the century, the word *homosexual* described behaviors, not identity. But as the word changed from an adjective to a noun, homophobia became increasingly significant in men's lives. Homophobia increases the gender differences between women and men, since "the possible imputation of homosexual interest to any bonds between men ensured that men had constantly to be aware of and assert their difference from both women and homosexuals," writes sociologist Lynne Segal.[37]

Industrialization, cultural ideals of companionate marriage and the separation of spheres, and the emergence of the modern homosexual—these simultaneous forces created the arena in which we have experienced intimacy and emotional life. Its division into two complementary gendered domains is part of the story of our gendered society.

LOVE AND GENDER

The separation of spheres also had a profound impact on our experiences of love. As with friendship, love has a history; its meanings and expressions change over time. "Passionate attachments between young people can and do happen in any society," writes historian Lawrence Stone, "but the social acceptability of the emotion has varied enormously over time and class and space, determined primarily by cultural norms and property arrangements." As with friendship, women have come to be seen as the love experts—notice how all the advice columns on love and relationships are written for and by women—while men's attempts to express love are evaluated on what have become "feminine" criteria. "Part of the reason that men seem so much less loving than women," argues sociologist Francesca Cancian, "is that men's behavior is measured with a feminine ruler." This has devalued and displaced one type of loving and replaced it with another. "His" expressions of love included sexual passion, the practical aspects of providing and protecting, ensuring material survival, and mutual aid. "Her" way of loving was sharing feelings, mutual emotional dependency, nurturing through talk.[38]

It wasn't always this way. Medieval troubadours of the eleventh to thirteenth centuries described undying passion as a hallmark of love for both women and men. But the romantic love they described was also seen as socially disruptive, a threat to the power of the church, the state, and the family. Thus, by the sixteenth and seventeenth centuries, "every advice book, every medical treatise, every sermon and religious homily . . . firmly rejected both romantic passion and lust as suitable bases for marriage." By the eighteenth century, attitudes had softened, and individuals were advised to make marital choices based on love and affection—provided, of course, that the two families approved and the individuals' social and economic status were roughly equal.[39]

It wasn't until the nineteenth century that love became the ordinary experience for couples, that it was "normal and indeed praiseworthy for young men and women to fall passionately in love, and that there must be something wrong with those who fail to have such an overwhelming experience sometime in late adolescence or early adulthood." But in the nineteenth-century marriage manuals, love is rarely mentioned as a reason to get married. In fact, love "is presented more as a product of marriage than its prerequisite." By the end of the century, though, "love had won its battle along the whole line in the upper sections of the middle class. It has since been regarded as the most important prerequisite to marriage."[40]

So, love as we know it—the basis for marriage, sexuality, and family—is relatively recent. Nor is it the foundation of marriage and/or sexual expression everywhere else in the world. As the basis for sexual activity, love turns out to be relatively rare. Love and sex turn out to be most highly associated in cultures where women and men are more unequal, and where women are materially dependent upon men. Where women and men are mutually dependent and relatively equal, love and sex tend not to be equated. Even in our society, love may or may not accompany sexual activity or family life, and it may wax and wane in its intensity. In a now classic article, sociologist William J. Goode noted that there was little evidence that the ideology of romantic love was widely or deeply believed by all strata of the American population.[41]

GENDERED LOVE, AMERICAN STYLE

Since the mid-nineteenth century, according to historians, love has come to mean tenderness, powerlessness, and emotional expression. And love has become increasingly a woman's business, the home its domain. The masculine workplace was rough and competitive, "a vast wilderness," a "rage of competitive battle," and demanded that men suppress their emotions; home must be the place where a man "seeks refuge from the vexations and embarrassments of business, an enchanting repose from exertion, a relaxation from care by the interchange of affection," as one New England minister explained in 1827. Women, said to possess "all the milder virtues of humanity," became the ministers of love. (This separation of emotional spheres was neither intended nor experienced as a gain for women. Indeed, women's emotionality—women were "accustomed to feel, oftener than to reason," as one Unitarian minister put it—was the chief justification for excluding women from the workplace, colleges and universities, and the voting booth.)[42]

Like friendship, then, the separation of spheres "feminized" love also, so that today love implies "an overemphasis on talking and feeling, a mystification of the material basis of attachment, and a tendency to ignore physical love and the practical aspects of nurturance and mutual assistance." Men's way of loving, focusing on "practical help, shared physical activities, spending time together, and sex," has been demoted to "less than" the feminine style. These different styles of loving are the products of the large-scale transformations that created the modern system of gender relations, and they are as much the cause of gender inequality as the result of preexisting gender differences. They are the result of gender inequality; these differences, as psychologist Carol Tavris tells us, emerged "because women are expected, allowed, and required to reveal certain emotions, and men are expected and required to deny or suppress them." They are the source of so much miscommunication between women and men it often feels as though we are from different planets, or at least, in Lillian Rubin's phrase, "intimate strangers."[43]

Consider, for example, the classic "he said/she said" tussle about whether we really love our partner. Here's what one husband said to Lillian Rubin:

> What does she want? Proof? She's got it, hasn't she? Would I be knocking myself out to get things for her—like to keep up this house—if I didn't love her? Why does a man do things like that if not because he loves his wife and kids? I swear, I can't figure out what she wants.

His wife says something very different: "It is not enough that he supports us and takes care of us. I appreciate that, but I want him to share things with me. I need for him to tell me his feelings."

These two statements aptly illustrate the differences between "his" and "her" ways of loving.[44]

Or do they? The empirical research on the gender of love reveals fewer differences, and of less significance, than we might otherwise expect. One recent review of the literature, for example, found that women's and men's experiences and attitudes were statistically similar on forty-nine of the sixty correlates of love. And those that we do find are occasionally the opposite of what we might have expected. Take, for example, the received wisdom that women are the romantic sex, men the rational, practical sex. After all, women are the domesticated emotional experts and the primary consumers of romance literature, emotional advice columns, and television talk-show platitudes. Some research confirms these stereotypes. One study found that men were more likely to respond to ephemeral qualities such as physical appearance, when they fell in love, and were far more likely to say they were easily attracted to members of the opposite sex. Yet most studies have found *men* to be the stronger believers in romantic love ideologies than women. (On the other hand, men also tend to be more cynical about love at the same time.)[45] Men, it seems, are more likely to believe myths about love at first sight, tend to fall in love more quickly than women, are more likely to enter relationships out of a desire to fall in love, and yet also tend to fall out of love more quickly. Romantic love, to men, is irrational, spontaneous, and compelling emotion that demands action. Who but a man, one might ask, could have said, as Casanova did, that "nothing is surer than that we will no longer desire them, for one does not desire what one possesses."[46]

Women, on the other hand, show a more "pragmatic orientation" toward falling in and out of love, and are also more likely to also like the men they love. Once in love, women tend to experience the state more intensely. One experiment found that after only four dates, men were almost twice as likely than women to define the relationship as love (27 percent to 15 percent). But by the twenty-first date, 43 percent of the women said that they were in love, while only 30 percent of the men did. The researchers write:

> If by "more romantic" we refer to the speed of involvement and commitment, then the male appears to be more deserving of that label. If, on the other hand, we mean the experiencing of the emotional dimension of romantic love, then the female qualifies as can-

didate for "more romantic" behavior in a somewhat more judicious and rational fashion. She chooses and commits herself more slowly than the male but, once in love, she engages more extravagantly in the euphoric and idealizational dimensions of loving.[47]

Despite the fact that men report falling out of love more quickly, it's women who initiate the majority of breakups. And women, it seems, also have an easier time accepting their former romantic partners as friends than the men do. After a breakup, men—supposedly the less emotional gender—report more loneliness, depression, and sleeplessness than women do. This is equally true after divorce: Married men live longer and emotionally healthier lives than divorced or single men; unmarried women live longer and are far happier than married women.[48]

Though some gender differences tend to both confirm and contradict traditional gender stereotypes, there is some evidence that these differences have narrowed considerably over the past few decades. In the late 1960s, William Kephart asked more than one thousand college students, "If a boy (girl) had all the other qualities you desired, would you marry this person if you were not in love with him (her)?" In the 1960s, Kephart found dramatic differences between men, who thought that marriage without love was out of the question, and women, who were more likely to admit that the absence of love wouldn't necessarily deter them from marriage. (Kephart attributed this to women's economic dependence, which allowed men the "luxury" of marrying for love.)[49]

Since the 1960s, sociologists have continued to ask this question, and each year fewer women and men say they are willing to marry for any reason but love. By the mid-1980s, 85 percent of both women and men considered such a marriage out of the question; and by 1991, 86 percent of the men and 91 percent of the women responded with an emphatic "no." The more dramatic shift among women indicates how much the women's movement has transformed women's lives: Women's economic independence now affords women, too, the luxury of marrying for love alone.[50]

But such studies yielded very different results in different countries, suggesting that our definitions of love may have more to do with cultural differences than they do with gender. When students in Japan and Russia were asked the same question in 1992, their answers differed dramatically from those of Americans. More Russian women (41 percent) and men (30 percent) answered yes than did either Japanese (20 percent of the men and 19 percent of the women) or the Americans (13 percent of the men and 9 percent of the women). And while the American and Japanese women were slightly less likely than the men to say yes, Russian women were much more likely than Russian men.[51]

And it may be that other factors enhance or diminish women's and men's ways of loving. Remember that couple cited earlier, whose statements about what they want from each other seemed to speak so loudly about intractable gender differences? These two statements, though, may say more about the transformation of love in a marriage than they do about deep-seated personality differences between women and men. Some startling research was undertaken by sociologist Cathy Greenblat on this issue. Greenblat asked a group of women and men two questions just before they were to get married. "How do you know you love this person?" "How do you know you are loved by this person?"[52]

Prior to marriage, the answers revealed significant gender differences that meshed in a happy symmetry. A man "knew" that he loved his future wife because he was willing to do so much for her, willing to sacrifice for her, eager to go out of his way to buy her flowers or demonstrate his love in some other visible way—willing, as one might say, to drop everything in the middle of the night and drive three hours in a blinding snowstorm because she was upset. Happily, conveniently, their future wives "knew" that they were loved precisely because the men were willing to go to such extraordinary lengths to demonstrate it. The women "knew" that they loved their future husbands because they wanted to take care of them, to nurture and support them, to express their emotions of caring and tenderness. And, happily, the men "knew" they were loved because the women took care of them, nurtured them, and were emotionally caring.

So far, so good—and perfectly symmetrical. Greenblat then interviewed twenty-five couples who had been married at least ten years. She added a new question, asking whether they questioned whether they loved their spouse or whether their spouse loved them. Overwhelmingly, women had no doubts that they still loved their husbands, but had significant doubts whether they were still loved by their husband. By contrast, the husbands had no doubts that they were loved by their wives, but had serious doubts about whether they loved their wives any longer.

It would easy to interpret such data as revealing a gender difference: Men fall in love sooner, but also fall out of love earlier than women. But such research may tell us more about the way that the structure of marriage transforms our ability to love and to be loved. After all, when you are married, you no longer have many opportunities to go well out of your way to do extraordinary things in order to demonstrate your love. You live together, come home from work to each other every day, and raise children together. While that may, in my estimation or yours, be heroic enough in itself, it does not lead men to feel that they are expressing their love in the way they "know" they love someone. Hence, they may begin to doubt whether they truly love their wives. By contrast, the nuclear family in the suburban single-family home enhances women's style of loving as domestic nurturing and caregiving. Thus, the wives were certain that they still loved their husbands, but were unsure that their husbands loved them.

To "read" such differences as revealing something essential about women and men would be to miss the structural impact of the modern family arrangement, and the way that structural arrangements enhance some relational styles and inhibit others. Even if women and men are not from different planets, the modern insular nuclear family may be foreign territory for men's ways of expressing the love they feel. It may mean that we need to expand our capacities for loving in different ways in different situations.

Our current feminization of love, psychologist Carol Tavris argues, has detrimental effects on women's lives:

> The feminization of love in America, the glorification of women's ways of loving, is not about the love between autonomous individuals. It celebrates a romantic, emotional love that promotes the myth of basic, essential differences between women and men. It supports the opposition of women's love and men's work. In so doing, it derails women from thinking about their own talents and aspirations, rewarding instead a narrowed focus on finding and keeping Mr. Right.[53]

Fortunately, love need not be feminized, as Francesca Cancian argues. Men's ways of loving—"the practical help and physical activities"—are, she notes "as much a part of love as the expression of feelings." And the feminization of love as the expression of feelings, nurturing, and intimacy also obscures women's capacity for instrumental, activity-centered forms of love, and thus, in effect, freezes men and women into patterns that mask some of their traits, as if right-handedness meant one could never even use one's left hand. Cancian poses an important question: "Who is more loving," she asks, "a couple who confide most of their experiences to each other but rarely cooperate or give each other practical help, or a couple who help each other through many crises and cooperate in running a household but rarely discuss their personal experiences?" Perhaps, Cancian suggests, what we need is a more embracingly universal definition of love, which has as its purpose individual development, mutual support, and intimacy—and which women and men are equally capable of experiencing.[54]

CONCLUSION

Love and friendship are perhaps the major avenues of self-exploration, and, along with sexuality (the subject of the next chapter), the chief routes we take in our society to know ourselves. "Love provides us with identities, virtues, roles through which we define ourselves, as well as partners to share our happiness, reinforce our values, support our best opinions of ourselves and compensate for the anonymity, impersonality or possibly frustration of public life," writes Robert Solomon. Our friends, Lillian Rubin writes, "are those who seem to us to call up the best parts of ourselves, even while they also accept our darker side."[55]

Yet friendship is so precarious. "Unlike a marriage," Lillian Rubin writes, friendship "is secured by an emotional bond alone. With no social compact, no ritual moment, no pledge of loyalty and constancy to hold a friendship in place, it becomes not only the most neglected social relationship of our time, but, all too often, our most fragile one as well." So, too, are love relationships, which require much care and nurturing in a world that seems to present an infinite number of distractions and subterfuges. Sexual encounters are more fragile still, holding at any particular moment only the most fleeting promise of sustained emotional connection.

To sustain our lives, to enable us to experience the full range of our pleasures, to achieve the deep emotional connections with lovers and friends, we must remember the ways that gender does *and does not* construct our emotional lives. To pretend that women and men are from different planets condemns us, at best, to occasional intergalactic travel, with interpreters and technical assistance. I'd prefer that the interpreters stay home, and that we learn to reveal more of ourselves. Love and friendship are deeply human experiences—ones we should be able to manage on our own. As British novelist E. M. Forster once wrote of passionate human connection—"[M]en and women are capable of sustained relations, not mere opportunities for an electrical discharge."

THE GENDERED BODY

We think of our bodies as either our own private possessions, over which we exercise complete control, or as a collection of biological impulses over which we have virtually no control at all. And though our culture is saturated with sexual jokes and innuendo, and we talk about sex incessantly, for most of us sexuality remains a pretty private experience, rarely discussed honestly and openly. For centuries, the body has been shrouded in myth, taboo, and ignorance.

Yet nothing could be more gendered than these most individual, private experiences. We inscribe our bodies with a wide range of cultural signs and symbols, and our sexualities are intimate expressions of well-established social norms and practices. Our bodies become social texts which we construct to be "read" by others. And significant changes in the past few decades—new surgical procedures, birth control, the Internet—have transformed this system of gendered signifying, making us more aware of our bodies than ever before, and enabling new groups to claim their own embodied agency, a kind of embodied democracy that has also been met, characteristically, with increased backlash.[1]

Our ideals of beauty and attractiveness are deeply gendered. For one thing, we know a lot more about standards of female beauty in other cultures than we know about men—in part because it's men who were creating those standards in the first place, and their valuation as men derived from other things, such as wealth and power. Specifically sexual standards of beauty often vary depending on the status of women. In societies where women's status is higher, smaller breasts are considered more attractive, probably because smaller breasts minimize the anatomical differences between women and men, and also because smaller breasts make it easier for women to move about quickly. In the United States, men's preferences for larger or smaller breasts on women tend to vary with economic trends—as do the hemlines on women's skirts. During periods of prosperity, when male breadwinners can afford to have their wives stay at home, larger breast sizes and shorter hemlines tend to be preferred, as these exaggerate the biological differences between women and men (and thus reinforce the social separation of spheres). During economic downturns, women's hemlines come down and smaller breast sizes tend to become the norm, as women and men both work to make ends meet, and the natural distinctions between women and men are minimized.

In many tropical cultures, women do not cover their breasts, but this doesn't mean that the men there are in a constant state of sexual frenzy. The breasts are simply not considered a sexual stimulus in those cultures, and attention may be focused elsewhere. And in some Islamic cultures, women are believed to be so sexually alluring (and men so unable to control themselves when confronted with temptation) that they practice *purdah*, which requires that they keep their entire bodies covered.

In the United States, women's beauty is placed at such a high premium and the standards of beauty are so narrow that many women feel trapped by what Naomi Wolf called the "beauty myth"—a nearly unreachable cultural ideal of feminine beauty that "uses images of female beauty as a political weapon against women's advancement." Just as Max Weber decried the "iron cage" of consumption in modern society, so, too, does Wolf decry the "Iron Maiden" created by this beauty myth, which entraps women in an endless cycle of cosmetics, beauty aids, diets, and exercise fanaticism, and makes women's bodies into "prisons their homes no longer were." Is this tyranny of slenderness an ironic outcome of women's increased independence—a kind of backlash attempt to keep women in their place just as they are breaking free? It's unlikely that it is any more than a coincidence, but it is worth noting that the first Miss America pageant was held in 1920—the same year women obtained the right to vote.[2]

Women are particularly concerned with breast size and weight. Breasts are "the most visible signs of a woman's femininity," writes philosopher Iris Young, "the sign of her sexuality." Women are often trapped in what we might call the Goldilocks dilemma, after the young girl of the fairy tale. As Goldilocks found the porridge "too hot" or "too cold" but never "just right," so too do women believe their breasts are either too large or too small—but never just right. In 2001, cosmetic surgeons performed nearly 220,000 breast augmentations and 99,428 breast reductions.

Women's weight often forces women to submit to what one writer labeled "the tyranny of slenderness." For example, the average weight of Miss America and *Playboy* pinups has decreased steadily since 1978, even though their average height and breast size has increased. In 1954, Miss America was 5' 8" and weighed 132 pounds. Today, the average Miss America contestant still stands 5' 8", but now weighs just 117 pounds. (An article in *Harper's Bazaar* in 1908 declared the normal weight for a healthy woman of 5' 8" to be 155 pounds; 133 would have been normal for a woman 5' 3' and 117 less than the prescribed weight of 120 pounds for a woman who stood 5' 1".) In 1975, the average fashion model weighed about 8 percent less than the average American woman; by 1990 that had grown to 23 percent. And though the average American woman today is 5' 4" tall and weighs 140 pounds, the average model is 5' 11" and weighs 117 pounds. Marilyn Monroe, perhaps the twentieth century's most recognizable sex symbol, wore a size 12 dress; contemporary sex symbols are more likely to wear a size 4. "Girls are terrified of being fat," writes Mary Pipher. "Being fat means being left out, scorned, and vilified. . . . Almost all adolescent girls feel fat, worry about their weight, diet and feel guilty when they eat." Perhaps most telling is that 42 percent of girls in first through third grades say they want to be thinner, and 81 percent of ten-year-olds are afraid of being fat. Forty-six percent of nine- to eleven-year-olds are on diets; by college the percentage has nearly doubled.[3]

Current standards of beauty for women combine two images—dramatic thinness and also muscular and buxom—that are virtually impossible to accomplish. Research on adolescents suggests that a large majority consciously trade off health concerns in their efforts to lose weight. As a result, increasing numbers of young women are diagnosed with either *anorexia nervosa* or *bulimia* every year. Anorexia involves chronic and dangerous starvation dieting and obsessive exercise; bulimia typically involves "bingeing and purging" (eating large quantities and then either vomiting or taking enemas to excrete it). While anorexia and bulimia are extreme and very serious problems, often requiring hospitalization, that can, if untreated, threaten a girl's life, they represent only the farthest reaches of a continuum of preoccupation with the body that begins with such "normal" behaviors as compulsive exercise or dieting.

It is important to remember that rates of anorexia and bulimia are higher in the United States than in any other country—by far. Estimates in the United States calculate that between 5 and 10 percent of all postpubescent girls and women are affected—that means about five to ten million girls and women.[4] In Britain the number is more like 165,000, and across Europe only 14.5 of every 10,000 women suffer from bulimia or anorexia, according to the European Medical Association. That's just over one-tenth of one per cent—and about fifty times less than the United States.[5] By contrast, many non-Western societies value plumpness, and there is a correlation between body weight and social class, and throughout Europe and the United States, nonwhite girls are far less likely to exhibit eating disorders than are white and middle-class girls. (Ironically, in societies where food is plentiful, ideals of thinness are imposed constantly, while in societies where the food supply is erratic, plumpness is more often the feminine ideal.)[6] Recent dramatic increases have, however, been observed among young middle- and upper-class Japanese women.[7]

While some stereotypic understandings would have it that such dramatic emphasis on thinness afflicts only middle- and upper-class white girls and women, the evidence suggests that these standards also define working-class and black ideals of the feminine body. Largeness "was one accepted—even revered—among Black folks," lamented an article in *Essence* magazine in 1994, but it "now carries the same unmistakable stigma as it does among Whites." And a study the following year found that black adolescent girls demonstrated significantly higher drive for thinness than did white adolescent girls. The media coverage of Oprah's dramatic weight loss, and the depiction of ultra-thin African American models and actresses may have increased black women's anxieties about their weight; indeed, it may be a perverse signal of assimilation and acceptance by the dominant culture that "their" ideal body type is now embraced by the formerly marginalized.[8]

It is also true that men have become increasingly concerned with their bodies, especially fitness and weight. While men have long been concerned about appearing strong and fit—witness the enormous success of Charles Atlas bodybuilding apparatus since the turn of the twentieth century—the building of strong muscles seems to increase as a preoccupation and obsession during periods when men are least likely to actually have to use their muscles in their work. That is, we want to look stronger during periods when we actually don't need it, recreating in our appearances what we no longer require in actuality. Today, successful new men's magazines such as *Men's Health* encourage men to see their bodies as women have been taught to see theirs—as ongoing projects to be worked on. (The magazine's circulation grew from 250,000 to more than 1.5 million in its first seven years—the most successful new magazine launch in history.) In part, this coincides with general concerns about health and fitness, and in part it is about looking young in a society that does not value aging. But more than that, it also seems to be about gender.

Men's bodily anxieties mirror those of women. While women are concerned with breast size and weight, men are concerned with muscularity—that is, both are preoccupied with those aspects of the male and female body that suggest and exaggerate innate biological differences between the sexes. It would appear that the more equal women and men become in the public sphere, the more standards of beauty would emphasize those aspects that are biologically different.

Standards of male muscularity have also increased dramatically. Many men experience what some researchers have labeled "Muscle Dysmorphia," a belief that one is too small, insufficiently muscular. Pope and his colleagues call it the "Adonis Complex"—the belief that men must look like Greek gods, with perfect chins, thick hair, rippling muscles, and washboard abdominals. The increasing packaging of men's bodies in the media—it is now common to see men's bodies displayed in advertising in ways that were conceivable only for women's bodies a generation ago—coupled with increased economic anxiety (which leads us to focus on the things we *can* control, like how we look), has led to a dramatic shift in men's ideas about their bodies.[9]

In 1999, Harrison Pope and his colleagues took G.I. Joe's proportions and translated them into real-life statistics (parallel to the descriptions of Barbie's changes). In 1974, GI Joe was 5 feet 10 inches tall, had a 31 inch waist, a 44 inch chest, and 12 inch biceps. Strong and muscular, it's true, but at least within the realm of the possible. GI Joe in 2002 is a little bit different. He's still 5 feet 10 inches tall, but his waist has shrunk to 28 inches, his chest has expanded to 50 inches, and his biceps are now 22 inches—almost the size of his waist. Such proportions would make one a circus freak, not a role model.[10]

Such hypertrophied ectomorphs make many men feel utterly inadequate. Nearly one-half of all men in one survey reported significant body image disturbance. A 1997 study reported in *Psychology Today* found 43 percent of the men were dissatisfied with their appearance, compared with only 15 percent twenty-five years earlier. As one college student told a journalist:

> When I look in the mirror, I see two things: what I want to be and what I'm not. I hate my abs. My chest will never be huge. My legs are too thin. My nose is an odd shape. I want what *Men's Health* pushes. I want to be the guy in the Gillette commercials.[11]

And increasing numbers of men are also exhibiting eating disorders. Pope and his colleagues believe that more than one million men suffer from some form of eating disorder; 10 percent of those seeking treatment for eating disorders are male. (According to one study, men are far less likely to seek treatment of eating disorders because they believe it to be a woman's illness.) While these problems may be more prevalent among gay men, increases among heterosexual men are also pronounced. A 1994 study of football players at Cornell found that 40 percent engaged in dysfunctional eating patterns and 10 percent manifest diagnosable eating disorders. A 1997 survey of 1,425 active duty naval men found that nearly 7 percent fit the criteria for bulimia, another 2.5 percent were anorexic, and over 40 percent fit the criteria for eating disorder and nearly 40 percent reported current binge eating. One in four reported compensatory behaviors such as fasting, vomiting, laxatives, and water pills—numbers that doubled when physical standards were being measured. And a recent survey of Australian college men found that one in five had used restrained eating, vomiting, laxative abuse, or cigarette smoking for weight control. About one in five also reported binge eating and weight control problems.[12]

And just as women have resorted to increasingly dangerous surgical and prosthetic procedures—such as having silicone-filled baggies placed in their breasts or being given mild localized doses of botulism to paralyze facial muscles and thereby "remove" wrinkles—so too are men resorting to increasingly dramatic efforts to get large. The use of anabolic steroids has mushroomed, especially among college-age men. Legal prescriptions for steroids have doubled since 1997, to more than 1.5 million, and countless more illegal sources provide less regulated doses. Steroids enable men to increase muscle mass quickly and dramatically, so that one looks incredibly big. Prolonged use also leads to dramatic mood changes, increased uncontrolled rage, and a significant shrinkage of the testicles.[13]

Eating disorders among women and "muscular dysmorphia" among men are parallel processes, extreme points on a continuum that begins with almost everyone. There are, for example, very few women who do not have a problematic relationship with food—virtually all women see food as something other than simple taste or nourishment, but mentally count the calories, determine whether this indulgence is worth it, calculate how much extra time they can spend in the gym to compensate, how much they weigh. And virtually all young men have a problematic relationship with violence. (As we'll see in the next chapter, violence is so closely equated with masculinity that it would be difficult to extricate the two.) And what signifies the capacity for violence but physical strength—at least looking strong. One can hear this in the voices of the anorexics and the obsessive bodybuilders. The young women, literally starving to death, talk constantly about how fat they are, and how if only they could lose weight they'd feel better about themselves, while their male counterparts, who are so muscle-bound that they cannot bend over to tie their shoes, talk about how "small" they are, and how much they have to eat and work out to get larger. If a measure of successful femininity is being thin, and a measure of masculinity is appearing strong and powerful, then anorexics and obsessive bodybuilders are not psychological misfits or deviants; they are overconformists to gender norms to which all of us, to some degree, are subject.[14]

Just as there has been an increase in the gap between rich and poor—the gap between the top 20 percent and the bottom 20 percent of American society is currently the highest in our history—so too has there been an increased bifurcation between the embodied "haves" and "have nots." Americans are both increasingly thin and increasingly overweight, exercising obsessively or sedentary couch potatoes, eating tofu and organic raw vegetables or Big Macs and supersized fried foods. This growing divide reflects different class and racial cultures, but it also is deeply gendered.

CHANGING THE BODY

Virtually all of us spend some time and energy in some forms of bodily beautification, by wearing fashionable clothes and jewelry, for example. But until recently, only a few marginalized "out groups" such as motorcycle gangs, practiced any forms of permanent bodily transformation—running the gamut beyond simply ear piercing, from piercing other body parts, to tattoos, cosmetic surgery, and even the rare case of sex-change operations. Today, body piercing involves far more than the earlobes, and can include the tongue, eyebrows, navel, nose, lips, nipples, and even the genitals. Increasing numbers of young people are also getting tattoos. Given their vaguely transgressive character in American society, tattoos and piercing denote a slight sexualized undertone—if only because they indicate that the bearer is aware of his or her body as an object of pleasure or desire.

Well over 10 million Americans have at least one tattoo, described by one psychiatrist as a "bumper sticker of the soul." The most common tattoo, found on one in four tattoo wearers, is "mom" or "mother." Design and placement are also highly sexually charged; we believe they say something about our selves and our sexuality. (This new popularity has also spawned a new industry—tattoo removal. According to one survey of people seeking removal, 45 percent said they got the tattoo because they thought it was fashionable; 22 percent because of peer pressure; 7 percent because of "sheer stupidity"; and 6 percent because they were in love. Thirteen per cent said they were under the influence of drugs or alcohol. One in ten regretted the decision "immediately," and another 28 percent voiced regret within the first month—which means that nearly four of every ten are sorry they acted so hastily.)[15]

One of the fastest growing methods of bodily transformation is cosmetic surgery. According to one study by the American Society of Plastic and Reconstructive Surgeons, the total number of cosmetic procedures increased from 413,208 in 1992 to 1.62 million in 2001. And the most common procedures increased by almost 500 percent. In addition to breast augmentation and reduction, these included 275,463 liposuctions (compared with 47,212 in 1992), 238,213 eyelid surgeries (59,461 in 1992), and 124,531 facelifts (40,077 in 1992).[16]

Though women continue to be the primary consumers of such cosmetic surgery, male patients have gone from 54,845 in 1992 to 330,072 in 2001, and now comprise 20 percent of all procedures. "More men are viewing cosmetic surgery as a viable way of looking and feeling younger," observed ASPRS President Dennis Lynch, M.D., "especially, to compete in the workplace."

This comment raises what may be most interesting from our gender perspective: not which gender is *having* the surgery, but which gender is the one *for whom* the surgery is being performed. It may be that, as one writer explains, "the traditional image of women as sexual objects has simply expanded: everyone has become an object to be seen," but the question remains: Seen by whom? Who do we imagine seeing us in our newly reconstructed state?[17]

For women, the answer is, usually men. Women's beauty—thinness, breast size, attractiveness—is valuable currency in the sexual marketplace, and given gender inequality, women have traded on their physical appearance to attract a mate. (Ironically, in one study, virtually all the male partners of women having plastic surgery thought the procedure was unnecessary.)[18]

For men, though, the answer is: men. Men also are the object of the "male gaze," and feel a need to look big, strong, and virile in front of other men. Take one extreme example of this, the case of penile enlargement surgery. This is a dramatic (and expensive) procedure—every year about fifteen thousand men pay about $6,000 to have it done—by which the penis can be lengthened by about two inches. (The average flaccid penis is about 3.5 inches long; erect it's about 5.1 inches long.) In one of the few studies that rely on data and not anecdotal evidence and thrilled testimonials, psychologist Randy Klein found that the average penile length before surgery was

2.6 inches (flaccid) and 5.4 inches (erect); after the surgery, penile length was 3.8 inches (flaccid) and 5.7 inches (erect). That is, the only significant difference in length was when the penis was flaccid.[19]

While one would think that men engage in this painful procedure to be "better" lovers, or to please women more, and indeed many men say that is part of their motivation. In many cases, however, it has far less to do with women's potential pleasure than men's visual perception. Men who have this procedure more often experience what one physician called "locker room syndrome"—the fear of being judged as inadequately masculine *by other men*. Take, for example, the testimonial letters from a satisfied customer:

> I was always afraid to get into situations where I would have to shower with other men or be seen by anyone. I can remember avoiding many of the sports and activities I loved dearly, all because I was afraid that I would be seen and made fun of. . . . I even avoided wearing shorts and tight clothes because of my fear that others would notice me.

"The thing I missed most was the changing room camaraderie and male bonding associated with these sports which was always something I enjoyed," writes another. "I felt ashamed to even go to the urinals in a public place and have made sure I never use these whilst other men are there too."[20]

Nowhere is gender inequality better observed than by the motivations for both women and men in changing their bodies. It is the male gaze—whether as potential sexual partner, potential sexual rival, or competitor in the marketplace or athletic field—that motivates such drastic measures.

SEXUAL BODILY TRANSFORMATION: TRANSGENDERISM

Some people feel constrained by gender role expectations and seek to expand these by changing their behavior. Though there are significant penalties for boys who are effeminate ("sissies") and some, but fewer, penalties for girls who are "tomboys," many adult men and women continue to bend, if not break gender norms in their bodily presentation. Some may go as far as to use the props of the opposite sex to challenge gender stereotypes; some people find erotic enjoyment in this, others do it to "pass" into a forbidden world. Again, this runs along a continuum: at one end are women who wear man-tailored clothing and power suits to work, since such clothing gives them the air of confidence as they downplay femininity and exude competence (which are often seen as antithetical); at the other end are those who wear full cross-gender regalia as a means of mockery and the pleasure of transgression. Transvestites regularly dress in the clothing of the opposite sex, disrupting the equation of biological sex and social gender by playing with gender (the socially and culturally prescribed adornments and dress).

Some people, though, feel that their biological sex doesn't match their internal sense of gender identity. Transgendered people feel a "persistent discomfort and sense of inappropriateness about one's assigned sex (feeling trapped in the wrong body)" as the diagnosis in the American Psychiatric Association's *Diagnostic and Statistical Manual* (DSM III) puts it. And rather than change their gender, they want to change their biological sex to match their felt gender identity. After two years of therapy and radical hormone therapies to mute or reverse secondary sex characteristics (such as body hair, voice, breasts), some of these people undergo Sex Reassignment Surgery (SRS), by which the original genitalia are surgically removed and new realistic medical constructions of vaginas and penises are created. Transgendered people offer living proof that the social construction of gender and sexuality is more than simply metaphoric.

Historically, transgenderism was quite rare; by 1980, only about four thousand had undergone these surgical interventions, and almost all of them were males seeking to become females. New medical and surgical procedures facilitated both male-to-female and female-to-male transsexual operations, and the inclusion of sex-change operations as procedures to be covered by Medicare (1978) and the listing of transsexualism in the DSM-III in 1980 allowed for insurance coverage for SRS. The increased visibility of transgendered people within the gay and lesbian movement has also increased the viability of SRS as a treatment option.

Typically, transgenderism is experienced as a general discomfort that becomes increasingly intense during puberty, that is, with the emergence of secondary sex characteristics. As one female-to-male transgendered person told an interviewer:

> I hate the changes in my body . . . I couldn't stand it . . . It affected my identity. I became very upset and depressed. As a matter of fact, by this time in my life, I spent most of my time in my room . . . I thought about suicide. . . . [21]

While transgenderism remains relatively uncommon, the implications of such procedures is enormous. Once, a discrepancy between one's biological sex and what one experienced internally as one's gender would privilege the body, as if it contained some essential truth about the person. If such conflicts were to be resolved by therapeutic interventions, they would "help" the person accept their body's "truth" and try and adjust their feelings about their gender. Transgenderism enables us to dissolve what is experienced as an arbitrary privileging of the body-at-birth, and give more weight to who we feel we are, bringing us close to a world in which we can freely choose our gender because we can freely change our sex.

SEXUALITY

Nowhere in our intimate lives is there greater expression of gender difference than in our sexual relationships. Yet even here, as we shall see, there are signs of change and convergence. As friendship and love have become "feminized"—that is, as the model of appropriate behavior has come to resemble what we labeled as traditionally "feminine" models of intimacy—sexuality has become increasingly "masculinized." The "masculinization of sex"—including the pursuit of pleasure for its own sake, the increased attention to orgasm, the multiplication of sexual partners, the universal interest in sexual experimentation, and the separation of sexual behavior from love—is partly a result of the technological transformation of sexuality (from birth control to the Internet) and partly the result of the sexual revolution's promise of greater sexual freedom with fewer emotional and physical consequences.

Much of that sexual revolution was a rejection of the Victorian double standard, which was, after all, merely the nineteenth-century version of the interplanetary theory of gender. According to these writers, women and men were different species. As the celebrated French historian Jules Michelet put it in 1881:

> [Woman] does nothing as we [men] do. She thinks, speaks, and acts differently. Her tastes are different from our tastes. Her blood even does not flow in her veins as ours does, at times it rushes through them like a foaming mountain torrent. . . . She does not eat like us—neither as much nor of the same dishes. Why? Chiefly, because she does not digest as we do. Her digestion is every moment troubled with one thing: She yearns with her very bowels. The deep cup of love (which is called the pelvis) is a sea of varying emotions, hindering the regularity of the nutritive function.[22]

Sex was invariably seen as bad for women—unhealthy and immoral—while it was tolerated or even encouraged for men. "The majority of women (happily for them) are not much troubled with sexual feelings of any kind," wrote one physician (obviously male) in the 1890s.[23]

Even when Alfred Kinsey undertook his pioneering studies of sexual behavior in the decade following World War II, this double standard was still firmly in place. As he wrote in 1953:

> [W]e have not understood how nearly alike females and males may be in their sexual responses, and the extent to which they may differ. We have perpetuated the age-old traditions concerning the slower responsiveness of the female, the greater extent of the erogenous areas on the body of the female, the earlier sexual development of the female, the idea that there are basic differences in the nature of orgasm among females and males, the greater emotional content of the female's sexual response, and still other ideas which are not based on scientifically accumulated data—and all of which now appear to be incorrect. It now appears that the very techniques which have been suggested in marriage manuals, both ancient and modern, have given rise to some of the differences that we have thought inherent in females and males.[24]

Kinsey believed that males and females have basically the same physical responses, though men are more influenced by psychological factors. Note in the passage above how Kinsey suggests that the advice of experts actually *creates* much of the difference between women and men. One study of gynecology textbooks published between 1943 and 1972 bears this out. The authors found that many textbooks asserted that women could not experience orgasm during intercourse. One textbook writer observed that "sexual pleasure is entirely secondary or even absent" in women; another described women's "almost universal frigidity." Given such assumptions, it's not surprising that women were counseled to fake orgasm; after all, they weren't capable of real ones. "It is good advice to recommend to the women the advantage of innocent simulation of sex responsiveness; as a matter of fact many women in their desire to please their husbands learned the advantage of such innocent deception," was the way one text counseled gynecologists to raise the issue with their female patients.[25]

The double standard persists today—perhaps less in what we actually do, and more in the way we think about it. Men still stand to gain status and women to lose it from sexual experience: he's a stud who scores; she's a slut who "gives it up." Boys are taught to try to get sex; girls are taught strategies to foil the boys' attempts. "The whole game was to get a girl to give out," one man told sociologist Lillian Rubin. "You expected her to resist; she had to if she wasn't going to ruin her reputation. But you kept pushing. Part of it was the thrill of touching and being touched, but I've got to admit, part of it was the conquest, too, and what you'd tell the guys at school the next day." "I felt as if I should want to get it as often as possible," recalled another. "I guess that's because if you're a guy, you're supposed to want it." "Women need a reason to have sex," commented comedian Billy Crystal. "Men just need a place."[26]

The sexual double standard is much more than a case of separate but equal sexual scripting, much more than a case of one sexuality for Martians and another for Venutians. The sexual double standard is itself a product of gender inequality, of sexism—the unequal distribution of power in our society based on gender. Gender inequality is reinforced by the ways we have come to assume that men are more sexual than women, that men will always try to escalate sexual encounters to prove their manhood, and that women—or, rather, "ladies"—either do not have strong sexual feelings, or that those they do must be constantly controlled lest they fall into disrepute. With such a view, sex becomes a contest, not a means of connection; when sexual pleasure happens, it's often seen as his victory over her resistance. Sexuality becomes, in the words of feminist lawyer Catharine MacKinnon, "the linchpin of gender inequality."[27]

Women are raised to believe that to be sexually active or "promiscuous" is to transgress the rules of femininity. These rules are enforced not just by men, of course, but also by other women, and institutionalized in church, state, and school. The pursuit of sex transforms good girls into bad girls, so most women accept the cultural standard of sexual minimalism—few partners, fewer positions, less pleasure, less sex without emotional commitment. Such an ideology keeps a woman waiting for her Prince Charming to liberate her, to arouse her with his tender kisses, and release the passion smoldering beneath her cooler surface.[28]

The sexual double standard is far more rigidly enforced than any ideological difference in men's and women's patterns of friendship and love. As a result, we are far more likely to observe significant gender differences in sexuality. Examples of these different scripts abound—from what we think about, what we want, and what we actually do. For example, consider what "counts" as sex. When they say the word *sex*, women and men often mean different things. In one study, monogamous heterosexual couples in their mid-forties were asked, "How many times did you make love last week?" Consistently, the researchers found, the men reported slightly higher numbers than the women. What could this indicate—better memories? masculine braggadocio? clandestine affairs? solitary pleasures? When the researchers asked more questions, they found the difference was the result of women and men counting different experiences as "making love." The women would count one sexual encounter once, while the men tallied up the number of their orgasms. Thus, while a woman might say, "Hmm, we made love three times last week," her husband might say, "Hmm, let me see, we did it three times, but one of those times we did it twice [meaning that he had two orgasms], so I guess the answer is four."

The differences in counting criteria reveal deeper differences in the understanding of sexual expression. Women's understanding that sex equals the entire encounter gives them a somewhat broader range of sexual activities that count as sex. Men's focus on orgasm as the defining feature of sex parallels their tendency to exclude all acts except intercourse from "having sex." Oral or manual stimulation are seen as "foreplay" for men, as "sex" for women. Men cannot tally the encounter on their mental scorecard unless intercourse also occurs. This often results in complex rules about what constitutes a "technical virgin." (The public seminar on what counts as "sexual relations" in the impeachment trial of President Clinton in the late 1990s bears this out. Since he and Monica Lewinsky did not have sexual intercourse, and instead did what girls in my high school used to call "everything but," Clinton argued that he did not lie when he denied having sex with Lewinsky. In his mind, as one of my pals in the locker room explained it to me, "it only counts if you put it in." And some recent medical evidence bears this out; a recent article in the *Journal of the American Medical Association* reported that only intercourse "counted" as sex for nearly two-fifths of those surveyed. Fifty-nine percent of respondents believed that oral-genital contact did not constitute having sex.[29]

Intercourse and orgasm are more important forms of sexual expression for men than they are for women. This leads to a greater emphasis on the genitals as the single most important erogenous zone for men. If men's sexuality is "phallocentric"— revolving around the glorification and gratification of the penis—then it is not surprising that men often develop elaborate relationships with their genitals. Some men name their penis—"Willie," "John Thomas," or "Peter"—or give them cute nicknames taken from mass-produced goods, such as "Whopper" and "Big Mac." Men may come to believe that their penises have little personalities (or, perhaps, what feel like big personalities), threatening to refuse to behave the way they are supposed to behave. If men do not personify the penis, they objectify it; if it is not a little person, then it is supposed to act like a machine, an instrument, a "tool." A man projects "the coldness and hardness of metal" onto his flesh, writes the French philosopher Emmanuel Reynaud.[30]

Few women name their genitals; fewer still think of their genitals as machines. Can you imagine if they called their clitoris "Shirley" or their labia "Sally Ann"? In fact, women rarely refer to their genitals by their proper names at all, generally describing vulva, labia, and clitoris with the generic "vagina" or even the more euphemistic "down there" or "private parts." And it would be rare indeed to see a woman having a conversation with her labia.[31]

So when they think about sex, men and women are often thinking about different things. Actually, thinking about sex at all seems to be a gendered activity. Men tend to think about sex more often than women. More than half of the men surveyed (54 percent) in the most recent large-scale sex survey conducted by the National Opinion Research Center (NORC) at the University of Chicago reported that they think about sex very frequently, compared with 19 percent of the women. Two-thirds of the women report that they think about sex less frequently, compared with 43 percent of the men. And 14 percent of the women say they rarely or never think about sex, compared with only 4 percent of the men.[32]

Forty years earlier, Alfred Kinsey and his colleagues had found that 89 percent of men who masturbated fantasized, while only 64 percent of women did. And what they "use" for their fantasies differs. Today, nearly one-fourth (23 percent of men and 11 percent of women) use X-rated movies or videos; 16 percent of men and 4 percent of women use sexually explicit books or magazines.[33] And what they fantasize about differs dramatically. A research assistant and I have collected more than one thousand sexual fantasies from students over the past decade. In those fantasies, definite gender patterns emerged. Men tend to fantasize about strangers, often more than one at a time, doing a variety of well-scripted sexual acts; women tend to fantasize about setting the right mood for lovemaking with their boyfriend or husband, but rarely visualize specific behaviors. Consider, for example these "typical" scenes, composites of fantasies we've collected. The following were reported by women:

> My boyfriend and I are on a deserted island. The palm trees flap in the soft breeze, the sand glistens. The sun is warm and we swim for a while in the cool blue water and then come back to the beach and lie there. We rub suntan oil on each others' bodies, and soon we are kissing passionately. Then we make love in the sand.
>
> My husband and I are at a ski resort, in a cabin and it's late at night. It's snowing outside, so we build a fire in the fireplace and lie down on the fur rug in front of it. We sip champagne by the roaring fire, and then he kisses me and takes my blouse off. Then we make love.

Compare them to this one, a composite of a typical man's fantasy:

> I'm walking down the street and these two unbelievably gorgeous blondes are walking towards me. Our eyes meet and we realize we have to have each other. One of them kneels in front of me and unzips my fly and begins to give me the best blow job I've ever had. The other pulls down her shorts and begins to play with herself. Then I do her while the first one gets eaten out by the one I'm fucking. We do it every way we can imagine, and then they get it on while I'm resting, but watching them turns me on, so we start up again. Then we all get up and walk away with these big smiles on our faces. We never see one another again.[34]

Men's fantasies are idealized renditions of masculine sexual scripts: genitally focused, orgasm centered, and explicit in the spatial and temporal sequencing of sexual behaviors. We know exactly who does what to whom in what precise order. Physical characteristics of the other participants are invariably highly detailed; these are most often strangers (or famous models or actresses) chosen for their physical attributes. Rarely do they include the physical setting for the encounter. Women's fantasies, on the other hand, are replete with descriptions that set the scene—geographic and temporal settings, with elaborate placement of props like candles, rugs, and wine glasses. They often involve present or past partners. Explicitly sexual description is minimal, and usually involves vague references to lovemaking.

Thus, we might say that women's *sexual* imaginations are impoverished at the expense of highly developed *sensual* imaginations; by contrast, men's sensual imaginations are impoverished by their highly developed sexual imaginations. (These differences hold for both heterosexual and homosexual women and men, a further indication that the basic component in our sexual scripts is gender, not sexual orientation.) While there has been some evidence of shifts in women's fantasies toward more sexually explicit scenes, and increasing comfort with explicit language, these fantasies do reveal both what we think and what we think we are supposed to think about when we think about sex.[35]

Where do these dramatically different mental landscapes come from? One place, of course, is sexual representation. Pornography occupies a special place in the development of men's sexuality. Nearly all men confess to having some exposure to pornography, at least as adolescents; indeed, for many men the first naked women they see are in pornographic magazines. And pornography has been the site of significant political protest—from an erotophobic right wing that considers pornography to be as degrading to human dignity as birth control information, homosexuality, and abortion, to radical feminist campaigns that see pornography as a vicious expression of misogyny, on a par with rape, spouse abuse, and genital mutilation.

While the right wing's efforts rehearsed America's discomfort with all things sexual, the radical feminist critique of pornography transformed the political debate, arguing that when men looked at pornographic images of naked women, they were actually participating in a culture-wide hatred and contempt for women. Pornographic images are about the subordination of women; pornography "makes sexism sexy," in the words of one activist. These are not fictional representations of fantasy; these are documentaries of rape and torture, performed for men's sexual arousal. Here is one pornographic director and actor, commenting on his "craft":

> My whole reason for being in the [pornography] Industry is to satisfy the desire of the men in the world who basically don't much care for women and want to see the men in my Industry getting even with the women they couldn't have when they were growing up. . . . So when we come on a woman's face or somewhat brutalize her sexually, we're getting even for their lost dreams. I believe this. I've heard audiences cheer me when I do something foul on screen. When I've strangled a person or sodomized a person or brutalized a person, the audience is cheering my action, and then when I've fulfilled my warped desire, the audience applauds.[36]

The claims of antipornography feminists—that pornography causes rape, or that it numbs us to the real effect of real violence in women's lives—have been difficult to demonstrate empirically. Few studies have shown such an empirical relationship, though several have documented some modest changes in men's attitudes immediately after exposure to violent pornography. Yet whether or not there is *any* empirical evidence that the pornography alone causes rape or violence, there remains the shocking difference between us: On any given day in the United States, there are men masturbating to images of women enduring sexual torture, genital mutilation, rape, and violence. Surely, this points to a dramatic difference between women's and men's sexualities—one can hardly imagine many women masturbating to reenactments of Lorena Bobbitt's ministrations to her husband. Violence is rarely sexualized for women; that such images can be such a routine and casual turn-on for many men should at least give us pause.[37]

Pornography also exaggerates the masculinization of sex. In typical porn video scenes, both women and men want sex—even when women don't want it, when they are forced or raped, it turns out that they wanted it after all. Both women and men are always looking for opportunities to have sex, both are immediately aroused and ready for penetration, and both have orgasms within fifteen seconds of penetration. Which gender's sexuality does that sound like? As a result, as antipornography activist John Stoltenberg writes, pornography "tells lies about women," but it "tells the truth about men."[38]

Given men's and women's different sexual mentalities, it's not surprising that we develop different sexualities, as evidenced in our attitudes and behaviors. For one thing, women's inclusion of their boyfriend or husband in their fantasies indicates that women's sexuality often requires an emotional connection to be fully activated. "For sex to really work for me, I need to feel an emotional *something*," one woman told Lillian Rubin. "Without that, it's just another athletic activity, only not as satisfying, because when I swim or run, I feel good afterward." Women's first sexual experiences are more likely to occur in the context of a committed relationship.[39]

Since women tend to connect sex and emotional connection, it makes sense that they would be less interested in one-night stands and in affairs and non-monogamy. In one survey, women were about 20 percent more likely to agree that one-night stands are degrading (47 percent of the men agreed, 68 percent of the women agreed). Men are more likely to be unfaithful to their spouse, though that gender gap has closed considerably in the past two decades. And, of course, the separation of sex and emotion means that men are more likely to have had more sexual partners than women. In figure 10.1, one can see these differences, and also observe how this gender gap has also been narrowing over the past few decades.[40]

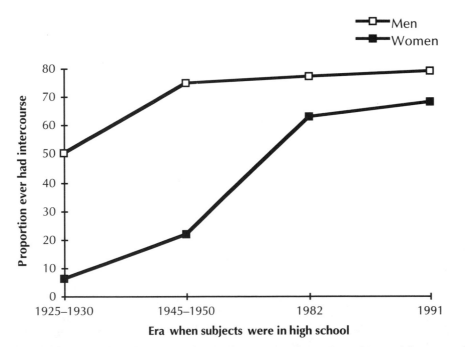

Figure 10.1. Trends in heterosexual experience among teens. From Pepper Schwartz and Virginia Rutter, *The Gender of Sexuality: Sexual Possibilities* (Pine Forge Press, 1998), p. 165. Used by permission of publisher.

Men's wider sexual repertoire usually includes desiring oral sex, about which women report being far less enthusiastic. As one woman explained:

> I like going down on him. It makes him feel good, truly good. I don't find it unpleasant. I don't say I wish I could do it all the time. I don't equate it with a sale at Bloomingdale's. That I could do all the time. But it's not like going to the dentist either. It's between two extremes. Closer to Bloomingdale's than to the dentist.[41]

But perhaps this has less to do with the intrinsic meaning of the act, and more to do with the gender of the actor. For example, when men describe their experiences with oral sex, it is nearly always from the position of power. Whether fellatio—"I feel so powerful when I see her kneeling in front of me"—or cunnilingus—"being able to get her off with my tongue makes me feel so powerful"—men experience the giving and receiving of oral sex as an expression of their power. By contrast, many women perceive both giving and receiving oral sex from the position of powerlessness—not necessarily because they are forced to do so, but because "it makes him happy" for them to either do it, or let him do it. So oral sex, like intercourse, allows him to feel "like a man," regardless of who does what to whom.

GENDERED SEXUAL SOCIALIZATION

Where does the sexual gender gap come from? Though we are constantly bombarded with sexual images in the media, and receive lessons about sexual morality from our parents, our teachers, and our religious institutions, most of our sexual learning comes during adolescence, and most of our adolescent sexual socialization is accomplished by our peers. We teach ourselves and each other about what feels good and why, and then we practice performing those activities until they do feel the way we're told they're supposed to feel.

Remember, for example, those junior high school "wrestling matches"—two adolescents trying to negotiate, usually without words, the extent of their sexual contact. Both the boy and the girl have goals, though they may be very different. "His" object, of course, is to score—and toward that end he has a variety of maneuvers, arguments, and other strategies his friends have taught him. "Her" object may be pleasure, but it is also to preserve and protect her reputation as a "good girl," which requires that she be seen as alluring but not "easy." "Young men come to sex with quite different expectations and desires than do young women," the NORC sex survey declared. "Young women often go along with intercourse the first time, finding little physical pleasure in it, and a substantial number report being forced to have intercourse."[42]

Let's follow one typical adolescent boy and girl as they negotiate their competing desires. If they have been dating for a while, he may decide it's time to escalate the sexual relationship, to move from kissing (first base) to touching her breast (second base). It is nearly universally "his" job to escalate, and "her" job to decide if she will let him. So he moves his hand toward her breast, on top of her blouse. She lets him.

Is our hero now thinking, "Mmmm. This feels good. Her breast is so soft and warm. I think I'll keep my hand here for a while"? Unlikely. If he's typical, he's already strategizing how to get underneath her blouse. And she's thinking—what? "Mmmm. This feels good. I like this better than when that other guy tried this a few weeks ago"? More likely she is thinking, "I know he's going to try to get underneath my blouse now. Do I want him to? How do I stop him without hurting his feelings?"

Each time he escalates, he barely has time to enjoy it before developing his strategy to get to the next stage. And each time, she has to decide whether and how to prevent him from doing so. Rarely is either of them fully experiencing the thrill and pleasure of exploring each other's body. Both are actually far ahead, in the future, plotting their next move. Much of our adolescent sexual socialization emphasizes the future over the present; it often takes place as much in the future tense as the present tense.

If they are not in the same "time zone," you'd think, at least, that they'd be on the same planet. (Of course, they might each be on Mars and Venus anyway!) But, even here, their attention is divided. He may be thinking, "Wow, I got to third base! I can't wait to tell the other guys!" while she is thinking, "Oh my God, I let him go too far. I hope none of my friends finds out!" So he promises not to tell anyone (even though that may be a lie) in return for her allowing him to go a bit farther. Spatially, too, they are in different places—each with same-sex peers, enhancing and preserving their reputations. As one feminist researcher put it, "Although their sexual interest is focused on the opposite sex, it is primarily to their same-sex peers that adolescents will look for validation of their sexual attitudes and accomplishments." Given this spatial and temporal separation—both in the future and with their same-sex peers—it's a wonder that pleasure and intimacy happen at all![43]

This dynamic helps to explain why there seems to be so much pressure on adolescents, and why there are so any breakdowns in communication, including boys attempting to go further than girls want them to. That young boys and young girls have sexual experiences for reasons other than intimacy and pleasure has been a truism in sex research. Psychologist Charlene Muehlenhard, for example, has been studying adolescents' sexual encounters for more than a decade. She found that more men (57.4 percent) than women (38.7 percent) reported that they had engaged in unwanted sexual intercourse due to being enticed—that is the other person made an advance that the person had difficulty refusing. More men (33.5 percent) than women (11.9 percent) had unwanted sexual intercourse because they wanted to get sexual experience, wanted something to talk about, or wanted to build up their confidence. And more men (18.4 percent) than women (4.5 percent) said they engaged in sexual intercourse because they did not want to appear to be homosexual, shy, afraid, or unmasculine or unfeminine. Peer pressure was a factor for 10.9 percent of the men but only 0.6 percent of the women.[44]

By the time we get to be adults, this socialized distance between women and men can ossify into the different experiences we are said to have. Each gender is seeking to express different feelings, for different reasons, with different repertoires, and so it may appear that we are originally from different planets. In the British film *Sammy and Rosie Get Laid*, a lesbian character suggests that heterosexuals are to be pitied: "The women spend all their time trying to come, and they're unsuccessful, and the men spend all their time trying not to come, and they're unsuccessful also."

She has a point. Since many men believe that adequate sexual functioning is being able to delay ejaculation, some develop strategies to prevent what they consider to be premature ejaculation—strategies that exaggerate emotional distancing, phallocentrism, the focus on orgasm, and objectification. Here's how Woody Allen once put it in a stand-up comedy routine from the mid-1960s. After describing himself as a "stud," Allen says:

> When making love, in an effort to [pause] to prolong [pause] the moment of ecstacy, I think of baseball players. All right, now you know. So the two of us are making love violently, and she's digging it, so I figure I'd better start thinking of baseball players pretty quickly. So I figure it's one out, and the Giants are up. Mays lines a single to right. He takes second on a wild pitch. Now she's digging her nails into my neck. I decide to pinch-hit for McCovey. [pause for laughter] Alou pops out. Haller singles, Mays takes third. Now I've got a first and third situation. Two outs and the Giants are behind one run. I don't know whether to squeeze or to steal. [pause for laughter] She's been in the shower for ten minutes already. [pause] I can't tell you anymore, this is too personal. [pause] The Giants won.

Readers may be struck by several things—the imputation of violence, how her pleasure leads to his decision to think of baseball players, the requirement of victory in the game, and the sexual innuendo contained in the sports language. The text also supplies a startling revelation of male sexual distancing. Here's a device that is so successful at delaying ejaculation (or any sexual connection) that the narrator is rendered utterly unaware of his partner's experience. "She's been in the shower for ten minutes already," Allen remarks, as if he's just noticed. Other men describe elaborate mental scripting of sports scenes, reciting multiplication tables, or, in the case of one of my students, a chemistry major, reciting, in order, the Periodic Table of the Elements. No wonder women often wonder what men are thinking about during sex!

And that doesn't factor in the variety of potions, creams, and ointments that are advertised in the backs of men's magazines, products men can apply to their penises before intercourse to enable them to delay ejaculation. Such creams have been incorporated into new "endurance" condoms. But what are these creams and ointments that promise delayed ejaculation? Most use benzocaine, a mild anesthetic (similar to the Novocain your dentist uses). Is it possible that men experience themselves as better lovers when they feel *less* pleasure?[45]

When it goes "right," we clearly observe the gendered qualities of sex. Another illustration of the genderedness of sex comes from research on what happens when things go wrong. For example, when men seek therapeutic evaluation for sexual problems, they rarely describe not experiencing enough pleasure. One man who experienced premature ejaculation reported that he felt like he "isn't a real man" because he "can't satisfy a woman." Another, with erectile problems, told a therapist that "a real man never has to ask his wife for anything sexually" and he "should be able to please her whenever he wants." Each of these men thus expressed a sexual problem in gender terms; each fears that his sexual problem damages his masculinity, makes him less of a real man. For them, sexuality is less about mutual pleasuring and more about hydraulic functioning. Is it any wonder that men use the language of the workplace (in addition to using metaphors from sports and war) to describe sexual experiences. We use the "tool" to "get the job done," which is, of course, to 'achieve' orgasm, or else we experience "performance anxiety." Men with sexual problems are rarely gender nonconformists, unable or unwilling to follow the rules of masculine sexual adequacy. If anything, they are overconformists to norms that define sexual adequacy by the ability to function like a well-oiled machine.[46]

It's in this gendered context that we can also understand the enormous popularity of Viagra, and other, new drugs about to come on the market that minister to men's sexual problems. Although most men who experience "erectile dysfunction" (the current term for what used to be called "impotence," a term that equates erections with power in the first place) also experience "morning erections"—which indicates that their problems are not physiological but psychological—Viagra and other drugs enable men to achieve and sustain erections. Viagra was the most successful new drug ever launched in the United States; more than 35,000 prescriptions were filled within the first two weeks on the market. Many men crowed that they had found the "magic bullet," the fountain of sexual youth. "You just keep going all night," gushed one man. "The performance is unbelievable."[47]

Certainly believable, however, was how these men experienced the demands of male sexuality in mechanical terms, and how relieved they were that the machine had been repaired. And no sooner did Viagra appear on the market than it was misunderstood. Viagra enables erections when there is adequate sexual desire—that is, when the men want to have sex and are aroused. Viagra does not work as an aphrodisiac, creating the desire in the first place. And what therapists call "inhibited sexual desire," or "low sexual interest"—once, interestingly, called frigidity in women—is now the leading sexual problem among men. Unfortunately, medical knowledge has yet to find a pharmaceutical remedy for that.[48]

CLOSING THE SEXUAL GENDER GAP

Despite the persistence of gender differences in sexual attitudes and behaviors, the sexual gender gap has been closing in recent years, as women's and men's sexual experiences come to more closely resemble one another's. Or, rather, women's has come to resemble men's. As I argued above, our experience of love has been feminized and our sexuality has been increasingly "masculinized." While men's sexual behavior has hardly changed, women's sexuality has changed dramatically, moving increasingly closer to the behavior of men. (This probably both thrills and terrifies men.)

Part of this transformation has been the result of the technological breakthroughs and ideological shifts that have come to be known as the sexual revolution. Since the 1960s, the pursuit of sexual pleasure for its own sake has been increasingly available to women, as adequate and relatively safe birth control and legal abortion have made it possible to separate fully sexual activity from reproduction. (Men, of course, always were able to pursue sexual pleasure for its own sake; thus, in this sense, women's sexuality has come to more closely resemble men's.) "I guess sex was originally to produce another body; then I guess it was for love; nowadays it's just for feeling good," was how one fifteen-year old boy summed up the shift. In addition, widespread sex education has made people more sexually aware—but not necessarily more sexually active. In one recent literature review of fifty-three studies that examined the effects of sex education and HIV education on sexual activity, twenty-seven found no changes in rates of sexual activity, twenty-two observed marked decreases, delayed onset of activity, and reduced number of sexual partners. Only three studies found any increase in sexual activity associated with sex education. It would appear that sex education enables people to make *better* sexual decisions, and encourages more responsibility, not less.[49]

Ideologically, feminism made the pursuit of sexual pleasure, the expression of women's sexual autonomy, a political goal. No longer would women believe that they were sexually disinterested, passive, and virtuous asexual angels. Women were as entitled to pleasure as men were. And, practically, they knew how to get it, once feminists exposed what one feminist called "the myth of the vaginal orgasm." Feminism was thus, in part, a political resistance to what we might call the "socialized asexuality" of feminine sexuality. "Part of my attraction to feminism involved the right to be a sexual person," recalls one woman. Another envisioned a feminism that "validates the right for a woman to say yes instead of no." In the past three decades, then, it's been women's sexuality that has been transformed, as women have sought to express their own sexual agency. Consider, for example, the transformation of the idea of sexual experience in the first place. While it used to be that men were expected to have some sexual experience prior to marriage, many women and men placed a premium of women's virginity. Not anymore. As Lillian Rubin writes, "[I]n the brief span of one generation—from the 1940s to the 1960s—we went from mothers who believed their virginity was their most prized possession to daughters for whom it was a burden." Virginity was no longer "a treasure to be safeguarded"; now, it was "a problem to be solved."[50]

Rates and motivations for masturbation have also begun to converge. What, after all, is masturbation but self-pleasuring—surely, an expression of sexual agency. The most recent large-scale national sex survey found that men's and women's motivations for masturbation were roughly similar. As are sexual attitudes. In the NORC sex survey, 36 percent of men and 53 percent of women born between 1933 and 1942 believed that premarital sex was almost always wrong. These numbers declined for both groups, but declined far more sharply for women, so that for those born between 1963 and 1974, only 16 percent of men and 22 percent of women believed that premarital sex was almost always wrong.[51]

Sexual behaviors, too, have grown increasingly similar. Among teenage boys, sexual experience has remained virtually the same since the mid-1940s, with about 70 percent of all high school–aged boys having had sexual intercourse (the rates were about 50 percent for those who went to high school in the late 1920s). But the rates for high school girls have changed dramatically, up from 5 percent in the 1920s to 20 percent in the late 1940s, to 55 percent in 1982 and 60 percent in 1991. And the age of first intercourse has steadily declined for both boys and girls. Similarly, although the rates of teenage virgins have declined for both girls and boys, they have declined more rapidly for girls. The number of teenagers who have had more than five different sexual partners by their eighteenth birthday has increased for both sexes; the rate of increase is also greater for girls as well.[52]

Just as adolescents' sexual experiences are becoming more similar, more "masculinized," a backlash political campaign has also been underway to stop teenage sex in its tracks. Abstinence campaigns encourage young people to "just say no" to sex, to refrain from sexual intercourse until marriage. Begun in the early 1990s in Southern Baptist churches, and fueled also in part by growing concern about sexually transmitted diseases, especially HIV, teenagers are now encouraged to take a "virginity pledge" and forswear sexual intercourse until marriage. Abstinence has such political currency that it has now been celebrated as a dramatic success; a recent cover story in *Newsweek* magazine portrayed two white teenagers, happily hugging under the headline "The New Virginity: Why More Teens Are Choosing Not to Have Sex." Inside, the magazine offered data that the total percentage of high school students who say they've had sex had dropped from more than 50 percent in 1991 to slightly more than 45 percent in 2001. Teen birth rates had likewise dropped from 6 percent to about 5 percent of all births.[53] Proponents point to the success of abstinence-based sex education and elaborate publicity campaigns in accounting for a 10 percent drop in teen sexual activity.

It does appear to have *some* effect, but is hardly a counterweight to the other messages teenagers are getting. Sociologist Peter Bearman analyzed data from more than ninety thousand students, and found that taking a virginity pledge does lead an average teenager to delay his or her first act of intercourse—by about eighteen months. And the pledges were only effective for students up to age seventeen. By the time they are twenty years old, over 90 percent of both boys and girls are sexually active. And the pledges were not effective at all if a significant proportion of students at the school were taking them. (That is, taking the pledge seems to be a way of creating a "deviant" subculture, what Bearman called an "identity movement"—add "virgins" to the Goths, Deadheads, jocks, nerds, preppies, and the rappers.) And, what's worse, when the pledgers finally did have sex, they were *far less likely* to use contraception.[54]

It also appears that only boys' rates are declining, not girls' rates. Why would this be so? Partly, sociologists Barbara Risman and Pepper Schwartz argue, is because girls are now presumed to be sexually active inside a romantic relationship, and so boys are more likely to begin their sexual lives with a girlfriend. (In the past, boys were more likely to begin their sexual careers furtively, with someone outside their social circle, a "bad girl.") The decline in boys' rates, then, "reflects girls' increasing negotiation power to restrict sex to relationships"; teen pregnancies are further testament to the increasing power of girls within romantic relationships, as they are far more likely to insist on safer sex practices. If that's the case, feminism—the empowerment of women and girls—may actually have had a dampening effect on boys' sexual behaviors, by empowering girls to insist on safer sex and relationship intimacy, while right-wing efforts to encourage students to "just say no" will actually increase teen pregnancy as fewer teenagers use contraception.[55]

For adults, rates of premarital sex and the number of sex partners also seem to be moving closer. In another survey, 99 percent of male college graduates and 90 percent of female college graduates said that they had had sex before marriage. Researchers in one survey of sexual behavior from the 1970s found far greater sexual activity and greater variety among married women in the 1970s than Kinsey had found in the late 1940s. Ninety per cent of all married women claimed to be happy with their sex lives; three-quarters were content with its frequency, while 25 percent wanted more. A study in the 1980s echoed this trend. Women and men displayed similar sexual desires—both wanted frequent sex, were happiest when initiating and refusing sex in equal amounts, and became discontent when sex was infrequent.[56]

What turns us on sexually is also similar. In the 1970s, psychologist Julia Heiman developed a way to measure women's sexual arousal. Samples of college women listened to two sorts of tapes—romantic and explicitly sexual—while wearing a tampon-like device that measured blood flow to the vagina. Like men, women were far more sexually aroused by explicit sex-talk than they were by romance. And interest in sexual variety also appears to be converging. Experiences of oral sex have increased dramatically for both women and for men. And, if one twenty-year-old college woman is to be believed, the meanings attached to oral sex seem to be shifting as well. "I was about 16 and I had this friend—not a boyfriend, a boy *friend*—and I didn't know what to give him for his birthday, so I gave him a blow job. I wanted to know what it was like; it was just for kicks," is what she told an interviewer, "without a trace of embarrassment or self-consciousness."[57]

It would appear that women are having more sex and enjoying it more than ever in our history. And so women are far less likely, now, to fake orgasm. When Lillian Rubin interviewed white working-class women in the mid-1970s for her study *Worlds of Pain,* she found that over 70 percent of the women said they faked orgasm at least some of the time. Now, she finds that the same percentage says that they never fake it.[58]

The evidence of gender conversion does not mean that there are no differences between women and men in their sexual expression. It still means different things to be sexual, but the rules are not enforced with the ferocity and consistency that they were in the past. "It's different from what it used to be when women were supposed to hold out until they got married. There's pressure now on both men and women to lose their virginity," is how one twenty-nine-year-old man put it. "But for a man it's a sign of manhood, and for a woman there's still some loss of value." Moreover, though both men and women feel entitled to pleasure, and both have their first sexual experience because they wanted to, men still seem to believe that that entitlement also covers acting on it—even when the woman doesn't want to. "I paid for a wonderful evening," commented one college man, "and I was entitled to sex for my effort." As a result of attitudes like these, cases of date and acquaintance rape continue to skyrocket on our campuses.[59]

About 15 percent of college women report having been sexually assaulted; more than half of these assaults were by a person that the woman was dating. Some studies have estimated the rates to be significantly higher, nearly double (27 percent) that of the study undertaken by Mary Koss and her colleagues.[60] And, while some pundits have expressed outrage that feminists have transformed college-age women into "victims," it is more accurate to express outrage that predatory males have turned college women into victims of sexual assault. Any number of rapes is unacceptable. But that significant numbers of college women are forced to change their behaviors because of the behaviors of these men—where they study, how late they stay in the library, which parties they go to, whom they date—is the outrage.

Among adults, women and men report quite different rates of forced sex. While 96.1 percent of men and 77.2 percent of women say they have never been forced to have sex against their will, those who have been forced display dramatic differences. Just slightly more than 1 percent of men (1.3 percent), but over one-fifth of all women (21.6 percent) were forced to have sex by the opposite sex, only about 2 percent of men (1.9 percent) and just .3 percent of women were forced by someone of the same sex. Men continue to be the principal sexual predators. Several studies estimate the likelihood that a woman will be the victim of a completed rape to be about one in five. The figure for an attempted rape is nearly double that.[61]

Women's increase in sexual agency, revolutionary as it is, has not been accompanied by a decrease in male sexual entitlement, nor by a sharp increase in men's capacity for intimacy and emotional connectedness. Thus, just as some feminist women have celebrated women's claim to sexual autonomy, others—therapists and activists—have deplored men's adherence to a "non-relational" model of sexual behavior. As with friendship and with love, it's men who have the problem, and psychologists such as Ronald Levant seek to replace "irresponsible, detached, compulsive, and alienated sexuality with a type of sexuality that is ethically responsible, compassionate for the well-being of participants, and sexually empowering of men."[62]

The notion of non-relational sex means that sex is, to men, central to their lives; isolated from other aspects of life and relationships; often coupled with aggression; conceptualized socially within a framework of success and achievement; and pursued despite possible negative emotional and moral consequences. Sexual inexperience is viewed as stigmatizing. Examples of male non-relational sexuality abound, report the critics. Men think about sex more often than women; have more explicit sexual fantasies; masturbate more often than women; buy more porn; have more sex partners; and have more varied sexual experiences than women.[63]

In a recent edited volume on this problem, psychologist Gary Brooks pathologizes male sexual problems as a "centerfold syndrome." Symptoms include: voyeurism, objectification, sex as a validation of masculinity, trophyism, and fear of intimacy. Ron Levant contributes a medical neologism, *alexithymia,* to describe the socially conditioned "inability to feel or express feelings." This problem must be serious; after all, it has a Greek name. Some authors also note the danger to women by men who have this type of "masculine" sex, who "deny the humanity of their partners, and . . . objectify and even violate the partner who is actually treated more as a prop." Others warn of "the damage ultimately done to men when they are socialized in a way that limits their ability to experience intimacy."[64]

Not all the studies of male non-relationality are so critical. Psychologists Glenn Good and Drury Sherrod argue that for many men nonrelational sex is a stage of development, not necessarily a way of being:

> Men progress through the NS [nonrelational sexuality] stage by mastering the developmental tasks associated with this stage . . . [which] includes gaining experience as a sexual being, gaining experience with interpersonal aspects of sexuality, developing identity, and developing comfort with intimacy. Men following this route develop internally directed senses of their behavior that allow them to form and sustain intimate, caring relationships with others.

In fact, Good and Sherrod argue, experience with nonrelational sexuality may be a positive experience, allowing adolescents "to reduce sexual tensions," and "gain sexual experiences, refine skills associated with sexual activities, and experience different partners and behaviors, thereby reducing curiosity about different partners in the future."[65]

The idea of non-relational sex as a "problem" for men is relatively recent, and is part of a general cultural discomfort with the excesses of the sexual revolution. In the

1970s, as Martin Levine and Richard Troiden point out, the significant sexual problems came from too little sexual experience—anorgasmia (the inability to achieve orgasm), especially for women, ejaculatory and erectile problems for men. Now the problem is sex "addiction," a relatively new term that makes having a lot of sex a problem, and "nonrelational sex," which makes pursuing sexual pleasure for its own sake also a problem. While it may be true that non-relational sexuality may be a problem for some men, especially for those for whom it is the only form of sexual expression, it is not necessarily the only way men express themselves sexually. Many men are capable of both relational and non-relational sexuality. Some men don't ever practice non-relational sexuality because they live in a subculture in which it is not normative; other men develop values that oppose it.[66] One possibly worthy goal might be to enlarge our sexual repertoires to enable both women and men to experience a wide variety of permutations and combinations of love and lust, without entirely reducing one to the other—as long as all these experiences are mutually negotiated, safe, and equal.

HOMOSEXUALITY AS GENDER CONFORMITY

Thus far, I've been describing the ways in which men and women are socialized toward "his" and "her" sexualities. I've deliberately avoided the obvious disclaimer that I was speaking about heterosexuality and not homosexuality, because this gendering of sexuality is as applicable to homosexuals as it is to heterosexuals. In fact, it may even be *more* obvious among gay men and lesbians, because in homosexual encounters there are two gendered men or two gendered women. That is, you have masculinity or femininity multiplied by two! Gender differences may even be exaggerated by sexual orientation.

This is, of course, contrary to our commonsense understandings of homosexuality, as well as those biological studies that suggest that gay men have some biological affinity with women, as opposed to heterosexual men. Indeed, our commonsense assumption is that gay men and lesbians are gender *non*conformists—lesbians are "masculine" women; gay men are "feminine" men. But such commonsense thinking has one deep logical flaw—it assumes that the gender of your partner is more important, and more decisive in your life, than your own gender. But our own gender—the collections of behaviors, attitudes, attributes, and assumptions about what it means to be a man or a woman—is far more important than the gender of the people with whom we interact, sexually or otherwise. Sexual behavior, gay or straight, confirms gender identity.

That doesn't mean that these commonsense assumptions haven't completely saturated popular discussions of homosexuality, especially in those advice books designed to help parents make sure that their children did not turn out "wrong." For example Peter and Barbara Wyden's book *Growing Up Straight: What Every Thoughtful Parent Should Know About Homosexuality,* argued that "pre-homosexual" boys were identifiable by their lack of early childhood masculinity, which could be thwarted by an overly "masculine" mother, that is, one who had a job outside the home and paid attention to feminist ideas![67]

A few empirical studies have also made such claims. For example, psychiatrist Richard Green tracked a small group of boys (about fifty-five) from preschool to young adulthood. All the boys were chosen for patterns of frequent cross-dressing at home.

They liked to play with girls at school, enjoyed playing with dolls, and followed their mothers around the house doing housework. Their parents were supportive of this behavior. These "sissy boys," as Green called them, were four times more likely to have homosexual experiences as nonfeminine boys. But this research has also been widely criticized: such gender nonconformity is extremely rare (there was great difficulty in finding even fifty-five boys), and thus cannot be the source of the great majority of homosexual behavior. Extreme patterns of nonconformity are not equivalent to milder measures, such as not liking sports, preferring music or reading, and indifference to rough-and-tumble play. The homosexual experience may be a result of the social reactions to their conduct (persecution by other boys, or the therapy to which they were often exposed), which thwarted their ability to establish conventional heterosocial patterns of behavior. It may have been the ostracism itself, and not the offending behavior, that led to the sexual experiences. When milder forms of gender nonconformity are examined, most boys who report such behavior turn out to be heterosexual. Finally, when studies by Green and his colleagues were extended to "tomboys" it was found that there was no difference in eventual sexual preference between girls who reported tomboy behavior and those who did not. (What Green and his colleagues seem to have found is that being a sissy is a far more serious offense to the gender order than being a tomboy.)[68]

The evidence points overwhelmingly the other way: that homosexuality is deeply gendered, and that gay men and lesbians are true gender conformists. To accept such a proposition leads to some unlikely alliances, with gay-affirmative writers and feminists lining up on the same side as an ultra-conservative writer such as George Gilder, who, in his unwavering critique of masculinity—both gay and straight—writes that lesbianism "has nothing whatever to do with male homosexuality. Just as male homosexuals, with their compulsive lust and promiscuous impulses, offer a kind of caricature of typical male sexuality, lesbians closely resemble other women in their desire for intimate and monogamous coupling."[69]

Since the birth of the gay liberation movement in the Stonewall riots of 1969—when gay men fought back against the police who were raiding a New York City gay bar—gay men have been particularly eager to demonstrate that they are not "failed" men, as earlier popular images portrayed them. In fact, many gay men became extremely successful as "real" men, enacting a hypermasculine code of anonymous sex, masculine clothing, and physical appearance including bodybuilding. The "clone" as he was called, comprising about 35 percent of all gay men, was perhaps even more successful at masculinity than were straight men. By the early 1980s, this notion had produced some curious inversions of traditional stereotypes. In one popular song from 1983, Joe Jackson commented on this:

See the nice boys, dancing in pairs
Golden earring, golden tan, blow wave in their hair
Sure they're all straight, straight as a line
All the gays are macho, can't you see their leather shine?[70]

By contrast, the sexual lives of lesbians were quite different. For many lesbians, gay liberation did not mean sexual liberation. In the lesbian community, there was more discussion of "the tyranny of the relationship" than of various sexual practices; lesbian couples in therapy complained of "lesbian bed death," the virtual cessation of sexual activity for the couple after a few years. One woman told an interviewer:

> As women we have not been socialized to be initiators in the sexual act. Another factor is that we don't have to make excuses if we don't want to do it. We don't say we have a headache. We just say no. We also do a lot more cuddling and touching than heterosexuals, and we get fulfilled by that rather than just the act of intercourse. . . . Another thing is that such a sisterly bond develops that the relationship almost seems incestuous after a while. The intimacy is so great. We know each other so well.[71]

While some lesbians did embrace a sexual liberationist ethic and sought arenas for sexual variety, most remained gender conformists.

This was underscored by the fact that feminism also played a large role in the social organization of lesbian life. During the early waves of the women's movement, lesbianism was seen as a political alternative, a decision not to give aid and comfort to the enemy (men). How could a woman be truly feminist, they asked, if she shared her life and bed with a man? The "political lesbian" represented a particular fusion of sexual and gender politics, an active choice that matched one's political commitment. "For a woman to be a lesbian in a male-supremacist, capitalist, misogynist, racist, homophobic, imperialist culture," wrote one woman, "is an act of resistance." While of course not all lesbians are feminists, even this construct of political lesbianism is a form of gender conformity. If one resists gender inequality, political lesbians argue, then one must opt out of sexual relationships with men, and choose to be sexual only with women *because they are women.* Gender remains the organizing principle of sexuality—even a sexuality that is understood as a form of resistance to gender politics.[72]

The weight of evidence from research on homosexuality bears out this argument that gay men and lesbians are gender conformists. Take, for example, the number of sexual partners. In one study, sex researchers found that most lesbians reported having had fewer than ten sexual partners, and almost half said they had never had a one-night stand. A 1982 survey of unmarried women between the ages of twenty and twenty-nine found an average of 4.5 sexual partners over the course of their lives. But the average gay male in the same study had had hundreds of partners, many one-night stands, and more than a quarter of them reported a thousand or more partners. Masters and Johnson found that 84 percent of males and 7 percent of females had had between fifty and one thousand or more sexual partners in their lifetimes; and that 97 percent of men and 33 percent of women had had seven or more relationships that had lasted four months or less. While 11 percent of husbands and 9 percent of wives in another study described themselves as promiscuous, 79 percent of gay men and 19 percent of lesbians made such a claim. (Among heterosexual cohabitors, though, 25 percent of the men and 22 percent of the women described themselves as promiscuous.) Gay men have the lowest rates of long-term committed relationships, while lesbians have the highest, and lesbians place much greater emphasis on emotional relationships than gay men. Thus, it appears that men—gay and straight—place sexuality at the center of their lives, and that women—straight or lesbian—are more interested in affection and caring in the context of a love relationship.[73]

Research on frequency of sexual activity bears this out. In one study, among heterosexual married couples, 45 percent reported having sex three or more times per week during the first two years of their marriage, and 27 percent of those married between two and ten years reported such rates. By contrast, 67 percent of gay men together up to two years, and 32 percent of those together two to ten years had sex three or more times per week. One-third of lesbians had sex three or more times per week in the first two years of their relationship; but only 7 percent did after two years. After ten years, the percentages reporting sex more than three times per week were 18 percent for married couples, 11 percent for gay men, and 1 percent for lesbians. Nearly half the lesbians (47 percent) reported having sex less than once a month after ten years together. One interviewer described a lesbian couple:

> She and her roommate were obviously very much in love. Like most people who have a good, stable, five year relationship, they seemed comfortable together, sort of part of one another, able to joke, obviously fulfilled in their relationship. They work together, have the same times off from work, do most of their leisure activities together. They sent me off with a plate of cookies, a good symbolic gesture of the kind of welcome and warmth I felt in their home.[74]

If heterosexuality and homosexuality are so similar, in that men and women express and confirm their gendered identities through sexual behavior, what then are the big differences between heterosexuals and homosexuals—aside, of course, from the gender of the partner? One difference is that gay relationships are more egalitarian. (See table 10.1.) When we ask, for example, who intiates sex, gay men and lesbians report identical rates, which are far more egalitarian than the rates for married or cohabiting couples. Because homosexuals' identities are defined by their sexuality, and because their sexuality is not procreative, gay men and lesbians have also been more sexually experimental, especially with non-penetrative sex. As one sex therapist writes, "gay men have more ways of sexually relating than do heterosexual men." And Masters and Johnson found that gay couples have longer lovemaking sessions than heterosexual couples.[75]

One other way that heterosexuality and homosexuality are similar, actually, is in the impact of homophobia on sexual behavior. Obviously, for gay people homophobia saturates all their interactions. The systematic devaluation of homosexuality, the stigma

Table 10.1. Who Initiates Sex

	Self	Equal	Partner
Husbands	51	33	16
Male Cohabitor	39	42	19
Gay Men	31	37	32
Lesbians	31	37	32
Female Cohabitor	15	46	39
Wives	12	40	48

Source: Adopted from Blumstein and Schwartz, *American Couples: Money-Work-Sex* (William Morrow, 1983).

attached to being homosexual, becomes a crucial element in one's identity. As sociologist Ken Plummer writes,

> [T]he perceived hostility of the societal reactions that surround . . . homosexuality . . . renders the business of becoming a homosexual a process that is characterized by problems of access, problems of guilt, and problems of identity. It leads to the emergence of a subculture of homosexuality. It leads to a series of interaction problems involved with concealing the discreditable stigma. And it inhibits the development of stable relationships among homosexuals to a considerable degree.[76]

To understand more fully the experience of stigma, try this little thought experiment, which was developed by two social psychologists: Imagine for a moment that you are an anxious person and that being anxious is against the law. You must try to hide your fears from others. Your own home may be a safe place to feel anxious, but a public display of apprehension can lead to arrest or, at least, to social ostracism. At work one day, an associate looks at you and says, "That's funny, for a crazy moment there I thought you were anxious." "Heck, no," you exclaim a bit too loudly, "*not me!*" You begin to wonder if your fellow worker will report his suspicions to your boss. If he does, your boss may inform the police, or will at least change your job to one that requires less contact with customer, especially with those who have children.[77]

Whereas it is clear that homophobia constructs gay experience, we are less aware of the power of homophobia to structure the experiences and identities of heterosexuals. While there is evidence that social attitudes toward homosexuality have been increasingly accepting in recent decades, homophobia is more than "acceptance," or the fear or hatred of homosexuals; it is also, for men, the fear of being perceived as unmanly, effeminate, or, worst of all, gay. These fears seem less keen among heterosexual women, though many worry about the dangers of homosexuals (nearly always men) to their children.[78]

Male heterosexuals often spend a significant amount of time and energy in masculine display so that no one could possibly get the "wrong" impression about them. In one study, many heterosexual men said they had sex in order to prove they weren't gay. Since our popular misperceptions about homosexuality usually center on gender inversion, compensatory behaviors by heterosexuals often involve exaggerated versions of gender stereotypic behaviors. In this way, homophobia reinforces the gender of sex, keeping men acting hypermasculine and women acting ultra-feminine. "Heterosexuality as currently construed and enacted (the erotic preference for the other gender) requires homophobia," write sex researchers John Gagnon and Stuart Michaels.[79]

What Else Affects Sexuality?

While gender remains one of the organizing principles of sexuality, other aspects of our lives also profoundly influence our sexual behaviors and expectations. For one thing, sexual behavior, as we've seen, varies widely among different cultures. Margaret Mead found that in some cultures, the idea of spontaneous sex is not encouraged for either women or for men. Among the Arapesh, she writes, the exceptions are believed to occur in women. "Parents warn their sons even more than they warn their daughters against permitting themselves to get into situations in which someone can make love to them." Another anthropologist reported that in one southwest Pacific society, sexual intercourse is seen as highly pleasurable and deprivation harmful to both sexes. And Bronislaw Malinowski saw significant convergence between women and men in the Trobriand Islands, where women initiate sex as often as men, and where couples avoid the "missionary" position because the woman's movements are hampered by the weight of the man so that she cannot be fully active.

In the contemporary United States, several variables other than gender affect sexuality, such as class, age, education, marital status, religion, race, and ethnicity. Take class, for example. Kinsey found that, contrary to the American ideology that holds that working-class people are more sensual because they are closer to their "animal natures," lower class position did not mean hotter sex. In fact, he found that upper- and middle-class people were more sophisticated in the "arts of love," demonstrating wider variety of activities and greater emphasis on foreplay, while lower-class people dispensed with preliminaries, and did not even kiss very much.

There is evidence that race and ethnicity also produce some variations in sexual behavior. For example, blacks seem to hold somewhat more sexually liberal attitudes than whites, and have slightly more sex partners, but they also masturbate less frequently, have less oral sex, and are slightly more likely to have same-sex contacts. Hispanics are also more sexually liberal than whites, and masturbate more frequently than blacks or whites; but they also have less oral sex than whites (yet more than blacks), and have fewer sex partners, either of the same or opposite sex, than whites or blacks.[80]

Age also affects sexuality. What turns us on at fifty will probably not be what turned us on at fifteen. Not only are there significant physiological changes that augur a decline in sexual energy and interest, but age is also related to marital status and family obligations. As Lillian Rubin writes,

On the most mundane level, the constant negotiation about everyday tasks leaves people harassed, weary, irritated, and feeling more like traffic cops than lovers. Who's going to do the shopping, pay the bills, take care of the laundry, wash the dishes, take out the garbage, clean the bathroom, get the washing machine fixed, decide what to eat for dinner, return the phone calls from friends and parents? When there are children, the demands, complications and exhaustion increase exponentially.[81]

Ah, children. By far one of the greatest "anaphrodisiacs"—sexual turn-offs—in our society is having children. Couples—gay and straight—with children report far less sexual activity than couples without children. There's less time, less freedom, less privacy—and less interest.

You've probably heard reports that women hit their sexual peak in the late thirties and early forties, while men peak before they turn twenty, after which they are increasingly likely to appreciate softer, more sensual activities. And you've probably heard that such differences reveal biological differences in male and female sexual anatomy. But that ignores the ways in which women's and men's sexualities are related to each other. That "his" sexuality shifts toward the more sensual just as "her" sexuality takes a sharp turn toward the explicitly sexual indicates more than a simple divergence in biological patterns, especially since it is not the case in other cultures when men and women biologically age "differently." What these reports suggest is that marriage has a pronounced effect on sexual expression, domesticating sex, bringing it into the domain historically reserved to women: the home. When men feel that sex is no longer dangerous and risky (which is, to them, exciting), their sexual repertoire may soften to include a wider range of sensual pleasures. When women feel that sex is no longer dangerous and risky (which they interpret as threatening), they feel safe enough to explore more explicitly sexual pleasures. Such an interpretation suggests, of course, that the differences we observe between women and men may have more to do with the social organization of marriage than with any inherent differences between males and females.

Yet despite this, the longer-range historical trend over the past several centuries has been to sexualize marriage, to link the emotions of love and nurturing to erotic pleasure within the reproductive relationship. Thus, sexual compatability and expression have become increasingly important in our married lives, as the increased amount of time before marriage (prolonged adolescence), the availability of birth control and divorce, and an ethic of individual self-fulfillment have combined to increase the importance of sexual expression throughout the course of our lives.

HEALTH, SEX, AND HIV

With the onset of the HIV epidemic, major changes occurred in the sexual patterns of gay men, including fewer partners, less anonymous sex, and increases in the practice of safer sex and the number of gay male couples. The emphasis on "safer sex" was seen by many as an effort to "feminize" sexuality, to return it to the context of emotional and monogamous relationships, thus abandoning the earlier gay liberationist ethic of sexual freedom. To men, the very phrase *safe sex* was experienced as an oxymoron—what's sexy—heat, passion, excitement, spontaneity—was the exact opposite of what's safe—soft, warm, cuddly. Many men feared that practicing safe sex would mean no longer having sex like men, and that programs encouraging such gender nonconformity would be doomed to failure. (This is not simply an issue for gay men, of course. Heterosexual women have been trying to get heterosexual men to practice a form of safe sex for decades, finding that their own sexual expressivity is less encumbered when both partners take responsibility for birth control. Fear of pregnancy and fear of HIV transmission both require that one fuse sexual pleasure with sexual responsibility.)[82]

Critics needn't have worried. Much of the work to minimize the risk for HIV among gay men has been to reaffirm masculine sexuality, to develop ways that men could still have "manly" sex while they also practiced safe sex. Gay organizations promoted safe sex clubs, pornographic videos, and techniques. As a result, gay men did begin to practice safe sex, without disconfirming their masculinity, though there is some evidence of recent backsliding by younger gay men, especially since HIV treatments now seem to augur longer and healthier lives for HIV-positive people than previously.

Of course, the epicenter of the HIV epidemic has shifted dramatically since the disease was first diagnosed in 1984. Globally, more than 21 million men, women, and children have died from AIDS, and another 42 million are living with it—that's one out of every 162 people on earth. The global epicenter of AIDS has shifted dramatically since it was first diagnosed in the United States. Seven out of every ten people infected live in Sub-Saharan Africa; adding South and South East Asia and Latin America brings the total up to 88 percent.[83] (See figure 10.2.)

It is noteworthy that rates of infection are roughly equally distributed between women and men throughout the underdeveloped world, where women's significantly lower status often renders them powerless to resist sexual advances, to insist on safer sex practices, or to have much access to health care. In Sub-Saharan Africa, nearly three-fifths of all HIV-positive cases are women. Among African adolescents, girls outnumber boys among the infected by about five to one. Empowering women, affording women equal rights, will prove the major mechanism to reduce HIV. Dr. Pascoal Mocumbi, prime minister of Mozambique, challenged Africans to "break the silence regarding the sexual behaviour and gender inequalities that drive the epidemic."[84]

Such gender symmetry is true around the world—except in the United States and Western Europe and Australia and New Zealand. In North America and Western Europe, the percentage of HIV-positive women is less than 25 percent; in Australia and New Zealand (where women's status is highest in the industrial world), only 7 percent.[85] In these places, AIDS remains a highly "gendered" disease. Although women and men are both able to contract the virus that causes AIDS—and, in fact, women are actually more likely to contract the disease from unprotected heterosexual intercourse than are men—and despite the fact that rates of new infection among women are increasing faster than among men, the overwhelming majority of all AIDS patients in the United States are men. (And rates of new infections are far higher among young black men than white men, an indication that class and race are also keys that drive the epidemic.)[86]

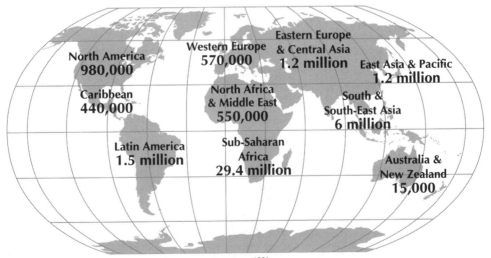

Total: **42 million**

Figure 10.2. Adults and children estimated to be living with HIV/AIDS as of end 2002. World Health Organization, 2002: http://www.who.int/hiv/facts/plwha_m.jpg

Seen in this way, AIDS is the most highly gendered disease in American history—a disease that both women and men could get, but one that overwhelmingly disproportionately affects one gender and not the other. It would be useful to understand masculinity—risk taking, avoidance of responsibility, pursuit of sex above all other ends—as a risk factor in the spread of the disease, in the same way as we understand it to be a risk factor in drunk driving accidents.[87]

GENDERED HEALTH

Understanding gender to be a major risk factor in explaining drunk driving reminds us that health and illness are also deeply gendered. Historically, it was men who took all the health-related risks, both in terms of behaviors, such as drinking and drugs, and by considering it unmasculine to seek health care treatment. Ignoring health issues, "playing through pain," was, in fact a symbol of masculinity. And it was women who took far fewer risks, took better care of their health, and took vitamins, exercised, and saw doctors more regularly. An old adage among those who study gender and health is that "women get sicker, but men die quicker."[88]

Researchers have long understood gender to be a primary factor in health-related behavior. As men's health researcher and advocate Will H. Courtenay puts it:

> A man who does gender correctly would be relatively unconcerned about his health and well-being in general. He would see himself as stronger, both physically and emotionally, than most women. He would think of himself as independent, not needing to be nurtured by others. He would be unlikely to ask others for help. He would spend much time out in the world and away from home. . . . He would face danger fearlessly, take risks frequently, and have little concern for his own safety.[89]

Race, class, and ethnicity complicate the picture. Middle-aged black men, for example, have much lower longevity (up to seven years less) and much higher rates of stress and lifestyle-related diseases (heart attack, stroke, diabetes) than their white counterparts. A report by the Kellogg Foundation concluded, "[F]rom birth, a black male on average seems fated to a life so unhealthy that a white man can only imagine it." While some part of this is attributable to age—young black males have astronomically higher health risks than whites—and to class—working-class men of all races also have lower longevity and higher morbidity than middle-class men—this holds true even for middle-aged black men at every level of the class hierarchy. While men, "overall, have a particular set of pressures to show strength and not reveal weakness," writes columnist Ellis Cose, "this feeling is intensified in black men." There is, he continued, "an ethic of toughness among black men, built up to protect yourself against racial slights and from the likelihood that society is going to challenge you or humiliate you in some way. This makes it hard to admit that you are in pain or need help."[90]

Yet even in health, there are signs of gender convergence. First, more women are disregarding traditional strictures of femininity and taking increased risks—in their sexual behaviors, and also in risk taking. Take drinking, for example. Of course, far more men drink to excess than women do, and it is heaviest among young white male students attending four-year institutions, and often revolves around fraternities and sports events. But an increasing number of women are binge drinking as well, especially in sororities, where 80 percent of women are binge drinkers, compared with 30 percent outside sororities. "To be able to drink like a guy is kind of a badge of honor," commented one senior at Syracuse University. "For me, it's a feminism thing." While few feminists would actually suggest that binge drinking is an index of women's liberation, many young women have come to feel that drinking, fighting, smoking, and other typically "masculine" behaviors are a sign of power—and therefore cool. "I don't think women gain any power in outdrinking a man," commented another Syracuse senior, "because it will always be a standard set by the man. In drinking and everywhere else, women need to start setting their own standards." As journalist Barbara Ehrenreich put it, "Gender equality wouldn't be worth fighting for if all it meant was the opportunity to be as stupid and self-destructive as men can be."[91]

And there are signs that more men are seeking health professionals, taking better care of their health—a domain that had been traditionally reserved to women. Efforts to develop men's health awareness has been especially successful in the underdeveloped world, where campaigns for reproductive health and family planning for women have branched out and begun to include men in health planning. In such campaigns, it is clear that the health interests of women and men are hardly the conflicting interests of Martians and Venutians. There is no zero-sum game; rather, our interests are complementary. Both women's and men's health needs confront dominant ideas about gender that inhibit men's health-seeking behavior and often prohibit women's. Gender inequality is bad for both women's and men's health.[92]

Of course, predictably, just as there are increasing signs of gender convergence, there is a small backlash chorus that argues that the dramatic gains in women's health have come at the expense of men. After all, they argue, the gender gap in life span has been slowly growing over the past century; though women outlived men by about one year in 1920, they now outlive men by almost six years. And men have a higher death rate for every one of the leading causes of death. And yet, they claim, men are vastly underserved in the national health research budgets. Just as predictably, though, these men rarely argue for *increased* funding for health care across the board. Rather, they see health care as a zero-sum game, and urge decreases for women and increases for men. And many of the "top ten" causes of death are related to lifestyle—such as heart disease, injuries, diabetes, HIV, suicide, and homicide. The "enemy" to these misguided minions is not feminist-inspired efforts to promote health awareness for women but an ideology of masculinity that encourages us to "live fast and die young," and an indifferent federal government that makes the United States the only industrial nation without a national program of funded health care.[93]

The women's health movement has made it abundantly clear that health is not a zero-sum game, in which one gender benefits at the expense of the other. Rather, efforts to promote women's health also invariably benefit men—from the decline in mortality of the women in our lives to the decline in mortality of fetuses and babies from poor prenatal treatment or illegal back-alley abortions; to women's decreased dependence on men. And efforts to promote men's health also benefit women, both directly in the quality and longevity of the lives of the men they care about, and also indirectly, since decreasing risk taking, drug and alcohol use, will also reduce the amount of violence that women endure from men.

Gender differences persist in our sexual expression and our sexual experiences, in our health experiences and our health seeking, but they are far less significant than they used to be, and the signs point to continued convergence. It may come as a relief to realize that our lovers are not from other planets, but are capable of the same joys and pleasures that we are.

Yet one health issue remains—perhaps our nation's number one public health issue: violence. And it is here that the gender gap is as wide as it is deep. In fact, it is the only area in which the gender gap is increasing, where there are truly significant differences between women and men.

CHAPTER 11

THE GENDER
OF VIOLENCE

To be or not to be: that is the question:
Whether 'tis nobler in the mind to suffer
The slings and arrows of outrageous fortune,
Or to take arms against a sea of troubles,
And by opposing end them?

—WILLIAM SHAKESPEARE
HAMLET

I am not insane. I am angry. I killed because people like me are
mistreated every day. I did this to show society, "Push us and we
will push back."

—LUKE WOODHAM, 1997

Two sentiments, a question and an answer, separated by four centuries. Does one suffer or does one seek revenge? Get mad or get even? Each has an unacceptably high price: Luke Woodham resolved it by stabbing his mother to death and then killing two students in his Pearl, Mississippi, high school in October 1997. Two months later, three students were killed in Paducah, Kentucky. And four students and a teacher were killed in Jonesboro, Arkansas, in March 1998. And in Littleton, Colorado, on April 20, 1999, twelve students and one teacher were gunned down by two students, who then took their own lives. Both Woodham and the two boys who opened fire in Jonesboro were said to be distraught after being snubbed by girls. Suffer a loss? Or, make someone pay?

As a nation, we are preoccupied by violence. We fret about "teen violence," complain about "inner city crime," or fear "urban gangs." We express shock at the violence in our nation's public schools, where metal detectors crowd the doorways, and knives and guns crowd out pencils and erasers in students' backpacks. Those public school shootings left us speechless and sick at heart. Yet when we think about these wrenching events, do we ever consider that, whether white or black, inner city or suburban, these bands of marauding "youths," or these troubled teenagers, are virtually all young men.

Nightly, we watch news reports of suicide bombings in the Middle East, or terrorist attacks on the United States, or our (and our allies') outposts abroad, or of racist attacks against Turks in Germany or Pakistanis in London, or of homophobic gay-bashing murders, or of Colombian drug lords and their legions of gun-toting thugs, or the well-armed right-wing militias. Do these reports ever mention that virtually every single one of these terrorists, suicide bombers, or racist gangs is male? Do they investigate how ideologies of masculinity may have contributed to the motivation for such heinous crimes?

Seldom do the news reports note that virtually all the violence in the world today is committed by men. Imagine, though, if the violence were perpetrated entirely by women. Would that not be *the* story, the only issue to be explained? Would not a gender analysis occupy the center of every single story? The fact that these are men seems so natural as to raise no questions, generate no analysis.

Take a couple of recent examples. In 1993, *Youth and Violence,* the American Psychological Associations Commission on Violence and Youth report, attributed rising rates of violence to access to guns, involvement in gangs, mass media violence, physical punishment, parental neglect, substance abuse, poverty, prejudice, and absence of antiviolence programs. The next year, the Carnegie Corporation devoted an entire issue of its quarterly journal to "Saving Youth from Violence" and came up with a list of factors that contribute to youth violence, among them: frustration, lack of social skills, being labeled as "dumb," poverty, abuse, neglect, drugs, alcohol, violent video games, and the availability of guns. In neither of these blue-ribbon panels' reports was the word *masculinity* ever mentioned.[1]

You would think the numbers alone would tell the story: Men constitute 99 percent of all persons arrested for rape; 88 percent of those arrested for murder; 92 percent of those arrested for robbery; 87 percent for aggravated assault; 85 percent of other assaults; 83 percent of all family violence; 82 percent of disorderly conduct. Men are overwhelmingly more violent than women. Nearly 90 percent of all murder victims are killed by men, according to the United States Department of Justice's Uniform Crime Reports.[2]

From early childhood to old age, violence is the most obdurate, intractable behavioral gender difference. The National Academy of Sciences puts the case starkly: "The most consistent pattern with respect to gender is the extent to which male criminal participation in serious crimes at any age greatly exceeds that of females, regardless of source of data, crime type, level of involvement, or measure of participation." "Men are always and everywhere more likely than women to commit criminal acts," write criminologists Michael Gottfredson and Travis Hirschi.[3] Yet how do we understand this obvious association between masculinity and violence? Is it a product of biology, a fact of nature, caused by something inherent in male anatomy? Is it universal? In the United States, what has been the historical association between gender and violence? Has that association become stronger or weaker over time? What can we, as a culture, do to prevent or at least ameliorate the problem of male violence?

There has surely been no shortage of explanations for male violence. Some researchers rely on biological differences between women and men, suggesting that "the durability, universality and generality of the relative aggressiveness of males" point definitively toward a genetic difference. So, for example, some scholars argue that androgens, male hormones, especially testosterone, are what drive male aggression. It is true that testosterone is highly correlated with aggressive behavior: Increased testosterone levels typically result in increased aggression. Other scholars have looked to more evolutionary explanations such as homosocial competition, which regards male violence as the result of the evolutionary competition for sexual access to females. Men fight with each other to create dominance hierarchies; the winners of those fights have their choice of females.[4]

But, as we've seen earlier, by itself the biological evidence is unconvincing. While testosterone is associated with aggression, it does not cause the aggression but only facilitates an aggressiveness that is already present. (It does nothing for nonaggressive males, for example.) Nor does the causal arrow always point from hormone to behavior. Winners in athletic competition experience increased testosterone levels *after* they win. Violence causes increased testosterone levels; hormonal increases cause violence. Nor does testosterone cause violence against those who are significantly higher on the dominance ladder. Increased testosterone will cause a midlevel male baboon, for example, to increase his aggression against the male just below him, but it will not embolden him to challenge the hierarchical order.[5]

In fact, there is also little evidence to support the evolutionary theory of homosocial competition. In some cultures, males are not in the least violent or competitive with each other. If "boys will be boys," as the saying goes, they will be so differently in different cultures. And, in some societies, including ours, males are especially violent against females—the very group they are supposedly competing for. (To murder or assault the person you are trying to inseminate is a particularly unwise reproductive strategy.) Sociologist Judith Lorber intelligently reframes the question:

> When little boys run around noisily, we say "Boys will be boys," meaning that physical assertiveness has to be in the Y chromosome because it is manifest so early and so commonly in boys. But are boys universally, the world over, in every social group, a vociferous, active presence? Or just where they are encouraged to use their bodies freely, to cover space, take risks, and play outdoors at all kinds of games and sports?[6]

Following Freud, some psychoanalysts have looked for an explanation of male violence in the Oedipal drama: The frustration of the young boy's sexual desires is translated into aggression (the frustration-aggression hypothesis). Stated more neutrally, the young boy must constantly and publicly demonstrate that he has successfully separated from his mother and transferred his identity to his father—that is, that he has become masculine. Male violence is a way to prove successful masculinity.

Or, at least, an adaptive strategy to avoid becoming prey themselves. In a fascinating study, Barbara Ehrenreich argues that the origins of war lie less in an innate propensity for aggression and a lust for predation than in the fear that we are slated to become someone else's dinner menu. The origins of society lie in defense—we became social not because of some deep need for sociability, but because only together could we defend ourselves successfully. Thus, she argues, the near-universal association of masculinity and war is compensatory and defensive, a "substitute occupation for underemployed male hunter-defenders."[7]

While not necessarily describing a cultural universal, these psychological models do help explain the particular association of masculinity with violence, especially among younger males. (There are, of course, many societies in which masculinity is not associated with violence.) In particular, psychologists have pointed out how violence is a form of masculine emotional expressiveness, as if the only legitimate emotion a man could express was rage. Hamlet's complex argument addressing the moral choices before him becomes Luke Woodham's self-justifying shrug.

Psychological explanations often assume universal generalizability. They take little account of either cross-cultural variation or the historical shifts in any culture over time. But such cultural and historical shifts are important if we are adequately to explain violence in the first place. In the 1980s, two social anthropologists reversed the question: What can we learn from those societies in which there is very little violence? They found that the definition of masculinity had a significant impact on the propensity toward violence. In societies in which men were permitted to acknowledge fear, levels of violence were low. But in societies where masculine bravado—the posture of strength and the repression and denial of fear—was a defining feature of masculinity, violence was likely to be high. It turns out that those societies in which bravado is prescribed for men are also those in which the definitions of masculinity and femininity are very highly differentiated.[8]

So societies in which gender inequality is highest are those where masculinity and femininity are seen to be polar opposites, and thus they are societies that mandate "masculine bravado." For example, Joanna Overing tells us that in the Amazon jungle, the extremely violent Shavante define manhood as "sexual bellicosity," a state both superior to and opposed to femininity, while their peaceful neighboring Piaroas define manhood *and womanhood* as the ability to cooperate tranquilly with others in daily life. In sum, these are a few of the themes that anthropologists have isolated as leading toward both interpersonal violence and intersocietal violence:

1. The ideal for manhood is the fierce and handsome warrior;
2. Public leadership is associated with male dominance, both of men over other men and of men over women;
3. Women are prohibited from public and political participation;
4. Most public interaction is between men, not between men and women or among women;
5. Boys and girls are systematically separated from an early age;
6. Initiation of boys is focused on lengthy constraint of boys, during which time the boys are separated from women, taught male solidarity, bellicosity, and endurance, and trained to accept the dominance of older groups of men;
7. Emotional displays of male virility, ferocity, and sexuality are highly elaborated;
8. The ritual celebration of fertility focuses on male generative abilities, not female ones;
9. Male economic activities and the products of male labor are prized over female.[9]

One of the most significant "causes" of male violence, then, is gender inequality. Taken together, these works provide some policy-oriented goals toward which we might look if we are to reduce the amount of gendered violence in society. First, it seems clear that the less gender differentiation between women and men, the less likely will be gendered violence. This means the more "like women" men can be seen—nurturing, caring, frightened—and the more "like men" women can be seen—capable, rational, competent in the public sphere—the more likely that aggression will take other routes besides gendered violence.[10]

Men's violence against women is the result of entitlement thwarted; men's violence against other men often derives from the same thwarted sense of entitlement. I imagine that there is a curvilinear relationship between male-to-male violence and male violence against women and the entitlement to patriarchal power. To find peaceful societies, we might want to look at cultures in which entitlement to power is either not thwarted or not present. Societies with the least male-male gendered violence would be those in which patriarchy is either intact and unquestioned, or else hardly present at all, and hasn't been for some time.

THE GENDER OF CRIME

If we are to understand the association of masculinity and violence, we must, therefore, be specific. First, we must look at different groups of men. Surely, violence is not evenly distributed among all groups of men, but varies by class, race, age, region, ethnicity, and sexuality. Second, we must explore the historical fluctuations of that association, and compare the contemporary United States with other industrial countries.

When we do that, an astonishing picture emerges. Stated most baldly: *Young American men are the most violent group of people in the industrialized world.* Our homicide rate is between five and twenty times higher than that of any other industrial democracy, and we imprison five to twenty times more people than does any other country on earth except Russia. (Some might say that our prison population is so much higher because our crime rate is higher; others argue the opposite case, that our crime rate is so high because our prison population is so high. I think both are partly true, but that the relationship between prison and crime is not what common sense would have us believe. Prisons not only deter crime; but they also teach criminals how to commit crime.) In 1992, young men between fifteen and twenty-four had a homicide rate of 37.2 per 100,000. This figure is about ten times higher than that of the next closest industrialized country, Italy, and more than sixty times greater than the same age group in England.[11]

And it's getting worse. Between 1985 and 1994, the number of homicides by fourteen to seventeen-year-old males more than tripled—as has the number of men in prison. In 1971, the American prison population was about two hundred thousand. Less than thirty years later it has mushroomed to more than 1.2 million convicted criminals incarcerated in the nation's fifteen hundred state and federal prisons, with another half-million sitting in the country's three thousand local jails. That's a rate of 645 per 100,000 Americans. On any given day, one out of every three African American men in their twenties is either in prison, in jail, on probation, or on parole. In 1996, six states, including California, were spending more on prisons than on their state colleges and universities.[12]

According to the California Highway Patrol, nine out of ten of those arrested for drunk driving are men; 84 percent of those who are jailed for fatal accidents resulting from drunk driving are men; and 86 percent of arson crimes are committed by men. In fact, the classic profile of the arsonist is entirely gendered. "Look for a passive, unmarried man between the ages of 18 and 30 who lacks a capacity to confront people," according to Allan Hedberg, a California psychologist who studies arsonists. "Big forest fires with massive fire trucks and Pandemonium are a way of making a masculine statement for an unstable young man who in the past has been wronged."[13]

On the other side of the police ledger, the statistics are also revealing. Although fewer than 5 percent of high-speed chases involve suspects wanted for violent felonies—most of them are suspected of traffic violations—one-fifth of all high-speed chases end in serious injury or death, most often of innocent bystanders. Why? Because it is almost always younger male officers who do the chasing. In one study in southern Florida, "winning a race" was cited by officers as the objective in a pursuit.[14]

Criminologist Marvin Wolfgang notes that violent crime rises any time there is an unusually high proportion of the population of young men between the ages of fifteen and twenty-four. Psychiatrist James Gilligan observes that the only two innate biological variables that are predictors of violence are youth and maleness. The relationship is immediately visible if plotted on a chart, as in these figures from mid-nineteenth-century Britain (see figure 11.1) And things aren't so different today, as you can see from a similar chart for the city of Chicago from 1965 to 1990 (see figure 11.2).

Taken separately, gender and age are the two most powerful predictors of violence. Men are far more violent than women, and the likelihood of violence by either gender

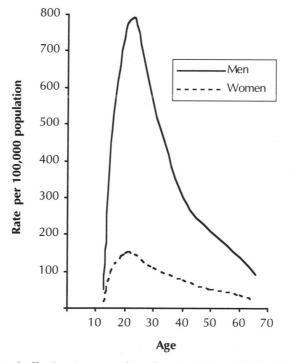

Figure 11.1. Criminal offenders by age and gender, England and Wales, 1842–1844. Based on data from F. G. P. Neison, *Contributions to Vital Statistics* . . . , 3d ed. (London, 1857), 303–304, as plotted by Travis Hirschi and Michael Gottfredson, "Age and the Explanation of Crime," *AJS* 89 (1983): 556.

Chicago 1965–1990

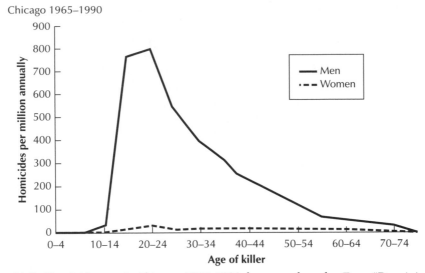

Figure 11.2. Homicide rates in Chicago, 1965–1990, by age and gender. From "Darwinism and the Roots of Machismo," *Scientific American.*

decreases as one ages. Consider, for example, at the data from a survey of high school seniors in 1994. Nearly one-fifth of high school boys report that they hurt someone so badly that he or she needed bandages or to see a doctor. One out of twenty girls reported that level of violence.

Nonetheless, we should not pretend that just because males are overwhelmingly more likely to commit an act of violence or a crime, women never do so. In fact, there is some interesting evidence about criminality among women. Certainly, women commit crimes. But which crimes they commit and their reasons for committing them are sometimes very different from men's. In the mid-1970s, two sociologists noted that crime rates for women were increasing significantly. Freda Adler and Rita Simon each argued that there was evidence of increasing rates of women's criminality. And each blamed feminism. "Is it any wonder," asked Adler, "that once women were armed with male opportunities they should strive for status, criminal as well as civil, through established male hierarchical channels?" Simon nuanced her claims a bit more, arguing that feminism actually decreased the rates of female violent crime, since women were less subject to direct male control, but that it increased the rates of property crimes.[15]

Some contemporary analysts blame feminism not for the increase in women's criminality, but for our ignorance of it. "Women commit the majority of child homicides in the United States, a greater share of physical child abuse, an equal rate of sibling violence and assaults on the elderly, about a quarter of child sexual abuse, an overwhelming share of the killings of newborns, and a fair preponderance of spousal assaults," writes Patricia Pearson, and yet we still think violence is entirely the province of the male. As we will see, many of these statistics hinge on curious misreadings of the data, but even if they were entirely accurate, the number of child or newborn homicides is so minuscule that even if women committed all of them, the gender ratio of homicide would barely move.[16]

What's more interesting is that while both claims may be politically useful to those who want to return women to their "natural" place in the home, they are not supported by the empirical evidence. First of all, the most interesting long-term historical evidence suggests that women's criminality has actually *decreased* since the eighteenth century. Court records reveal a steady decline in women's arrests and prosecutions since the eighteenth century, brought about, in part, by changes in the definition of femininity and the "cult of domesticity" that made women angels of their households:

> By the end of the nineteenth century, there was a clear separation of home and work, a firmer sexual division of labor, the exclusion of women from the public sphere and from productive work, and the confinement of women to reproductive and domestic work in the home. . . . [T]here was also a decline in female criminal court involvement during this period.[17]

Despite the increases in crime rates for women over the past few decades, the base numbers were so small to begin with that *any* modest increase would appear to be a larger percentage increase than among men. In fact, the sex differential in crime has remained roughly the same when seen as a number per 100,000 of population. Then it becomes clear that, as one criminologist put it simply, "relative to males, the profile of the female offender has not changed."[18]

Violent crimes by women actually seem to have fallen. Among females, murder is the most prevalent form of violent crime, and nearly two-thirds of those women convicted of murder killed a relative, intimate, or someone else they knew (compared to less than one-third of the men). Over the past twenty years, the rate at which men were killed by their wives has fallen by close to two-thirds, while the rate at which women were killed by their intimate partners fell by one-third, which was the overall decline in the nation's homicide rate from 1981 to 1998.[19] (Although women convicted of murder receive, on average, a sentence more than three years shorter than men convicted of murder, this sentencing differential seems to have less to do with the gender of the murderer and more to do with the circumstances of the murder, the past criminal history of the murderer, and relationship of the murdered—that is, men who murdered an intimate partner tend to receive sentences roughly equal in length to those of the women.)[20] At least part of the explanation for this precipitous decline in women's homicide rate must be the expansion of services for battered women, so that now a woman whose intimate partner batters and/or rapes her has alternatives that support her leaving the relationship.[21]

There have been some reported increases in women's property crime, especially fraud, forgery, and embezzlement, but most of that increase has been in petty theft—that is, shoplifting, credit card fraud, passing bad checks. Crimes that seem to be most attractive to women are those that, like shoplifting, enable women to express their desires without taking responsibility for them. They want, they desire, they crave—but they know that femininity requires the suppression of desire. Shoplifting is "stealing beauty," as in the title of a recent film; stealing sexuality, adulthood, lust, and passion—

without loss of reputation, the celebrated recent case of Winona Ryder notwithstanding. As criminologist Jack Katz argues:

> [T]he young girls seem especially seduced by items of makeup, jewelry, and clothes: things used to cover up the naked female self, to give the body the appearance of the mature female, and to make the self dazzlingly attractive to a world blinded to the blemishes underneath. Females take symbols of adult female identity—cosmetics, jewelry and sexy underwear.[22]

If, Katz argues, shoplifting is the prototypical "female" crime because it is about satisfying desire without taking responsibility, then the stick-up is the prototypical "male" crime: fast, aggressive, dangerous, and violent. (Men outnumber women in arrests for robbery by about fifteen to one.) And directly personal. The "badass" stick-up guy is phallic power—hard and tough, using his gun to threaten penetration. Street robbery may make little rational sense as a way of making money, but it is still enormously appealing to young males; it's a way of "doing gender":

> Unless it is given sense as a way of elaborating, perhaps celebrating, distinctively male forms of action and ways of being, such as collective drinking and gambling on street corners, interpersonal physical challenges and moral tests, cocky posturing and arrogant claims to back up "tough" fronts, stickup has almost no appeal at all.[23]

Yet the evidence on gender and violence does not lead to the conclusion that all men are violent rapacious beasts and all women angelic and nonviolent little lambs. Societies that have high rates of male crime also tend to have high rates of female crime. We need to remember that the three most common arrest categories—for both women and men—are driving under the influence (DUI), larceny-theft, and "other except traffic" (a category that includes mostly criminal mischief, public disorder, and minor offenses). Taken together, these three offenses account for 48 percent of all male arrests and 49 percent of all female arrests. It's when crime turns violent that the gender patterns emerge most starkly.[24]

There is evidence of female aggression and violence, of course—but it remains dramatically different from men's violence. For example, women's violence tends to be defensive, while men are more often the initiators of violent acts. And while men's violence may be instrumental—designed to accomplish some goal—or expressive of emotion, women's violence often is the outcome of feeling trapped and helpless. For example, the types of violent crimes women are either as likely or more likely to commit than men—child homicide, child abuse, assaults on the elderly, murder of newborns—as well as female-initiated spousal abuse or spousal murder, seem to stem from terror and helplessness.[25]

The gendered patterns of violence among children are also revealing. Among three-year-olds, for example, the most frequent acts of violence are from boy-to-boy; girl-to-girl violence, by contrast, is the least frequent. Boy-to-girl violence is far more frequent than girl-to-boy. In one study, two Finnish psychologists contrasted physical, verbal, and "indirect" forms of aggression. They found that girls at all ages (except the youngest) were more likely to engage in indirect aggression (telling lies behind the person's back, trying to be someone's friend as revenge to another, saying to others, "Let's not be friends with him or her"). Boys at all ages were more likely to engage in direct aggression (kicking, hitting, tripping, shoving, arguing, swearing, and abusing) and verbal aggression. Girls at all ages were also more likely to use peaceful means (talking to clarify things, forgetting about it, telling a teacher or parent) to resolve problems, and were also more likely to withdraw or sulk.[26]

We have some evidence that the gender gap in violence is decreasing. One study from Finland found that girls in the 1980s were much less violent than in the 1990s, both from self-reports and in the eyes of their peers. The study also found greater acceptance of violence among the girls. But in the late 1990s, the study found, violence has a more positive connotation for girls, "something that makes the girl feel powerful, strong, and makes her popular"—in short, doing for girls what violence and aggression have historically done for boys.[27]

A spate of recent books about girls' aggression throws new light on these issues.[28] Some, like Rachel Simmons, argue that such indirect aggression may have devastating effects on girls' development, self-esteem, and aspirations:

> Unlike boys, who tend to bully acquaintances or strangers, girls frequently attack within tightly knit friendship networks, making aggression harder to identify and intensifying the damage to the victims. Within the hidden culture of aggression, girls fight with body language and relationships instead of fists and knives. In this world, friendship is a weapon, and the sting of a shout pales in comparison to a day of someone's silence. There is no gesture more devastating than the back turning away.

But girls' indirect forms of aggression are not the expression of some innately devious feminine wiles, but the consequences of gender inequality. "Our culture refuses girls access to open conflict, and it forces their aggression into nonphysical, indirect and covert forms. Girls use backbiting, exclusion, rumors, name-calling, and manipulation to inflict physical pain on targeted victims," Simmons writes. Indirect horizontal aggression is the safest and easiest way to express one's anger. Were girls permitted the kind of aggression that boys are, they won't express their anger in such backhanded ways.[29]

Evidence of women's increased violence—that is, of a decreasing gender gap—is still scant and spotty. In the United States, women constitute only 6.3 percent of the prison population (about 75,000 inmates)—a 9.1 percent increase since 1995. One-half the women prisoners are incarcerated in just four states—Florida, Texas, California, and New York. The female inmate population tends to mirror the male inmate population demographically (not in terms of offenses), including a disproportionate number of nonwhite, poor, and undereducated and unemployed women. Violence remains perhaps the most gendered behavior in our culture.[30]

GENDERED VIOLENCE: AN INSTITUTIONAL PROBLEM

After he had successfully tested a nuclear bomb in November 1952, creating a fusion explosion about one thousand times more powerful than the fission bomb that destroyed Hiroshima seven years earlier, Edward Teller, the Nobel Prize–winning nuclear physicist, wrote the following three word telegram to his colleagues: "It's a boy." No one had to point out to Teller the equation of military might—the capacity for untold violence—and masculinity. Such a terrible tragic connection remains fixed for both the military heroes of our masculine fantasies and for the bespectacled scientists who create the technology that enables those Rambo-wannabes to conquer the world.

It would be easy to catalog all the phallic images and rhetoric in that vast historic parade of military heroes in decorated uniforms and scientists in white lab coats, suggesting that proving masculinity is a common currency for both warrior and wonk, gladiator and geek. Pop psychologists have yet to run out of sexually tinged phrases to describe this; one feminist calls masculine militarism a case of "missile envy"; another writes about how men "created civilization in the image of a perpetual erection: a pregnant phallus." But these images turn gender into a screen against which individuals project their psychological fears and problems, reducing war and the state's use of institutional violence to a simple aggregation of insecure men desperate to prove their masculinity. While this argument is not entirely without merit, as we shall see, it leaves us without an understanding of the institutional violence that is implicit in the construction of the modern bureaucratic state. For that we need to explore the link between the two realms, how "militarism perpetuates the equation between masculinity and violence" and how war "encodes violence into the notion of masculinity generation after generation."[31]

Though masculinity may be associated historically with war, the way we fight today would leave many men without the ability to test and prove their manhood in a conventional military way. After all, most soldiers today are not combatants. Most are in support services—transport, administration, technical support, maintenance. The increasingly technological sophistication of war has only sped up this process—nuclear weapons, "smart bombs," automatic weaponry, self-propelled military vehicles, and long-distance weapons all reduce the need for Rambo-type primitive warriors and increase the need for cool, rational button pushers.[32]

Yet there is something powerful in the ways that our political leaders seek to prove an aggressive and assertive masculinity in the political arena. War and its technology confer upon men a "virile prestige," as French philosopher Simone de Beauvoir put it. Think of Andrew Jackson's man-making slaughter of the Seminoles, or Theodore Roosevelt thundering about the strenuous life as he charged up San Juan Hill. For much of our history, our political leaders have tried to balance manly restraint with equally manly belligerence. Military prowess and the willingness to go to war have been tests of manhood. Explaining why Lyndon Johnson continued to escalate the war in Vietnam, a biographer writes:

> He wanted the respect of men who were tough, real men, and they would turn out to be hawks. He had unconsciously divided people around him between men and boys. Men were activists, doers, who conquered business empires, who acted instead of talked, who made it in the world of other men, and had the respect of other men. Boys were the talkers and the writers and the intellectuals, who sat around thinking and criticizing and doubting instead of doing.

(In case you find such sentiments strange, think about the cliché "those who can, do, and those who can't do, teach.") When opponents criticized the war effort, Johnson attacked their masculinity. When informed that one member of his administration was becoming a dove on Vietnam, Johnson scoffed, "Hell, he has to squat to piss!" And, as he celebrated the bombings of North Vietnam, Johnson declared proudly that he "didn't just screw Ho Chi Minh. I cut his pecker off."[33]

Such boasts continue to plague American politics. Jimmy Carter's reluctance to intervene in Iran led one security affairs analyst to comment that the United States was "spreading its legs for the Soviet Union" and led to the election of our last cowboy president, Ronald Reagan, who promised to rescue America from its post-Vietnam lethargy—which he accomplished, in part, by invading small countries like Grenada. As one political commentator put it, Reagan "made mincemeat of Mr. Carter and Mr. Mondale, casting them as girly-boys who lacked the swagger necessary to lead the world." George H. W. Bush inherited the right to that same masculine mantle when he invaded Panama and the Persian Gulf for Operation Desert Storm. Bill Clinton's popularity ratings soared when, during his impeachment hearings in 1998, he threatened and eventually undertook air strikes against Iraq. And George W. Bush's bellicose posturing and threats to invade Iraq have proved popular enough to ensure Republican electoral victories, and to knock the corporate scandals of his friends' companies, the failure of the war against terrorism, and an economic recession off the front page.[34]

Such presidential sentiments both trickle down to those who were charged with creating and fighting those wars and bubble up to policymakers from the defense strategists who are trained to prosecute those wars and who are today calculating the megatonnage and kill ratios for future ones. "There is among some people a feeling of compulsion about the pursuit of advanced technologies—a sense that a man must be continually proving his virility by pioneering on the frontiers of what is only just possible." In an article about masculinity and the Vietnam War, journalist I. F. Stone illustrated this compulsive proving of masculinity among those who planned the war. At a briefing about the escalation of the bombing of North Vietnam, one Pentagon official described the U.S. strategy as two boys fighting: "If one boy gets the other in an arm lock, he can probably get his adversary to say 'uncle' if he increases the pressure in sharp, painful jolts and gives every indication of willingness to break the boy's arm." And recently, when a German politician indicated he was concerned about popular opposition to Euromissile deployment, one American defense strategist opined that "[T]hose Krauts are a bunch of limp-dicked wimps."[35]

Carol Cohn conducted an ethnographic analysis of defense intellectuals. She recalls that "lectures were filled with discussion of vertical erector launchers, thrust-to-weight ratios, soft lay-downs, deep penetration, and the comparative advantage of protracted versus spasm attacks—or what one military advisor to the National Security Council has called 'releasing 70 to 80 per cent of our megatonnage in one orgasmic whump.' There was serious concern about the need to harden our missles, and the need to 'face it, the Russians are a little harder than we are.' Disbelieving glances would occasionally pass between me and my ally—another woman—but no one else seemed to notice."[36]

It would be simplistic to reduce the complexities of military and political decisions to psychological "pissing contests," but it is equally important to include a discussion of gender in our investigations. From the top political leaders to military strategists and technological experts, issues of gender play themselves out in the formulation of military policy. And public opinion also plays an important role in these demonstrations of sexual potency. Recall, for example, how during the Gulf War, our enemy Saddam Hussein was constantly sexualized on bumper stickers that read "Saddam, Bend Over" and "U.S.A.—Up Saddam's Ass," insults that equated military conflict with homosexual rape. One widely reprinted cartoon showed Saddam Hussein bending over as if in Muslim prayer, with a huge approaching U.S. missile about the penetrate him from behind. Thus was the sexual nature of military adventurism played out in sexual paraphernalia.

AMERICA: A HISTORY OF GENDERED VIOLENCE

Although we commonly think that all states require the use of violence—that the creation and maintenance of politics requires both a police force and military to subdue both ourselves and others—the equation of violence and masculinity remains a particularly strong one for Americans. The United States has a long and bloody history of specifically gendered violence, in which both individual men and Americans as a nation have demonstrated and proved manhood. It's not just our political and military leaders—although, as we have seen, they certainly have had their issues as well. One psychologist speaks of a "civic advocacy of violence as socially acceptable, appropriate and necessary." Our most venerated cultural heroes were soldiers—or, at least, the actors who played them in the movies.[37]

Historians suggest that this particularly American, and particularly tragic, code of violence arrived in the eighteenth century, brought and developed by Scottish and Irish immigrants to the American south, where brawling, dueling, fighting, hunting, and drinking became the means to express manhood. Andrew Jackson's mother told her son, arguably the most mean-tempered and violent president in our nation's history, that "the law affords no remedy that can satisfy the feelings of a true man." The American frontier—perhaps the single largest collection of younger males in the history of the industrialized world—provided a legacy of violence to American life. Violence has always been highest in those places where young men gather, especially away from the "civilizing" effect of women.[38]

In the aftermath of the Civil War, after the South had suffered a humiliating and emasculating defeat, young boys took to placing chips of wood on their shoulders, daring other boys to knock them off so they could legitimately fight with them. Only in America is "having a chip on one's shoulder" considered a badge of honor among boys. More than that, violence was seen as legitimate—as long as it was retaliatory. If someone else knocked that chip off, kicking his ass was a reasonable response. In her penetrating analysis of American violence, anthropologist Margaret Mead described the typically American refusal to initiate aggression but to retaliate far out of proportion to the original offense in "an aggression which can never be shown except when the other fellow starts it" and which is "so unsure of itself that it had to be proved." Remember these words the next time you watch two young boys square off in a playground. "You wanna start something?" one of them yells. "No, but if you start it, I'll finish it!" replies the other. No one wants to take responsibility for the initial act of aggression, but everyone wants to finish the fight.[39]

Violence has long been understood as the best way to ensure that others publicly recognize one's manhood. Fighting was once culturally prescribed for boys, who, the theory went, needed to demonstrate gender identity. In one of the best-selling advice manuals of the first part of the twentieth century, parents learned that:

> There are times when every boy must defend his own rights if he is not to become a coward and lose the road to independence and true manhood. . . . The strong willed boy needs no inspiration to combat, but often a good deal of guidance and restraint. If he fights more than, let us say, a half dozen times a week,—except, of course, during his first week at a new school—he is probably over-quarrelsome and needs to curb. The sensitive, retiring boy, on the other hand, needs encouragement to stand his ground and fight.

In this best-seller, boys were encouraged to fight once a day, except during the first week at a new school, when, presumably they would fight more often![40]

Lurking beneath such advice was the fear that boys who were not violent would not grow up to be real men. The spectre of the "sissy"—encompassing the fears of emasculation, humiliation, and effeminacy that American men carry with them—is responsible for a significant amount of masculine violence. Violence is proof of masculinity; one is a "real" man, because one is not afraid to be violent. Psychiatrist James Gilligan speaks of "the patriarchal code of honor and shame which generates and obligates male violence"—a code that sees violence as the chief demarcating line between women and men.[41]

The contemporary code of violence of the streets descended from old southern notions of honor—a man had to be ready to fight to prove himself in the eyes of others. Southern whites called it "honor"; by the turn of the century it was called "reputation." By the 1950s northern ghetto blacks spoke of "respect," which has now been transformed again into not showing "disrespect," or "dissing." It's the same code of violence, the same daring. Listen to one New York gang member, describing the reasons that his gang requires random knife slashings as initiation rituals. "Society claims we are notorious thugs and killers but we are not," he says. "We're a family of survivors, . . . proud young black men living in the American ghetto. Harlem princes trying to rise up and refusing to be beaten down." Another man recalls his days in a juvenile detention facility where "you fought almost every day because everybody trying to be tougher than the next person." Another street hood gives a contemporary slant to the old "chip on the shoulder" when he describes what he calls the "accidental bump," when you're walking around Spanish Harlem "with your chest out, bumping into people and hoping they'll give you a bad time so you can pounce on them and beat 'em into the goddamn concrete." Sociologist Vic Seidler writes that "as boys, we have to be constantly on the alert to either confront or avoid physical violence. We have to be alert to defend ourselves. . . . Masculinity is never something we can feel at ease with. It's always something we have to be ready to prove and defend." And criminologist Hans Toch adds that "in cultures of masculinity, the demonstrated willingness to fight and the capacity for combat are measures of worth and self-worth."[42]

Masculinity is still often equated with the capacity for violence. From the locker room to the chat room, men of all ages learn violence is a socially sanctioned form of expression. Male socialization is a socialization to the legitimacy of violence—from infantile circumcision, to being hit by parents and siblings, to routine fights with other boys, to the socially approved forms of violence in the military, sports, and prison (the United States is only industrialized country that still employs capital punishment), to epigrams that remind us not to get mad but to get even, and that the working world is the Hobbesian war of each against all, a jungle where dogs eat dogs.

VIOLENCE AGAINST WOMEN

Men learn that violence is an accepted form of communication between men, and between women and men. It's so commonplace, so deeply woven into the fabric of daily life that we accept violence as a matter of course—within families, between friends, between lovers. Most victims of violence know their attackers; many known them intimately. Nearly one in five victims of violence treated in hospital emergency rooms was injured by a spouse, a former spouse, or a current or former boyfriend or girlfriend. Violence can be a private, personal, and intimate language, just as it can be a mode of public address between societies and social groups.

The gender imbalance of intimate violence is staggering. Of those victims of violence who were injured by spouses or ex-spouses, women outnumber men by about nine to one. Eight times as many women were injured by their boyfriends as men injured by girlfriends. The United States has among the highest rates in the industrial world for rape, domestic violence, and spousal murder. Domestic violence is the leading cause of injury to women in the nation, claiming nearly four million victims a year. Between one-third and one-half of all women are assaulted by a spouse or partner at some point during their lives. Between 30 percent and 40 percent of all women who are murdered are murdered by husband or boyfriends, according to the FBI. Every six minutes, a woman in the United States is raped; every eighteen seconds a woman is beaten, and every day four women are killed by their batterers.[43]

It doesn't have to be this way, of course. As we saw earlier, societies may be located on a continuum from rape-free to rape-prone. Anthropologist Peggy Reeves Sanday found that the best predictors of rape-proneness were levels of militarism, interpersonal violence in general, ideologies of male toughness, and distant father-child relationships. Those societies in which rape was relatively rare valued women's autonomy (a woman continued to own property in her own name after marriage) and valued children (men were involved in child rearing). Stated most simply, "the lower the status of women relative to men, the higher the rape rate." What does that tell us about women's status in the United States?[44]

In fact, the United States has the highest rate of reported rape in the industrial world—about eighteen times higher than England's. Between 12 percent and 25 percent of all American women have experienced rape, and another 12 to 20 percent have experienced attempted rape. That means that between one-fourth and nearly one-half of all women have been sexually assaulted, and between two-thirds and four-fifths of these rapes involve acquaintances. One calculation estimates that between 20 and 30 percent of all girls now twelve years old will suffer a violent sexual attack during the rest of their lives.[45]

What is, perhaps, more frightening, is that of those twelve-year-old girls, 16 percent of them have *already* been raped. According to the U.S. Department of Justice, half the women raped in 1992 (a typical year) were juveniles under eighteen years old, and 16 percent were younger than twelve. Another study found that 96 percent of those female rape victims under twelve knew their attackers. In one of five cases, their rapist was also their father. While there is some evidence that suggests that females under eighteen are also the most likely to file false reports of rape with the police (though virtually none of these allegations ever got to trial and all were retracted in the interview stage), these false reports seem to be the result of fears of pregnancy, and the hope that declaring they were raped would permit them to get an abortion, since in many states, abortion is only legal in cases of rape or threat to the mother's health. But these cases of rape of young girls can hardly be subsumed under some vague and insulting heading of relationship "miscommunication."[46]

The recent expose of pervasive child sexual abuse by Catholic priests (and the Church's subsequent efforts to cover up these crimes) reminds us of how vulnerable boys are as well. While these revelations have been shocking, pedophile sexual abuse should not be confused with homosexual rape; pedophilia is a "sexual orientation" not a variation of homosexuality. Pedophile priests are erotically attracted not to members of their own sex, but to children (some choose boys, others choose girls, and some are indiscriminate). The erotic charge comes from the presumed seductive innocence of the child, not the attraction of one's own gender. And boys are no more vulnerable to same-sex sexual assault by their peers (as opposed to adults) in the Catholic Church than they are in any other mostly single-sex and gender unequal institution.

As we've seen in earlier chapters, different theoretical schools offer different explanations for all sorts of rape. Arguments that rape is simply the reproductive strategy for losers in the sexual arena are unconvincing. Equally unconvincing are psychological arguments that rape is an isolated, individual act, committed by sick individuals who experience uncontrollable sexual impulses. After all, almost three-fourths of all rapists plan their rapes. And only about 5 percent of rapists can be categorized as psychotic. Nor is it persuasive to blame alcohol or drugs as the cause of men losing control. Why, then, wouldn't women lose control of themselves in the same way?

An adequate explanation of rape has to recognize that it is men who rape women, and ask the more frightening question: Why do so many "otherwise" typical, normal men commit rape? As sociologist Allan Johnson puts it, how can such a pervasive event be the work of a few lunatics? "It is difficult to believe that such widespread violence is the responsibility of a small lunatic fringe of psychopathic men," he writes. "That sexual violence is so pervasive supports the view that the focus of violence against women rests squarely in the middle of what our culture defines as 'normal' interaction between men and women." The reality is that rape is committed by all-American regular guys. And, on campus, "[c]ollege women are at greater risk of being raped or aggressed against by the men they know and date than they are by lunatics in the bushes."[47]

Surveys of college women reveal the prevalence of rape, while surveys of college men indicate how casually it can be viewed. Mary Koss's research on campus date and acquaintance rape, although the subject of vicious backlash attacks, remains the most impressive and thorough research we have on rape's frequency and scope. She found that nearly half (44 percent) of all women surveyed have experienced some forms of sexual activity when they didn't want to; 15 percent experienced attempted rape, 12 percent were coerced by drugs and alcohol, and a full 25 percent had sexual intercourse when they didn't want to because they were "overwhelmed" by a man's overwhelming arguments and pressure; and nearly one in ten (9 percent) were forcibly raped.[48]

No wonder feminist writer Susan Griffin called rape "the all-American crime," engaged in by normal all-American guys. Yet it is also equally true that most men do not commit rape. In several surveys, many men indicated that they would consider it— provided the conditions were "right" and they knew that they would not get caught. In a survey of American college men, more than one-fourth (28 percent) indicated that they would be likely to commit rape and use force to get sex; 6 percent said they would commit rape but not use force; and 30 percent said they might use force but would not commit rape. Forty per cent indicated that they would neither use force nor commit rape—less than half! In another survey, 37 percent indicated some likelihood of committing rape if they were certain they would not be caught.[49]

Something still holds men back—well, at least some men! Is it simply the fear of being caught? Or is it that they can't quite take demonstrating their masculinity to that next level. In a sense, what we see is not that rapists are nonconformists, psychologically unbalanced perverts, who couldn't otherwise get sex, but that rapists are actually *over*conformists—exceptionally committed to a set of norms about masculinity that makes every encounter with every women potentially, even inevitably, about sexual conquest, that turns every date into a contest, and that turns a deaf ear to what a woman might want because, after all, women aren't men's equals to begin with. "The most striking characteristic of sex offenders," writes one researcher, "is their apparent normality." Bernard Lefkowitz, author of a chillingly detailed portrait of a gang-rape of a mentally retarded girl by several high-status high school athletes in Glen Ridge, New Jersey, argues that "[f]or a lot of boys, acting abusively toward women is regarded as a rite of passage. It's woven into our culture." So, any discussion of rape has to take account of the ordinariness of the crime within the normative definition of masculinity, and of the empirical reality that despite all that, most men do not and never will commit rape. If rape is normative, are non-rapists not real men?[50]

In a fascinating study of convicted rapists, sociologist Diana Scully develops these themes. Scully found that rapists have higher levels of consensual sexual activity than other men, and are as likely to have significant relationships with women, and are as likely to be fathers as are other men. This should effectively demolish the evolutionary arguments that men who rape do so out of sexual frustration, desire for relationships with women, or are "losers" in the sexual marketplace. Rape was used by men "to put women in their place," she writes. "Rape is a man's right," one convicted rapist told her. "If a woman doesn't want to give it, a man should take it. Women have no right to say no. Women are made to have sex. It's all they are good for. Some women would rather take a beating, but they always give in; it's what they are for." Men rape, Scully concludes, "not because they are idiosyncratic or irrational, but because they have learned that in this culture sexual violence is rewarding" and because "they never thought they would be punished for what they did."[51]

Rape is a crime that combines sex and violence, that makes sex the weapon in an act of violence. It's less a crime of passion than a crime of power, less about love or lust than about conquest and contempt, less an expression of longing than an expression of entitlement. You might think that when men think about rape, then, they think about the power they feel.

You'd be wrong. Listen to the voice of one young man, a twenty-three-year-old stockboy named Jay in a San Francisco corporation, who was asked by author Tim Beneke to think about under what circumstances he might commit rape. He has never committed rape. He's simply an average guy, trying to imagine the circumstances under which he would commit an act of violence against a woman. Here's what Jay says:

> Let's say I see a woman and she looks really pretty and really clean and sexy and she's giving off very feminine, sexy vibes. I think, wow I would love to make love to her, but I know she's not interested. It's a tease. A lot of times a woman knows that she's looking really good and she'll use that and flaunt it and it makes me feel like she's laughing at me and I feel degraded. . . . If I were actually desperate enough to rape somebody it would be from wanting that person, but also it would be a very spiteful thing, just being able to say "I have power over you and I can do anything I want with you" because really I feel that they have power over me just by their presence. Just the fact that they can come up to me and just melt me makes me feel like a dummy, makes me want revenge. They have power over me so I want power over them.[52]

Jay speaks not from a feeling of power, but from a feeling of powerlessness. "They have power over me so I want power over them." In his mind, rape is not the initiation of aggression against a woman, but a form of revenge, a retaliation following an injury already done to him. But by whom?

Beneke explores this apparent paradox by looking at language. Think of the terms we use in this culture to describe women's beauty and sexuality. We use a language of violence, of aggression. A woman is a "bombshell," a "knockout," a "femme fatale." She's "stunning," "ravishing," "dressed to kill." We're "blown away," "done in." Women's beauty is experienced by men as an act of aggression: it invades men's thoughts, elicits unwelcome feelings of desire and longing, makes men feel helpless, powerless, vulnerable. Then, having committed this invasive act of aggression, women reject men, say no to sex, turn them down. Rape is a way to get even, to exact revenge for rejection, to retaliate. These feelings of powerlessness, coupled with the sense of entitlement to women's bodies expressed by the rapists Diana Scully interviewed, combine in a potent mix—powerlessness and entitlement, impotence and a right to feel in control. The astonishing, shamefully high United States rape rate comes from that fusion.

Thus, rape is less a problem of a small number of sick individuals and more a problem of social expectations of male behavior, expectation that stem from gender inequality (disrespect and contempt for women) and may push men toward sexual predation. A completed rape is only the end point on a continuum that includes sexual coercion as well as the premeditated use of alcohol of drugs to dissolve a woman's resistance. In the most famous study of college men's behaviors, Mary Koss and her colleagues found that one in thirteen men admitted to forcing (or attempting to force) a woman to have sex against her will, but 10 percent had engaged in unwanted sexual contact and another 7.2 percent had been sexually coercive. In another study, Scott Boeringer found that more than 55 percent had engaged in sexual coercion, 8.6 percent had attempted rape, and 23.7 percent had provided drugs or alcohol to a woman in order to have sex with her when she became too intoxicated to consent or resist (which is legally considered rape in most jurisdictions). Such numbers belie arguments that rape is simply the crime of sick individuals.[53]

Men's feelings of both powerlessness and entitlement are also part of the backdrop to the problem of violence in the home. Though the family is supposed to be a refuge from the dangerous outside world, a "haven in a heartless world," it turns out that the home is, for women and children, the single most dangerous place they can be. Not even the legal "protection" of marriage keeps women safe from the threat of rape, and levels of violence against women in the home are terrifyingly high. Family violence researcher Murray Straus and his colleagues concluded that "the American family and the American home are perhaps as or more violent than any other American institution or setting (with the exception of the military, and only then in time of war)."[54]

Marriage certainly doesn't protect women from rape. In one study of 644 married women, 12 percent reported having been raped by their husbands. One researcher estimates that between 14 percent and 25 percent of women are forced by their husbands to have sexual intercourse against their will during the course of their marriage. In yet another study of 393 randomly selected women, a date or a spouse were more than three times more likely to rape a woman than a stranger, a friend, or an acquaintance. Fully one-half of the sample reported more than twenty incidents of marital rape, and 48 percent indicated that rape was part of the common physical abuse by their husbands. In that study, David Finklehor and Kirsti Yllo also found that nearly three-fourths of the women who had been raped by their husbands had successfully resisted at least once; that 88 percent reported that they never enjoyed being forced; and that less than one-fourth (22 percent) had been sexually victimized as children.[55]

One of the more dramatic changes in rape laws has been the removal of exemptions of husbands from prosecutions for rape. As recently as 1985, more than half of the states in the United States still expressly prohibited prosecution for marital rape, on the grounds that women had no legal right to say no to sex with their husbands. When a woman says "I do," it apparently also meant "I will . . . whenever *he* wants to." Although by 1993, all states had declared marital rape a crime "at least where force is used," according to the National Clearinghouse on Marital and Date Rape, as of 1996, the exemption still applies in several states where the couple is living together (not separated), and only five states have extended such protection to unmarried couples who live together. Family researcher Richard Gelles described the scope of this problem in his testimony before the New Hampshire state legislature in 1981, when that state was considering removing the marital exemption from prosecution:

> In reality, marital rape is often *more traumatic* than stranger rape. When you have been intimately violated by a person who is supposed to love and protect you, it can destroy your capacity for intimacy with anyone else. Moreover, many wife victims are trapped in a reign of terror and experience repeated sexual assaults over a period of years. When you are raped by a stranger you have to live with a frightening memory. *When you are raped by your husband, you have to live with your rapist.*[56]

Marital rape is a significant problem in other countries as well, where husbands remain excluded from prosecution, since a man is legally entitled to do whatever he wants with his property. And wife abuse is also a chronic problem in other countries. In Hong Kong and Quito, Ecuador, for example, estimates run that as many as 50 percent of all married women are regularly beaten by their husbands.[57]

Though domestic violence is certainly a problem in other countries, it also appears that rates of wife abuse in the United States are among the highest in the world. Battery is the single major cause of injury to women in the United States. More than two million women are beaten by their partners every year. According to the Bureau of Justice Statistics, 85 percent of all victims of domestic violence are women. Between two thousand and four thousand women a year are murdered by their husbands or boyfriends. Another study found that nearly one-half of all women murdered in New York City were killed by their husbands or boyfriends. (Only about 3 percent of all male homicides are committed by wives, ex-wives, or girlfriends.)[58]

As we've seen earlier, not only are the rates for spousal murder significantly different for women and men, so are the events leading up to it. R. Emerson and Russell Dobash and their colleagues argue that

> men often kill wives after lengthy periods of prolonged physical violence accompanied by other forms of abuse and coercion; the roles in such cases are seldom if ever reversed. Men perpetrate familial massacres, killing spouse and children together; women do not. Men commonly hunt down and kill wives who have left them; women hardly ever behave similarly. Men kill wives as part of planned murder-suicides; analogous acts by women are almost unheard of. Men kill in response to revelations of wifely infidelity; women almost never respond similarly, though their mates are more often adulterous.[59]

It is also worth noting that these disparate rates of spousal homicide in Western societies are relatively modest compared with the rates in developing societies, where the ratio is even greater. Where patriarchal control is relatively unchallenged, assault, rape, and even murder may be seen less as a crime and more as a prerogative.[60]

Despite the overwhelming evidence of the problems of domestic violence against women, we often hear a small chorus of voices shouting about "husband abuse." When one sociologist claims that husbands' abuse by wives is the most underreported form of domestic violence, suddenly legions of antifeminists trot out such arguments in policy discussions. Some of these studies suggest that women are "as likely" to hit men as men are to hit women, and that women commit 50 percent of all spousal murders, and provide "facts" such as that 1.8 million women suffered one or more assaults by a husband or boyfriend, and more than 2 million men were assaulted by their wives or girlfriends; that 54 percent of all violence labeled as "severe" was committed by women; or that among teenage dating couple, girls were more violent than boys. (Ironically, the people who claim equivalent rates of domestic violence are often the same people who argue that women and men are biologically different, and that women are not biologically aggressive enough to enter the military or serve on police forces.) One obviously confused journalist suggests that since "only" 3 to 4 percent of women are battered each year, "we ought to consider it "the unfortunate behavior of a few crazy men." (If 3 to 4 percent of all men were stricken with testicular or prostate cancer each year, or were victims of street assault, this same journalist would no doubt consider it a national emergency and try to mobilize the entire medical community or the National Guard—and perhaps both!)[61]

If these data were true, you might ask, why are there no shelters for battered men, no epidemics of male victims turning up in hospital emergency rooms, no legions of battered men coming forward to demand protection? (Well, that's not entirely true. O. J. Simpson did call himself an "abused husband" after he beat up his former wife Nicole. And one shelter for battered men did open in Vancouver, Canada, but closed within two months because no one came to it.) Partly, these pundits tell us, because men who are victims of domestic violence are so ashamed of the humiliation, of the denial of manhood, that they are unlikely to come forward, and more likely to suffer in silence the violent ministrations of their wives—a psychological problem that one researcher calls "the battered husband syndrome." "Because men have been taught to 'take it like a man' and are ridiculed when they feel that have been battered by women, women are nine times more likely to report their abusers to the authorities," observe two writers. And partly, they tell us, because the power of the "feminist lobby" is so pervasive that there has been a national cover-up of this demonstrably politically incorrect finding. As one polemicist puts it,

> While repeated studies consistently show that men are victims of domestic violence at least as often as are women, both the lay public and many professionals regard a finding of no sex difference in rates of physical aggression among intimates as surprising, if not unreliable, the stereotype being that men are aggressive and women are exclusively victims.[62]

Such assertions are not supported by empirical research at all, and the inferences drawn from them are even more unwarranted. For example, in the original study of "The Battered Husband Syndrome," sociologist Susan Steinmetz surveyed fifty-seven couples. Four of the wives, but not one husband, reported having been seriously beaten. From this finding, Steinmetz concluded that men simply don't report abuse, and that there must be a serious problem of husband abuse, and that some 250,000 men were hit every year—this, remember, from a finding that no husbands were abused. By the time the media hoopla over these bogus data subsided, the figure had ballooned to 12 million battered husbands every year![63]

One problem is the questions asked in the research. Those studies that found that women hit men as much as men hit women asked couples if they had ever, during the course of their relationship, hit their partner. An equal number of women and men answered yes. The number changed dramatically, though, when they were asked who initiated the violence (was it offensive, or defensive), how severe it was (did she push him before or after he'd broken her jaw?), and how often the violence occurred. When these three questions were posed, the results looked like what we knew all along: the amount, frequency, severity and consistency of violence against women is far greater than anything done by women to men—Lorena Bobbitt notwithstanding.[64]

Another problem stems from who was asked. The studies that found comparable rates of domestic violence asked only one partner about the incident. But studies in which both partners were interviewed separately found large discrepancies between reports from women and from men. The same researchers who found comparable rates have suggested that such results be treated with extreme caution, because men underreport severe assaults. (Perhaps it is felt to be equally unmanly to beat up a woman as to be beaten up by one, since "real men" never raise a hand against a woman.)[65]

A third problem results from *when* the informants were asked about domestic violence. The studies that found comparability asked about incidents that occurred in a single year, thus equating a single slap with a reign of domestic terror that may have lasted decades. And, while the research is clear and unequivocal that violence against women increases dramatically following divorce or separation, the research that found comparable results excluded incidents that occurred after separation or divorce. About 76 percent of all assaults take place at that time though—with a male perpetrator more than 93 percent of the time.[66]

Finally, the research that suggests comparability is all based on the Conflict Tactics Scale, a scale that does not distinguish between offensive and defensive violence, equating a vicious assault with a woman hitting her husband while he is, for instance, assaulting their children. Nor does it take into account the physical differences between women and men, which lead to women being six times more likely to require medical care for injuries sustained in family violence. Nor does it include the nonphysical means by which women are compelled to remain in abusive relationships (income disparities, fears about their children, economic dependency). Nor does it include marital rape or sexual aggression. As one violence researcher asks, "Can you call two people equally aggressive when a woman punches her husband's chest with no physical harm resulting and a man punches his wife's face and her nose is bloodied and broken? These get the same scores on the CTS."[67]

Supporters of battered men, by the way, rarely dispute the numbers of battered women—they only claim the number of battered men is equivalent. This is curious, because they typically do not advocate for more funding for domestic violence, but, rather, for *less* funding for women's programs. Such politically disingenuous efforts have earned the disapproval of even the researcher whose work is used most commonly to support their claims.[68]

Of course, some research suggests that women are fully capable of using violence in intimate relationships, but at nowhere near the same rates or severity. According to the U.S. Department of Justice, females experienced more than ten times as many incidents of violence by an intimate as men did. On average, women experienced about 575,000 violent victimizations, compared with about 49,000 for men. Perhaps it's a bit higher—perhaps as much as 3 or 4 percent of all spousal violence is committed by women, according to criminologist Martin Schwartz. About one in eight wives reports having ever hit her husband. And when women are violent, they tend to use either the least violent tactics or the most violent ones. Women shove, slap, and kick as often as men, Straus and his colleagues found. But they also use guns almost as often as men do.[69]

Domestic violence varies as the balance of power in the relationship shifts. When all the decisions are made by one spouse, rates of spouse abuse—whether committed by the woman or the man—are at their highest levels. Violence against women is most common in those households in which power is concentrated in the hands of the husband. Interestingly, rates of violence against husbands are *also* higher (though much less likely) in homes in which the power is concentrated in the hands of the husband, or, in the extremely rare cases, in the hands of the wife. Concentration of power in men's hands leads to higher rates of violence, period—whether against women or against men. Rates of wife abuse and husband abuse both plummet as the relationships become increasingly equal, and there are virtually no cases of wives hitting their husbands when all decisions are shared equally, that is, when the relationships are fully equal.[70]

Women and men do not commit acts of violence at the same rate, or for the same reasons. Family violence researcher Kersti Yllo argues that men tend to use domestic violence instrumentally, for the specific purpose of striking fear and terror in their wives' hearts, to ensure compliance, obedience, and passive acceptance of the husband's rule in the home. Women, by contrast, tend to use violence expressively, to express frustration or immediate anger—or, of course, defensively, to prevent further injury. But rarely is women's violence systematic, purposive, and routine. As two psychologists recently put it:

> [I]n heterosexual relationships, battering is primarily something that men do to women, rather than the reverse. . . . [T]here are many battered women who are violent, mostly, but not always, in self-defense. Battered women are living in a culture of violence, and they are part of that culture. Some battered women defend themselves: they hit back, and might even hit or push as often as their husbands do. But they are the ones who are beaten up.[71]

In the results of a survey that simply adds up all violent acts, women and men might appear to be equally violent. But the nation's hospital emergency rooms, battered women's shelters, and county morgues suggest that such appearances are often deadly deceptive.

Violence against women knows no class, racial, or ethnic bounds. "Educated, successful, sophisticated men—lawyers, doctors, politicians, business executives—beat their wives as regularly and viciously as dock workers." Yet there are some differences. For example, one of the best predictors of the onset of domestic violence is unemployment. And a few studies have found rates of domestic violence to be higher in African American families than in white families. One study found that black men hit their wives four times as often as white men did, and that black women hit their husbands twice as often as white women did. While subsequent studies have indicated a decrease in violence among black families, the rates are still somewhat higher than for white families.[72]

Among Latinos the evidence is contradictory: one study found significantly less violence in Latino families than in Anglo families, while another found a slightly higher rate. These contradictory findings were clarified by separating different groups of Latinos. Kaufman Kantor and colleagues the found that Puerto Rican husbands were about twice as likely to hit their wives as Anglo husbands (20.4 percent to 9.9 percent), and about ten times more likely than Cuban husbands (2.5 percent). In many cases, however, these racial and ethnic differences disappear when social class is taken into account. Sociologist Noel Cazenave examined the same National Family Violence Survey and found that blacks had *lower* rates of wife abuse than whites in three of four income categories—the two highest and the lowest. Higher rates among blacks were reported only by those respondents in the $6,000–$11,999 income range (which included 40 percent of all blacks surveyed). Income and residence (urban) were also the variables that explained virtually all the ethnic differences between Latinos and Anglos. The same racial differences in spousal murder can be explained by class: Two-thirds of all spousal murders in New York City took place in the poorest sections of the Bronx and Brooklyn.[73]

Of course, gay men and lesbians can engage in domestic violence as well. A recent informal survey of gay victims of violence in six major cities found that gay men and lesbians were more likely to be victims of domestic violence than of antigay hate crimes. One study presented to the Fourth International Family Violence Research conference found that abusive gay men had profiles similar to those of heterosexual batterers, including low self-esteem and an inability to sustain intimate relationships.[74]

Domestic violence is another way in which men exert power and control over women. And yet, like rape, domestic violence is most likely to occur not when the man feels most powerful, but when he feels relatively powerless. Violence is restorative, a means to reclaim the power that he believes is rightfully his. As one sociologist explains, "abusive men are more likely to batter their spouses and children whenever they feel they are losing power or control over their lives." Another reminds us that "[m]ale physical power over women, or the illusion of power, is nonetheless a minimal compensation for the lack of power over the rest of one's life."[75]

CONCLUSION

Violence is epidemic in American society today. The United States is, by far, the most violent industrial nation in the world—despite our being the society with the highest rates of incarceration, and the only industrialized nation that uses the death penalty to deter violence. Did I say "despite"? Don't I mean "because"?

Violence takes an enormous social toll, not just on its victims, but in the massive costs of maintaining a legal system, prisons, and police forces. And it takes an incalculable psychic cost—an entire nation that has become comfortable living in fear of violence. (Turn on the evening news in any city in America for the nightly parade of murders, fires, parental abuse, and fistfights masquerading as sports). "To curb crime we do not need to expand repressive state measures, but we do need to reduce gender inequalities," writes criminologist James Messerschmidt. And assuaging that fear, as criminologist Elizabeth Stanko puts it, "will take more than better outdoor lighting."[76]

Of course, better lighting is a start. And we have to protect women from a culture of violence that so often targets them. But we also have to protect boys "from a culture of violence that exploits their worst tendencies by reinforcing and amplifying the atavistic values of the masculine mystique." After all, it is men who are overwhelmingly the victims of violence—just as men are overwhelmingly its perpetrators.[77]

Often, biological explanations are invoked as evasive strategies. "Boys will be boys," we say, throwing up our hands in helpless resignation. But even if all violence were biologically programmed by testosterone or the evolutionary demands of reproductive success, the epidemic of male violence in America would still beg the political question: Are we going to organize our society so as to maximize this propensity for violence, or to minimize it? These are political questions, and they demand political answers—answers that impel us to find alternative, nonviolent routes for men to express themselves as men.

Frankly, I believe that men are better than that, better than biologically programmed violent and rapacious beasts. A colleague recently devised a way to suggest that men can do better. For the Rape Awareness Week at his university, he created "splash guards" to be distributed in the men's rooms on campus. (For those who don't know, a splash guard is the plastic grate that is placed in men's public urinals that prevents splatter.) He had thousands made up with a simple and hopeful slogan. It says simply: "You hold the power to stop rape in your hand."

I believe that we can also do far better than we have in reducing violence in our society, and withdrawing our tacit silent, and thereby complicit support for it. When right-wingers engage in this sort of "male-bashing"—asserting that men are no better than testosterone-crazed violent louts (and that therefore women must leave the workplace and return home to better constrain us)—most men know these slurs to be false. But they are false with a ring of truth to them. For as long as men remain in their postures of either silent complicity or defensive denial, one might very well get the idea that we do condone men's violence. "All violent feelings," wrote the nineteenth-century British social critic John Ruskin, "produce in us a falseness in all our impressions of external things." Until we transform the meaning of masculinity, we will continue to produce that falseness—with continued tragic consequences.

A DEGENDERED SOCIETY?

The principle which regulates the existing social relations between the two sexes—the legal subordination of one sex to the other—is wrong in itself, and now one of the chief hindrances to human improvement; and . . . it ought to be replaced by a principle of perfect equality, admitting no power or privilege on the one side, nor disability on the other.

—JOHN STUART MILL
THE SUBJECTION OF WOMEN (1869)

We sit perched at the beginning of a new millennium, looking over into an uncharted expanse of the future. What kind of society do we want to live in? What will be the gender arrangements of that society?

To see gender differences as intransigent leads also to a political resignation about the possibilities of social change and increased gender equality. Those who proclaim that men and women come from different planets would have you believe that the best we can hope for is a sort of interplanetary détente, an uneasy truce in which we exasperatingly accept the inherent and intractable foibles of the other sex, a truce mediated by ever-wealthier psychological interpreters who can try and decode their impenetrable language.

I think the evidence is clear that women and men are far more alike than we are different, and that we need far fewer cosmic interpreters and far more gender equality to enable both women and men to live the lives we want to live. The future of gender differences is intimately tied to the future of gender inequality. As gender inequality is reduced, the differences between women and men will shrink.

And besides, the interplanetary model of gender differences entirely ignores the historical record. For the past century, we have steadily moved to lessen gender inequality—by removing barriers to women's entry into all arenas of the public sphere, protecting women who have been victimized by men's violent efforts to delay, retard, or resist that entry. And as we have done so, we have found that women can perform admirably in arenas once believed to be only suitable for men, and that men can perform admirably in arenas once held to be exclusively women's domain. Don't believe me; ask those women surgeons, lawyers, and pilots. And ask those male nurses, teachers, and social workers, as well as all those single fathers, if they are capable of caring for their children.

In this book, I've made several arguments about our gendered society. I've argued that women and men are more alike than we are different, that we're not at all from different planets. I've argued that it is gender inequality that produces the differences we do observe, and that also produces the cultural impulse to search for such differences, even when there is little or no basis for them in reality. I've also argued that gender is not a property of individuals that is accomplished by socialization, but a set of relationships produced in our social interactions with one another and within gendered institutions, whose formal organizational dynamics reproduce gender inequality and produce gender differences.

I've also pointed to evidence of a significant gender convergence taking place over the past half-century. Whether we looked at sexual behavior, friendship dynamics, efforts to balance work and family life, or women's and men's experiences and aspirations in education or the workplace, we find the gender gap growing ever smaller. (The lone exception to this process, as we saw in the last chapter, is violence.)

To celebrate this gender convergence in behavior and attitudes is not to advocate degendering people. It's not a plea for androgyny. Some psychologists have proposed androgyny as a solution to gender inequality and gender differences. It implies a flattening of gender differences, so that women and men will think, act, and behave in some more "neutralized" gender nonspecific ways. "Masculinity" and "femininity" will be seen as archaic constructs as everyone becomes increasingly "human."

Such proposals take a leap beyond the ultimately defeatist claims of immutable difference offered by the intergalactic theorists. After all, proponents of androgyny at least recognize gender differences as socially constructed and that change is possible.

But androgyny remains unpopular as a political or psychological option because it would eliminate differences between people, mistaking equality for sameness. To many of us, the idea of sameness feels coercive, a dilution of difference into a bland, tasteless amalgam in which individuals would lose their distinctiveness. It's like Hollywood's vision of communism as a leveling of all class distinctions into a colorless, amorphous mass in which everyone would look, act, and dress the same—as in those advertisements that feature poorly but identically dressed Russians. Androgyny often feels like it would enforce life on a flat, and ultimately barren degendered landscape. Is the only way for women and men to be equal to become the same? Can we not imagine a vision of equality based on respect for and embracing of difference?

Fears about androgyny confuse gendered people with gendered traits. It's not that women and men need to be more like each other than we already are but that all the psychological traits and attitudes and behaviors that we, as a culture, label as "masculine" or "feminine" need to be redefined. These traits and attitudes, after all, also carry positive and negative values, and it is through this hierarchy, this unequal weighting, that gender inequality becomes so deeply entwined with gender difference. To degender people does not by itself eliminate gender inequality.

In fact, calls for androgyny paradoxically reify the very gender distinctions that they seek to eliminate. Advocates frequently urge men to express more of their "feminine" sides; women, to express more of their "masculine" sides. Such exhortations, frankly, leave me deeply insulted.

Let me give you an example. As I was sitting in my neighborhood park a couple of years ago with my newborn son in my arms, a passerby commented, "How wonderful it is to see men these days expressing their feminine sides." I growled, underneath my conspicuously false smile. While I tried to be pleasant, what I wanted to say was this: "I'm not expressing anything of the sort, ma'am. I'm being tender, and loving and nurturing toward my child. As far as I can tell, I'm expressing my *masculinity!*"

Why, after all, are love, nurturing, and tenderness defined as feminine? Why do I have to be expressing the affect of the other sex in order to have access to what I regard as human emotions? Being a man, everything I do expresses my masculinity. And I'm sure my wife would be no less insulted if, after editing a particularly difficult article, or writing a long, involved essay, she were told how extraordinary and wonderful it is to see women expressing their masculine sides—as if competence, ambition, and assertiveness were not human properties to which women *and* men could equally have access.

Love, tenderness, nurturing; competence, ambition, assertion—these are *human* qualities, and all human beings—both women and men—should have equal access to them. And when we do express them, we are expressing, respectively, our gender identities, not the gender of the other. What a strange notion indeed, that such emotions should be labeled as masculine or feminine, when they are so deeply human, and when both women and men are so easily capable of so much fuller a range of feelings.

Strange, and also a little sad. "Perhaps nothing is so depressing an index of the inhumanity of the male supremacist mentality as the fact that the more genial human traits are assigned to the underclass: affection, response to sympathy, kindness, cheerfulness," was the way feminist writer Kate Millett put it in her landmark book, *Sexual Politics,* first published in 1969.[1]

So much has changed since then. The gendered world that I inhabit is totally unlike that of my parents. My father could have gone to an all-male college, served in an all-male military, and spent his entire working life in an all-male work environment. Today that world is but a memory. Women have entered every workplace, the military and its training academies (both federal and state supported), and all but three or four colleges today admit women. Despite persistent efforts from some political quarters to turn back the clock to the mid-nineteenth century, those changes are permanent; women will not go back to the home where some people think they belong.

These enormous changes will only accelerate in the next few decades. The society of the third millennium will increasingly degender traits and behaviors without degendering people. We will still be women and men, equal yet capable of appreciating our differences, different yet unwilling to use those differences as the basis for discrimination.

Imagine how quickly the pace of that change might accelerate if we continue to degender traits, not people. What if little boys and girls saw their mothers and their fathers go off to work in the morning, with no compromise to their masculinity or femininity. Those little boys and girls would grow up thinking that having a job—being competent, earning a living, striving to get ahead—was something that *grownups* did, regardless of whether they were male or female grownups. Not something that men did, and women did only with guilt, social approbation, and sporadically and irregularly depending on their fertility. "And when I grow up," those children would say, "I'm going to have a job also."

And when both mothers and fathers are equally loving and caring and nurturing toward their children, when nurture is something that *grownups* do—and not something that mothers do routinely and men do only during halftime on Saturday afternoon—then those same children will say to themselves, "And when I get to be a grownup, I'm going to be loving and caring toward my children."

Such a process may sound naively optimistic, but the signs of change are everywhere around us. In fact, the historical evidence points exactly in that direction. It was through the dogged insistence of that nineteenth-century ideology, the separation of spheres, that two distinct realms for men and women were imposed, with two separate sets of traits and behaviors that accompany each sphere. This was the historical aberration, the anomaly—its departure from what had preceded it and from the "natural" propensity of human beings goes a long way in explaining the vehemence with which it was imposed. Nothing so natural or biologically determined has to be so coercive.

The twentieth century witnessed the challenge to separate spheres, undertaken, in large part, by those who were demoted by its ideological ruthlessness—women. That century witnessed an unprecedented upheaval in the status of women, possibly the most significant transformation in gender relations in world history. From the rights to vote and work, asserted early in the century, to the rights to enter every conceivable workplace, educational institution, and the military, in the latter half, women have shaken the foundations of the gendered society. And they were left at the end of the century having accomplished half a revolution—a transformation of their opportunities to be workers and mothers.

This half-finished revolution has left many women frustrated and unhappy. For some reason, they remain unable to "have it all"—to be good mothers and also to be effective and ambitious workers. With astonishing illogic, some pundits explain women's frustrations as stemming not from the continued resistance of men, the intransigence of male-dominated institutions to accept them, or the indifference of politicians to enact policies that would enable these women to balance their work and family lives, but rather to the effort of women to expand their opportunities and to claim a full share of humanity. It is a constant source of amazement how many women have full-time jobs exhorting women not to take full-time jobs.

The second half of the transformation of gender is just beginning, and will be, I suspect, far more difficult to accomplish than the first. That's because there was an intuitively obvious ethical imperative attached to enlarging the opportunities for and eliminating discrimination against women. But the transformation of the twenty-first century involves the transformation of men's lives.

Men are just beginning to realize that the "traditional" definition of masculinity leaves them unfulfilled and dissatisfied. While women have left the home, from which they were "imprisoned" by the ideology of separate spheres, and now seek to balance work and family lives, men continue to search for a way back into the family, from which they were exiled by the same ideology. Some men express their frustration and confusion by hoping and praying for a return to the old gender regime, the very separation of spheres that made both women *and* men unhappy. Others join various men's movements, such as PromiseKeepers, the Million Man March, or troop off to a mythopoetic men's retreat in search of a more resonant, spiritually fulfilling definition of masculinity.

The nineteenth-century ideology of separate spheres justified gender inequality based on putative natural differences between the sexes. What was normative—enforced by sanction—was asserted to be normal, as part of the nature of things. Women have spent the better part of a century making clear that such an ideology did violence to their experiences, effacing the work outside the home that women actually performed, and enforcing a definition of femininity that allowed only partial expression of their humanity.

It did the same for men, of course—valorizing some emotions and experiences, discrediting others. As with women, it left men with only partially fulfilled lives. Only recently, though, have men begun to chafe at the restrictions that such an ideology placed on their humanity.

At the turn of the twenty-first century, it might be wise to recall the words of a writer at the turn of the twentieth century. In a remarkable essay written in 1917, the New York City writer Floyd Dell spelled out the consequences of separate spheres for both women and men.

> When you have got a woman in a box, and you pay rent on the box, her relationship to you insensibly changes character. It loses the fine excitement of democracy. It ceases to be a companionship, for companionship is only possible in a democracy. It is no longer a sharing of life together—it is a breaking of life apart. Half a life—cooking, clothes and children; half a life—business, politics and baseball. It doesn't make much difference which is the poorer half. Any half, when it comes to life, is very near to none at all.

Like feminist women, Dell understands that these separate spheres that impoverish the lives of both women and men are also built upon gender inequality. (Notice how he addresses his remarks to men who "have got a woman in a box.") Gender inequality produced the ideology of separate spheres, and the ideology of separate spheres, in turn, lent legitimacy to gender inequality. Thus, Dell argues in the opening sentence of his essay that "feminism will make it possible for the first time for men to be free."[2]

The direction of the gendered society in the new century and the new millennium is not for women and men to become increasingly *similar,* but for them to become more *equal.* For those traits and behaviors heretofore labeled as masculine and feminine—competence and compassion, ambition and affection—to be accepted as distinctly human qualities, accessible to both women and men who are grown-up enough to claim them. It suggests a form of gender proteanism—a temperamental and psychological flexibility, the ability to adapt to one's environment with a full range of emotions and abilities. The protean self, articulated by psychiatrist Robert Jay Lifton, is a self that can embrace difference, contradiction, and complexity, a self that is mutable and flexible in a rapidly changing world.[3] Such a transformation does not require that men and women become more like each other, but, rather, more deeply and fully themselves.

Personally, I'm optimistic. Not long ago, I was playing a game with my then three-year-old son Zachary, which we call "opposites." You know the game: I say a word, and he tells me the opposite. It's simple and fun, and we have a great time playing it. One evening, my mother was visiting, and the three of us were walking in our neighborhood park playing Opposites. Scratchy/smooth, tall/short, high/low, fast/slow—you get the idea. Then my mother asked, "Zachary, what's the opposite of boy?"

My whole body tensed. Here it comes, I thought, Mars and Venus, gender binary opposition, all the things I argue against in this book.

Zachary looked up at his grandmother and said, "Man."

Here, at last, on Planet Earth, there's one small voice that knows we're not from Mars and Venus, after all. And, as he ages, he'll also learn that the differences we see are created by the inequalities we have inherited.

NOTES

NOTES TO CHAPTER 1

1. John Gray, *Men Are from Mars, Women Are from Venus* (New York: HarperCollins, 1992), 5.
2. *J.E.B. v. Alabama,* 114 S Ct., 1436, (1994).
3. Barbara Risman, *Gender Vertigo* (New Haven: Yale University Press, 1998), 25. See also Judith Lorber, *Paradoxes of Gender* (New Haven: Yale University Press, 1994).
4. Catharine Stimpson, *Where the Meanings Are* (New York: Methuen, 1988).
5. See Michael Kimmel, *Manhood in America: A Cultural History* (New York: The Free Press, 1996).
6. I also tell this story in *Manhood in America.*
7. Torri Minton, "Search for What It Means to Be White," *San Francisco Chronicle,* May 8, 1998.
8. Simmel is cited in Lewis Coser, "Georg Simmel's Neglected Contributions to the Sociology of Women," *Signs* 2, no. 4 (1977):872.
9. Cited in Coser, 872.
10. Cited in James Brooke, "Men Held in Beatings Lived on the Fringes," *New York Times,* October 16, 1998, A16. Valerie Jenness, the sociologist who was quoted in the story, told me that she was misquoted, and that of course she had mentioned gender as well as age—which suggests that the media's myopia matches that of the larger society.
11. Virginia Woolf, *Three Guineas* [1938] (New York: Harcourt, 1966), 142.
12. R. W. Connell, *Gender and Power* (Stanford: Stanford University Press, 1987), 183; Erving Goffman, *Stigma* (Englewood Cliffs, NJ: Prentice-Hall, 1963), 128.
13. Connell, *Gender and Power,* 183, 188, 187.
14. Cited in Risman, *Gender Vertigo,* 141.
15. Carol Tavris, "The Mismeasure of Woman," *Feminism and Psychology* (1993):153.
16. Cynthia Fuchs Epstein, *Deceptive Distinctions* (New Haven: Yale University Press, 1988).
17. Deborah Tannen, *You Just Don't Understand* (New York: William Morrow, 1991).
18. William O'Barr and Jean F. O'Barr, *Linguistic Evidence: Language, Power and Strategy—The Courtroom* (San Diego: Academic Press, 1995); see also Alfie Kohn, "Girl Talk, Guy Talk," *Psychology Today,* February 1988, 66.
19. Alex Witchel, "Our Finances, Ourselves," *New York Times,* June 4, 1998, 13.
20. Ibid.
21. Rosabeth M. Kanter, *Men and Women of the Corporation* (New York: Harper and Row, 1977).
22. Kathleen Gerson, *Hard Choices* (Berkeley: University of California Press, 1985); *No Man's Land* (New York: Basic Books, 1993).
23. Risman, *Gender Vertigo,* 70:
24. David Almeida and Ronald Kessler, "Everyday Stressors and Gender Differences in Daily Distress," *Journal of Personality and Social Psychology* 75, no. 3 (1998).
25. See Nancy Stedman, "In a Bad Mood—for a Good Reason," *New York Times,* October 24, 1998, for an example of a journalist who actually understood the story.

26. Risman, *Gender Vertigo,* 21.
27. Gayle Rubin, "The Traffic in Women," in *Toward an Anthropology of Women,* ed. R. R. Reiter, 179–80. (New York: Monthly Review Press, 1975).
28. Catharine MacKinnon, *Towards a Feminist Theory of the State* (Cambridge: Harvard University Press, 1989), 218–19.
29. Michael Kimmel, Diane Diamond, and Kirby Schroeder, "'What's This About a Few Good Men?' Negotiating Sameness and Difference in Military Education from the 1970s to the Present," in *Masculinities and Education,* ed. N. Lesko (Thousand Oaks, CA: Sage Publications, 1999).

Notes to Chapter 2

1. Jerre Levy, cited in Jo Durden-Smith and Diane deSimone, *Sex and the Brain* (New York: Warner Books, 1983), 61.
2. Rev. John Todd, *Woman's Rights* (Boston: Lee and Shepard, 1867), 26.
3. Barbara Ehrenreich and Dierdre English, *For Her Own Good: 150 Years of the Experts' Advice to Women* (New York: Doubleday, 1979), 111.
4. Cited in Carl Degler, *In Search of Human Nature: The Decline and Revival of Darwinism in American Social Thought* (New York: Oxford University Press, 1991), 107.
5. Todd, *Woman's Rights,* 25.
6. California State Historical Society Library, San Francisco, ms. #2334. For a summary of the way biological arguments were used to exclude women from public participation, see Michael Kimmel, "Introduction," in *Against the Tide: Pro-Feminist Men in the United States, 1776–1990, a Documentary History,* ed. M. Kimmel and T. Mosmiller (Boston: Beacon, 1992).
7. Cited in Stephen Jay Gould, *The Mismeasure of Man* (New York: W. W. Norton, 1981), 104–105.
8. Edward C. Clarke, *Sex in Education; or, A Fair Chance for the Girls* (Boston: Osgood and Co., 1873), 152.
9. See Cynthia Eagle Russet, *Sexual Science: The Victorian Construction of Womanhood* (Cambridge: Harvard University Press, 1989).
10. There are several important texts that provide good ripostes to the biological arguments. Among them are Ruth Bleir, ed., *Feminist Approaches to Science* (New York: Pergamon, 1986); Lynda Birke, *Women, Feminism, and Biology: The Feminist Challenge* (New York: Methuen, 1986). Anne Fausto-Sterling's *Myths of Gender: Biological Theories About Women and Men* (New York: Basic Books, 1985) is indispensible. Deborah Blum, *Sex on the Brain: The Biological Differences Between Men and Women* (New York: Viking, 1997) provides a good summary. Robert Nadeau, *S/He Brain: Science, Sexual Politics, and the Myths of Feminism* (New York: Praeger, 1996) illustrates the conservative and antifeminist uses to which this research can so effortlessly be put.
11. Richard Dawkins, *The Selfish Gene* (New York: Oxford University Press, 1976), 152; Edward O. Wilson, *On Human Nature* (Cambridge: Harvard University Press, 1978), 167.
12. Anthony Layng, "Why We Don't Act Like the Opposite Sex?" *USA Today,* January 1993; Donald Symons, "Darwinism and Contemporary Marriage," in *Contemporary Marriage: Comparative Perspectives on a Changing Institution,* ed. Kingley Davis (New York: Russell Sage Foundation, 1985), cited in Carl Degler, "Darwinians Confront Gender; or, There Is More to It Than History," in *Theoretical Perspectives on Sexual Difference,* ed. D. Rhode (New Haven: Yale University Press, 1990), 39.
13. Edward Wilson, *Sociobiology: The New Synthesis* (Cambridge: Harvard University Press, 1974).

14. Lionel Tiger, "Male Dominance?" *The New York Times Magazine,* October 25, 1970.

15. See, for example, Judy Stamps "Sociobiology: Its Evolution and Intellectual Descendents" *Politics and Life Science,* 14(2) 1995.

16. David Barash, *The Whisperings Within* (New York: Harper and Row, 1979), 54; see also W. M. Shields and L. M. Shields, "Forcible Rape: An Evolutionary Perspective," *Ethology and Sociobiology* 4(1983):119.

17. Randy Thornhill and Craig T. Palmer, "Why Men Rape," *The Sciences,* January 2000, 30.

18. Thornhill and Palmer, *A Natural History of Rape* (Cambridge: MIT Press, 2000), 53.

19. Richard Alexander and K. M. Noonan, "Concealment of Ovulation, Parental Care, and Human Social Evolution," in *Evolutionary Biology and Human Social Behavior,* ed. N. Chagnon and W. Irons (North Scituate, MA: Duxbury, 1979), 449.

20. Richard Lewontin, "Biological Determinism as a Social Weapon," in *Biology as a Social Weapon,* ed. the Ann Arbor Science for the People Editorial Collective (Minneapolis: Burgess, 1977), 15; Stephen Jay Gould, *Ever Since Darwin: Reflections in Natural History* (New York. W. W. Norton, 1977), 254.

21. Carol Tavris and Carole Wade, *The Longest War* (New York: Harcourt Brace, 1984).

22. Mary McDonald Pavelka, "Sexual Nature: What Can We Learn from a Cross-Species Perspective?" in *Sexual Nature, Sexual Culture* ed. Abrahamson and S. Pinkerton (Chicago: University of Chicago Press, 1995), 22.

23. Lloyd DeMause, "Our Forbears Made Childhood a Nightmare," *Psychology Today,* April 1975.

24. Randy Thornhill and Craig T. Palmer, "Why Men Rape," *The Sciences,* January 2000, 32, 34; see also Thornhill and Palmer, *A Natural History of Rape.* See also my critique of their book, "An Unnatural History of Rape," in *Evolution, Gender, and Rape,* ed. Cheryl Travis (Cambridge: MIT Press, 2003). Even other evolutionary psychologists have dismissed Thornhill and Palmer's apologetics. See Michael Gard and Benjamin Bradley, "Getting away with Rape," *Psychology, Evolution and Gender* 2, no. 3 (December 2000):313–319.

25. I. Singer and J. Singer, "Periodicity of Sexual Desire in Relation to Time of Ovulation in Women," *Journal of Biosocial Science* 4 (1972):471–81; see also Elisabeth A. Lloyd, "Pre-Theoretical Assumptions in Evolutionary Explanations of Female Sexuality," in *Feminism and Science,* ed. E. F. Keller and H. E. Longino (New York: Oxford University Press, 1996).

26. N. Burley, "The Evolution of Concealed Ovulation," *The American Naturalist* 114 (1979); Mary McDonald Pavelka, "Sexual Nature," 19. See also Sarah Blaffer Hrdy, *The Woman That Never Evolved* (Cambridge: Harvard University Press, 1981).

27. Stephen Beckerman, R. Lizzarralde, C. Ballew, S. Schroeder, C. Fingelton, A. Garrison, and H. Smith, "The Bari Partible Paternity Project: Preliminary Results," *Current Anthropology* 39, no. 1 (1998):164–67.

28. Steven Gangestad, Randy Thornhill, and Christine Garver, "Changes in Women's Sexual Interests and Their Partners' Mate-Retention Tactics Across the Menstrual Cycle: Evidence for Shifting Conflicts of Interest," in *Proceedings of the Royal Society,* 2002. Not surprisingly, Gangestad repudiated the journalist's interpretation, since it's pretty much the mirror image of his argument that it is more in males' interest to be promiscuous, and in females' interest to be monogamous. Personal communication, 12/16/02.

29. See Evelyn Fox Keller, *A Feeling for the Organism: The Life and Work of Barbara McClintock* (San Francisco: W. H. Freeman, 1983).

30. See Natalie Angier, "Men, Women, Sex, and Darwin," *New York Times,* February 21, 1999; see also her *Women: An Intimate Geography* (Boston: Houghton Mifflin, 1999).

31. Paul Ehrlich, *Human Natures: Genes, Cultures, and the Human Prospect* (New York: Penguin, 2002).

32. Emile Durkheim, *The Division of Labor in Society* [1893] (New York: The Free Press, 1984), 21; see also Ehrenreich and English, *For Her Own Good,* 117. Of course, Durkheim's asser-

tion of the progressive historical divergence could be due not to evolution but to women's increased confinement and restriction.

33. James C. Dobson, *Straight Talk to Men and Their Wives* (Dallas: Word Publishing Co., 1991), 177; Adam Begley, "Why Men and Women Think Differently," *Newsweek,* May 12, 1995, 51.

34. See Elizabeth Fee, "Nineteenth Century Craniology: The Study of the Female Skull," *Bulletin of the History of Medicine* 53 (1979).

35. Turner is cited in *South Side Observer,* April 29, 1896; C. A. Dwyer, "The Role of Tests and their Construction in Producing Apparent Sex-related Differences," in *Sex-Related Differences in Cognitive Functioning,* ed. M. Wittig and A. Peterson, 342 (New York: Academic Press, 1979).

36. Doreen Kimura's summary of these brain differences, *Sex and Cognition* (Cambridge: The MIT Press, 1999), catalogs a large variety of brain differences in spatial, verbal, and other forms of reasoning. She feels comfortable stating that "we can say with certainty that there are substantial stable sex differences in cognitive functions like spatial rotation ability, mathematical reasoning, and verbal memory; and in motor skills requiring accurate targeting and finger dexterity" (181). Since she never tells the reader about the shape of the distribution of these traits, we have no idea whether such differences actually mean anything at all, if they are categorical, or if the distribution is larger among women and among men than it is between women and men—which is the case in virtually every one of these studies. Such is typically the case when authors argue from ideology rather than evidence. A better source is Lesley Rogers, *Sexing the Brain* (New York: Columbia University Press, 2001), which is, at least intellectually honest and does not conceal or obscure conflicting information.

37. Norman Geschwind, cited in Durden-Smith and deSimone, *Sex and the Brain,* 171. Other influential studies on horomone research include G. W. Harris, "Sex Hormones, Brain Development and Brain Function," *Endocrinology* 75 (1965).

38. Ruth Bleier, *Science and Gender: A Critique of Biology and Its Theory on Women* (New York: Pantheon, 1984).

39. A. W. H. Buffery and J. Gray, "Sex Differences in the Development of Spacial and Linguistic Skills," in *Gender Differences: Their Ontogeny and Significance,* ed. C. Ounsted and D. C. Taylor (London: Churchill Livingston, 1972); Jerre Levy, "Lateral Specialization of the Human Brain: Behavioral Manifestation and Possible Evolutionary Basis," in *The Biology of Behavior,* ed. J. A. Kiger (Corvallis, Eugene: University of Oregon Press, 1972); see also Anne Fausto-Sterling, *Myths of Gender: Biological Theories About Womern and Men* (New York: Basic Books, 1986), 40.

40. Jean Christophe Labarthe, "Are Boys Better Than Girls at Building a Tower or a Bridge at 2 Years of Age," *Archives of Disease in Childhood* 77 (1997):140–44.

41. Joseph Lurito. See also Robert Lee Hotz, "Women Use More of Brain When Listening, Study Says," *The Los Angeles Times,* November 29, 2000.

42. Durden-Smith and deSimone, *Sex and the Brain,* p. 60.

43. Levy, "Lateral Specialization."

44. Janet Hyde, "How Large Are Cognitive Differences? A Metanalysis," *American Psychologist* 26 (1981); Janet Hyde, Elizabeth Fennema, and S. J. Laman, "Gender Differences in Mathematics Performance: A Meta-Analysis," *Psychlogical Bulletin* 107 (1990).

45. Michael Peters, "The Size of the Corpus Callosum in Males and Females: Implications of a Lack of Allometry," *Canadian Journal of Psychology* 42, no. 3 (1988); Christine de Lacoste-Utamsing and Ralph Holloway, "Sexual Dimorphism in the Human Corpus Callosum," *Science,* June 25, 1982; but also see William Byne, Ruth Bleier, and Lanning Houston, "Variations in Human Corpus Callosum Do Not Predict Gender: A Study Using Magnetic Resonance Imaging," *Behavioral Neuroscience* 102, no. 2 (1988).

46. See Michael Gurian, *The Wonder of Girls* (New York: Pocket Books, 2002); see also Caryl Rivers, "Pop Science Book Claims Girls Hardwired for Love," *Women's E-News,* June 29, 2002.
47. Cited in Le Anne Schreiber, "The Search for His and Her Brains," *Glamour,* April 1993; Kimura, cited in Rivers, "Pop Science Book."
48. Marcel Kinsbourne, "The Developmen of Lateralization," in *Biological and Neurological Mechanisms,* ed. H. W. Reese and M. D. Franzen (Mahwah, NJ: Erlbaum, 1996).
49. Several books are useful summaries of this research, including Dean Hamer and Peter Copeland, *The Science of Desire* (New York: Simon and Schuster, 1994); Simon LeVay, *Queer Science: The Use and Abuse of Research into Homosexuality* (Cambridge: MIT Press, 1996); Lee Ellis and Linda Ebertz, eds., *Sexual Orientation: Toward Biological Understanding* (New York: Pareger, 1997). Several other works provide valuable rejoinders to the scientific research; see, for example, Vernon Rosario, ed., *Science and Homosexualities* (New York: Routledge, 1997); Timothy Murphy, *Gay Science: The Ethics of Sexual Orientation Research* (New York: Columbia University Press, 1997); John Corvino, ed., *Same Sex: Debating the Ethics, Science, and Culture of Homosexuality* (Lanham: Rowman and Littlefield, 1997). A double issue of *Journal of Homosexuality* 28, nos. 1–2 (1995) was devoted to this theme. For a strong dissenting opinion, see William Byne, "Why We Cannot Conclude That Sexual Orientation Is Primarily a Biological Phenomenon," *Journal of Homosexuality* 34, no. 1 (1997); William Byne, "Science and Belief: Psychobiological Research on Sexual Orientation," *Journal of Homosexuality* 28, no. 2 (1995).
50. Michel Foucault, *The History of Sexuality* (New York: Pantheon, 1978). See also Jonathan Ned Katz, *The Invention of Heterosexuality* (New York: E. Dutton, 1993).
51. Gunter Dorner, W. Rohde, F. Stahl, L. Krell, and W. Masius, "A Neuroendocrine Predisposition for Homosexuality in Men," *Archives of Sexual Behavior* 4, no. 1 (1975):6.
52. Simon LeVay, "The 'Gay Brain' Revisited," at nerve.com (2000); Simon LeVay, "A Difference in Hyopthalamic Structure Between Homosexual and Heterosexual Men," *Science,* 253 (30 August 1991); Simon LeVay,*The Sexual Brain* (Cambridge: M.I.T Press, 1994); Simon LeVay and Dean Hamer, "Evidence for a Biological Influence in Male Homosexuality," *Scientific American* 270 (1994). See also "Born or Bred?" *Newsweek,* February 24, 1992.
53. P. Yahr, "Sexually Dimorphic Hypothalamic Cell Groups and a Related Pathway That Are Essential for Masculine Copulatory Behavior," in *The Development of Sex Differences and Similarities in Behavior,* ed. M. Haug, R. Whalen, C. Aron, and K. Olsen, 416 (Dordrecht: Kluwer Academic Publishers. 1993).
54. See *Chronicle of Higher Education,* 10 November 1995.
55. See, for example, Dennis McFadden and Edward G. Pasanen, "Comparison of the Auditory Systems of Heterosexual and Homosexuals: Click-evoked Otoacoustic Emissions," *Proceedings of the National Academy of Sciences* 95, March 1998, 2709–13; and McFadden and Pasanen, "Spontaneous Otoacoustic Emissions in Heterosexuals, Homosexuals, and Bisexuals," *Journal of the Acoustical Society of America* 105, no. 4 (April 1999):2403–13; and Dennis McFadden and Craig Champlin, "Comparison of Auditory Evoked Potentials in Heterosexual, Homosexual, and Bisexual Males and Females," *Journal of the Association for Research in Otolaryngology* 1 (2000):89–99.
56. Marc Breedlove in Pat McBroom, "Sexual Experience May Affect Brain Structure," at http://www.berkeley.edu/news/berkeleyan/1997/1119/sexexp.html; see also Jim McKnight, "Editorial: The Origins of Male Homosexuality," *Psychology, Evolution and Gender* 2, no. 3 (December 2000):226.
57. See F. Kallmann, "Comparative Twin Study on the Genetic Aspects of Male Homosexuality," *Journal of Nervous Mental Disorders* 115 (1952):283–98. Kallman's findings may have been an artefact of his sample, which was drawn entirely from institutionalized mentally ill

patients—some of whom had been institutionalized because they were gay. See also Richard Lewontin, Steven Rose, and Leon Kamin, *Not in Our Genes: Biology, Ideology, and Human Nature* (New York: Pantheon, 1984).

58. J. Michael Bailey and Richard Pillard, "A Genetic Study of Male Sexual Orientation," *Archives of General Psychiatry* 48 (December 1991); J. Michael Bailey and Richard Pillard, "Heritable Factors Influence Sexual Orientation in Women," *Archives of General Psychiatry* 50 (March 1993).

59. This is equally a problem in Frederick Whitam, Milton Diamond, and James Martin, "Homosexual Orientation in Twins: A Report on 61 Pairs and Three Triplet Sets," *Archives of Sexual Behavior* 22, no. 3 (1993).

60. Richard Pillard and James Weinreich, "Evidence of a Familial Nature of Male Homosexuality," *Archives of General Psychiatry* 43 (1986).

61. See Peter Bearman and Hannah Bruckner, "Opposite Sex Twins and Adolescent Same-Sex Attraction," *American Journal of Sociology* (March 2002).

62. Steven Goldberg, *The Inevitability of Patriarchy* (New York: Simon and Schuster, 1973), 93.

63. See James McBride Dabbs (with Mary Godwin Dabbs), *Heroes, Rogues, and Lovers: Testosterone and Behavior* (New York: McGraw Hill, 2000), 8; Andrew Sullivan, "The He Hormone," *The New York Times Magazine,* April 2, 2000, 48. Dabbs rampages through the literature about testosterone, claiming to be able to predict (cause and effect) behaviors ranging from rape to fraternity keg parties, from choice of occupation to likelihood to commit crimes, simply by the level of testosterone. About the only statement that that Dabbs makes that is less than completely hyperbolic is that "[s]ometimes male bluster is hardwired into the brain by early testosterone" (66). Well, at least some people's bluster may be.

64. There is some evidence that AndroGel is dangerous and should not be taken without significant testing. Testosterone may shrink the testes (since they no longer need to produce it), but also may exacerbate prostate cancer, acting like food to a growing tumor. See Jerome Groopman, "Hormones for Men," *The New Yorker,* July 29, 2002, 34–38.

65. Robert Sapolsky, *The Trouble with Testosterone* (New York: Simon and Schuster, 1997), 155.

66. Theodore Kemper, *Testosterone and Social Structure* (New Brunswick: Rutgers University Press, 1990). Arthur Kling, "Testosterone and Aggressive Behavior in Man and Non-human Primates," in *Hormonal Correlates of Behavior,* ed. B. Eleftheriou and R. Sprott (New York: Plenum, 1975); see also E. Gonzalez-Bono, A Salvador, J. Ricarte, M. A. Serrano, and M. Arendo, "Testosterone and Attribution of Successful Competition," *Aggressive Behavior* 26, no. 3 (2000):235–40.

67. Anu Aromaki, Ralf Lindman, and C. J. Peter Eriksson, "Testosterone, Aggressiveness, and Antisocial Personality," *Aggressive Behavior* 25 (1999):113–23; Sapolsky, cited in Richard Lacayo, "Are You Man Enough?" *Time,* April, 24, 2000.

68. Peter B. Gray, Sonya Kahlenberg, Emily Barrett, Susan Lipson, and Peter T. Ellison, "Marriage and Fatherhood Are Associated with Lower Testosterone in Males," *Evolution and Human Behavior* 23 (2002):193–201; see also the coverage of this study, William Cromie, "Marriage Lowers Testosterone," *The Harvard Gazette,* September 19, 2002; Ellen Barry, "The Ups and Downs of Manhood," *The Boston Globe,* July 9, 2002.

69. See, for example, Jed Diamond, *Male Menopause* (Napierville, IL: Sourcebooks, 1998); and Groopman, "Hormones for Men."

70. John Money and Anke Ehrhardt, *Man and Woman, Boy and Girl* (Baltimore: The Johns Hopkins University Press, 1972).

71. Anke Ehrhardt and S. W. Baker, "Fetal Androgens, Human Central Nervous System Differentiation, and Behavior Sex Differences," in *Sex Differences in Behavior,* ed. R. Friedman, R. M. Richart, and R. L. Vande Wiele, 49 (Huntington: Krieger, 1978).

72. Fausto-Sterling, *Myths of Gender,* 136–37.

73. Irvin Yalom, Richard Green, and N. Fisk. "Prenatal Exposure to Female Hormones—Effect on Psychosexual Development in Boys," *Archives of General Psychiatry* 28 (1973).

74. Gloria Steinem, "If Men Could Menstruate," in *Outrageous Acts and Everyday Rebellions* (New York: Holt, Rinehart and Winston, 1983).

75. Durden-Smith and deSimone, *Sex and the Brain,* 92.

76. Gunter Dorner, B. Schenk, B. Schmiedel, and L. Ahrens, "Stressful Events in Prenatal Life of Bisexual and Homosexual Men," *Explorations in Clinical Endocrinology* 81 (1983):87. See also Dorner, et al., "Prenatal Stress as a Possible Paetiogenic Factor of Homosexuality in Human Males," *Endokrinologie* 75(1983); and G. Dorner, F. Gotz, T. Ohkawa, W. Rohde, F. Stahl, and R. Tonjes, "Prenatal Stress and Sexual Brain Differentiation in Animal and Human Beings," *Abstracts,* International Academy of Sex Research, 13th Annual Meeting, Tutzing: June 21–25, 1987.

77. The other side is presented in a clever article by Gunter Schmidt and Ulrich Clement, "Does Peace Prevent Homosexuality?" *Journal of Homosexuality* 28, no. 1–2 (1995).

78. Terrance Williams, Michelle Pepitone, Scott Christensen, Bradley Cooke, Andrew Huberman, Nicolas Breedlove, Tess Breedlove, Cynthia Jordan, and S. Marc Breedlove, "Finger Length Ratios and Sexual Orientation," *Nature* 404, March 30, 2000, 455; see also S. J. Robinson, "The Ratio of 2nd to 4th Digit Length and Male Homosexuality," *Evolution and Human Behavior* 21 (2000):333–45. Also see Tim Beneke, "Sex on the Brain," *The East Bay Express,* September 22, 2000, for a superb profile of Breedlove and his research.

79. Marc Breedlove, personal communication with the author, February 13, 2001; see also Susan Rubinowitz, "Report: Index Finger Size May Indicate Homosexuality," *The New York Post,* March 30, 2000.

80. See Alice Domurat Dreger, *Hermaphrodites and the Medical Invention of Sex* (Cambridge: Harvard University Press, 1998); Gert Hekma, "'A Female Soul in a Male Body': Sexual Inversion as Gender Inversion in Nineteenth Century Sexology," in *Third Sex, Third Gender,* ed. Gilbert Herdt (Cambridge: The MIT Press, 1993).

81. See Julliane Imperato-McGinley et al., "Steroid 5-alpha Reductase Deficiency in Man: An Inherited Form of Pseudohermaphroditism," *Science* 186 (1974); Julliane Imperato-McGinley et al., "Androgens and the Evolution of Male-Gender Identity Among Male Pseudohermaphrodites with 5-alpha Reductase Deficiency," *New England Journal of Medicine* 300 (1979):1235. For an excellent summary of the research, see Gilbert Herdt, "Mistaken Sex: Culture, Biology, and the Third Sex in New Guinea," in *Third Sex, Third Gender.*

82. Herdt, "Mistaken Sex."

83. Cited in Tavris and Wade, *The Longest War,* 208–209.

84. Dobson, *Straight Talk,* 184.

85. Goldberg, *The Inevitability of Patriarchy,* 233–34; see also Fausto-Sterling, *Myths of Gender,* 124.

86. A recent effort to use hormone research and evolutionary imperatives is J. Richard Udry, "Biological Limits of Gender Construction," *American Sociological Review* 65 (June 2000): 443–57. Udry's thesis is elegantly demolished by Eleanor Miller and Carrie Yang Costello, "Comment on Udry," *American Sociological Review* 65 (June 2000):592–98.

87. Lewontin et al., *Not in Our Genes,* 147.

88. Alice Rossi, *Gender and the Life Course* (Chicago: Aldine, 1982).

89. Darrell Yates Rist, "Are Homosexuals Born That Way?" *The Nation,* October 19, 1992, 427. "Born or Bred?" *Newsweek,* February 24, 1992.

90. Karen De Witt, "Quayle Contends Homosexuality Is a Matter of Choice, Not Biology," *The New York Times,* September 14, 1992; Ashcroft cited in Eric Alterman, "Sorry, Wrong President," *The Nation,* February 26, 2001, 10. See John Leland and Mark Miller, "Can Gays Convert?" *Newsweek,* August 17, 1998. While it is certain that some therapeutic interven-

tions can lead people to change their sexual behavior and sexual object choice, the evidence that people's orientations change is less than convincing.

91. John D'Emilio, *Making Trouble: Essays on Gay History* (New York: Routledge, 1992), 187.
92. See, for example, Martin Levine, *Gay Macho: The Life and Death of the Homosexual Clone* (New York: New York University Press, 1997); see also John Gagnon and William Simon, *Sexual Conduct* (Chicago: Aldine, 1973).
93. Vera Whisman, *Queer by Choice* (New York: Routledge, 1992).
94. Charlotte Bunch, "Lesbians in Revolt," in *Feminist Frameworks*, ed. A. Jaggar and Rothenberg, 144 (New York: McGraw-Hill, 1984).
95. LeVay, *The Sexual Brain*, 6.
96. Ruth Hubbard, "The Political Nature of Human Nature," in *Theoretical Perspectives on Sexual Difference*, ed. Deborah Rhode, 69 (New Haven: Yale University Press, 1990).
97. Robert A. Padgug, "On Conceptualizing Sexuality in History," *Radical History Review* 20 (1979):9.
98. Richard Hofstadter, *Social Darwinism in American Thought* (New York: Random House, 1944), 204.
99. Adam Begley, "Why Men and Women Think Differently," *Newsweek* May 12, 1995.

NOTES TO CHAPTER 3

1. See, for example, Karen Sacks, "Engels Revisited: Women, Organization of Production, and Private Property," in *Women, Culture, and Society,* ed. M. Rosaldo and L. Lamphere (Stanford: Stanford University Press, 1974), and *Sisters and Wives: The Past and Future of Sexual Equality* (Westport: Greenwood, 1979).
2. Margaret Mead, *Sex and Temperament in Three Primitive Societies* (New York: William Morrow, 1935). Critics such as Derek Freeman have suggested that Mead, like the biologists she was criticizing, simply found what she was looking for, especially in Samoa, where she apparently fabricated some details. Yet challenges to the core insight in her work in New Guinea, that of cultural variation in gender roles, are unsubstantiated and unconvincing.
3. Mead, *Sex and Temperament,* 57–58, 29, 35, 84, 128, 101.
4. Margaret Mead, *Male and Female* (New York: William Morrow, 1949), 69; *Sex and Temperament,* 171.
5. Mead, *Sex and Temperament,* 197, 190, 189; *Male and Female,* 98.
6. Mead, *Sex and Temperament,* 228.
7. Adrienne Zihlman, "Woman the Gatherer: The Role of Women in Early Hominid Evolution," in *Gender and Anthropology,* ed. S. Morgen (Washington, DC: American Anthropological Association, 1989), 31.
8. Friedrich Engels, *On the Origin of the Family, Private Property, and the State* (New York: International Publishers, 1970).
9. Eleanor Leacock, "Women's Status in Egalitarian Society: Implications for Social Evolution," *Current Anthropology* 19, no. 2 (1978):252; see also Eleanor Leacock, "Montagnais Women and the Jesuit Program for Colonization," in *Women and Colonization,* ed. M. Etienne and E. Leacock (New York: Praeger, 1980).
10. Sacks, "Engels Revisited" and *Sisters and Wives.*
11. Marvin Harris *Cows, Pigs, Wars, and Witches: The Riddle of Culture* (New York: Random House, 1974); and *Cannibals and Kings* (New York: Random House, 1977).
12. Lionel Tiger and Robin Fox, *The Imperial Animal* (New York: Holt, 1971).
13. Claude Lévi-Strauss *The Elementary Structures of Kinship* (London: Tavistock, 1969); see also Collier and Rosaldo, "Politics and Gender in Simple Societies," in *Sexual Meanings: The Cul-*

tural Construction of Gender and Sexuality, ed. S. B. Ortner and H. Whitehead (Cambridge: Cambridge University Press, 1981).

14. Bacon, Barry, and Child, "Cross Cultural Survey"
15. Judith Brown, "A Note on the Division of Labor by Sex," *American Anthropologist* 72, no. 5 (1970).
16. Scott Coltrane; Mead, *Male and Female,* 190, 189.
17. Daphne Spain, *Gendered Spaces* (Chapel Hill: University of North Carolina Press, 1992); "The Spatial Foundations of Men's Friendships and Men's Power," in *Men's Friendships,* ed. Peter Nardi (Newbury Park, CA: Sage Publications, 1992), 76.
18. Thomas Gregor, *Mehinaku: The Drama of Daily Life in a Brazilian Indian Village* (Chicago: University of Chicago Press, 1977), 255; see also 305–306; In another passage, Gregor recounts a child's game in which a girl pretends to invade the men's house, and the boys pretend to gang rape her (114). See also Thomas Gregor, "No Girls Allowed," *Science* 82, December 1982.
19. Peggy Reeves Sanday, *Female Power and Male Dominance* (New York: Cambridge University Press, 1981), 75, 128. See also Maria Lepowsky, "Gender in an Egalitarian Society: A Case Study from the Coral Sea," in *Beyond the Second Sex: New Directions in the Anthropology of Gender,* ed. R. Sanday and R. G. Goodenough (Philadelphia: University of Pennsylvania Press, 1990.)
20. See Tavris and Wade, *The Longest War,* 330–31.
21. See Peggy Reeves Sanday, *Fraternity Gang Rape* (New York: New York University Press, 1991).
22. John W. Whiting, Richard Kluckhohn, and Albert Anthony, "The Function of Male Initiation Ceremonies at Puberty," in *Readings in Social Psychology,* ed. E. Maccoby, T. M. Newcomb, and E. L. Hatley (New York: Henry Holt, 1958).
23. Edgar Gregersen, *Sexual Practices* (New York: Franklin Watts, 1983), 104.
24. Marc Lacey, "African Activists Urge End to Female Mutilation" in *International Herald Tribune,* February 7, 2003, p. 10.
25. Cited in Rogaia Mustafa Abusharaf, "Unmasking Tradition," *The Sciences,* March/April 1998, 23.
26. See for example, Joseph Zoske, "Male Circumcision: A Gender Perspective," *Journal of Men's Studies* 6, no. 2 (Winter 1998); see also Michael Kimmel, "The Kindest Uncut," *Tikkun,* 16, no. 3 (May 2001).
27. Karen Paige and Jeffrey Paige, *The Politics of Reproductive Ritual* (Berkeley: University of California Press, 1981).
28. Tavris and Wade, *The Longest War,* 314; see also Paige and Paige, *The Politics of Reproductive Ritual;* Fatima Mernissi, *Beyond the Veil: Male-Female Dynamics in a Modern Muslim Society* (New York: Wiley, 1975).
29. Michael Olien, *The Human Myth* (New York: Harper and Row, 1978); M. K. Martin and B. Voorhies, *Female of the Species* (New York: Columbia University Press, 1975).
30. Walter Williams, *The Spirit and the Flesh* (Boston: Beacon Press, 1986).
31. Sabine Lang, *Men as Women, Women as Men* (Austin: University of Texas Press, 1998).
32. Gregersen, *Sexual Practices,* 270.
33. Martin and Voorhies, *Female of the Species,* 97.
34. Cited in Clyde Kluckholn, *Mirror for Man* (Greenwich, CT: Greenwood, 1970).
35. Gilbert Herdt, *Guardians of the Flutes* (Chicago: University of Chicago Press, 1981), 1, 165, 282.
36. F. E. Williams, *Papuans of the Trans-Fly* (Oxford: Oxford University Press, 1936), 159; see also E. L. Schiefflin, *The Sorrow of the Lonely and the Burning of the Dancers* (New York: St. Martin's Press, 1976); R. Kelly, *Etero Social Structure* (Ann Arbor: University of Michigan Press, 1977); J. Carrier, "Sex Role Preference as an Explanatory Variable in Homosexual Be-

havior," *Archives of Sexual Behavior* 6 (1977); Stephen O. Murray, *Homosexualities* (Chicago: University of Chicago Press, 2000).

37. William Davenport, "Sex in Cross-Cultural Perspective," in *Human Sexuality in Four Perspectives,* ed. F. Beach and M. Diamond (Baltimore: The Johns Hopkins University Press, 1977); see also Gilbert Herdt, ed., *Ritualized Homosexuality in Melanesia* (Berkeley: University of California Press, 1984), 66.

38. Gregersen, *Sexual Practices,* 257.

39. Ibid.

40. Davenport, "Sex in Cross-Cultural Perspective."

41. Ernestine Friedel, *Women and Men: An Anthropologist's View* (New York: Holt, Rinehart, 1975).

42. Gregersen, *Sexual Practices.*

43. Kluckholn, 1948; see also Gregersen, *Sexual Practices,* 289.

44. Ibid.

45. Nancy Tanner and Adrienne Zihlman, "Women in Evolution," *Signs* 1, no. 3 (Spring 1976); Nancy Tanner, *Becoming Human* (New York: Cambridge University Press, 1981); Adrienne Zihlman, "Motherhood in Transition: From Ape to Human," in *The First Child and Family Formation,* ed. W. Miller and L. Newman (Chapel Hill: Carolina Population Center, 1978).

46. Helen Fischer, *The Anatomy of Love* (New York: Norton, 1992), 57.

47. Michelle Rosaldo, "The Use and Abuse of Anthroplogy: Reflections on Feminism and Cross-Cultural Understanding," *Signs* 5, no. 3 (Spring 1980):393; Bonnie Nardi, review of Peggy Reeves Sanday's *Female Power and Male Dominance, Sex Roles* 8, no. 11 (1982):1159.

48. Marija Gimbutas, *The Goddesses and Gods of Old Europe, 7000–3500 B.C.* (Berkeley: University of California Press, 1982) and Marija Gimbutas, *The Living Goddesses* (Berkeley: University of California Press, 1999). See also Riane Eisler, *The Chalice and the Blade* (New York: HarperCollins, 1987).

49. Eisler, *The Chalice and the Blade,* 45, 58.

50. Frances Fukuyama, "Women and the Evolution of World Politics," *Foreign Affairs,* September 1998, 27.

51. Peggy Reeves Sanday, *Women Center: Life in a Modern Matriarchy* (Boston: Beacon, 2002), 116.

52. Eleanor Leacock, "Montagnais Women," 200.

Notes to Chapter 4

1. Sigmund Freud, "The Dissection of the Psychical Personality," in *New Introductory Lectures on Psychoanalysis* [1933] (New York: W. W. Norton, 1965), 74.

2. Ibid.

3. See Sigmund Freud, *Civilization and Its Discontents* (New York: W. W. Norton, 1970).

4. Sigmund Freud, *Letters of Sigmund Freud, 1873–1939,* ed. Ernst Freud (London: Hogarth Press, 1961), 419–20.

5. See, for example, Jeffrey Masson, *The Assault on Truth* (New York: Farrar Straus and Giroux, 1984); and Alice Miller, *Thou Shalt Not Be Aware: Society's Betrayal of the Child* (New York: Farrar, Straus and Giroux, 1984), *For Your Own Good* (New York: Farrar Straus and Giroux, 1983).

6. Lewis Terman and Catherine Cox Miles, *Sex and Personality* (New York: McGraw-Hill, 1936); see also Henry Minton, "Feminity in Men and Masculinity in Women: American Psychiatry and Psychology Portray Homosexuality in the 1930s," *Journal of Homosexuality* 13, no. 1 (1986).

7. George Henry, "Psychogenic Factors in Overt Homosexuality," *American Journal of Psychiatry* 93 (1937); cited in Minton, "Femininity in Men," 2. Note, however, that Henry's secondary claim is not that these tendencies will simply emerge, but that the social *response* to these traits will exaggerate and sustain them; i.e., that overt responses of homophobia will actually encourage the tendency toward homosexuality.

8. See Jean Piaget, *Plays, Dreams and Imitation in Children* (New York: Norton, 1951); *The Language and Thought of the Child* (London: Routledge, 1952), and *The Moral Judgment of the Child* (New York: Free Press, 1965).

9. Lawrence Kohlberg, "A Cognitive-Developmental Analysis of Children's Sex Role Concepts and Attitudes," in *The Development of Sex Differences,* ed. E. Maccoby (Stanford: Stanford University Press, 1966) and Lawrence Kohlberg and Edward Zigler, "The Impact of Cognitive Maturity on the Development of Sex Role Attitudes in the years 4 to 8," *Genetic Psychology Monographs* 75 (1967).

10. Albert Bandura and Althea Huston, "Identification as a Process of Incidental Learning," *Journal of Abnormal and Social Psychology* 63 (1961); Albert Bandura, Dorothea Ross, and Sheila Ross, "A Comparative Test of the Status Envy, Social Power, and Secondary Reinforcement Theories of Identifactory Learning," *Journal of Abnormal and Social Psychology* 67 (1963); Walter Mischel, "A Social-Learning View of Sex Differences," in *The Development of Sex Differences.*

11. See Karen Horney, "On the Genesis of the Castration Complex in Women," in *Psychoanalysis and Women,* ed. J. B. Miller (New York: Bruner/Mazel, 1973).

12. Bruno Bettelheim, *Symbolic Wounds* (New York: Collier, 1962); Wolfgang Lederer, *The Fear of Women* (New York: Harcourt Brace Jovanovich, 1968).

13. Nancy Chodorow, *The Reproduction of Mothering* (Berkeley: University of California Press, 1978); Jessica Benjamin, *The Bonds of Love* (Nerw York: Pantheon, 1984); Dorothy Dinnerstein, *The Mermaid and the Minotaur* (New York: Harper and Row, 1977); Lillian Rubin, *Intimate Strangers* (New York: Harper and Row, 1983). Three of these writers—Chodorow, Benjamin, and Rubin—have Ph.D.s in sociology and also are practicing therapists, a combination that, in my view, enabled them to explore the social consequences of the individual devaluation of women with rare acuity.

14. Chodorow, *The Reproduction of Mothering;* see also Chodorow, "Family Structure and Feminine Personality," in *Women, Culture, and Society,* ed. M. Rosaldo and L. Lamphere (Stanford: Stanford University Press, 1974).

15. Chodorow, "Family Structure," 50.

16. Carol Gilligan, *In a Different Voice* (Cambridge: Harvard University Press, 1982), 173.

17. Belenky et al., *Women's Way of Knowing* (New York: Basic Books, 1987); Tannen, *You Just Don't Understand;* Robert Bly, *Iron John* (Reading: Addison-Wesley, 1991).

18. See H. Crothers, *Meditations on Votes for Women* (Boston: Houghton, Mifflin, 1914), 74.

19. Carol Gilligan, "Reply," in "On *In a Different Voice:* An Interdisciplinary Forum," *Signs* 11, no. 2 (1986):327; Affidavit of Carol Gilligan in *Johnson v. Jones,* D Ct, S.C., filed 1/7/93, 3.

20. Carol Tavris, "The Mismeasure of Woman," *Feminism and Psychology* 3, no. 2 (1993):153.

21. Tannen, *You Just Don't Understand,* 24, 25; see also Deborah Tannen, *Gender and Discourse* (New York: Oxford University Press, 1994).

22. Tannen, *You Just Don't Understand,* 181.

23. Eleanor Maccoby and Carol Jacklin, *The Psychology of Sex Differences* (Stanford: Stanford University Press, 1974), 362.

24. Joseph Pleck offered a superb summary of these studies in "The Theory of Male Sex Role Identity: Its Rise and Fall, 1936 to the Present," in *In the Shadow of the Past: Psychology Views the Sexes,* ed. M. Lewin (New York: Columbia University Press, 1984). Much of my summary draws from his essay.

25. Adorno, Teodor, et al., *The Authoritarian Personality* (New York: Harper and Row, 1950).

26. Walter Miller and E. Guy Swanson, *Inner Conflict and Defense* (New York: Holt, 1960).
27. Talcott Parsons, "Certain Primary Sources and Patterns of Aggression in the Social Structure of the Western World," *Psychiatry,* 10 (1947):309.
28. Sandra Bem, "The Measurement of Psychological Androgyny," *Journal of Consulting and Clinical Psychology* 42 (1974); Sandra Bem, "Androgyny vs. the Tight Little Lives of Fluffy Women and Chesty Men," *Psychology Today,* September 1975; Sandra Bem, "Beyond Androgyny: Some Presumptuous Prescriptions for a Liberated Sexual Identity," in *The Future of Women: Issues in Psychology,* ed. J. Sherman and F. Denmark (New York: Psychological Dimensions, 1978). See also Alexandra Kaplan and Mary Anne Sedney, *Psychology and Sex Roles: An Androgynous Perspective* (Boston: Little Brown, 1980), quote is on 6; Janet Spence, Robert Helmreich, and Joy Stapp, "The Personal Attributes Questionaire: A Measure of Sex-Role Stereotypes and Masculinity-Femininity," *JSAS Catalog of Selected Documents in Psychology* 4 (1974).
29. Sandra Bem, *Lenses of Gender* (New Haven: Yale University Press, 1993), 124.
30. Joseph Pleck, *The Myth of Masculinity* (Cambridge: The MIT Press, 1981).
31. See, for example, James M. O'Neil, "Assessing Men's Gender Role Conflict," in *Problem Solving Strategies and Interventions for Men in Conflict,* ed. D. Moorer and F. Leafgren (Alexandria, VA: American Association for Counseling and Development, 1990); J. M. O'Neil, B. Helms, R. Gable, L. David, and L. Wrightsman, "Gender Role Conflict Scale: College Men's Fear of Femininity," *Sex Roles* 14 (1986):335–50; Joseph Pleck, "The Gender Role Strain Paradigm: An Update," in *A New Psychology of Men,* ed. R. Levant and W. Pollack (New York: Basic Books, 1995); James Mihalik, Benjamin Locke, Harry Theodore, Robert Cournoyer, and Brendan Lloyd, " A Cross-National and Cross-Sectional Comparison of Men's Gender Role Conflict and Its Relatinshop to Social Intimacy and Self-Esteem," *Sex Roles* 45 no. 1/2 (2001):1–14.
32. Warren Farrell, *The Myth of Male Power* (New York; Simon and Schuster, 1993).
33. That's not to say that Pleck doesn't try valiantly to do so. His "Men's Power over Women, Other Men, and in Society," in *Women and Men: The Consequences of Power,* ed. D. Hiller and R. Sheets (Cincinnati: University of Cincinnati Women's Studies, 1977) takes the theory as far as it will go, which is quite far in my view. But the theory is still unable to theorize both difference and institutionalized gender relations adequately.
34. Jean-Paul Sartre, *Anti-Semite and Jew* (New York: Schocken Press, 1965), 60.

NOTES TO CHAPTER 5

1. M. Pines, "Civilizing of Genes," *Psychology Today,* September 1981.
2. Helen Z. Lopata and Barrie Thorne, "On the Term 'Sex Roles,'" *Signs,* 3 (1979):719.
3. Tim Carrigan, Bob Connell, and John Lee, "Toward a New Sociology of Masculinity," *Theory and Society* 14 (1985). See also Connell, *Gender and Power;* R. W. Connell, *Masculinities* (Berkeley: University of California Press, 1995); Judith Stacey and Barrie Thorne, "The Missing Feminist Revolution in Sociology," *Social Problems* 32, no. 4 (1985) for elaboration and summaries of the sociological critique of sex role theory.
4. Deborah Rhode, *Speaking of Sex* (Cambridge: Harvard University Press, 1997), 42.
5. Stacey and Thorne, "The Missing Feminist Revolution," 307.
6. Carrigan, Connell, and Lee, 587; see also Connell, *Gender and Power.*
7. David Tresemer, "Assumptions Made About Gender Roles," *Another Voice: Feminist Perspectives on Social Life and Social Science,* ed. M. Millman and R. M. Kanter, 323 (New York: Anchor Books, 1975); R. Stephen Warner, David Wellman, and Leonore Weitzman, "The Hero, the Sambo, and the Operator: Three Characterizations of the Oppressed," *Urban Life and Culture* 2 (1973).

8. Carrigan, Connell, and Lee, "Toward a New Sociology of Masculinity," 587.

9. Hannah Arendt, *On Revolution* (New York: Viking, 1971).

10. Evelyn Fox Keller, *A Feeling for the Organism* (New York: W. H. Freeman, 1985).

11. Janet Saltzman Chafetz, "Toward a Macro-Level Theory of Sexual Stratification," *Current Perspectives in Social Theory* 1 (1980).

12. Erving Goffman, "The Arrangement Between the Sexes," *Theory and Society* 4 (1977):316.

13. Kanter, *Men and Women of the Corporation.* See also Rosabeth Moss Kanter, "Women and the Structure of Organizations: Explorations in Theory and Behavior," in *Another Voice: Feminist Perspectives on Social Life and Social Science,* ed. M. Millman and R. M. Kanter (New York: Anchor Books, 1975).

14. Joan Acker, "Hierarchies, Jobs, Bodies: A Theory of Gendered Organizations," *Gender & Society* 4, no. 2 (1990):146; see also Joan Acker, "Sex Bias in Job Evaluation: A Comparable Worth Issue," in *Ingredients for Women's Employment Policy,* ed. C. Bose and G. Spitze (Albany: SUNY Press, 1987); "Class, Gender, and the Relations of Distribution," *Signs: Journal of Women in Culture and Society* 13 (1988) Joan Acker, *Doing Comparable Worth: Gender, Class, and Pay Equity* (Philadelphia: Temple University Press, 1989); and Joan Acker and Donald R. Van Houten. "Differential Recruitment and Control: The Sex Structuring of Organizations," *Administrative Science Quarterly* 19, no. 2 (1974).

15. Acker, "Hierarchies, Jobs, Bodies," 146–147.

16. Judith Gerson and Kathy Peiss. "Boundaries, Negotiation, Consciousness: Reconceptualizing Gender Relations," *Social Problems* 32, no. 4 (1985):320.

17. Acker, "Hierarchies, Job, Bodies," 258.

18. Candace West and Don Zimmerman, "Doing Gender," *Gender & Society* 1, no. 2 (1987):140.

19. Suzanne J. Kessler, "The Medical Construction of Gender: Case Management of Intersexed Infants," *Signs* 16, no. 1 (1990):12, 13.

20. The phrase comes from R. W. Connell; I take it from the title of Barbara Risman, *Gender Vertigo.*

21. Cited in West and Zimmerman, "Doing Gender," 133–34.

22. Carey Goldberg, "Shunning 'He' and 'She,' They Fight for Respect," *The New York Times,* September 8, 1996, 24.

23. Cited in Carey Goldberg, "Shunning 'He' and 'She,' " 24.

24. Harold Garfinkle, *Studies in Ethnomethodology* (Englewood Cliffs: Prentice-Hall, 1967), 128, 132.

25. Suzanne Kessler, "The Medical Construction of Gender," 25.

26. Nocholas Groth, Ann Burgen, and Suzanne Sgroi, *Sexual Assault of Children and Adolescents* (San Francisco; Jossey-Bass, 1978).

27. Carol Sheffield, *Feminist Jurisprudence,* (New York: Routledge, 1997):203.

28. I will explore the sociology of rape in significantly more detail in chapter 11.

29. West and Zimmerman, "Doing Gender," 140; Barrie Thorne, 1980, 110; E. Thompson, *The Making of the English Working Class* (New York: Pantheon, 1963), 11.

30. James Messerschmidt, *Masculinities and Crime* (Lanham, MD: Rowman and Littlefield, 1993), 121.

31. Carrigan, Connell, and Lee, "Toward a New Sociology of Masculinity." 589; Karen D. Pyke, "Class-Based Masculinities: The Interdependence of Gender, Class and Interpersonal Power," *Gender & Society* 10, no. 5 (1996):530.

NOTES TO CHAPTER 6

1. The debate over family values is too extensive to be summarized here. See, for a few examples, Barbara Dafoe Whitehead, "Dan Quayle Was Right," *The Atlantic,* April 1993; David

Popenoe, *Life Without Father: Compelling New Evidence that Fatherhood and Marriage Are Indispensable for the Good of Children and Society* (New York: The Free Press, 1996) and his "Modern Marriage: Revising the Cultural Script," in *Promises to Keep: Decline and Renewal of Marriage in America,* ed. D. Popenoe, J. B. Elshtain, and D. Blankenhorn (Lanham, MD: Rowman and Littlefield, 1996). On the other side, see Judith Stacey, *Brave New Families* (New York: Basic Books, 1990) and *In the Name of the Family: Rethinking Family Values in a Postmodern Age* (Boston: Beacon 1997), as well as Stephanie Coontz, *The Way We Never Were: American Families and the Nostalgia Trap* (New York: Basic Books, 1995), and *The Way We Really Are: Coming to Terms with America's Changing Families* (New York: Basic Books, 1998).

2. Katha Pollitt, cited in Stephanie Coontz, *The Way We Really Are,* 95.

3. See, for example, "Push to Help Families Thrive Comes Under Attack," *USA Today,* 15 June 2001, 13A; Eric Nagourney, "Study Finds Families Bypassing Marriage," *The New York Times,* February 15, 2000; and "The Decline of Marriage," *Scientific American,* December 1999; see generally James Q. Wilson, *The Marriage Problem: How Our Culture Has Weakened Families* (New York: HarperCollins, 2002).

4. Scott Coltrane, *Gender and Families* (Newbury Park: Pine Forge Press, 1998), 48–49; Coontz, *The Way We Really Are,* 30.

5. On the transformation of the idea of marriage see, for example, Edward Shorter, *The Making of the Modern Family* (New York: Basic Books, 1977); Arlene Skolnick, *Embattled Paradise: The American Family in an Age of Uncertainty* (New York: Basic Books, 1993); Christopher Lasch, *Women and the Common Life: Love, Marriage, and Feminism* (New York: Norton, 1997), especially 162. On husbands' brutality, see for example Steven Mintz and Susan Kellogg, *Domestic Revolutions: A Social History of the American Family* (New York: The Free Press, 1988), 58.

6. Mintz and Kellogg, *Domestic Revolutions,* 50; see also Page Smith, *Daughters of the Promised Land: Women in American History* (Boston: Little Brown, 1970); John Demos, "The Changing Faces of Fatherhood: A New Exploration in American family History," in *Father and Child: Developmental and Clinical Perspectives,* ed. S. Cath, A. Gurwitt, and J. Ross, 429 (Boston: Little, Brown, 1982).

7. John Demos, *Past, Present, and Personal: The Family and Life Course in American History* (New York: Oxford University Press, 1986), 32; see also Tamara Hareven, *Family Time and Industrial Time* (New York: Cambridge University Press, 1982). Tennyson, "The Princess" is cited in Skolnick, *Embattled Paradise,* 35.

8. Cited in Popenoe, *Life Without Father,* 95.

9. Gerda Lerner, "The Lady and the Mill Girl: Changes in the Status of Women in the Age of Jackson," *American Studies Journal* 10, no. 1 (Spring 1969):9, 7; Theodore Dwight, *The Father's Book* (Springfield, MA: G. and C. Merriam, 1834). See, generally, Kimmel, *Manhood in America,* chapters 1 and 2.

10. Lasch, *Women and the Common Life,* 162.

11. Bonnie Thornton Dill, "Our Mothers' Grief: Racial-Ethnic Women and the Maintenance of Families," *Journal of Family History,* 13, no. 4 (1988):428.

12. John Gillis, "Making Time for Family: The Invention of Family Time(s) and the Reinvention of Family History," *Journal of Family History* 21 (1996); John Gillis, *A World of Their Own Making: Myth, Ritual, and the Quest for Family Values* (New York: Basic Books, 1996).

13. Skolnick, *Embattled Paradise,* 33; *Harper's* cited in Demos, "The Changing Faces of Fatherhood," 442; see also Ralph LaRossa, "Fatherhood and Social Change," *Family relations* 37 (1988); and Ralph LaRossa, *The Modernization of Fatherhood: A Social and Political History* (Chicago: University of Chicago Press, 1997); Robert Griswold, *Fatherhood in America: A History* (New York: Basic Books, 1993).

14. Skolnick, *Embattled Paradise,* 41; Mintz and Kellogg, *Domestic Revolutions,* 110.
15. See Stephen D. Sugarman, "Single Parent Families," in *All Our Families: New Policies for a New Century,* ed. M. Mason, A. Skolnick, and S. Sugarman, 20–21. (New York: Oxford University Press, 1998).
16. See LaRossa, *Modernization of Fatherhood.*
17. Mintz and Kellogg, *Domestic Revolutions,* 179; Coontz, *The Way We Really Are,* 30; Mintz and Kellog, *Domestic Revolutions,* 237.
18. William Chafe, *The Unfinished Journey: America Since World War II* (New York: Oxford University Press, 1986), 125; Morris Zelditch, "Role Differentiation in the Nuclear family: A Comparative Study," in *Family, Socialization and Interaction Process,* ed. T. Parsons and R. F. Bales, 339 (New York: The Free Press, 1955).
19. Archibald MacLeish, "Poem in Prose"; Helen Smith, personal communication. I am grateful to Helen for pushing me to acknowledge how the family of the 1950s worked for so many middle-class suburban Americans, including, I suppose, myself.
20. Griswold, *Fatherhood in America,* 204; Lasch, *Women and the Common Life,* 94; Ruth Schwartz Cowan, *More Work for Mother: The Ironies of Household Technology from the Open Hearth to the Microwave* (New York: Basic Books, 1983), 216; Lerner cited in Skolnick, *Embattled Paradise,* 115.
21. See, for example, Barbara Ehrenreich, *The Hearts of Men* (New York: Doubleday, 1983) on the "male revolt" from breadwinner status. Also see Kimmel, *Manhood in America,* especially chapter 7.
22. See Skolnick, *Embattled Paradise,* 148.
23. Nancy A Crowell and Ethel M. Leeper, eds., *America's Fathers and Public Policy* (Washington, DC: National Academy Press, 1994), 1.
24. Anna Quindlen, "Men at Work," *The New York Times,* February 18, 1990.
25. Coontz, *The Way We Really Are,* 79; Arlene Skolnick, *The Intimate Environment* (New York: HarperCollins, 1996), 342; Judith Bruce, Cynthia B. Lloyd, and Ann Leonard, *Families in Focus: New Perspectives on Mothers, Fathers, and Children* (New York: The Population Council, 1995); Dirk Johnson, "More and More, the Single Parent Is Dad," *The New York Times,* August 31, 1993, 1.
26. Andrew Cherlin, "By the Numbers," *The New York Times Magazine,* April 5, 1998.
27. Arlie Hochschild (with Anne Machung), *The Second Shift: Working Parents and the Revolution at Home* (New York: Viking, 1989), 258.
28. J. K. Footlick, "What Happened to the Family?" *The 21st Century Family,* special edition, *Newsweek,* Winter-Spring 1990, 14.
29. Scott Coltrane, *Family Man: Fatherhood, Housework, and Gender Equity* (New York: Oxford University Press, 1996), 203; Lillian Rubin, *Worlds of Pain* (New York: Basic Books, 1976), 131; Cherlin, "By the Numbers," 39; Coltrane, *Family Man,* 203.
30. Jessie Bernard, *The Future of Marriage* (New York: World, 1972); Walter R. Gove, "The Relationship Between Sex Roles, Marital Status, and Mental Illness," *Social Forces* 51 (1972); Walter Gove and M. Hughes, "Possible Causes of the Apparent Sex Differences in Physical Health: An Empirical Investigation," *American Sociological Review* 44 (1979); Walter Gove and Jeanette Tudor. "Adult Sex Roles and Mental Illness," *American Journal of Sociology* 73 (1973); "The Decline of Marriage," *Scientific American,* December 1999.
31. Natalie Angier, *The New York Times,* 1998, 10.
32. See Linda J. Waite and Maggie Gallagher, *The Case for Marriage: Why Married People Are Happier, Healthier, and Better Off Financially* (New York: Doubleday, 2000). See also, for example, Hynubae Chun and Injae Lee, "Why Do Married Men Earn More: Productivity or Marriage Selection?," *Economic Inquiry* 39, no. 2 (April 2001):307–19; and Leslie Stratton "Examining the Wage Differential for Married and Cohabiting Men," *Economic Inquiry* 40,

no. 2 (April 2002):199–212. See also Paula England's review of *The Case for Marriage* in *Contemporary Sociology* 30, no. 6 (2001).

33. Bebin and statistics cited in Elaine Carey, "Kids Put a Damper on Marital Bliss: Study," *Toronto Star,* August 15, 1997, A1, A14.

34. J. Condry and S. Condry, "Sex Differences: A Study in the Eye of the Beholder," *Child Development* 47 (1976).

35. B. Lott, *Women's Lives: Themes and Variations in Gender Learning* (Monterey: Brooks/Cole, 1987). See also L. A. Schwartz and W. T. Markham, "Sex Stereotyping in Children's Toy Advertisements," *Sex Roles* 12 (1985); and S. B. Ungar, "The Sex Typing of Adult and Child Behavior in Toy Sales," *Sex Roles* 8 (1982).

36. See Carol Jacklin, "Female and Male: Issues of Gender," *American Psychologist* 44 (1989), for a report on this and related research.

37. See, for example, Barrie Thorne, "Boys and Girls Together . . . But Mostly Apart: Gender Arrangements in Elementary Schools," in *Relationships and Development,* ed. W. Hartup and Z Rubin (Hillsdale, NJ: Lawrence Erlbaum, 1986).

38. See, for example, Barrie Thorne and Zella Luria, "Sexuality and Gender in Children's Daily Worlds," *Social Problems* 33 (1986).

39. Barrie Thorne, *Gender Play* (New Brunswick: Rutgers University Press, 193), 3.

40. Hochschild, *The Second Shift;* Paul Amato and Alan Booth, "Changes in Gender Role Attitudes and Perceived Marital Quality," *American Sociological Review* 60 (1995).

41. Pat Mainardi, "The Politics of Housework," in *Sisterhood Is Powerful,* ed. R. Morgan (New York: Vintage, 1970).

42. Ballard and Foote are cited in Cowan, *More Work for Mother,* 43; Campbell is cited in Susan Strasser, *Never Done: A History of American Housework* (New York: Pantheon, 1982), 62.

43. Johnson, "More and More, The Single Parent Is Dad," A 15.

44. Coltrane, *Family Man,* 46; Dana Vannoy-Hiller and William W. Philliber. *Equal Partners: Successful Women in Marriage* (Newbury Park: Sage Publications, 1989), 115; Hochschild, *The Second Shift.*

45. Arlie Hochschild, "Ideals of Care: Traditional, Postmodern, Cold-Modern, and Warm-Modern," *Social Politics* (Fall 1995):318.

46. Anna Quindlen, cited in Deborah Rhode, *Speaking of Sex* (Cambridge: Harvard University Press, 1997), 8.

47. On men's involvement in family work, see Joseph Pleck, "Men's Family Work: Three Perspectives and Some New Data," *The Family Coordinator* 28 (1979); "American Fathering in Historical Perspective," in *Changing Men: New Directions in Research on Men and Masculinity,* ed. M. S. Kimmel (Beverly Hills, CA: Sage Publications, 1987); *Working Wives/Working Husbands* (Newbury Park: Sage Publications, 1985); "Families and Work: Small Changes with Big Implications," *Qualitative Sociology* 15 (1992); "Father Involvement: Levels, Origins, and Consequences," in *The Father's Role,* ed. M. Lamb, 3rd ed. (New York: John Wiley, 1997).

48. Julie Press and Eleanor Townsley. "Wives' and Husbands' Housework Reporting: Gender, Class, and Social Desirability," *Gender & Society* 12, no. 2 (1998):214.

49. Hiromi Ono, "Husbands' and Wives' Resources and Marital Dissolution in the United States," *Journal of Marriage and the Family* 60, (1998):674–89.

50. Ono; see also Dirk Johnson, "Until Dust Do Us Part," *Newsweek,* March 25, 2002, 41; see also Sanjiv Gupta, "The Effects of Transitions in Marital Status on Men's Performance of Housework," *Journal of Marriage and the Family* (August 1999).

51. *Ladies Home Journal,* September 1997; John Gray, "Domesticity, Diapers, and Dad," *Toronto Globe and Mail,* June 15, 1996.

52. See Bart Landry, *Black Working Wives: Pioneers of the American Family Revolution* (Berkeley: University of California Press, 2001); Margaret Usdansky, "White Men Don't Jump Into Chores," *USA Today,* August 20, 1994; Julia Lawlor, "Blue Collar Dads Leading Trend in Caring for Kids, Author Says," *The New York Times,* April 15, 1998.

53. Cited in Coltrane, *Family Man,* 162: see also Scott Coltrane and Michele Adams, "Men's Family Work: Child Centered Fathering and the Sharing of Domestic Labor," in *Working Families: The Transformation of the American Home,* ed. Rosanna Hertz and Nancy Marshall (Berkeley: University of California Press, 2001).

54. Mick Cunningham, "Parental Influences on the Gendered Division of Housework," *American Sociological Review* 66 (April 2001):184–203; see also Janet Simons, "Life with Father," *Rocky Mountain News,* August 20, 2001.

55. Barbara Vobejda, "Children Help Less at Home, Dads Do More," *Washington Post,* 24 November 1991, A1.

56. Jerry Adler, "Building a Better Dad," *Newsweek,* June 17, 1996; Tamar Lewin, "Workers of Both Sexes Make Trade-Offs for Family, Study Shows," *The New York Times,* October 29, 1995, 25.

57. Benjamin Spock and Steven J. Parker, *Dr. Spock's Baby and Child Care,* 7th ed. (New York: Pocket Books, 1998), 10.

58. United Nations, *The World's Women, 1970–1990: Trends and Statistics* (New York: The United Nations, 1991); Pat Schroeder, cited in Rhode, *Speaking of Sex,* 7.

59. Lewin, "Workers of Both Sexes Make Trade-Offs," 25.

60. "Sex, Death, and Football," *The Economist,* June 13, 1998, 18; Robert D. Mintz and James Mahalik, "Gender Role Orientation and Conflict as Predictors of Family Roles for Men," *Sex Roles* 34, no. 1–2 (1996):805–21; Barbara Risman, "Can Men 'Mother'? Life as a Single Father," *Family Relations* 35 (1986); see also Caryl Rivers and Rosalind Barnett. "Fathers Do Best," *The Washington Post,* June 20, 1993, C5.

61. Andrew Cherlin, "By the Numbers," *The New York Times Magazine,* April 5, 1998, 41.

62. Cherlin, "By the Numbersl;" Donald Hernandez, "Children's Changing Access to Resources: A Historical Perspective," *Social Policy Report* 8, no. 1 (Spring 1994):22.

63. Dirk Johnson, "Until Dust Do Us Part," *Newsweek,* March 25, 2002, 41.

64. Jane R. Eisner, "Leaving the Office for Family Life," *The Des Moines Register,* March 27, 1998, 7A.

65. Jay Belsky, "A Reassessment of Infant Day Care" and Thomas Gamble and Edward Zigler, "Effects of Infant Day Care: Another Look at the Evidence," both in *The Parental Leave Crisis: Toward a National Policy,* ed. E. Zigler and M. Frank (New Haven: Yale University Press, 1988); see also Susan Chira, "Study Says Babies in Child Care Keep Secure Bonds to Mother," *The New York Times,* April 21, 1996. For a handy summary of these data, see "Child Care in the United States, 1972 vs. 1999," a flyer from the National Council of Jewish Women at www.ncjw.org.

66. Susan Chira, "Can You Work and Have Good Happy Kids?" *Glamour,* April 1998.

67. Cherlin, "By the Numbers," 40.

68. See S. M. Bianchi and Daphne Spain, *American Women in Transition* (New York: Russell Sage Foundation, 1986); E. G. Menaghan and Toby Parcel. "Parental Employment and Family Life: Research in the 1980s," *Journal of Marriage and the Family* 52 (1990); Glenna Spitze, "Women's Employment and Family Relations: A Review," *Journal of Marriage and the Family* 50 (1988).

69. Philip Blumstein and Pepper Schwartz, *American Couples* (New York: William Morrow, 1983), 155; Chira, "Can You Work," 269.

70. Joan K. Peters, *When Mothers Work: Loving Our Children Without Sacrificing Our Selves* (Reading, MA: Addison-Wesley, 1997).

71. Popenoe, *Life Without Father,* 63; National Center for Health Statistics. "Births, Marriages, Divorces, and Deaths for January, 1995" *Monthly Vital Statistics Report* 44, no. 1. Hyattsville, MD: Public Health Service.

72. Popenoe, *Life Without Father,* 6, 34; see also Tamar Lewin, "Is Social Stability Subverted If You Answer 'I Don't'?" *The New York Times,* November 4, 2000, B-11, 13.

73. Pittman, cited in Olga Silverstein, "Is a Bad Dad Better Than No Dad?" *On the Issues,* (Winter 1997):15; David Blankenhorn, *Fatherless America: Confronting Our Most Urgent Social Problem* (New York: Basic Books, 1993), 30; Robert Bly, *Iron John* (Reading, MA: Addison-Wesley, 1990), 96; Popenoe, *Life Without Father,* 12.

74. Carey Goldberg, "Single Dads Wage Revolution One Bedtime Story at a Time," *The New York Times,* June 17, 2001, A1, 16.

75. Cherlin, "By the Numbers," 40; Kristin Luker, "Dubious Conceptions: The Controversy over Teen Pregnancy," *The American Prospect* 5 (1991); Paul Amato and Alan Booth, *A Generation at Risk: Growing Up in an Era of Family Upheaval* (Cambridge: Harvard University Press, 1997), 229; Amato and J. Gilbreth, "Nonresident Fathers and Children's Well-Bring: A Meta-Analysis," *Journal of Marriage and the Family* 61 (1999):557–73.

76. Martin Sanchez-Jankowski, *Islands in the Street: Gangs and American Urban Society* (Berkeley: University of California Press, 1991), 39.

77. Blaine Harden, "Finding Common Ground on Poor Deadbeat Dads," *The New York Times,* February 3, 2002, 3.

78. David Popenoe, "Evolution of Marriage and Stepfamily Problems," in *Stepfamilies: Who Benefits? Who Does Not?,* ed. A. Booth and J. Dunn, 528 (Wayne, NJ: Lawrence Erlbaum, 1994).

79. United Nations, *Demographic Yearbook.* Department for Economic and Social Information and Policy Analysis, Statistical Division, November, 1996; United States Bureau of the Census, "Current Population Report: Marital Status and Living Arrangements, March, 1996" (Washington, D.C.: United States Government Printing Office, 1997); "Divorce, American Style," *Scientific American,* March 1999.

80. Lawrence Stone, "A Short History of Love," *Harper's Magazine,* February 1988, 32.

81. Constance Ahrons, *The Good Divorce* (New York: HarperCollins, 1994).

82. Demie Kurz, *For Richer, For Poorer: Mothers Confront Divorce* (New York: Routledge, 1995); Leonore Weitzman, *The Divorce Revolution: The Unexpected Social and Economic Consequences for Women and Children in America* (New York: Free Press, 1985); Patricia A. McManus and Thomas A. DiPrete, "Losers and Winners: The Financial Consequences of Separation and Divorce for Men," *American Sociological Review* 66 (April 2001):246–68; Paul Amato, "The Impact of Divorce on Men and Women in India and the United States," *Journal of Comparative Family Studies* 25, no. 2 (1994).

83. Popenoe, *Life Without Father,* 27; Frank Furstenberg and Andrew Cherlin, *Divided Families: What Happens to Children When Parents Part?* (Cambridge: Harvard University Press, 1991); Debra Umberson and Christine Williams. "Divorced Fathers: Parental Role Strain and Psychological Distress," *Journal of Family Issues* 14, no. 3 (1993).

84. Valerie King, "Nonresident Father Involvement and Child Well-Being," *Journal of Family Issues* 15, no. 1 (1994); Edward Kruk, "The Disengaged Noncustodial Father: Implications for Social Work Practice with the Divorced Family," *Social Work* 39, no. 1 (1994).

85. Judith Wallerstein and J. Kelly, *Surviving the Breakup: How Children and Parents Cope with Divorce* (New York: Basic Books, 1980); Judith Wallerstein and Susan Blakeslee, *Second Chances: Men, Women, and Children a Decade After Divorce* (New York: Ticknor and Fields, 1989), 11; Judith Wallerstein, Julia Lewis, and Sandra Blakeslee, *The Unexpected Legacy of Divorce: A 25 Year Landmark Study* (New York: Hyperion, 2000).

86. For criticism of Wallerstein's study, see, for example, Andrew Cherlin, "Generation Ex," *The Nation*, December 11, 2000; Katha Pollitt, "Social Pseudoscience," *The Nation*, October 23, 2000, 10 (and subsequent exchange, December 4, 2000); Thomas Davey, "Considering Divorce," *The American Prospect*, January 1–15, 2001; Walter Kirn, "Should You Stay Together for the Kids," *Time*, September 25, 2000; and Elisabeth Lasch-Quinn, "Loving and Leaving," *The New Republic*, May 6, 2002.

87. See E. Mavis Heatherington and John Kelly, *For Better or for Worse: Divorce Reconsidered* (New York: W. W. Norton, 2002); Leonard Beeghley, *What Does Your Wife Do? Gender and the Transformation of Family Life* (Boulder: Westview Press, 1996), 96; Donna Ruane Morrison and Andrew Cherlin, "The Divorce Process and Young Children's Well-Being: A Prospective Analysis," *Journal of Marriage and the Family* 57, no. 3 (1995); Amato, "Impact of Divorce."

88. Joan B. Kelly, "Mediated and Adversarial Divorce: Respondents Perceptions of Their Processes and Outcomes," *Mediation Quarterly* 24 (Summer 1989):125.

89. J. Block, J. Block, and P. F. Gjerde, "The Personality of Children Prior to Divorce: A Prospective Study," *Child Development* 57 (1986); Skolnick, *Embattled Paradise*, 212; for British study, see Jane Brody, "Problems of Children: A New Look at Divorce," *The New York Times*, June 7, 1991.

90. Amato and Booth, *A Generation at Risk*, 230, 234, 201; Paul Amato and Alan Booth, "The Legacy of Parents' Marital Discord: Consequences for Children's Marital Quality," *Journal of Personality and Social Psychology* 81, no. 4 (2001):627–38; see also Amato,"The Impact of Divorce"; "The Implications of Research Findings on Children in Stepfamilies," in *Stepfamilies: Who Benefits? Who Does Not?*, ed. A. Booth and J. Dunn (Wayne, NJ: Lawrence Erlbaum, 1994); "Single-Parent Households as Settings for Children's Development, Well-Being and Attainment: A Social Networks/Resources Perspective," *Sociological Studies of Children* 7 (1995); Paul Amato and Alan Booth. "Changes in Gender Role Attitudes and Perceived Marital Quality," *American Sociological Review* 60 (1995); Paul Amato, Laura Spencer Loomis, and Alan Booth. "Parental Divorce, Marital Conflict, and Offspring Well-Being During Early Adulthood," *Social Forces* 73, no. 3 (1995). "Low conflict," by the way, is unhappy but not physically violent.

91. B. Berg and R. Kelly. "The Measured Self-Esteem of Children from Broken, Rejected, and Accepted Families," *Journal of Divorce* 2 (1979); R. E. Emery, "Interparental Conflict and Children of Discord and Divorce," *Psychological Bulletin* 92 (1982); H. J. Raschke and V. J. Raschke, "Family Conflict and the Children's Self-Concepts," *Journal of Marriage and the Family* 41 (1979); J. M. Gottman and L. F. Katz. "Effects of Marital Discord on Young Children's Peer Interaction and Health," *Developmental Psychology* 25 (1989); D. Mechanic and S. Hansell, "Divorce, Family Conflict, and Adolescents' Well-being," *Journal of Health and Social Behavior* 30 (1989); Paul Amatio and Juliana Sobolewski, "The Effects of Divorce and Marital Discord on Adult Children's Psychological Well Being," *American Sociological Review* 66 (December 2001):900–21.

92. Block, Block, and Gjerde, "The Personality of Children"; President of Council cited in Coontz, *The Way We Really Are*, 108; Gallup poll data cited in Skolnick, *The Intimate Environment*, 304.

93. Coontz, *The Way We Really Are*, 83.

94. Amato and Booth, *A Generation at Risk*, 207; see also Susan Jekielek,"The Relative and Interactive Impacts of Parental Conflict and Marital Disruption on Children's Emotional Well-Being," paper presented at the annual meeting of the American Sociological Association, New York, 1996; Carl Degler, *At Odds: Women and the Family in America from the Revolution to the Present* (New York: Oxford University Press, 1980); Terry Arendell, "Divorce

American Style," *Contemporary Sociology* 27, no. 3 (1998):226. See also Terry Arendall, *Mothers and Divorce: Legal, Economic, and Social Dilemmas* (Berkeley: University of California Press, 1986); "After Divorce: Investigations into Father Absence," *Gender & Society* (December 1992); *Fathers and Divorce* (Newbury Park: Sage Publications, 1995).

95. Griswold, *Fatherhood in America,* 263; Nancy Polikoff, "Gender and Child Custody Determinations: Exploding the Myths," in *Families, Politics, and Public Policy: A Feminist Dialogue on Women and the State,* ed. I. Diamond, 184–85 (New York: Longman, 1983); Robert H. Mnookin, Eleanor Maccoby, Catherine Albiston, and Charlene Depner. "Private Ordering Revisited: What Custodial Arrangements Are Parents Negotiating?" in *Divorce Reform at the Crossroads,* ed. S. Sugarman and H. Kaye (New Haven: Yale University Press, 1990), especially 55; Eleanor Maccoby and Robert Mnookin. *Dividing the Child: Social and Legal Dilemmas of Custody* (Cambridge: Harvard University Press, 1992), especially 101.

96. Maccoby, quoted in Johnson, "More and More, the Single Parent Is Dad," A 15; Furstenberg and Cherlin, *Divided Families*; Frank Furstenberg, "Good Dads-Bad Dads: Two Faces of Fatherhood," in *The Changing American Family and Public Policy,* ed. A. Cherlin (Lanham, MD: Urban Institute Press, 1988); William J. Goode, "Why Men Resist," in *Rethinking the Family: Some Feminist Questions,* ed. B. Thorne and M. Yalom (New York: Longman, 1982).

97. Amato and Booth, *A Generation at Risk,* 74.

98. See, for example, Kelly, "Long Term Adjustments," 131; D. Leupnitz, *Child Custody: A Study of Families After Divorce* (Lexington: Lexington Books, 1982); D. Leupnitz, "A Comparison of Maternal, Paternal, and Joint Custody: Understanding the Varieties of Post-Divorce Family Life," *Journal of Divorce* 9 (1986); V. Shiller, "Loyalty Conflicts and Family Relationships in Latency Age Boys: A Comparison of Joint and Maternal Custody," *Journal of Divorce* 9 (1986).

99. Kelly, "Longer Term Adjustment," 136; Crowell and Leeper, *America's Fathers and Public Policy,* 27.

100. For more about the U.S. fatherhood movement, see Anna Gavanas, "Domesticating Masculinity and Masculinizing Domesticity in Contemporary U.S. Fatherhood Politics," *Social Politics* (forthcoming 2003).

101. Michael J. Kanotz, "For Better or for Worse: A Critical Analysis of Florida's Defense of Marriage Act," *Florida State University Law Review* 25, no. 2 (1998).

102. Gilbert Zicklin, "Deconstructing Legal Rationality: The Case of Lesbian and Gay Family Relationships," *Marriage and Family Review* 21, no. 3/4 (1995):55.

103. Cited in *The New York Times,* September 27, 1991.

104. Laura Benkov, *Reinventing the Family: Lesbian and Gay Parents* (New York: Crown, 1994); Skolnick, *The Intimate Environment,* 293–94; Blumstein and Schwartz, *American Couples*; Lawrence Kurdek, "The Allocation of Household Labor in Gay, Lesbian, and Heterosexual Married Couples," in *Families in the United States: Kinship and Domestic Politics,* ed. K. Hansen and A. Ilta Garey (Philadelphia: Temple University Press, 1998).

105. John Gagnon and William Simon, *Sexual Conduct* (Chicago: Aldine, 1973), 213.

106. J. Schulenberg, *Gay Parenting* (New York: Doubleday, 1985); F. W. Bozett, ed., *Gay and Lesbian Parents* (New York: Praeger, 1987); Katherine Allen and David H. Demo. "The Families of Lesbians and Gay Men: A New Frontier in Family Research," *Journal of Marriage and the Family* 57 (1995); Ann Sullivan, ed., *Issues in Gay and Lesbian Adoption: Proceedings of the Fourth Annual Peirce-Warwick Adoption Symposium* (Washington, DC: Child Welfare League of America, 1995), 5; John J. Goldman, "N.J. Gays Win Adoption Rights," *Los Angeles Times,* December 18, 1997.

107. Mary Ann Mason, Arlene Skolnick, and Stephen D. Sugarman, *All Our Families: New Policies for a New Century* (New York: Oxford University Press, 1998), 8; Bozett, *Gay and Lesbian Parents.*

108. Judith Stacey, "Gay and Lesbian Families: Queer Like Us," in *All Our Families: New Policies for a New Century,* M. Mason, A. Skolnick, and S. Sugarman, 135 (New York: Oxford University Press, 1998).

109. Judith Stacey and Timothy J. Biblarz, "(How) Does the Sexual Orientation of Parents Matter," *American Sociological Review* 66 (April 2001):159–83; see also Michael Bronski, "Queer as Your Folks," *The Boston Phoenix,* August 3, 2001, and Erica Goode, "A Rainbow of Differences in Gays' Children," *The New York Times,* July 17, 2001.

110. Donald Clark, cited in Stacey, "Gay and Lesbian Families."

111. cited in Richard Gelles, *The Violent Home* (Beverly Hills, CA: Sage Publications, 1972), 14.

112. Elizabeth Thompson Gershoff, "Corporal Punishment by Parents and Associated Child Behaviors and Experiences: A Meta-Analytic and Theoretical review," *Psychological Bulletin* 128, no. 4 (2002):539–79. Gershoff's critics suggest that the negative effects are the result of "inept harsh parenting" and not specifically spanking. See Diana Baumrind, Robert Larzelere, and Philip A. Cowan, "Ordinary Physical Punishment: Is it Harmful?" *Psychological Bulletin* 128, no. 4 (2002):580–89.

113. Abraham Bergman, Roseanne Larsen, and Beth Mueller, "Changing Spectrum of Child Abuse," *Pediatrics,* 77 (1986).

114. Murray Straus, Richard Gelles, and Suzanne Steinmetz, *Behind Closed Doors: Violence in the American Family* (New York: Anchor, 1981), 94; see also Murray Straus, *Beating the Devil Out of Them* (New York: Jossey-Bass, 1994).

115. Richard Gelles, *Family Violence* (Newbury Park: Sage Publications, 1987), 165.

116. Skolnick, *The Intimate Environment,* 426.

117. *Harvard Men's Health Watch* 2, no. 11 (June 1998).

118. David H. Demo, "Parent-Child Relations: Assessing Recent Changes," *Journal of Marriage and the Family* 54, no. 1 (1990):224.

119. Hochschild, *The Second Shift,* 269.

120. Cited in Quindlen, "Men at Work."

121. Andrew Greeley, "The Necessity of Feminism," *Society* 30, no. 6 (September 1993):13–14.

122. Lasch, *Women and the Common Life,* 119.

123. Coltrane, *Family Man,* 223–25.

NOTES TO CHAPTER 7

1. In M. G. Lord, *Forever Barbie: The Unauthorized Biography of a Real Doll* (New York: William Morrow, 1994).

2. Deborah Rhode, *Speaking of Sex* (Cambridge: Harvard University Press, 1997), 56.

3. Edward C. Clarke, *Sex in Education; or, A Fair Chance for the Girls* (Boston: Osgood, 1873), 128, 137.

4. W. W. Ferrier, *Origin and Development of the University of California* (Berkleley: University of California Press, 1930); see also Myra Sadker and David Sadker, *Failing at Fairness: How Schools Shortchange Girls* (New York: Simon and Schuster, 1994), 22.

5. Henry Fowle Durant, "The Spirit of the College" [1977], reprinted in Michael S. Kimmel and Thomas Mosmiller, *Against the Tide: Pro-Feminist Men in the United States, 1776–1990, A Documentary History* (Boston: Beacon Press, 1992), 132.

6. Henry Maudsley, "Sex in Mind and in Education" [1874], in *Desire and Imagination: Classic Essays in Sexuality,* ed. R. Barreca, 208–209 (New York: Meridian, 1995).

7. Sadker and Sadker, *Failing at Fairness,* 14. These stereotypes can break down when complicated by other, racially based stereotypes; for example Asian American girls are expected to like math and science more than white girls.

8. David Karp and William C. Yoels. "The College Classroom: Some Observations on the Meanings of Student Participation," *Sociology and Social Research* 60, no. 4 (1976); American Association of University Women, *How Schools Shortchange Girls: A Study of Major Findings on Girls and Education* (Washington, DC: American Association of University Women, 1992), 68; Sadker and Sadker, *Failing at Fairness*, 5.

9. Sadker and Sadker, *Failing at Fairness*, 42–43.

10. Peggy Orenstein, *Schoolgirls* (New York: Doubleday, 1994), 11, 12.

11. See Leonore Weitzman and Diane Russo, *The Biased Textbook: A Research Perspective* (Washington, DC: Research Center on Sex Roles and Education, 1974).

12. Leonore Weitzman et al., "Sex Role Socialization in Picture Books for Preschool Children," *American Journal of Sociology* 77, no. 6 (1972).

13. Rhode, *Speaking of Sex*, 56.

14. Angela M. Gooden and Mark A. Gooden, "Gender Representation in Notable Children's Picture Books: 1995–1999," *Sex Roles* 45, no. 1/2) (July 2001):89–101.

15. *National Television Violence Study*, 2 vol. (Thousand Oaks, CA: Sage Publications, 1998), V. 2, 97. I will return to this issue in the last chapter.

16. On IQ, see Lewis Terman and M. Oden. "The Promise of Youth," in *Genetic Studies of Genius*, ed. L. Terman, (Stanford: Stanford University Press, 1935). On girls perceived for appearance and not achievement, see Sadker and Sadker, *Failing at Fairness*, 55, 134. On girls downplaying their talents, see American Association of University Women, *Shortchanging Girls, Shortchanging America* (Washington, DC: American Association of University Women, 1991), 48; Carolyn Heilbrun, cited in Orenstein, *Schoolgirls*, 37.

17. American Association of University Women, *Hostile Hallways: The AAUW Survey on Sexual Harassment in America's Schools* (Washington, DC: American Association of University Women, 1993); Sandler cited in Sadker and Sadker, *Failing at Fairness*, 111.

18. Jill Smolowe, "Sex with a Scorecard," *Time*, April 5, 1993, 41; Jane Gross, "Where 'Boys Will Be Boys' and Adults Are Bewildered," *The New York Times*, March 29, 1993, A-1.

19. See, for example, William Pollack, *Real Boys: Rescuing Our Sons from the Myths of Boyhood* (New York: Random House, 1998).

20. Christine Hoff Sommers, *The War Against Boys* (New York: Scribners, 1999). Sommers, cited in Debra Viadero, "Behind the 'Mask of Masculinity,'" *Education Week*, May 13, 1998; Thompson, cited in Margaret Combs, "What About the Boys?" *Boston Globe*, Jule 26, 1998. For more of this backlash argument, see Michael Gurian *The Wonder of Boys* (New York: Jeremy Tarcher/Putnam, 1997) and Judith Kleinfeld, "Student Performance: Male Versus Female," *The Public Interest* (Winter 1999). For dissenting opinions, see my review of Gurian, "Boys to Men," *San Francisco Chronicle*, January 12, 1997; Mills "What About the Boys"; and R. W. Connell, "Teaching the Boys," *Teachers College Record*, 98(2), Winter, 1996.

21. Gilligan, *In a Different Voice*; Lyn Mikel Brown and Carol Gilligan, *Meeting at the Crossroads* (New York: Ballantine, 1992).

22. Pollack, cited in Debra Viadero, "Behind the Mask." See also William Pollack, *Real Boys: Rescuing Our Boys from the Myths of Boyhood* (New York: Random House, 1998).

23. Wayne Martino, "Masculinity and Learning: Exploring Boys' Underachievement and Underrepresentation in Subject English," *Interpretation* 27, no. 2 (1994); "Boys and Literacy: Exploring the Construction of Hegemonic Masculinities and the Formation of Literate Capacities for boys in the English Classroom," *English in Australia* 112 (1995); "Gendered Learning Experiences: Exploring the Costs of Hegemonic Masculinity for Girls and Boys in Schools," in *Gender Equity: a Framework for Australian Schools* (Canberra: Publications and Public Communications, Department of Urban Services, ACT Government, 1997). Catharine Stimpson, quoted in Tamar Lewin, "American Colleges Begin to Ask, Where Have All the Men Gone?" *The New York Times*, December 6, 1998.

24. Martino, "Gendered Learning Experiences," 133, 134.

25. Martain Mac an Ghaill, *The Making of Men: Masculinities, Sexualities, and Schooling* (Buckingham, Open University Press, 1994), 59; David Gillborne, *Race, Ethnicity, and Education* (London: Unwin Hyman, 1990), 63; James Coleman, *The Adolescent Society* (New York: Harper and Row, 1961).

26. Brendan Koerner, "Where the Boys Aren't," *U.S. News and World Report,* February 8, 1999; Tamar Lewin, "American Colleges Begin to Ask, Where Have all the Men Gone?" *The New York Times,* December 6, 1998; Michael Fletcher, "Degrees of Separation," *The Washington Post,* June 25, 2002; Jamilah Evelyn, "Community Colleges Start to Ask, Where Are the Men?" *The Chronicle of Higher Education,* June 28, 2002; Ridger Doyle, "Men, Women, and College," *Scientific American,* October 1999.

27. From The American Psychological Association, "All that Violence is Numbing" available at www.apa.org; statistics first appeared in 1992 in *U.S. News and World Report.*

28. "Boys will be boys" are, not so incidentally, the last four words of Hoff Sommers's antifeminist screed.

29. Cited in Michael S. Kimmel, "The Struggle for Gender Equality: How Men Respond," *Thought and Action: The NEA Higher Education Journal* 8, no. 2 (1993).

30. Catell, cited in William O'Neil, *Divorce in the Progressive Era* (New Haven: Yale University Press, 1967), 81; Admiral F. E. Chadwick, "The Woman Peril," *Educational Review* (February 1914):47; last cited in Sadker and Sadker, *Failing at Fairness,* 214.

31. United States Department of Education, 1996.

32. National Science Foundation, *Characteristics of Doctoral Students,* cited in Linda Schliebenger, *Has Feminism Changed Science?* (Cambridge: Harvard University Press, 1999), 34.

33. Cornelius Riordan, "The Future of Single-Sex Schools," in *Separated by Sex: A Critical Look at Single-Sex Education for Girls* (Washington, DC: American Association of University Women Educational Foundation, 1998) 54.

34. Orenstein, *Schoolgirls,* 27.

35. Elizabeth Tidball "Perspective in Academic Women and Affirmative Action," *Educational Record,* 1973.

36. Cynthia Fuchs Epstein, *Deceptive Distinctions* (New Haven: Yale University Press, 1991).

37. Crosby, Faye et al., "Taking Selectivity into Account, How Much Does Gender Composition Matter?: A Reanalysis of M. E. Tidball's Research," *National Women's Studies Association Journal* 6 (1994); see also Cynthia Fuchs Epstein, "The Myths and Justifications of Sex Segregation in Higher Education: VMI and The Citadel," *Duke Journal of Gender Law and Policy* 4 (1997) and Cynthia Fuch Epstein, "Multiple Myths and Outcomes of Sex Segregation," *New York Law School Journal of Human Rights* 14 (1998).

38. Christopher Jencks and David Riesman, *The Academic Revolution* 300, 298. Riesman supported the continuation of VMI and Citadel's single-sex policy. Despite his own findings, See also David Riesman, "A Margin of Difference: The Case for Single-Sex Education," in *Social Roles and Social Institutions: Essays in Honor of Rose Laub Coser,* ed. J. R. Blau and N. Goodman (Boulder: Westview Press, 1991).

39. Carol Tavris, *The Mismeasure of Woman* (New York: Simon and Schuster, 1992), 127; R. Priest, A. Vitters, and H. Prince, "Coeducation at West Point," *Armed Forces and Society* 4, no. 4 (1978):590.

40. Epstein, "Multiple Myths and Outcomes," 191.

41. See Margaret Talbot, "Sexed Ed," *The New York Times Magazine,* September 22, 2002.

42. VMI I, 766 F. Supp, 1435; VMI V, 116 S. Ct. 2264, Brief for Petitioner; see also Valorie K. Vojdik, "Girls' Schools After VMI: Do They Make the Grade?" *Duke Journal of Gender Law and Policy* 4 (1997):85; Epstein, "Myths and Justifications," 108.

43. *Faulkner v. Jones,* 858 F. Supp 552 1994; Citadel Defendants' Proposed Findings of Fact, 1434.

44. Josiah Bunting quote in Citadel case. Cited in Vojdik, "Girls' Schools After VMI," 76. (As someone who began his college career at an all-male college and later transferred to a co-educational one, I could readily testify that men at the single-sex school were far more distracted by the absence of women than were the men at the coeducational school by their presence! With no women around, most of the young men couldn't stop thinking about them!)
45. John Dewey, "Is Coeducation Injurious to Girls?" *Ladies Home Journal,* June 11, 1911, 60.
46. Thomas Wentworth Higginson, "Sex and Education," *The Woman's Journal,* 1874, editorial, p. 1; reprinted in *History of Woman Suffrage,* 6 vols., S. B. Anthony, E. C. Stanton eds. (Rochester, NY: National American Woman Suffrage Association Press, 1881–1922), vol. 3.
47. Mike Bowler, "All-Male, All-Black, All Learning," *The Baltimore Sun,* 15 October 1995; Susan Estrich, "For Girls' Schools and Women's College, Separate Is Better," *The New York Times,* May 22, 1994.
48. See Kim Gandy, "Segregation Won't Help," *USA Today,* May 10, 2002.
49. "Harlem Girls School vs. The Three Stooges," *The New York Observer,* March 30, 1998, 4.
50. Pamela Haag, "Single-Sex Education in Grades K-12: What Does the Research Tell Us?" in *Separated by Sex: A Critical Look at Single-Sex Education for Girls* (Washington, DC: American Association of University Women Educational Foundation, 1998), 34; Valerie Lee, "Is Single-Sex Secondary Schooling a Solution to the Problem of Gender Inequity?" in *Separated by Sex: A Critical Look at Single-Sex Education for Girls,* 43; Riordan, "The Future of Single-Sex Schools," 53; Connie Leslie, "Separate and Unequal?" *Newsweek,* March 23, 1998, 55; Clark, cited in Charles Whitaker, "Do Black Males Need Special Schools?" *Ebony,* March 1991, 18.
51. Amanda Datnow, Lea Hubbard, and Elisabeth Woody, "Is Single Gender Schooling Viable in the Public Sector? Lessons from California's Pilot Program" (Toronto: Ontario Institute for Studies in Education, 2001).
52. Sadker and Sadker, *Failing at Fairness,* 125–26.
53. See, for example, Christine Stolba, "We've Come the Wrong Way Baby," *The Women's Quarterly* (Spring 2002). On the other side, see the Title IX FAQ Packet, published by the WEEA Equity Resource Center at www.edc.org/womensequity. Such criticism will continue as the Bush administration is currently reviewing Title IX; see Welch Suggs, "Can a Commission Change Title IX?" *Chronicle of Higher Education,* July 12, 2002.

NOTES TO CHAPTER 8

1. See Irene Padavic and Barbara Reskin, *Women and Men at Work,* 2nd ed. (Thousand Oaks, CA: Pine Forge, 2002), 26–27.
2. See Felice Schwartz, "Management Women and the New facts of Life," *Harvard Business Review,* January–February 1989.
3. Jerry Jacobs, "Men in Female-Dominated Fields: Trends and Turnover," in *Doing "Women's Work": Men in Nontraditional Occupations,* ed. Christine L. Williams, 49–63 Beverly Hills: Sage Press, 1993
4. Taylor, cited in Ashley Montagu, *The Natural Superiority of Women* (New York: Anchor, 1952), 28; *Workplace 2000,* cited in Rosalind Barnet and Caryl Rivers, *She Works/He Works* (New York: Simon and Schuster, 1992), 64
5. Kimmel, *Manhood in America;* Willard Gaylin, *The Male Ego* (New York: Viking, 1992), cited also in Michael Kimmel, "What Do Men Want?" *Harvard Business Review,* November–December 1993.
6. Gaylin, *The Male Ego,* 64.

7. Arthur Miller, *Death of a Salesman* [1949](New York: Penguin, 1989), 22, 23.

8. Marc Feigen-Fasteau, *The Male Machine* (New York: Dell, 1974), 120.

9. Cited in Londa Schiebinger, *Has Feminism Changed Science?* (Cambridge: Harvard University Press, 1999), 76.

10. See Arlie Hochschild, *The Managed Heart* (Berkeley: University of California Press, 1982).

11. Katha Pollitt, "Killer Moms, Working Nannies," *The Nation,* November 24, 1997.

12. John Baden, "Perverse Consequences (P.C.) of the Nanny State," *The Seattle Times,* January 17, 1996; Del Jones, "Hooters to Pay $3.75 Million in Sex Suit," *USA Today,* 1 October 1997, 1A.

13. Barbara Reskin, "Sex Segregation in the Workplace," in *Women and Work: A Handbook,* ed. P. Dubeck and K. Borman, 94 (New York: Garland, 1996), 94; see also Barbara Reskin, ed., *Sex-Segregation in the Workplace: Trends, Explanations, Remedies* (Washington, DC: National Academy Press, 1984); Barbara Reskin, "Bringing the Men Back In: Sex Differentiation and the Devaluation of Women's Work," *Gender and Society* 2, no. 1 (1988); and Barbara Reskin and Patricia Roos, eds., *Job Queues, Gender Queues: Explaining Women's Inroads into Male Occupations* (Philadelphia: Temple University Press, 1990).

14. Padavic and Reskin, *Women and Men at Work,* 65, 67; see also Andrea Beller, and Kee-Ok Kim Han, "Occupational Sex Segregation: Prospects for the 1980s," in *Sex-Segregation in the Workplace: Trends, Explanations, Remedies,* ed. B. Reskin, 91 (Washington, DC: National Academy Press, 1984).

15. Dana Dunn, "Gender-Segregated Occupations," in *Women and Work,* ed. P. Dubeck and K. Borman, 92 (New York: Garland, 1996).

16. Margaret Mooney Marini and Mary C. Brinton, "Sex Typing in Occupational Socialization," in *Sex-Segregation in the Workplace: Trends, Explanations, Remedies,* ed. B. Reskin, 224 (Washington, DC: National Academy Press, 1984); Jerry A. Jacobs, *Revolving Doors: Sex Segregation and Women's Careers* (Stanford: Stanford University Press, 1989), 48.

17. Samuel Cohn. *The Process of Occupational Sex-Typing: The Feminization of Clerical Labor in Great Britain* (Philadelphia: Temple University Press, 1985).

18. Yilu Zhao, "Women Soon to Be Majority of Veterinarians," *The New York Times,* June 9, 2002, 24.

19. Katharine Donato, "Programming for Change? The Growing Demand Among Computer Specialists," in *Job Queues, Gender Queues: Explaining Women's Inroads into Male Occupations,* ed. B. Reskin and Roos, 17. (Philadelphia: Temple University Press, 1990).

20. Charlotte Perkins Gilman, *His Religion and Hers* [1923], edited with a new introduction by Michael Kimmel (Walnut Creek: Altamira Press, 2003), 72

21. William Bielby and James Baron, "Undoing Discrimination: Job Integration and Comparable Worth," in *Ingredients for Women's Employment Policy,* ed. C. Bose and G. Spitze, 226 (Albany: SUNY Press, 1987); Reskin, "Bringing the Men Back In," 64.

22. Reed Abelson, "6 Women Sue Wal-Mart, Charging Job and Promotion Bias," *The New York Times,* June 20, 2001, C1, 17.

23. *EEOC v. Sears, Roebuck and Co.,* 628 F Supp 1264 (N.D. Ill 1986); 839 F 2d 302 (7th Cic. 1988).

24. Asra Q. Nomani, "A Fourth Grader's Hard Lesson: Boys Earn More Money Than Girls," *Wall Street Journal,* 7 July 1995, B1.

25. Census 2000, http://www.census.gov/Press-Release/www/2002/demoprofiles.html; see also Ronnie Steinberg, "How Sex Gets into Your Paycheck," in *Women's VU,* Vanderbilt University Women's Center 20, no. 2 (1997):1.

26. A. D. Bernhardt, M. Morris, and M. S. Handcock, "Women's Gains or Men's Losses? A Closer Look at the Shrinking Gender Gap in Earnings," *American Journal of Sociology,* 101 (1995): 302–28; see also Deborah Rhode, *Speaking of Sex: The Denial of Gender Equality* (Cambridge: Harvard University Press, 1997), 175; Tamar Lewin, "Women Losing Ground to Men in

Widening Income Difference," *The New York Times,* September 15, 1997, 1, 12. See also David Cay Johnston, "As Salary Grows, So Does a Gender Gap," *The New York Times,* May 12, 2002. Government data can be seen at http://www/dol/gov/dol/wb/public/wb_pubs/wagegap2.htm.

27. Elizabeth Becker, "Study Finds a Growing Gap Between Managerial Salaries for Men and Women," *The New York Times,* January 24, 2002, 18; Shannon Henry, "Wage Gap Widens," *The Washington Post,* January 23, 2002.

28. Mary Corcoran, Greg Duncan, and Michael Ponza, "Work Experience, Job Segregation, and Wages," in *Sex-Segregation in the Workplace: Trends, Explanations, Remedies,* ed. B. Reskin, 188 (Washington, DC: National Academy Press, 1984); Michelle Budig and Paula England, "The Wage Penalty for Motherhood," *American Sociological Review* 66 (2001):204–25.

29. Becker, "Study Finds Growing Gap"; Judith Lorber, "Women and Medical Sociology: Invisible Professionals and Ubiquitous Patients," in *Another Voice,* ed. M. Millman and R. M. Kanter, 82 (Garden City, NY: Anchor, 1975).

30. Cited in Julie Mathaei, *An Economic History of Women in America* (New York: Schocken, 1982), 192.

31. Lynn Martin, *A Report on the Glass Ceiling Initiative* (Washington, DC: U.S. Department of Labor, 1991), 1.

32. *Good for Business: Making Full Use of the Nation's Human Capital* (Washington, DC: U.S. Government Printing Office, 1995); Ruth Simpson, "Does an MBA Help Women?—Career Benefits of the MBA," *Gender, Work and Organization* 3, no. 2 (April 1996):119.

33. Farrell, *The Myth of Male Power,* 105–106.

34. Kanter, *Men and Women of the Corporation,* 209.

35. Ibid., 216, 221, 230.

36. Lynn Zimmer, "Tokenism and Women in the Workplace: The Limits of Gender-Neutral Theory," *Social Problems* 35, no. 1 (1988):64; Nina Toren and Vered Kraus, "The Effects of Minority Size on Women's Position in Academia," *Social Forces* 65 (1987):1092.

37. Christine Williams, "The Glass Escalator: Hidden Advantages for Men in the 'Female' Professions," *Social Problems* 39, no. 3 (1992); *Still a Man's World: Men Who Do 'Women's Work'* (Berkeley: University of California Press, 1995); see also Marie Nordberg, "Constructing Masculinity in Women's Worlds: Men Working as Pre-School Teachers and Hairdressers," *NORA: Nordic Journal of Women's Studies* 10, no. 1 (2002):26–37.

38. Williams, "The Glass Escalator," 296.

39. Williams, "The Glass Escalator," 296; Alfred Kadushin, "Men in a Woman's Profession," *Social Work* 21 (1976):441.

40. Heidi Hartmann, "Capitalism, Patriarchy, and Job Segregation by Sex," *Signs* 1, no. 3 (1976): 139.

41. Cited in Rhode, *Speaking of Sex,* 144.

42. See Catharine MacKinnon, *Sexual Harassment of Working Women* (Cambridge: Harvard University Press, 1977).

43. *Henson v. Dundee,* 682 F 2d, 897, 902.

44. Susan Crawford, "Sexual Harassment at Work Cuts Profits, Poisons Morale," in *Wall Street Journal,* 19 April 1993, 11F; Elizabeth Stanko, *Intimate Intrusions* (London: Routledge, 1985); E. Couric, "An NJL/West Survey, Women in the Law: Awaiting their Turn," *National Law Journal,* 11 December 1989; 1997 study by Klein Associates.

45. Ellen Neuborne, "Complaints High from Women in Blue Collar Jobs," *USA Today,* 3–6 May 1996.

46. De'Ann Weimer, "Slow Healing at Mitsubishi," *U.S. News and World Report,* 22 September 1997, 74, 76.

47. Rhode, *Speaking of Sex,* 28.

48. Stanko, *Intimate Intrusions,* 61.

49. Crawford, "Sexual Harassment at Work Cuts profits," 11F.
50. Steinberg, "How Sex Gets into Your Paycheck," 2.
51. See Barbara Reskin and Irene Padavic, *Women and Men at Work* (Thousand Oaks, CA: Pine Forge Press, 1995).
52. Sara Evans and Barbara Nelson, *Wage Justice: Comparable Worth and the Paradox of Technocratic Reform* (Chicago: University of Chicago Press, 1989), 13; Reskin, "Bringing the Men Back In."
53. Cited in Rhode, *Speaking of Sex,* 165, 169.
54. See, for example, Felice Schwartz, Gigi Anders, "The Mami Track," *Hispanic,* July 1993.
55. See *The Week,* 36.
56. Ronnie Steinberg and Alice Cook, "Policies Affecting Women's Employment in Industrial Countries," in *Women Working,* ed. A. Stromberg and S. Harkess, 326 (Mountain View, CA: Mayfield, 1988).
57. Karen Oppenheim Mason, "Commentary: Strober's Theory of Occupational Sex Segregation," in *Sex-Segregation in the Workplace: Trends, Explanations, Remedies,* ed. B. Reskin, 169 (Washington, DC: National Academy Press, 1984), 169.
58. See Sylvia Ann Hewlett, *Creating a Life: Professional Women and the Quest for Children* (New York: Talk Miramax Books, 2002); Sylvia Ann Hewlett, "Executive Women and the Myth of Having It All," *Harvard Business Review,* April 2002, 66–73. But see also the enormous critical response from feminists, including Katha Pollitt, "Backlash Babies," *The Nation,* May 13, 2002, and Garance Franke-Ruta, "Creating a Lie," *The American Prospect* 13, no. 12 (July 1, 2002).
59. See, for example, C. E. Miree and I. H. Frieze, "Children and Careers: A Longitudinal Study of the Impact of Young Children on Critical Career Outcomes of MBAs," *Sex Roles* 41 (1999): 787–808; J. E. Olson, I. H. Frieze, and E. G. Detlefsen, "Having It All? Combining Work and Family in a Male and Female Profession," *Sex Roles* 23 (1990):515–33. See also the summary of this research in Maureen Perry-Jenkins, Rena Repetti, and Ann Crouter, "Work and Family in the 1990s," *Journal of Marriage and the Family* 62, no. 4 (2000):981–98.
60. See Lisa Belkin, "Tony Blair's Baby: Some Decisions Last Longer," *The New York Times,* April 12, 2000, G1; Ellen Goodman, "Well Done, Mrs. Blair," *The Boston Globe,* April 14, 2000.
61. See Editorial, "A Family Values Fraud," *Glamour,* May 1999, 186.
62. Faye Crosby, *Spouse, Parent, Worker: On Gender and Multiple Roles* (New Haven: Yale University Press, 1990); Joan Peters, *When Mothers Work: Loving Our Children Without Sacrificing Ourselves* (New York: Addison-Wesley, 1997).

NOTES TO CHAPTER 9

1. Cited in Drury Sherrod, "The Bonds of Men: Problems and Possibilities in Close Male Relationships," in *The Making of Masculinities: The New Men's Studies,* ed. H. Brod, 230. (Boston: Allen and Unwin, 1987); cited in Rubin, *Intimate Strangers,* 59.
2. Mary Wollstonecraft, *A Vindication of the Rights of Women* [1792] (London: Penguin, 1969), 56; Simone de Beauvoir, *The Second Sex* (New York: Vintage, 1959), 142.
3. Lionel Tiger, *Men in Groups* (New York: Vintage, 1969).
4. Jack Balswick, "The Inexpressive Male: A Tragedy of American Society," in *The Forty-Nine Percent Majority,* ed. D. David and R. Brannon (Reading, MA; Addison-Wesley, 1976); Mirra Komarovsky, *Blue Collar Marriage* (New York: Vintage, 1964); Joseph Pleck, "The Male Sex Role: Definitions, Problems, and Sources of Change," *Journal of Social Issues* 32, no. 3 (1976): 273.
5. Lewis, Robert. "Emotional Intimacy Among Men," *Journal of Social Issues* 34 (1978); see also Pleck, "The Male Sex Role."

6. Paul Wright, "Men's Friendships, Women's Friendships, and the Alleged Inferiority of the Latter," *Sex Roles* 8, no. 1 (1982):3; Daniel Levinson, *The Seasons of a Man's Life* (New York: William Morrow, 1978), 335.

7. Francesca Cancian, "The Feminization of Love," *Signs* 11 (1986); and *Love in America: Gender and Self-Development* (Cambridge: Cambridge University Press, 1987).

8. See S. E. Taylor, L. C. Klein, B. Lewis, T. L. Gruenwald, R. A. R. Gurung, and J. A. Updegraff, "Biobehavioral Female Responses to Stress: Tend and Befriend, Not Fight or Flight," *Psychological Review* 107, no. 3 (2000):411–29.

9. Sandra Brehm, *Intimate Relationships* (New York: Random House, 1985), 346.

10. Mayta Caldwell and Letita Peplau, "Sex Differences in Same-Sex Friendships," *Sex Roles* 8, no. 7 (1982); Beth Hess, "Friendship," in *Aging and Society,* ed. M. Riley, M. Johnson, and A. Foner (New York: Russell Sage, 1972).

11. Lynne Davidson and Lucille Duberman. "Friendship: Communication and Interactional Patterns in Same-Sex Dyads," *Sex Roles* 8, no. 8 (1982):817.

12. Lillian Rubin, *Just Friends* (New York: Harper and Row, 1985), 60–61, 62–63; Rubin, *Intimate Strangers,* 130, 135.

13. Brehm, *Intimate Relationships;* Paul Wright, "Men's Friendships"; Davidson and Duberman, "Friendship"; R. Bell, *Worlds of Friendship* (Beverly Hills: Sage Publications, 1981).

14. Karen Walker, " 'I'm Not Friends the Way She's Friends': Ideological and Behavioral Constructions of Masculinity in Men's friendships," *masculinities* 2, no. 2 (1994):228; Rubin, *Intimate Strangers,* 104. On the impact of the telephone more generally, see Claude Fischer, *To Dwell Among Friends* (Chicago: University of Chicago Press, 1982).

15. Stuart Miller, *Men and Friendship* (Boston: Houghton Mifflin, 1983).

16. Graham Allen, *Friendship—Developing a Sociological Perspective* (Boulder, CO: Westview, 1989), 66.

17. Wright, "Men's Friendships," 19.

18. N. L. Ashton, "Exploratory Investigation of Perceptions of Influences on Best-friend Relationships," *Perception and Motor Skills* 50 (1980); Shavaun Wall, Sarah M, Pickert, and Louis V. Paradise, "American Men's Friendships: Self-Reports on Meaning and Changes," *The Journal of Psychology* 116 (1984).

19. Helen Hacker, "Blabbermouths and Clams: Sex Differences in Self-Disclosure in Same-Sex and Cross-sex Friendship Dyads," *Psychology of Women Quarterly* 5, no. 3 (Spring 1981).

20. Scott Swain,"Men's Friendship with Women: Intimacy, Sexual Boundaries, and the Informant Role," in *Men's Friendships,* ed. Nardi, 84, 77 (Newbury Park: Sage Publications, 1992). For a more general review of this literature, see Maccoby and Jacklin, *The Psychology of Sex Differences.*

21. Barbara Bank, "Friendships in Australia and the United States: From Feminization to a More Heroic Image," *Gender & Society* 9, no. 1 (1995):96.

22. Theodore F. Cohen, "Men's Families, Men's Friends: A Structural Analysis of Constraints on Men's Social Ties," in *Men's Friendships,* ed. P. Nardi, 117 (Newbury Park: Sage Publications, 1992); Allen, *Friendship,* 75.

23. Shanette Harris, "Black Male Masculinity and Same Sex friendships," *The Western Journal of Black Studies* 16, no. 2 (1992):77; Martin Simmons,

24. Harris, "Black Male Masculinity," 78, 81; see also Clyde W. Franklin II, " 'Hey Home'—'Yo, Bro': Friendship Among Black Men," in *Men's Friendships,* ed. P. Nardi (Newbury Park: Sage Publications, 1992).

25. Helen M. Reid and Gary Alan Fine, "Self-Disclosure in Men's Friendships: Variations Associated with Intimate Relations," *Men's Friendships,* ed. P. Nardi (Newbury Park: Sage Publications, 1992); Jeanne Tschann, "Self-Disclosure in Adult Friendship: Gender and Marital

Status Differences," *Journal of Social and Personal Relationships* 5 (1988); Wright, "Men's Friendships," 16–17.

26. Rubin, *Intimate Strangers,* 154, 150.

27. Gerald Suttles, "Friendship as a Social Institution," in *Social Relationships,* ed. G. McCall, M. McCall, N. Denzin, G. Suttles, and S. Kurth, 116 (Chicago: Aldine, 1970).

28. Miller, *Men and Friendship,* 2, 3; Rubin, *Intimate Strangers,* 103.

29. On experiment, see Lillian Faderman, *Surpassing the Love of Men* (New York: Columbia University Press, 1981); quote from Swain, "Covert Intimacy," 83–84.

30. Peter Nardi and Drury Sherrod, "Friendship in the Lives of Gay Men and Lesbians," *Journal of Social and Personal Relationships* 11 (1994); Rubin, *Intimate Strangers,* 105.

31. Cited in Rubin, *Intimate Strangers,* 130.

32. Peter Nardi, "The Politics of Gay Men's Friendships," in *Men's Lives,* ed. M. Kimmel and M. Messner, 4th ed., 250 (Boston: Allyn and Bacon, 1998).

33. Rubin, *Intimate Strangers,* 205, 58, 159.

34. Sherrod, "The Bonds of Men," 231.

35. Rubin, *Intimate Strangers,* 206.

36. Sherrod, "The Bonds of Men," 221; E. Anthony Rotundo, "Romantic Friendships: Male Intimacy and Middle-Class Youth in the Northern United States, 1800–1900," *Journal of Social History* 23, no. 1 (1989):21.

37. Foucault, cited in Nardi, *Men's Friendships,* 184; Lynne Segal, *Slow Motion: Changing Masculinities, Changing Men* (New Brunswick, NJ: Rutgers University Press, 1990), 139.

38. Lawrence Stone, "Passionate Attachments in the West in Historical Perspective," in *Passionate Attachments: Thinking About Love,* ed. W. Gaylin and E. Person, 33 (New York: The Free Press, 1988); Cancian, *Love in America,* 70.

39. Stone, "Passionate Attchments," 28.

40. Ibid., 32; Michael Gordon and M. Charles Bernstein, "Mate Choice and Domestic Life in the Nineteenth Century Marriage Manual," *Journal of Marriage and the Family* (November 1970):668, 669.

41. William J. Goode, "The Theoretical Importance of Love," *American Sociological Review* 24, no. 1 (1959).

42. Cited in Cancian, *Love in America,* 21, 19, 23; see also Mary Ryan, *The Cradle of the Middle Class: The Family in Oneida County, N.Y., 1790–1865* (New York: Cambridge University Press, 1981).

43. Cancian, *Love in America,* 121; Carol Tavris, *The Mismeasure of Women* (New York: Simon and Schuster, 1992), 263; Rubin, *Intimate Strangers.*

44. Rubin, *Worlds of Pain,* 147.

45. Elaine Hatfield, "What Do Women and Men Want from Love and Sex," in *Changing Boundaries,* ed. E. Allegier and N. McCormick (Mountain View, CA; Mayfield, 1983).

46. William Kephart, "Some Correlates of Romantic Love," *Journal of Marriage and the Family* 29 (1967); Kenneth Dion and Karen Dion, "Correlates of Romantic Love," *Journal of Consulting and Clinical Psychology* 41 (1973); Charles Hill, Zick Rubin, and Letitia Anne Peplau, "Breakups Before Marriage: The End of 103 Affairs," in *Divorce and Separation: Context, Causes, and Consequences,* ed. G. Levinger and O. C. Moles (New York: Basic Books, 1979); Charles Hobart, "Disillusionment in Marriage and Romanticism," *Marriage and Family Living* 20 (1958); Charles Hobart, "The Incidence of Romanticism During Courtship," *Social Forces* 36 (1958); David Knox and John Spoakowski, "Attitudes of College Students Toward Love," *Journal of Marriage and the Family* 30 (1968); George Theodorson, "Romanticism and Motivation to Marry in the United States, Singapore, Burma, and India," *Social Forces* 44 (1965).

47. Dion and Dion, "Correlates of Romantic Love"; Zick Rubin, "Measurement of Romantic Love," *Journal of Personality and Social Psychology* 16, no. 2 (1970); Arlie Hochschild, "Attending to, Codifying, and Managing Feelings: Sex Differences in Love," paper presented at the annual meetings of the American Sociological Association, August 1975; Eugene Kanin, Karen Davidson, and Sonia Scheck. "A Research Note on Male-Female Differentials in the Experience of Heterosexual Love," *Journal of Sex Research* 6 (1970):70.
48. Hill, Rubin, and Peplau, "Breakups Before Marriage."
49. Kephart, "Some Correlates of Romantic Love."
50. Simpson et al, 1986; Allgeier and Allgeier, 1991.
51. Susan Sprecher, E. Aron, E. Hatfield, A. Cortese, E. Potapava, and Levitskaya, "Love: American Style, Russian Style, and Japanese Style," paper presented at the Sixth Annual Conference on Personal Relationships, Orono, Maine, 1992.
52.. Cathy Greenblat, personal communication. This research has not yet been published.
53. Tavris, *The Mismeasure of Woman*, 284.
54. Cancian, "The Feminization of Love," 705, 709.
55. Rubin, *Just Friends*, 41.

NOTES TO CHAPTER 10

1. It is ironic, perhaps, that some of these developments that have made us more aware of our bodies have also enabled us to change (surgery) or conceal (Internet) them.
2. Naomi Wolf, *The Beauty Myth* (New York: William Morrow, 1991), 10, 184.
3. See Debra Gimlin, *Body Work: Beauty and Self-Image in American Culture* (Berkeley: University of California Press, 2002), 5; "How to Get Plump," *Harper's Bazaar,* August 1908, 787; Mary Pipher, *Reviving Ophelia* (New York: Ballantine, 1996); M. E. Collins, "Body Figure Perceptions and Preferences among Preadolescent Children," *International Journal of Eating Disorders* 10 (1991):199–208; A. Gustafson-Larson and R. Terry, "Weight-Related Behaviors and Concerns of Fourth Grade Children," *Journal of the American Dietetic Association* 92, no. 7 (1992):818–22; see also www.healthywithin.com/STATS.htm.
4. See L. Smolak and R. Striegel-Moore, "The Implications of Developmental Research for Eating Disorders," in *The Developmental Psychopathology of Eating Disorders: Implications for Research, Prevention, and Treatment,* ed. M. Smolak, Levine, and R. Striegel-Moore, 235–57 (Mahwah, NJ: Erlbaum, 1996).
5. "Europe Targets Eating Disorders," at http://news.bbc.uk/1/hi/health/197334.stm and "Eating Disorders Factfile," at http://news.bbc.co.uk/1/hi/health/medical_notes/187517.stm.
6. See A. Furnham and N. Alibhai, "Cross-Cultural Differences in the Perception of Female Body Shapes," *Psychological Medicine* 13, no. 4 (1983):829–37; D. B. Mumford, "Eating Disorders in Different Cultures," *International Review of Psychiatry,* 5, no. 1 (1993):109–13; N. Shuriquie, "Eating Disorders: A Transcultural Perspective," *Eastern Mediterranean Health Journal* 5, no. 2 (1999):354–60, also at http://www.emro.who.int/Publications/EMHJ/0502/20.htm. I am grateful to Lisa Machoian for her help in obtaining this material.
7. Sonni Efron, "Eating Disorders on the Increase in Asia," at http://www.dimensionsmagazine.com/news/asia/html.
8. Deborah Gregory, "Heavy Judgment," *Essence,* August 1994, 57–58; G. B Schreiber, K. M. Pike, D. E. Wilfley, and J. Rodin, "Drive for Thinness in Black and White Preadolescent Girls," *International Journal of Eating Disorders* 18, no. 1 (1995):59–69.
9. See Susan Bordo, *The Male Body* (New York: Farrar Straus, and Giroux, 2000).
10. Harrison Pope, Katharine Phillips, and Roberto Olivardia, *The Adonis Complex: The Secret Crisis of Male Body Obsession* (New York: The Free Press, 2000).

11. Cited in Richard Morgan, "The Men in the Mirror," *Chronicle of Higher Education,* September 27, 2002, A 53.

12. Pope et al., *The Adonis Complex.*

13. Gina Kolata, "With No Answers on Risks, Steroid Users Still Say 'Yes,'" *The New York Times,* December 2, 2002, A-1, 19.

14. See, for example, Christine Webber, "Eating Disorders," at http://netdoctor.co.uk/diseases/facts/eatingdisorders.htm

15. See "Motivation for Tattoo Removal," *Archives of Dermatology,* December 1996.

16. See www.plasticsurgery.org, the website of the American Society of Plastic Surgeons: http:///www.plasticsurgery.org/mediactr/92sexdis.htm

17. See Lynne Luciano, *Looking Good: Male Body Image in Modern America* (New York: Hill and Wang, 2001).

18. Gimlin, *Body Work,* 102.

19. See Sam Fields, "Penis Enlargement Surgery," at www.4–men.org/penisenlargementsurgery.html and Randy Klein, "Penile Augmentation Surgery," *Electronic Journal of Human Sexuality,* 2 March, 1999, chapter 2, 1; chapter 5, 8–9.

20. Letters testimonial to Dr. E. Douglas Whitehead at www.penile-enlargement-surgeon.com/diary.html

21. Cited in Devor, 1997.

22. Jules Michelet, cited in Darlaine C. Gardetto, "The Social Construction of the Female Orgasm, 1650–1890," paper presented at the annual meetings of the American Sociological Association, Atlanta, 1988, 18.

23. Cited in Barbara Ehrenreich and Deidre English, *For Her Own Good: 150 Years of Medical Advice to Women* (New York: Anchor, 1974).

24. Alfred Kinsey, Wendell Pomeroy, and Charles Martin, *Sexual Behavior in the Human Female* (Philadelphia: W. B. Saunders, 1953), 376.

25. Pauline Bart, "Male Views of Female Sexuality: From Freud's Phallacies to Fisher's Inexact Test," paper presented at the Second National Meeting of the special section of Psychosomatic Obstetrics and Gynecology, Key Biscayne, Florida, 1974, 6–7.

26. Lillian Rubin, *Erotic Wars* (New York: Farrar, Straus and Giroux, 1991), 28, 42; Bill Crystal, quoted in *The Week,* May 10, 2002, 17.

27. Catharine MacKinnon, *Only Words* (Cambridge: Harvard University Press, 1996), 185.

28. The best recent work on this dilemma for girls is Deborah Tolman, *Dilemmas of Desire: Teenage Girls Talk About Sexuality* (Cambridge: Harvard University Press, 2002).

29. Stephanie Sanders and June Machover Reinisch, "Would You Say You 'Had Sex' If . . . ," JAMA 281, January 20, 1999.

30. Emmanuel Reynaud, *Holy Virility,* trans. R. Schwartz (London: Pluto Press, 1983), 41.

31. See, for example, Carol Tavris, *The Mismeasure of Woman* (New York: Simon and Schuster, 1992); Harriet Lerner, *Women in Therapy* (New York: Harper and Row, 1989) chapter 2.

32. Edward Laumann, John Gagnon, Robert Michael, and Stuart Michaels, *The Social Organization of Sexuality* (Chicago: University of Chicago Press, 1994).

33. Ibid, 135.

34. Michael Kimmel and Rebecca Plante, "Sexual Fantasies and Gender Scripts: Heterosexual Men and Women Construct Their Ideal Sexual Encounters" in *Gendered Sexualities,* vol. 6 of *Advances in Gender Research,* ed. Patricia Gagné and Richard Tewksbury, 55–78 (Amsterdam: JAI Press, 2002).

35. See also E. Barbara Hariton and Jerome Singer, "Women's Fantasies During sexual Intercourse: Normative and Theoretical Implications," *Journal of Consulting and Clinical Psychology* 42, no. 3 (1974); Daniel Goleman, "Sexual Fantasies: What Are Their Hidden Meanings?" *The New York Times,* February 28, 1983; Daniel Goleman, "New View of Fantasy:

Much Is Found Perverse," *The New York Times,* May 7, 1991; Robert May, *Sex and Fantasy: Patterns of Male and Female Development* (New York: W. W. Norton, 1980); David Chick and Steven Gold, "A Review of Influences on Sexual Fantasy: Attitudes, Experience, Guilt, and Gender," *Imagination, Cognition and Personality* 7, no. 1 (1987–88); Robert A. Mednick, "Gender Specific Variances in Sexual Fantasy," *Journal of Personality Assessment* 41, no. 3 (1977); Diane Follingstad and C. Dawne Kimbrell, "Sexual Fantasies Revisited: An Expansion and Further Clarification of Variables Affecting Sex Fantasy Production," *Archives of Sexual Behavior,* 15, no. 6 (1986); Danielle Knafo and Yoram Jaffe. "Sexual Fantasizing in Males and Females," *Journal of Research in Personality* 18 (1984).

36. Robert Stoller, *Porn* (New Haven: Yale University Press, 1991), 31.
37. For a review of the empirical literature on pornography, see Michael Kimmel and Annulla Linders, "Does Censorship Make a Difference?: An Aggregate Empirical Analysis of Pornography and Rape," *Journal of Psychology and Human Sexuality.*
38. John Stoltenberg, "Pornography and Freedom," in *Men Confront Pornography,* ed. M. Kimmel (New York: Crown, 1990).
39. Rubin, *Erotic Wars,* 102; Tavris and Wade, *The Longest War,* 111.
40. Philip Blumstein and Pepper Schwartz, *American Couples* (New York: William Morrow, 1983), 279; Pepper Schwartz and Virginia Rutter, *The Gender of Sexuality* (Thousand Oaks: Pine Forge Press, 1998), 60–61. Of course, there are also systematic gender biases in the reporting of sexual experiences: men tend to overstate their experiences and women tend to understate theirs. So such wide discrepancies should be viewed with a skeptical eye.
41. Blumstein and Pepper Schwartz, *American Couples,* 234.
42. Laumann, et al., *The Social Organization of Sexuality,* 347.
43. Stevi Jackson, "The Social Construction of Female Sexuality," in *Feminism and Sexuality: A Reader,* ed. S. Jackson and S. Scott, 71 (New York: Columbia University Press, 1996).
44. Charlene Muehlenhard, "'Nice Women' Don't Say Yes and 'Real Men' Don't Say No: How Miscommunication and the Double Standard Can Cause Sexual Problems," *Women and Therapy* 7 (1988):100–101.
45. See Dwight Garner, "Endurance Condoms," *The New York Times Magazine,* December 15, 2002, 84.
46. See Jeffrey Fracher and Michael Kimmel, "Hard Issues and Soft Spots: Counseling Men About Sexuality," in *Handbook of Counseling and Psychotherapy with Men,* ed. M. Scher, M. Stevens, G. Good, and G. Eichenfeld (Newbury Park: Sage Publications, 1987).
47. Cited in Bordo, *The Male Body,* 61. There is actually some evidence of Viagra-related violence against women and a sort of sexual "road rage."
48. See Bruce Handy, "The Viagra Craze," *Time,* May 4, 1998, 50–57; Christopher Hitchens, "Viagra Falls," *The Nation,* May 25, 1998, 8.
49. Rubin, *Erotic Wars,* 13; on rates of change in sexual activity, see A. C Grunseit, S. Kippax, M. Baldo, A. Aggleton, and G. Slutkin, "Sexuality Education and Young People's Sexual Behavior: A Review of Studies," *Journal of Adolescent Research* (in press), manuscript from UNAID, 1997.
50. Amber Hollibaugh, "Desire for the Future: Radical Hope in Passion and Pleasure," in *Feminism and Sexuality: A Reader;* Rubin, *Erotic Wars,* 5, 46.
51. On rates of masturbation, see Laumann et al., *The Social Organization of Sexuality,* 86; Schwartz and Rutter, *The Gender of Sexuality,* 39. On sexual attitudes, see Lauman et al., *The Social Organization of Sexuality,* 507.
52. Laumann et al., *The Social Organization of Sexuality;* Schwartz and Rutter, *The Gender of Sexuality,* 165.
53. *Newsweek,* December 9, 2002, 61–71.
54. Peter S. Bearman and Hannah Bruckner, "Promising the Future: Virginity Pledges and First

Intercourse," *American Journal of Sociology* 106, no. 4 (2001):859–912; see also Alan Guttmacher Institute. Occasional Report. "Why Is Teenage Pregnancy Declining? The Role of Abstinence, Sexual Activity, and Contraceptive Use," 1996, at www.agi.org.

55. See Barbara Risman and Pepper Schwartz, "After the Sexual Revolution: Gender Politics in Teen Dating," *Contexts* 1 no. 1 (2002):16–24.

56. Lauman et al., *The Social Organization of Sexuality;* see also Schwartz and Rutter, *The Gender of Sexuality,* 102–103; see Sam Janus, *The Janus Report on Sexual Behavior* (New York: John Wiley, 1993), 315–16; Blumstein and Schwartz, *American Couples;* see also Lynne Segal, ed. *New Sexual Agendas* (New York: New York University Press, 1997), 67.

57. Gina Kolata, "Women and Sex: On This Topic, Science Blushes," *The New York Times,* June 21, 1998, 3; young woman cited in Rubin, *Erotic Wars,* 14.

58. Rubin, *Erotic Wars,* 120.

59. Cited in Rubin, *Erotic Wars,* 58; Mary Koss, L. A. Goodman, A. Browne, L. F. Fitzgerald, G. Keita, and N. F. Russo, *No Safe Haven: Male Violence Against Women at Home, at Work, and in the Community* (Washington, DC: American Psychological Association, 1994).

60. Mary Koss, T. Dinero, C. A. Seibel, and S. L. Cox, "Stranger and Acquaintance Rape: Are There Differences in the Victim's Experience?" *Psychology of Women Quarterly* 12, no. 1 (1988).

61. Laumann et al., *The Social Organization of Sexuality,* 336; see also Koss et al., *No Safe Haven.*

62. Ronald F. Levant, "Nonrelational Sexuality in Men" in *Men and Sex: New Psychological Perspectives,* ed. R. Levant and G. Brooks, 27. (New York: John Wiley, 1997).

63. See, for example, J. O. Billy, G. K. Tanfer, W. R. Grady, and D. H. Klepinger, "The Sexual Behavior of Men in the United States," *Family Planning Perspectives* 25, no. 2 (1993); Laumann et al., *The Social Organization of Sexuality.*

64. Gary Brooks, *The Centerfold Syndrome* (San Francisco: Jossey-Bass, 1995); and also Gary Brooks, "The Centerfold Syndrome," in *Men and Sex: New Psychological Perspectives,* ed. R. Levant and G. Brooks (New York: John Wiley, 1997). See also Levant, "Nonrelational Sexuality," 19; Joni Johnston, "Appearance Obsession: Women's Reactions to Men's Objectification of Their Bodies," in *Men and Sex,* 79, 101.

65. Glenn Good and Nancy B. Sherrod, "Men's Resolution of Nonrelational Sex Across the Lifespan," in *Men and Sex: New Psychological Perspectives,* ed. R. Levant and G. Brooks, 189, 190 (New York: John Wiley, 1997).

66. See Good and Sherrod, "Men's Resolution of Nonrelational Sex," 186.

67. Peter Wyden and Barbara Wyden, *Growing Up Straight: What Every Thoughtful Parent Should Know About Homosexuality* (New York: Trident Press, 1968).

68. Richard Green, *The "Sissy Boy" Syndrome* (New Haven: Yale University Press, 1986).

69. George Gilder, *Men and Marriage* (Gretna: Pelican Publishers, 1985).

70. Joe Jackson, "Real Men" (1983); for a sociological investigation of the gender organization of clone life, see Martin Levine, *Gay Macho: the Life and Death of the Homosexual Clone,* ed. M. S. Kimmel (New York: New York University Press, 1998).

71. Cited in Steve Chapple and David Talbot, *Burning Desires: Sex in America* (New York: Doubleday, 1989), 356.

72. Cheryl Clarke, "Lesbianism: An Act of Resistance," in *Feminism and Sexuality,* p. 155.

73. Alan Bell and Martin Weinberg, *Homosexualities* (New York: Simon and Schuster, 1978); William Masters and Virginia Johnson and Richard Kolodny, *Human Sexuality* (New York: Harper and Row, 1978); Blumstein and Schwartz, *American Couples,* 317.

74. Data from Blumstein and Schwartz, *American Couples;* woman is quoted in Bell and Weinberg, *Homosexualities,* 220.

75. Margaret Nichols, "Lesbian Sexuality: Issues and Developmental Theory," in *Lesbian Psychologies,* Boston Lesbian Psychologies Collective, ed. (Urbana: University of Illinois Press, 1987); Masters, Johnson, and Kolodny, *Human Sexuality.*

76. Kenneth Plummer, *Sexual Stigma* (New York: Routledge, 1975), p. 102.

77. Gerald Davison and John Neale, *Abnormal Psychology: An Experimental-Clinical Approach* (New York: John Wiley, 1974), 293.

78. See Jeni Loftus, "America's Liberalization in Attitudes Toward Homosexuality, 1973–1998," *American Sociological Review* 66 (October 2001):762–82.

79. Muelenhard, "Nice Women Don't Say Yes"; John Gagnon and Stuart Michaels, "Answer No Questions: The Theory and Practice of Resistance to Deviant Categorization," unpublished manuscript, 1989, 2. On the impact of homophobia on heterosexual men's lives, see also Richard Goldstein, "The Hate That Makes Men Straight," *The Village Voice,* December 22, 1998.

80. See Laumann et al., *The Social Organization of Sexuality,* 518–29, 177, 192, 82–84, 98, 302–309.

81. Rubin, *Erotic Wars,* 165.

82. See on these changes generally, Levine, *Gay Macho.*

83. World Health Organization; http://www.who.int/hiv/facts/plwha_m.jpg.

84. Michele Landsberg, "U.N. Recognizes Women Double Victims of AIDS," *Toronto Star,* July 1, 2001.

85. World Health Organization, http://www.who.int/hiv/facts/plwha_m.jpg.

86. Lawrence K. Altman, "Swift Rise Seen in H.I.V. Cases from Gay Blacks," *The New York Times,* June 1, 2001, A-1.

87. See Michael Kimmel and Martin Levine, "A Hidden Factor in AIDS: 'Real' Men's Hypersexuality," *The Los Angeles Times,* 3 June 1991. Of course, the route taken by women to high-risk behaviors is also gendered. While men are often eager to demonstrate manhood by engaging in such high-risk behaviors, women typically become IV drug users in the context of a "romantic" relationship or as part of a sexual initiation. And some women are also exposed to risk from HIV by male sexual partners who lie to them about their HIV status. I am grateful to Rose Weitz for pointing this out to me.

88. See Will Courtenay, "Engendering Health: A Social Constructionist Examination of Men's Health Beliefs and Behaviors," *Psychology of Men and Masculinity* 1, no. 1 (2000):4–15; "Men's Health," editorial in *British Medical Journal,* January 13, 1996, 69–70. For more about men's health specifically, see M. Sandra Wood and Janet M. Coggan, eds., *Men's Health on the Internet* (Binghamton, NY: Haworth Information Press, 2002).

89. Will H. Courtenay, "Engendering Health"; see also Lesley Doyal, "Sex, Gender, and Health: The Need for New Approach," *British Medical Journal,* November 3, 2001, 1061–63.

90. Linda Villarosa, "As Black Men Move into Middle Age, Dangers Rise," *The New York Times,* September 23, 2002, F-1, 8.

91. See Diana Jean Schemo, "Study Calculates the Effects of College Drinking in the U.S.," *The New York Times,* April 10, 2002, A-21; Jodie Morse, "Women on a Binge," *Time,* April 1, 2002, 57–61; Barbara Ehrenreich, "Libation as Liberation?" *Time,* April 1, 2002, 62.

92. See Judith Lorber, *Gender and the Social Construction of Illness* (Newbury Park, CA: Pine Forge Press, 1997).

93. See, for example, "Whatever Happened to Men's Health?" published by Men's Health America; www.egroups.com/group/menshealth.

NOTES TO CHAPTER 11

1. *Youth and Violence: Psychology's Response,* volume 1 (Washington, DC: American Psychological Association Commission on Violence and Youth, 1993); "Saving Youth from Violence," *Carnegie Quarterly* 39, no. 1 (Winter 1994).

2. United States Department of Justice, Uniform Crime Reports, 1991, 17; Diane Craven, "Sex Differences in Violent Victimization, 1994" (Washington, DC: U.S. Department of Justice (NCJ-164508), 1994); see also Martin Daly and Margo Wilson, *Homicide* (Chicago: Aldine, 1988).

3. National Academy of Sciences, cited in Michael Gottfredson and Travis Hisrchi, *A General Theory of Crime* (Stanford: Stanford University Press, 1990), 145. See also Steven Barkan, "Why Do Men Commit Almost All Homicides and Assault?" in *Criminology: A Sociological Understanding* (Englewood: Prentice-Hall, 1997); Lee Bowker, ed., *Masculinities and Violence* (Thousand Oaks: Sage Publications, 1998).

4. See James Q. Wilson and Richard Herrnstein, *Crime and Human Nature* (New York: Simon and Schuster, 1985), 121. For descriptions of various biological theories of violence, see, also, chapter 1 above.

5. I summarize these arguments in chapter 1.

6. Lorber, *Paradoxes of Gender,* 39. On the sociology of men's violence, see, especially, Michael Kaufman, *Cracking the Armour: Power, Pain, and the Lives of Men* (Toronto: Viking, 1993) and Michael Kaufman, "The Construction of Masculinity and the Triad of Men's Violence," in *Men's Lives,* ed. M. Kimmel and M. Messner, 4th ed. (Boston: Allyn and Bacon, 1997); See, also, Jackson Toby, "Violence and the Masculine Ideal: Some Qualitative Data," *The Annals of the American Academy of Political and Social Science* 364 (March 1966).

7. Barbara Ehrenreich, *Blood Rites: Origins and History of the Passions of War* (New York: Metropolitan Books, 1997), 45, 127.

8. Signe Howell and Roy Willis, *Societies at Peace* (New York: Routledge, 1983).

9. Howell and Willis, *Societies at Peace,* 38.

10. See also Elizabeth Stanko, *Everyday Violence* (London: Pandora, 1990), 71.

11. Fox Butterfield. *All God's Children: The Bosket Family and the American Tradition of Violence* (New York: Avon, 1995), 329.

12. Butterfield, *All God's Children,* 325; see also Wray Herbert, "Behind Bars," *U.S. News and World Report,* March 23, 1998, 33. See also Jay Livingston, "Crime and Sex: It's a Man's World," in *Crime and Criminology,* 2nd ed. (Englewood Cliffs: Prentice-Hall, 1996).

13. Cited in June Stephenson, *Men Are Not Cost Effective* (Napa: Diemer, Smith, 1991), 248.

14. Joe Sharkey, "Slamming the Brakes on Hot Pursuit," *The New York Times,* December 14, 1997, Wk, 3.

15. Freda Adler, *Sisters in Crime* (New York: McGraw-Hill, 1975), 10; Rita Simon, *Women and Crime,* (Washington, DC: U.S. Government Printing Office, 1975), 40.

16. See Patricia Pearson, *When She Was Bad: Violent Women and the Myth of Innocence* (New York: Viking, 1998); see also Larissa MacFarquhar, "Femmes Fatales," *The New Yorker,* March 9, 1998, 88–91.

17. Malcolm Feely and Deborah L. Little, "The Vanishing Female: The Decline of Women in the Criminal Process," *Law and Society Review* 25, no. 4 (1991):739.

18. Darrell J. Steffensmeier, "Trends in Female Crime: It's Still a Man's World" in *The Criminal Justice System and Women,* ed. B. R. Price and N. J. Sokoloff, 121 (New York: Clark, Boardman, 1982).

19. John O'Neil, "Homicide Rates Fall Among Couples," *The New York Times,* October 23, 2001, E-8.

20. Erich Goode, personal communication, 12/05/02; Jerome Skolnick, personal communication, 12/05/02; See also Erich Goode, *Deviant Behavior,* 5th ed. (Englewood Cliffs, NJ: Prentice-Hall, 2000), 127 and Kathleen Daly, *Gender Crime and Punishment* (New Haven: Yale University Press, 1994).

21. See Laura Dugan, Daniel Nagin, and Richard Rosenfeld, "Explaining the Decline in Intimate Partner Homicide: The Effects of Changing Domesticity, Women's Status, and Domestic Vio-

lence Resources," *Homicide Studies* 3, no. 3 (1999):187–214 and Richard Rosenfeld, "Changing Relationships Between Men and Women: A Note on the Decline in Intimate Partner Homicide," *Homicide Studies* 1, no. 1 (1997):72–83; Chris Huffine, personal communication.

22. Jack Katz, *Seductions of Crime: Moral and Sensual Attractions in Doing Evil* (New York: Basic Books, 1988), 71.

23. Katz, *Seductions of Crime,* 247; see also James Messerschmidt, *Masculinities and Crime* (Lanham, MD: Rowman and Littlefield, 1993), esp. 107, and Jody Miller "The Strengths and Limits of 'Doing Gender' for Understanding Street Crime," *Theoretical Criminology* 6, no. 4 (2002):433–60.

24. Darrell Steffensmeier and Ellie Allan, "Criminal Behavior: Gender and Age," in *Criminology: A Contemporary Handbook,* ed. J. F. Sheley, (Mountain View, CA: Wadsworth, 1995).

25. David Adams, "Biology Does Not Make Men More Aggressive Than Women," in *Of Mice and Women: Aspects of Female Aggression,* ed. K. Bjorkvist and Niemela, 14 (San Diego: Academic Press, 1992); see also Pearson, *When She was Bad.* But see also Coramae Richey Mann, *When Women Kill* (Albany: SUNY Press, 1996).

26. Adam Fraczek, "Patterms of Aggressive-Hostile Behavior Orientation Among Adolescent Boys and Girls," in *Of Mice and Women: Aspects of Female Aggression,* ed. K. Bjorkvist and P. Niemela (San Diego: Academic Press, 1992); Kirsti M. J. Lagerspetz and Kaj Bjorqvist, "Indirect Aggression in Boys and Girls," in *Aggressive Behavior: Current Perspectives,* ed. L. R. Huesmann (New York: Plenum, 1994).

27. Vappu Viemero, "Changes in Female Aggression over a Decade," in *Of Mice and Women: Aspects of Female Aggression,* ed. K. Bjorkvist and Niemela, 105 (San Diego: Academic Press, 1992).

28. See, for example, Rachel Simmons, *Odd Girl Out: The Hidden Culture of Aggression in Girls* (New York: Harcourt, 2002); Rosalind Wiseman, *Queen Bees and Wannabes: A Parents Guide to Helping Your Daughter Survive Cliques, Gossip, Boyfriends, and Other Realities of Adolescence* (New York: Crown, 2002); Sharon Lamb, *The Secret Lives of Girls: Sex, Play, Aggression, and Their Guilt* (New York: Free Press, 2002). See also Margaret Talbot, "Mean Girls," *The New York Times Magazine,* February 24, 2002, 24–29, 40, 58, 64–65; and Carol Tavris, "Are Girls Really as Mean as Books Say They Are?" *Chronicle of Higher Education,* July 5, 2002, B7–9.

29. Simmons, *Odd Girl Out.*

30. See, for example, Ann Donahue, "Population of Female Inmates Reaches Record," *USA Today,* 21 July 1997; Steefensmeier and Allen, "Criminal Behavior," 85.

31. Helen Caldicott, *Missile Envy* (New York: William Morrow, 1984); Barbara Ehrenreich, "The Violence Debate Since Adam and Eve," in *Test the West: Gender Democracy and Violence* (Vienna: Federal Minister of Women's Affairs, 1994), 34.

32. R. W. Connell, "Masculinity, Violence and War," in *Men's Lives,* ed. M. Kimmel and M. Messner, 3rd ed., 129 (Boston: Allyn and Bacon, 1995).

33. David Halberstam, *The Best and the Brightest* (New York: Random House, 1972), 531.

34. Maureen Dowd, "Rummy Runs Rampant," *The New York Times,* October 30, 2002, A-29.

35. Cited in Brian Easlea, *Fathering the Unthinkable: Masculinity, Scientists, and the Nuclear Arms Race* (London: Pluto Press, 1983), 117; see also his "Patriarchy, Scientists, and Nuclear Warriors," in *Beyond Patriarchy: Essays by Men on Pleasure, Power, and Change,* ed. M. Kaufman (Toronto: Oxford University Press, 1987); I. F. Stone, "Machismo in Washington," in *Men and Masculinity,* ed. J. Pleck and J. Sawyer (Englewood Cliffs: Prentice-Hall, 1974); Carol Cohn, " 'Clean Bombs' and Clean Language," in *Women, Militarism, and War: Essays in History, Politics, and Social Theory,* ed. J. B. Elshtain, 137 (Savage, MD: Rowman and Littlefield, 1990).

36. Cohn, " 'Clean Bombs,' " 35.

37. Wayne Ewing, "The Civic Advocacy of Violence," in *Men's Lives,* ed. M. Kimmel and M. Messner, 1st ed. (New York: Macmillan, 1989).

38. Jackson's mother, cited in Butterfield, *All God's Children,* 11; see also Eric A. Johnson and Eric H. Monkkonen, eds., *The Civilization of Crime* (Urbana: University of Illinois Press, 1996); David Courtwright, *Violent Land: Single Men and Social Disorder from the Frontier to the Inner City* (Cambridge: Harvard University Press, 1997). Also, see the trilogy by Richard Slotkin, *Regeneration Through Violence: The Mythology of the American Frontier, 1600–1860* (New York: Atheneum, 1973); *The Fatal Environment: The Myth of the Frontier in the Age of Industrialization* (New York: Atheneum, 1985); *Gunfighter Nation: The Myth of the Frontier in Twentieth Century America* (New York: Atheneum, 1992).
39. Margaret Mead, *And Keep Your Powder Dry* (New York: William Morrow, 1965), 151, 157.
40. J. Adams Puffer, *The Boy and His Gang* (Boston: Houghton Mifflin, 1912), 91.
41. James Gilligan, *Violence* (New York: Putnam, 1996).
42. Butterfield, *All God's Children,* 206–207; Kit Roane, "New York Gangs Mimic California Original," *The New York Times,* September 14, 1997, A-37; others cited in Katz, *Seductions of Crime,* 88, 107; Vic Seidler, "Raging Bull," *Achilles Heel* 5 (1980):9; Hans Toch, "Hypermasculinity and Prison Violence," in *Masculinities and Violence,* ed. L. Bowker, 170 (Newbury Park: Sage Publications, 1998).
43. Data from *The New York Times,* August 25, 1997; United States Department of Justice, *Family Violence,* 1997; Reva Siegel, "The 'Rule of Love': Wife Beating as Prerogative and Privacy," *Yale Law Journal* 105, no. 8 (June 1996); Deborah Rhode, *Speaking of Sex: The Denial of Gender Inequality* (Cambridge: Harvard University Press, 1997), 108; Stephenson, *Men Are Not Cost Effective,* 285; See also Neil Websdale and Meda Chesney-Lind, "Doing Violence to Women: Research Synthesis on the Victimization of Women," in *Masculinities and Violence,* ed. L. Bowker (Newbury Park: Sage Publications, 1998).
44. Sanday, *Female Power and Male Dominance;* quote from Larry Baron and Murray Straus, "Four Theories of Rape: A Macrosociological Analysis," *Social Problems* 34, no. 5 (1987):481.
45. See, for example, Diana Scully, *Understanding Sexual Violence: A Study of Convicted Rapists* (New York: HarperCollins, 1990); Diana Russell, *Rape in Marriage* (New York: Macmillan, 1982) and *Sexual Exploitation* (Beverly Hills, CA: Sage Publications, 1984); Rhode, *Speaking of Sex,* 119–20; Allan Johnson, "On the Prevalence of Rape in the United States," *Signs* 6, no. 1 (1980):145. For more on this, see also Diana Scully, and J. Marolla, " 'Riding the Bull at Gilley's': Convicted Rapists Describe the Rewards of Rape," *Social Problems* 32 (1985).
46. United States Department of Justice, "Child Rape Victims, 1992" (NCJ-147001) (June 1994); Eugene Kanin, "False Rape Allegations," *Archives of Sexual Behavior* 23, no. 1 (1994).
47. Johnson, "On the Prevalence of Rape," 145; Scully, *Understanding Sexual Violence,* 53.
48. Mary Koss, Christine A. Gidycz, and Nadine Misniewski, "The Scope of Rape: Incidence and Prevalence of Sexual Aggression and Victimization in a National Sample of Higher Education Students," *Journal of Consulting and Clinical Psychology* 55, no. 2 (1987).
49. John Briere and Neil Malamuth, "Self-Reported Likelihood of Sexually Aggressive Behavior: Attitudinal Versus Sexual Explanations," *Journal of Research in Personality* 17 (1983); Todd Tieger, "Self-Rated Likelihood of Raping and Social Perception of Rape," *Journal of Research in Personality* 15 (1991).
50. J. L. Herman, "Considering Sex Offenders: A Model of Addiction," *Signs* 13 (1988); Bernard Lefkowitz, *Our Guys* (Berkeley: University of California Press, 1997); Don Terry, "Gang Rape of Three Girls Leaves Fresno Shaken and Questioning," *The New York Times,* April 28, 1998; see also Jane Hood, " 'Let's Get a Girl': Male Bonding Rituals in America," in *Men's Lives,* ed. M. Kimmel and M. Messner, 4th ed. (Boston: Allyn and Bacon, 1997).
51. Scully, *Understanding Sexual Violence,* 74, 140, 166, 159.
52. Tim Beneke, *Men on Rape* (New York: St. Martin's Press, 1982), 81.
53. See Koss, Gidycz, and Misniewski, "The Scope of Rape," and also Scot Boeringer, "Pornography and Sexual Aggression: Associations of Violence and Nonviolent Depictions with Rape and Rape Proclivity," *Deviant Behavior* 15 (1994):289–304.

54. Murray Straus et al., *Behind Closed Doors* (Garden City: Anchor Books, 1981).
55. Diana Russell, *Rape in Marriage* (New York: Macmillan, 1982); David Finklehor and Kirsti Yllo. *License to Rape: Sexual Abuse of Wives* (Newbury Park: Sage Publications, 1985), 217, 208. On marital rape generally, see also Raquel Kennedy Bergen, "Surviving Wife Rape: How Women Define and Cope with the Violence," *Violence Against Women* 1, no. 2 (1995):117–38; and the special issue of *Violence Against Women* she edited, 5, no. 9 (September 1999); Raquel Kennedy Bergen, *Wife Rape: Understanding the Response of Survivors and Service Providers* (Thousand Oaks: Sage Publications, 1996); Anne L. Buckborough, "Family Law: Recent Developments in the Law of Marital Rape," in *Annual Survey of American Law,* 1989; "To Have and to Hold: The Marital Rape Exemption and the Fourteenth Amendment" Note, *Harvard Law Review* 99 (1986).
56. Gelles, cited in Joanne Schulman, "Battered Women Score Major Victories in New Jersey and Massachusetts Marital Rape Cases," *Clearinghouse Review* 15, no. 4 (1981):345.
57. Ehrenreich, "The Violence Debate," 30.
58. R. Bachman and L. E. Saltzman, "Violence Against Women: A National Crime Victimization Survey Report" (NCJ No. 154348) (Washington, DC: U.S. Department of Justice, 1994); Murray Straus and Richard Gelles, eds., *Physical Violence in American Families* (New Brunswick, NJ: Transaction Publishers, 1990); A. L. Kellerman and J. A. Marcy, "Men, Women, and Murder: Gender Specific Differences in Rates of Fatal Violence and Victimization," *Journal of Trauma* 33, no. 1 (1992). See also Evan Stark and Anne Flitcraft, "Violence Among Intimates: An Epidemiological Review," in *Handbook of Family Violence,* ed. V. van Hasselt et al. (New York: Plenum, 1988).
59. R. Emerson Dobash, Russell Dobash, Margo Wilson, and Martin Daly, "The Myth of Sexual Symmetry in Marital Violence," *Social Problems* 39 (1992):81; see also R. Emerson Dobash and Russell Dobash, *Violence Against Wives* (New York: The Free Press, 1979); "The Case of Wife Beating," *Journal of Family Issues* 2 (1981).
60. Walter DeKeserdy and Martin Schwartz, *Contemporary Criminology* (Mountain View, CA: Wadsworth, 1996).
61. Armin Brott, "The Battered Statistic Syndrome," *The Washington Post,* July 1994.
62. R. L. McNeely and G. Robinson-Simpson, "The Truth About Domestic Violence: A Falsely Framed Issue," *Social Work* 32, no. 6 (1987).
63. Susan Steinmetz, "The Battered Husband Syndrome," *Victimology* 2 (1978); M. D. Pagelow, "The 'Battered Husband Syndrome': Social Problem or Much Ado About Little?" in *Marital Violence,* ed. N. Johnson (London: Routledge and Kegan Paul, 1985); Elizabeth Pleck, Joseph Pleck, M. Grossman, and Pauline Bart, "The Battered Data Syndrome: A Comment on Steinmetz's Article," *Victimology* 2 (1978); G. Storch, "Claim of 12 Million Battered Husbands Takes a Beating," *Miami Herald,* 7 August 1978; Jack C. Straton, "The Myth of the 'Battered Husband Syndrome,'" *masculinities* 2, no. 4 (1994); Kerrie James, "Truth or Fiction: Men as Victims of Domestic Violence?" in *The Australian and New Zealand Journal of Family Therapy* 17, no. 3 (1996); Betsy Lucal, "The Problem with 'Battered Husbands,'" *Deviant Behavior* 16 (1995):95–112.
    Since the first edition of this book was published, I became increasingly distressed that social science research was being so badly misused for political ends. So I undertook an attempt to thoroughly investigate the case of "gender symmetry." See Michael Kimmel, "'Gender Symmetry in Domestic Violence: A Substantive and Methodological Research Review," *Violence Against Women* 8, no. 11 (November 2002):1332–63. Useful current data can be found in Callie Marie Rennison, "Intimate Partner Violence and Age of Victim, 1993–1999," U.S. Dept. of Justice, Bureau of Justice Statistics, October 2001.
64. See James, "Truth or Fiction" who found the same results in a sample of Australian and New Zealand couples.
65. J. E. Stets and Murray Straus, "The Marriage License as a Hitting License: A Comparison of

Assaults in Dating, Cohabiting, and Married Couples," *Journal of Family Violence* 4, no. 2 (1989); J. E. Stets and Murray Straus, "Gender Differences in Reporting Marital Violence and its Medical and Psychological Consequences," in *Physical Violence in American Families,* ed. M. Straus and R. Gelles (New Brunswick, NJ: Transaction Publishers, 1990).

66. United States Department of Justice, Bureau of Justice Statistics, *Family Violence,* 1984.

67. Glanda Kaufman Kantor, Jana Janinski, and E. Aldorondo, "Sociocultural Status and Incidence of Marital Violence in Hispanic Families," *Violence and Victims* 9, no. 3 (1994); and Jana Janinski. "Dynamics of Partner Violence and Types of Abuse and Abusers," at http://www.nnfr.org/nnfr/research/pv_ch1.html; Kersti Yllo, personal communication.

68. See Gelles, "Domestic Violence: Not an Even Playing Field," and Richard Gelles, "Domestic Violence Factoids" both available from Minnesota Center Against Violence and Abuse (www.mincava.umn.edu). See also, Kimmel, " 'Gender Symmetry.' "

69. Bachman and Saltzman, "Violence Against Women," 6; Straus and Gelles, *Physical Violence.* Given that Schawrtz's estimate of the actual rates are exactly the same as those that journalist Armin Brott used earlier, I wonder if he would say that we ought to consider this "the unfortunate behavior" of a few crazy women.

70. See, for example, Kersti Yllo, "Through a Feminist Lens: Gender, Power, and Violence," in *Current Controversies on Family Violence,* ed. R. J. Gelles, and D. Loseke (Thousand Oaks, CA: Sage Publications, 1993).

71. Neil Jacobson and John Gottman, *When Men Batter Women* (New York: Simon and Schuster, 1998), 36.

72. C. Saline, "Bleeding in the Suburbs," *Philadelphia Magazine,* March 1984, 82; Straus et al., *Behind Closed Doors;* R. L. Hampton, "Family Violence and Homicides in the Black Community: Are They Linked?" in *Violence in the Black Family: Correlates and Consequences,* (Lexington, MA; Lexington Books, 1987); R. L. Hampton and Richard Gelles, "Violence Towards Black Women in a Nationally Representative Sample of Black Families," *Journal of Comparative Family Studies* 25, no. 1 (1994).

73. Noel Cazenave and Murray Straus, "Race, Class, Network Embeddedness, and Family Violence: A Search for Potent Support Systems," in *Physical Violence in American Families,* ed. M. Straus and R. Gelles (New Brunswick, NJ: Transaction, 1990); Pam Belluck, "Women's Killers and Very Often Their Partners," *The New York Times,* March 31, 1997, B1.

74. Vicki Haddock, "Survey Tracks Gay Domestic Violence," *San Francisco Examiner,* 22 October 1996.

75. Cited in Stephenson, *Men Are Not Cost Effective,* 300; Dorie Klein, "Violence Against Women: Some Considerations Regarding Its Causes and Elimination," in *The Criminal Justice System and Women,* ed. B. Price and N. Sokoloff, 212 (New York: Clark Boardman, 1982).

76. Messerschmidt, James. *Masculinities and Crime* (Totowa: Rowman and Littlefield, 1993), 185; Elizabeth Stanko "The Image of Violence," *Criminal Justice Matters* 8 (1992):3.

77. Myriam Miedzian, *Boys Will Be Boys: Breaking the Link Between Masculinity and Violence* (New York: Doubleday, 1991), 298.

Notes to Epilogue

1. Kate Millett, *Sexual Politics* (New York: Random House, 1969).

2. Floyd Dell, "Feminism for Men," *The Masses,* February 1917; reprinted in *Against the Tide: Profeminist Men in the United States, 1776–1990 (A Documentary History),* ed. M. S. Kimmel and T. Mosmiller (Boston: Beacon Press, 1992).

3. Robert Jay Lifton, *The Protean Self* (New York: Basic Books, 1994). See also Cynthia Fuchs Epstein, "The Multiple Realities of Sameness and Difference: Ideology and Practice," *Journal of Social Issues* 53, no. 2 (1997).

INDEX